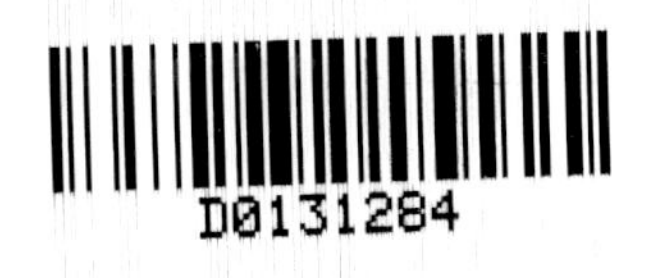
D0131284

GRAY WORK

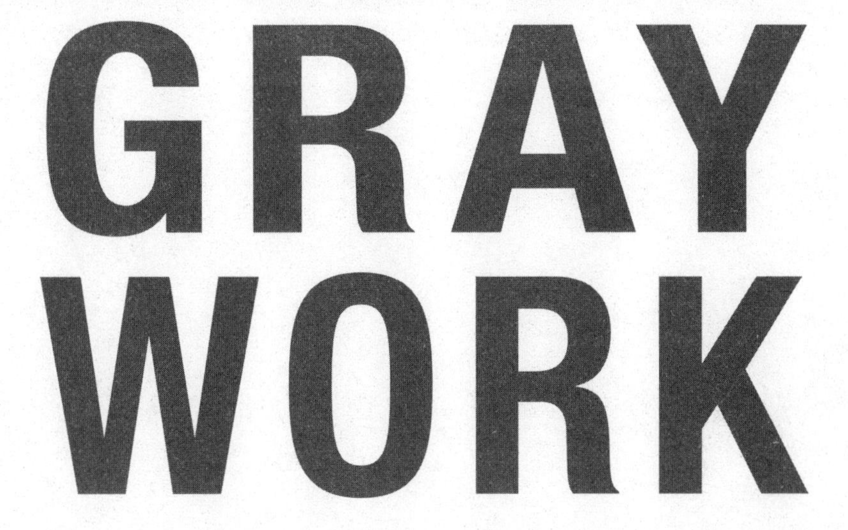

CONFESSIONS OF AN AMERICAN PARAMILITARY SPY

JAMIE SMITH

wm
WILLIAM MORROW
An Imprint of HarperCollins*Publishers*

All photographs are courtesy of the author.

HarperCollins books may be purchased for educational, business, or sales promotional use. For information please e-mail the Special Markets Department at SPsales@harpercollins.com.

FIRST EDITION

Designed by Lisa Stokes

Library of Congress Cataloging-in-Publication Data has been applied for.

ISBN 978-0-06-227169-3

15 16 17 18 19 OV/RRD 10 9 8 7 6 5 4 3 2 1

I wish to dedicate this book to my God and Savior Jesus Christ, without whom I'd be lost; to my family, who have been my ever-present rock; and to those who fight for our country, both military and civilian—your sacrifice cannot be appreciated, nor rewarded enough. To the fine men and women of SCG, LLC who worked tirelessly in the face of much adversity, but who always gave 100 percent. Finally, to Morgan, Cole, and Mallory, I hope this helps you understand why your dad was gone so much, missed so many birthdays and special times. I love you . . . to pieces.

Everything in this book is my opinion or recollection. I have changed many of the names, mainly to protect sources and the identities of people who are still working dangerous jobs in dangerous parts of the world. In a few instances, I have also compressed the timeline of the events described or created a composite character. Honoring the confidentiality agreement I signed when hired by the Central Intelligence Agency, and then by the Federal Bureau of Investigation, I submitted the manuscript for their review and have removed information considered classified. Both the FBI and CIA Publication Review Boards were courteous in their review process. The CIA has required that I—as is required of every former employee—include this disclaimer:

All statements of fact, opinion, or analysis expressed are my own and do not reflect in any way the official position or views of the CIA or any other U.S. Government agency. Nothing in the contents should be construed as asserting or implying U.S. Government authentication of information or Agency endorsement of the author's views. This material has been reviewed by the CIA to prevent the disclosure of classified information.

—Jamie Smith
February 2015

All men dream: but not equally. Those who dream by night in the dusty recesses of their minds wake in the day to find it was vanity: but the dreamers of the day are dangerous men, for they may act their dreams with open eyes, to make it possible.

—T. E. Lawrence, *Seven Pillars of Wisdom: A Triumph*

CONTENTS

III Afghanistan

IV Syria, Iran, Mali

GRAY WORK

PROLOGUE

Last week of Ramadan, August 2011
Tripoli, Libya

IN THE DARK HOURS OF THE EARLY MORNING, my cell buzzed and a thin voice gave me the news: bad guys with guns were heading our way. This was a city at war and the thugs who kept Muammar Qadhafi in power were savages. But like hyenas, they were most dangerous when desperate and cornered. For days I'd carefully dodged Qadhafi's hit teams from the Mukhabarat el-Jamahiriya as they stepped up their hunt for the rebels. I'd kept one step ahead of them at each turn. But now, somehow, overnight, they'd found me.

I got up from the couch I was sleeping on in the front room of the three-story concrete villa and grabbed my rifle—an AK-47. As far as I could tell, I was the only American operator in this part of Libya. Qadhafi's men were hunting the rebels, the opposition. It was going to be a long, hot night.

"Sumo, wake up." The young Asian, a twenty-something freelance photographer, was snoring just a few feet from me on another couch. I'd met him a few days earlier at the docks in Malta as I'd waited to board the old Korean-run, Filipino-crewed, Libyan-flagged fishing boat that brought us into this war-torn nation. It was his first time in this region, and he thought I worked for a news agency. I doubted his chances of surviving this war zone alone, so I let him tag along; I figured I could pawn him off to a real news crew at the first opportunity.

"We're out of here in two minutes," I said, pulling the shoulder strap of my tan Kifaru Tailgunner pack over my head and swinging it around to my front. Weighing nearly twelve pounds and about the size of a large football, it held my essentials: a loaded pistol given to me when I came ashore along with three spare mags of ammo, four loaded rifle magazines—also a gift upon arrival—a PVS-14-3 night vision monocular, a Medford TS-1 fixed-blade knife, a Garmin Oregon 400t GPS, and a Foretrex 401 GPS for a backup. There was a Ranger lensatic compass, signal mirror, Quest protein bars, gunshot kit, Thuraya satphone, laminated map, Cipro antibiotics, Imodium, infrared strobe, Velcro U.S. flag patch, passport, five grand in U.S. cash, extra batteries for everything, and most important, a laminated copy of two letters giving me authorization for being here.

Then I shouldered my Kifaru AG-1 main pack with everything else I brought in, including a compact sleeping bag, a change of clothes, fold-out solar panel to charge my electronics, a Panasonic Toughbook computer, spare satphone antenna, more batteries for everything, CamelBak water purification bottle system, a dark brown Catoma one-man shelter, more protein bars, a larger first-aid kit, and other odds and ends. I put the big fifty-pound pack on last, just in case I had to ditch it. That way I'd still have the smaller bag—the Tailgunner with my essentials for survival—hooked to my body.

I pulled the mag out from my AK-47 to make sure it was topped off, then hooked it back into the rifle, tugged on it to make sure it was seated, and then chambered a round. Last thing I wanted was to have my magazine fall out of my gun. It was a training habit from decades on firing ranges, but it was important. After getting my gear ready and wiping the cobwebs from my brain, I formed a loose plan that revolved around one concept—get the crap out of here. I woke the rest of our party: Sleepy—a former Libyan ambassador who'd defected and who'd brought me to this place; Hakin, his good friend who owned the house we were visiting; and the boy—his preteen son.

Sleepy opened his eyes wide from a deep sleep, then squinted, recoiling at the sound of my voice as if stung by a wasp. "Mr. Jamie, what is going on?"

"Kamel called. Qadhafi's men are heading here right now. They know you and I are here, and they also think our host is General Hakim." The man whose villa we were borrowing, Mr. Hakin, apparently had a name similar to that of a rebel leader. The caller, Kamel, was a significant leader in the Misrata rebellion. He was good at fund-raising, and coordinating the influx of men and weapons. He apparently also had really strong connections into the intel networks in Tripoli. If we didn't die tonight, I'd be happily adding him to the list of people to whom I owed my life.

We didn't have time to screw around. I didn't know when Kamel's team had intercepted the call or how far away the hit team might even be. Our only security right now was speed—just get out of here.

"Meet me at the front of the house and be ready to leave in two minutes."

Tripoli was exploding, but my company's operation in Libya was shaping up. We had a forward-staging base in Malta, manned by one of our support staffers, and an Operations Center in Charlotte, North Carolina, run by Odell International. My partner, D, and I had been in and out of the country, collecting critical information on the state of the insurrection and pushing it back to Washington, D.C. We had estimates of the strength of the rebel brigades, which were set up to help secure the country, the extent of radical Islamist penetrations of the insurgency and those brigades, the locations and destinations of shipments of deadly surface-to-air missiles (Man-Portable Air Defense Systems, called MANPADS), and anything else that seemed germane. We'd been responding to the Department of Defense and other RFIs (or requests for information) about certain people and places. When it was all wrapped up, I knew I'd have to brief Congresswoman Myrick, the Anti-Terrorism Caucus, and others on what we found. But first, I had to get out of Libya alive, and I wasn't eager to make another run into the crazy streets, where a confrontation could easily leave me dead and bleeding out.

THE PREVIOUS DAY AROUND lunchtime, I was in the courtyard trying to get a satphone signal to send a SITREP (situation report) back to our Ops Center when a loud crack ripped the air, and then another. Within seconds, Hakin's phone started playing a ridiculous ringtone on the highest volume setting and he announced that there was a sniper in our neighborhood, as if the shots weren't evidence enough.

Hakin, an out-of-shape, middle-aged businessman with a growing paunch before the war, now ran upstairs and came back with his AK-47 and two magazines. Then he ran out the front door. *This is the way people get killed,* I remember thinking.

Hakin lived in one of the ritziest areas of the city—it reminded me of the west side of Houston—but it was as dangerous as the worst gang turf in Southern California. The dictator's sons had homes nestled among the tree-lined boulevards that sat between Gergarish Road and Gorji Street, just a few blocks from the psychiatric hospital. How fitting that Hakin, who had no formal training in fighting, wanted to go hunting snipers. He belonged in that asylum, I half joked to myself.

"They say it's a single shooter. He's up a few blocks that way," Hakin said, pointing toward the rear of his house in his broken English. I wasn't here to hunt snipers; my job was to relay information to D.C., not go on a foot patrol with a guy who barely knew how to work his rifle. But I needed to keep building trust with these people, and of course Hakin had opened his home to me, a port in a dangerous storm. Hospitality is an ancient sacrament in Muslim countries. I cursed under my breath as I pulled on my Oakleys, shouldered my rifle, checked the mag and chamber, and nodded to Hakin, saying, "*Yah-la serbi*"—"Go . . . quickly."

Leaving the house, we circled left and moved low along a wall toward the street corner. I dropped prone to the concrete and crawled to the edge, poking my eyeball around and studying the empty, tree-lined street. But for a few cars, rocks, and trash, there was nothing really to see.

Hakin's phone rang again, startling both of us. I yanked my head back from the corner, yell-whispering at him to end that noise. Junk like that we called a "noise ND," short for negligent discharge. Have an ND, whether with a gun, flashlight, phone, or radio, and you direct the enemy to your position from the noise or light—and you never want to do that. It makes everyone around you hate you. "Hakin! Shut that thing off before you get us shot! Just take a deep breath," I told him as he got off the phone; he removed his wire-rimmed glasses and wiped the sweat with his sleeve as it dripped down into his now saucer-size eyes.

"The sniper is in Qadhafi's son's house on the roof. It is not far from here," he whispered.

The home of Qadhafi's heir-apparent was abandoned now. It had become a place for squatters and now, a sniper. I couldn't see it from my position, but Hakin seemed to have a clear line of sight from his. Here's a hint: if you can see the enemy, he most likely can see you, too.

Another pair of shots came from the house—it sounded like the same weapon as before, a high-powered rifle firing supersonic ammo. But I noticed that each shot produced a single report. If he'd been aiming in our direction there would have been two—the sound of the bullet breaking the sound barrier, followed by the muzzle discharge a second or so later. This guy was shooting anything that moved, but we weren't in his sights right now. We had to stay out of view of that house.

Long ago I learned the basic rubric for shooting and moving under fire. It was motion, distance, angles, cover, and concealment, MDACC for short. First, we needed to keep moving, because it's harder to hit a moving target. Our direction was important, too: we needed to move at an angle to the shooter, not on a straight line, which was far easier to hit. Lastly, Hakin and I also needed to find cover to stop bullets and conceal our position—cars, trees, or walls. There's a significant difference between cover, which stops a bullet, and concealment, which might not. This sniper had the advantage at a distance because we were assuming he had a scoped weapon and we didn't. But if we could get in the house at close quarters, that scope would become as useless as an ejection seat on a helicopter.

I grabbed Hakin by the shoulder and pointed to the wall across the street, then bolted for it, running low. I slid into the sidewalk and curb on the other side and motioned for him to come, while I covered his movement. Then, as we moved down the wall, another shot rang out. This time I heard two reports. The guy was firing our way now. Hakin stopped and reached for that dern ringing phone again. I was up near the wall as tightly as I could get, my rifle aimed toward the end of the street where the house was, though I still couldn't see it behind the row of trees blocking our view of the rooflines.

He took the call, then, eyes wild, gave me the update. "People from the neighborhood have seen him on the roof. He's on the far side of the house—not this side. Many people are coming to kill him in that direction."

We started to move forward, when the sniper's next two rounds were answered by an absolute onslaught of automatic weapons fire from the street off to our front right. We both hit the ground, hugging up against the corner of the wall, covering our heads.

It's never a bad thing to have reinforcements in a gunfight—or any fight, for that matter—but your life can depend on them knowing whether you're a friend or foe. With us situated on the opposite side of the building, it might be easy for them to mistake us for the sniper and shift fire onto us instead.

When the shooting let up, we moved quickly, crouching low, reaching the gate of a house next to the one the sniper was using. I mule-kicked the gate and we pushed inside. I scanned over my sights and cleared the courtyard, then turned my sights up high left toward the roofline of the other house. Three more cracks of a rifle brought another massive barrage of automatic fire tearing through the air, followed by a wild, yelling, chaotic commotion out in the street. I heard doors and glass being broken and the sounds of people running and yelling, shooting and more yelling. Someone had the same idea we did: get into that house.

An eight-foot wall separated our courtyard from the house where the sniper was hiding. I grabbed a white plastic chair, stood on it, and pulled myself over the wall, spider-dropped landing in a crouch, bringing my rifle up again, and looking for something to shoot. I heard scraping sounds and labored breathing behind me and realized Hakin was struggling to follow—pull-ups apparently weren't in his daily PT regimen. He finally dropped in a sweating, exhausted heap onto the ground next to me. To our right sat a ransacked SUV, stripped to the bone. Hakin got in front of me, saw someone he knew moving in the house, and yelled something in Arabic. Running, they headed to a door, went in, and started for the stairs. We followed them, tight, because I knew that a stranger like me—a Westerner—was just as likely to be shot as the sniper. I gripped Hakin's with my nonfiring hand, keeping him close, practically wearing him as we climbed to the second level.

More shooting and shouting punched and echoed down through the stone and marble structure as we raced up the ornately curved stairs to the next level. Blood was on the steps and the wall—smeared where someone had placed a hand going up or down.

We pushed through a door onto the flat roof of the building and found a bleeding black guy dressed in a dark gray, stained hooded sweat-shirt, flip-flops, and baggy, oversize camouflage pants. It was our sniper. He was shot nearly everywhere and was bleeding out. The low plaster and concrete wall in front of where he lay had been shredded by a storm of lead and full-metal-jacketed rounds. The mob had knocked him down in a hail of bullets, then rushed up and shot him many more times at point-blank range for good measure. A martyr might have called it a good way to die, but truthfully it was just the risk he ran working for a madman.

It was around this time when the townsfolk noticed me. Hakin immediately spoke up on my behalf and stood between us, their faces becoming less threatening by the second. A few reached to shake my hand. Many seemed surprised to find an American helping to protect their neighborhood.

BUT ALL THAT WAS YESTERDAY. As we hit the street again, at news of a hit team coming our way, I knew that tonight could easily be a different story.

Sumo, Sleepy, and Hakin were waiting by the front door with the kid—Hakin's son—all dressed in a mix of pajamas, flip-flops, jeans, and house shoes. The old man had on a blue terry-cloth robe with the belt dangling along the floor; the kid had a brown sheet around his shoulders. Were the killers coming for us, for this family tonight, because of what happened yesterday on the roof? Had I been compromised somehow by the locals?

"We're going to move out into the street and go up the road to your grandfather's house," I said to Hakin.

"I'm going to be in the front; everyone get right behind someone and stay quiet. Don't bunch up and don't walk in the middle of the road—stay right behind me and watch where you step. Don't make noise. Stay tight and you're last," I said, pointing to Sleepy. "Make sure we don't lose anybody. Everybody clear on this?" Sleepy translated, and nodded yes, so I opened the door and stepped out into the blackness.

Gun at my shoulder, I scanned the courtyard through my sights, moving across the open ground toward the gate. In the distance, to my right toward the marina, tracer fire licked up into the night sky and then I heard the report. From the delay, about ten seconds, I judged it to be roughly two miles from us.

Slowly, carefully I took my nonfiring hand and worked the squeaky metal gate handle, worrying the entire time that everyone in the neighborhood would hear it. I scanned up one side and down the other, then, slipping through to the street, we turned left, hugging the edge, away from the center of the road but keeping a few feet from the walls and buildings.

Moving down the middle of a road, gets you noticed, and that's how you get shot. Tonight, anyone could have seen our black silhouettes against the flat paved road. All the streetlights had been shot out, but the moonlight picked up anything shiny, so we made our way along the sidewalks, under the canopy of the trees but also where broken concrete, rocks, and debris littered the ground, making walking quietly a challenge.

I moved as quickly as I could, scanning over my rifle sights up, down, left, and right—rooftops, corners, under cars, any movement got my attention. My rifle stock and elbows were tucked in and the weight of my pack was cutting sharply into my shoulders. My senses were on fire and my eyes were opened so wide that my forehead ached as I tried to take in as much ambient light as I could. I directed my vision slightly off center to where I wanted to go, to allow the rod cells in my eyes to make maximum use of their abilities, since my cones had gone off duty when it got dark. My night-vision device stayed in my pack; I didn't have the head mount for it and mainly used it for static observation anyway—besides, I needed both hands free. My twenty-one-plus years of experience and training was all that stood between my gaggle of refugees and serious problems. At night in this hostile city, controlled by Qadhafi's hit teams, they could be coming from any direction. If we were shot down in the street, who would ever know? I was an American contractor; I wasn't officially here, at least according to my government. I'd gotten off a boat, had no passport stamp, and could just disappear into the haze that was Libya at war.

As we moved to a four-way intersection, blocked in every direction with rocks, chairs, tables, and tires, a machine gun ripped the night air nearby, much closer this time. I heard a vehicle engine start up—was it bad guys, or just some fellow reparking his car? At least I didn't have to worry about them driving up on us. We threaded our way through the makeshift barricades and made our turn south. Just a few blocks to go.

Lights from a vehicle washed over the intersection we'd just passed through. More automatic weapons fire, but I had no idea what they were shooting at. Now it was closer still. Nearby I could hear the engine of a truck or car racing and men yelling—were they searching the adjacent streets? Were the killers close? I couldn't tell if the trucks and shooting were friendly or not. But if we didn't hurry, we stood a good chance of being caught out in the open and gunned down.

Moving quickly but not running, my senses alive to every sound, every shadow, I had a strange thought of my dad back home in Mississippi, where I was raised. I sure could have used his help tonight. Once when our farm pond became infested with aggressive water moccasins, Dad strapped on his Smith & Wesson .357 Magnum revolver loaded with rat shot, got on the orange Kubota tractor, and rumbled out. A few minutes later, from the house, we children heard the battle. He shot snake after snake with that pistol. Most, we later saw, were hit right in their black heads.

When the Libyans and I reached the block where the house was, I told them to hide up against the wall under a tree, then I edged up close to the property. I heard nothing—no movement inside the gated courtyard. I motioned them forward. When we reached the front gate to the three-story house, I slowly worked the gate handle. It was locked.

I looked back to Hakin and made an unlocking motion with my left hand as if I had a key, then whispered to Sumo, "Does he have a key?" pointing to Hakin. He passed the question back.

Hakin shook his head no.

"Get the kid over that wall and tell him to open this gate."

Sumo and Sleepy lifted the featherweight preteen onto the top of the eight-foot security wall, which luckily was not covered with broken glass. While they did this, I looked for work, scanning both ends of the street for someone to shoot.

Moments later, metal scraped, hinges screamed, and the gate opened. Didn't they know about WD-40 over here? I slipped inside and scanned the immediate area for threats, then motioned everyone in. Counting them off as they filed past, I looked up and down the street once more, then shut the gate behind the last man. Sleepy wedged a piece of wood into the handle on the inside to keep it from being opened again from the street.

As we hustled across the courtyard to the front door of the house, Hakin took a knee in the garden and started digging. Grinning broadly in the pale moonlight, he held a brass key to the front door and blew dirt off it. We hustled inside and I sent everybody up the stairs to the roof.

A door opened out onto a terrace surrounded by a three- or four-foot wall. I saw plastic lawn chairs, the obligatory satellite TV dish, a clothesline holding laundry snapping softly in the gentle, salty Mediterranean breeze, a water bucket, and a few other housekeeping items scattered around.

"Lock the door and brace it, then you guys get down and get some rest. I'll keep watch," I told Sumo and Sleepy. I was pouring sweat and was exhausted—from the movement, from the events earlier in the day, from the boat ride—from just about everything. But from three floors up, I could see both ends of the street in either direction. I heard the low staccato sounds of automatic weapons in the distance. I didn't know where the bad guys were, but if anyone figured out we were here, they'd have to drive straight at us down that street. From up high, behind the cover of this thick concrete wall, I figured I could do a decent job on them. But the image of the sniper, perforated and bled out, stuck in my head. No stronghold was impregnable. I didn't know what the morning would bring. I never do. That's my job.

TODAY OUR NEW COMPANY NAME IS GRAY SOLUTIONS, but our mission is the same and we are who the big guys—governments, agencies, and international organizations—call when they don't want anyone to know they've got skin in the game. By 2011, when I hit Libya as a private contractor, I was seasoned in the business—a professional trained in battle, espionage, intelligence, and planning.

Today, at forty-five, I'm more operationally seasoned and more physically fit than ever in my life. My men and I can shoot an eight-inch target at twenty feet away in a dead sprint and can draw handguns and hit targets the size of the bottom of a Coke can in .85 seconds, on average. The teams that my company puts together today are subtle, quiet, yet any of them alone can unleash destruction with accuracy unrivaled by almost any private outfit on earth.

I previously served as a blue-badged federal employee in the Central

Intelligence Agency's ████████████████████ In it were some of the savviest paramilitary warriors America ever turned out. Every unit—Delta, ST6, Force Recon—will say they're the top, and everyone will argue they are better and badder or take on hairier missions that the other groups. Bottom line, they're all great units made up of true American heroes and I'm not here for a schoolyard debate about whose dad is toughest. Each unit has its own focus and specialties. But ██ men go through tremendously difficult selection and training and are capable of engaging the enemy anywhere on earth, under any conditions. Hard men, doing hard work, ██ operators work out on a limb with no backup team waiting in the wings to pull their butts out of the fire. They are the president's most lethal paramilitary tools.

I also served as a contractor with the CIA's █████████████, the teams that take Case Officers out into hot spots around the globe and make sure they make it home alive.

In the course of my time with the CIA, I learned to shoot practically any weapon I put my hands on; use a vehicle as a weapon or a means of escape with the precision of a surgeon's scalpel; detect surveillance in a crowded New Delhi street; blow up a truck with items found in your kitchen cabinets; or hit a guy just once to end it all. We could fight aboard commercial aircraft using just what was readily available, navigate a small boat and link up with submarines off the coast of a hostile country, or set up surveillance outposts on top of mountains in Pakistan and live for months. ██ specialists could penetrate nearly any structure on earth, steal whatever was required—even the safe itself—and leave nothing but smoking holes in the floor where the bolts had been—not even DNA. Masters of mayhem, yet men who could blend into a crowd in nearly any place on earth, do the job, and then disappear like morning mist when it sees the sun.

One day ██ operators are armed to the teeth running hard to a target and another you could find them carrying suitcases stuffed with millions of dollars for tribal leaders, buying supplies and loyalty, and making things happen in a very different way. Covert predators who leave no fingerprints and who are proud to claim the designation of operator.

The term "operator" was created decades ago to bridge the gap between the soldier and the spy. But today it seems that everyone who's ever held a gun claims the label.

An operator is someone who can fight his way out of a problem but wears no uniform; he is skilled at fighting, espionage, and gathering information, making drops, detecting surveillance, and meeting agents, but he or she lives in a kind of gray zone, playing chess in the dark. This isn't a life of 007 suits, ties, or cocktail parties, but Carhartts, beards, sunburned faces, AK-47s, and Bedouin tents. █████ is how the CIA gets its hands dirty; it is the dagger inside the cloak.

Today, I'm on the private side and we're known as "contractors," a term that can apply to a wide variety of skill sets and jobs. Construction workers hired to build barracks on a U.S. base in Kabul are contractors, as were truck drivers who hauled fuel to army units in Iraq, and former soldiers, sailors, and police officers who stand guard at U.S. embassies. But there is another type of contractor—a specialized contractor who works what's called the black side.

My team and I quietly help agencies like the CIA with things to which they don't want to be connected. We work for the FBI collecting information or snatching suspects in places—such as Iran—where they can't send their personnel. We work for foreign heads of state who have been dethroned by illegal coups and we put them back into power. We work for members of Congress, as well as Fortune 100 companies, gathering information on their foreign competitors or protecting their executives when they have to go into questionable countries. We work for the Department of Defense, training members of their various services to protect generals and admirals stationed in extremely hostile places. We work for the Nuclear Emergency Support Teams (NEST), teaching them to detect surveillance, to escape pursuit, and to use a vehicle like a weapon. We are force multipliers and we get the job done.

We are contractors in that we get paid the same way—by check or wire, most of the time. But there have been a few times when I was paid in cash slid across a restaurant table in a manila envelope from an undisclosed U.S. federal agency. But our role, our way of life, and our tradecraft—the way we do our job—is far, far different from standing guard at an embassy, guarding a CIA base, or driving a fuel truck. In a fight, there's no preliminary shoving match, no shouting. We don't say anything at all, we just move with as much speed, violence, and efficiency as humanly possible. It's not pretty, it probably doesn't make for good TV, but there are no points for style—just winning. We don't yell for a breacher to come blow down a door like in the movies—our guys see what's needed, step around the stack, set their charges without a word being spoken, and the door disappears with a loud bang and a gray cloud of smoke. We don't crack silly jokes in helicopters flying to a target; we don't get smashed in bars on the weekend and get into bar fights. It's like the difference between watching freshmen on a college campus and a grad student—one is just happy to be there and the other is ready to get about their business. We are mature, most of us have families, most go to church, and we know our business. Simply, we are professional warriors who inhabit the gray world where leaving a track behind can get you killed or embarrass your client.

In the world's most brutal places, you learn the little things or you die. Stop at the wrong vehicle checkpoint in Syria and you'll find yourself folded in half and stuffed into a car tire to be beaten to death with iron rods in a pale, concrete office somewhere. Say the wrong thing at a meeting with an Afghan warlord and you'll be buried out back in the goat pen by morning. Choose the wrong hotel in Karachi and you'll get a visit from the Pakistani Inter-Services Intelligence Agency, and have a fair chance of disappearing into a black hole from which there is no rescue. ████ we don't get black, diplomatic passports that give us immunity—we're on our own.

Fail to notice the street sweeper who takes a little too much interest in your car as you leave your hotel in Iran and you'll meet the Revolutionary Guard, be arrested, and end up tortured and killed like Beirut Station Chief Bill Buckley. Iran will never acknowledge they have you and U.S. government officials will publicly deny they ever knew you. You'll discover that the dank green walls of Evin Prison never let in the light of day.

Our world is savage, hard, and governed by two-hundred-proof Darwinian logic—either you make yourself strong and smart and survive, or you get slaughtered. I have tried to live by that all around the globe, from Libya to Iraq to Russia to Pakistan. At home it takes days to readjust to a life of Starbucks and Wal-Mart and sometimes I still drive to the local grocery store like I'm in a place where people still want to kill me—freaking my children out.

What the government has allowed me to tell of my story will give you a glimpse into the way the world really works behind the news, and a look into the future. At a time when the conventional military's footprint is shrinking around the globe, we are part of the new wave of American warfare—like it or not.

The business of life is about accumulating memories and experiences. This is not a treatise on geopolitics. These are a few of mine.

Welcome to my gray world.

I

The Rise of the Rebels

CHAPTER 1

Libya

Late February 2011
Washington, D.C.

Then I heard the voice of the Lord saying, "Whom shall send?
And who will go for us?"
And I said, "Here am I. Send me!"

Isaiah 6:8 (NIV)

I PULLED MY COAT UP TIGHTER AROUND MY NECK to ward off the frigid East Coast wind as it whistled through the parking garage and stole away any vestige of warmth I had left. Shouldering my daypack, I hit the button on my key fob and listened for the chirp-chirp telling me my car was locked. I could hear car tires turning on pavement, engines running, and the occasional horn on the streets below from someone running late to work. In the distance an ambulance announced its need to get somewhere. My phone vibrated against my belt as I stepped into the elevator to go up to my office. My secretary, Barbara, said I had a call waiting from a staff member from the office of Congresswoman Sue Myrick (R-NC). I knew her well—she was a woman whom the terrorists wanted dead and my company, SCG, LLC had provided her with armed security since the shooting of Congresswoman Gabrielle Giffords in Arizona on January 8, 2011. Congresswoman Myrick was permanently at risk, but that didn't stop her.

A fit, slight woman of seventy with short, dark hair and a quick smile, Myrick—who took office in 1995—founded the Congressional Anti-Terrorism Caucus and chaired the House Subcommittee on Terrorism, HUMINT [HUMan INTelligence], Analysis, and Counterintelligence. Closely tied to the intelligence community, she was a tough-minded American patriot and deputy minority whip in the House. Her driving concern was the rise of radical militant Islam, and she faced death threats nearly every day from Africa, the Middle East, and around the world. It was so bad that she had to change her congressional e-mail address regularly. I took the call on the way up.

"Sue was wondering," said her aide who handled military affairs, "if your team might have any insight into the Libyan crisis and the rebels, in particular. We know you've probably got resources beyond normal government channels and she trusts you guys and wants your input."

SCG, LLC WAS A SMALL, QUIET OUTFIT that provided a full suite of services—from intelligence and security support to special operations and tactical training—all for an elite, select client list of governments, corporations, agencies, and families around the globe. We were not a security company, but we provided that service and have had our people in Kabul, Islamabad, Cairo, and even on the U.S. Gulf Coast helping establish order for the state of Mississippi following Hurricane Katrina's wrath. We were not a training company, but we taught soldiers, sailors, airmen, marines, FBI agents, SWAT personnel, CIA staff, and allied foreign troops for more than ten years in everything from Pashtun language and combat medicine, to lock picking and driving armored trucks. We were not a private military or intelligence company, but we put boots on the ground in every major conflict zone since 9/11, provided intelligence on terrorists and coups, and even provided a highly focused "opposition research" service to select political clientele.

In a way, we were a hybrid of the Defense Department and CIA, but on a far, far smaller and leaner scale. We had several departments: Operations, Training, Intel, Logistics, and Admin, and each one worked to support the others. We had all the essential bells and whistles—from satellite phones, to encrypted voice calls, e-mail, and text messaging. We could track our people or our sensitive equipment anywhere on earth and see their position on one of the big screens in our Operations Center. Once my folks tracked me as I walked down into the vast red mountain canyons near Petra in southern Jordan to meet an asset—not an easy feat with the signal being blocked by the towering cliffs lining that path. We had video teleconferencing and could pull up our teams nearly anywhere on earth, except the north or south poles, for a face-to-face meeting. We used armored vehicles when necessary—many looked like taxicabs or beaters—a tactic we developed for Iraq and Afghanistan way before others were doing it. We also had B-7, near-presidential-level-protected Suburbans complete with run-flat tires, sat-com units, full medical trauma kits, automatic fire extinguishers under the hood, and door handles that shocked bad guys if they tried opening them.

Our men and women come from the best in the covert operations and intelligence world—CIA, Delta, ST6 (SEAL Team 6), 22nd SAS (Special Air Service), FBI HRT (Hostage Rescue Team), Britain's MI5 and MI6. We had our own in-house B&E (breaking and entering) specialists and we had the contract to teach the U.S. Navy's famous Red Cell team, based now at Little Creek, Virginia, and called by another name entirely, on how to break into protected buildings housing secure servers and other high-tech hardware. But we didn't take just any client and didn't accept just any contract—we were choosy and thus able to offer top-notch service anywhere on God's green (and brown) earth. We even brought in a psychologist who ran tests on every operator, instructor, and ops manager to determine what the optimum psychological profile looked like for future hires. We once took an American client to a Middle Eastern nation during the height of the Iranian war threat, and our team not only took all the standard security precautions, but went so far as to recon evacuation routes out in the event of a regional war; this included even identifying "borrowing" a boat from a local marina and sailing it to Cyprus in case all other legal travel options like airplanes and cars failed. I'd learned all these lessons about quality control the hard way, from my time as vice president of Blackwater USA, and also as the founding director of Blackwater Security Company.

BUT ON THIS COLD WINTER DAY I had to meet with Congresswoman Myrick: my team and I had escorted her abroad, and we had reported to her on the Egyptian revolt and the Muslim Brotherhood. I'd gone there, seen it firsthand, and had become her unofficial intelligence adviser, along with Dr. Walid Phares, who advised her on counterterrorism issues. In 2012, he would be appointed as one of the senior national security advisers to presidential candidate Mitt Romney and was a cochair of his Working Group on the Middle East and North Africa. Why Walid wasn't advising the National Security Council (NSC) was a mystery, because he definitely knew what he was talking about—as I came to find out over the next few months and years.

"I'll e-mail you what we have and I can be there when she's free. Just name the date," I said to Myrick's aide.

"The day after tomorrow," he said, adding that the congresswoman wasn't getting anything responsive to her questions from the Obama administration. "She thinks you guys might be able to give a more balanced view."

AT THE MEETING IN D.C., Congresswoman Myrick waved me to a chair like a gracious schoolteacher receiving a wayward pupil. Just off the reception area, her office was well appointed, with her desk in front of a large window, paintings hung from the wall amid mementos from her home state. We sat informally and talked about the president's apparent hesitancy to support the Libyan rebels and what Qadhafi's opponents might need. I suggested that to help them it would be important to identify the rebel sympathies and build relationships with their leaders, while staying alert to the fact that we needed to be careful to avoid dealing with militant Islamists; but I emphasized that I wasn't an expert on Libyan politics or the rebellion.

Of course, I got the context: all through the Middle East, threats to existing U.S. interests went hand in hand with the advancement of radical Islamist fundamentalists. The Arab Spring had unfolded in mid-December 2010 in Tunisia, as the tired and oppressed took to the streets, protested unemployment, sorry living conditions, the high cost of food, and lack of freedom. When a simple, lowly street vendor set himself on fire, Facebook and Twitter made his martyrdom a worldwide tsunami that struck North Africa and the Persian Gulf. In less than thirty days Tunisia had a new government, and that was just the start.

Other waves started in Algeria, Jordan, and Oman, but in Egypt they became tidal forces. The bloody rebellion there climaxed in February 2011, with the fall of the long-ruling dictator Hosni Mubarak and the subsequent destabilization and eventual takeover of the country by the terrorist-group-turned-political-party the Muslim Brotherhood.

Momentum built in other nations ruled by Sunni governments that had long suppressed their minority Shiite populations. Some saw it all as underdog freedom fighters toppling bullies who lined their pockets as their peoples suffered. I saw something else.

In the Muslim world, much of the violence that takes place is due to clashes between Shiites and the other major sect, the Sunni. The differences go back to a dispute over who was in charge of the Muslim faith after Muhammad died 632 years after Jesus, God's son, walked the earth. I'm oversimplifying, but the Sunnis thought the new leader should be elected, and Shiites thought the leadership should stay within the family of Muhammad. The Sunnis, a larger faction, won the day, and the Prophet Muhammad's close friend and adviser, Abu Bakr, became the first HMIC, the Head-Muslim-in-Charge. Officially, they called him their caliph and he ruled as sort of a head of state over the caliphate, the name for a Muslim state run by one religious leader. Since then the Shiites have fought the Sunnis for control because they don't recognize the authority of the elected Muslim leaders—who for the most part have been Sunnis. That explains why, in a very oversimplified way, religious violence erupts regularly around the world, as each group attempts to seize control from the other . . . in this peaceful religion.

But during the Arab Spring fleeing despots left vacuums in nations raging with sectarian tensions like these, all stoked by radical Islamists—some with terrorist sympathies and links to groups such as al-Qa'ida. Militant, fundamentalist Islamists, the terrorists, and the Iranian thugocracy basically saw opportunity there. The Muslim Brotherhood, terrorists bent on promoting radical Islam, were eager to assume power in Cairo. Across the region, questionable leaders were poised to exploit the chaos while Iran unspooled plots stretching from Saudi Arabia to Morocco. Vital U.S. relationships wavered as the geopolitics of the Middle East transformed; at the same time, places we'd had terrible relations with, like Libya and Syria, were now potentially opening up to us, if we'd just get involved and engage them.

But the MENA (Middle East and North Africa) area has always

been an enigma to the West, thanks to left-of-center media reports. Religious conservatives there are perceived by liberal Western academics as the victims, while U.S. religious conservatives are portrayed in just the opposite way. The United States is treated as the bad guy out to conquer land and steal oil, when in reality the United States has overthrown evil, cruel dictators like Saddam Hussein, who boiled victims alive. Once the dictators were gone, the U.S. tried to help the people set up their own governments. Then the media says that terrorists like the Muslim Brotherhood are really just poor folks oppressed, trying to gain freedom while the area's real religious minority—the Jews—are painted as the bad guys, the oppressors.

Reports like that only serve to complicate what was already a very complex place. In a way, I can understand journalists' goals—simplifying complex patterns allows people to see underlying critical truths they might otherwise miss. But because reality is, by its very nature, complex, too much simplification leads to an unsophisticated view of the world—and that seemed to be what was happening at the beginning of 2011.

So the questions about Libya were not wholly unexpected. Who were our friends? Who were our enemies? How could we steer them away from the militant Islamists, fundamentalists, and terrorists? If Qadhafi fell, who would take over? With whom would they ally themselves? For the sake of American influence, we had to seize the chance to befriend—or at least not antagonize—the new leaders. But we would have to move quickly because the bad guys were also moving.

Myrick's concern was threefold. First, she didn't want U.S. aid money falling into the wrong hands: if we were going to help the Libyan rebels, we had to know who they were, so supplies didn't wind up going to bad guys. Second, she wanted intervention directed toward stopping Qadhafi murdering his own people. Third, she wanted to see the United States build a relationship with the dictator's successor. Helping defeat Qadhafi could win us friends throughout the Middle East, creating new channels for intelligence and economic partnerships, while preventing al-Qa'ida from getting its people into a new government where it could co-opt Libya, as it had done in Afghanistan and was working to do in Yemen and Iraq.

We had to get on the ground and map the human terrain. You can't forge relationships over a phone line or predict what someone will do based on satellite imagery or an analyst's theory. You have to study the people, their goals, and alliances up close. You must listen to them. My team had to go there to be of any service to the congresswoman.

"What will you need from us?" That was my opening—the magic words.

"Send me," I simply said. It was our company motto at SCG, our ethos for everyone who worked there; we all had the same mind-set . . . send me.

They both looked at me like I'd lost my mind. The place we were talking about going—Libya—was halfway around the world, a literal minefield of alliances, tribes, spies, assassins, and American-hating Islamist jihadis; it was a place no person in his right mind would choose to visit. Every major player on the planet was looking, staring actually, at Libya, trying to get a handle on what was in play and how he or she could benefit. Politicians and the press were focused on the battles of the rebel factions, pitching it as a David and Goliath drama for the next news cycle. Mistakes would be costly and visible: a false move could demolish the solid reputation of our company, and of course, our lives would be at stake every moment we were out there.

In Libya, the difference between friend and enemy was almost impossible to identify; the complexities were baffling and made worse by the confusing mix of tribes and ethnicities that made up the rebel factions. It was as confusing to explain to those who are unfamiliar with the area as it is trying to articulate to a child why *flammable* and *inflammable* mean the same thing. But there was another kind of battle raging, one that would affect our every move and the outcome of the mission . . . and it was happening right here in Washington, where Libya appeared to be more of a political election football than anything else.

The United States was gearing up for a presidential election year and all the incumbents on both sides seemed to be trying to exploit the situation. Obama's people appeared risk-averse, promising an end to the fighting—pulling out of Afghanistan and yanking the majority of troops from Iraq. He would ultimately allow the negotiations on the Status of Forces Agreement with Iraq to fail, giving him an excuse to withdraw our troops without taking blame—claiming it was out of his control. But this resulted in the Iraqi Shiite prime minister Nouri al-Maliki inviting the Iranians to move in and essentially take over. Maliki also fired nearly all of the U.S.-trained generals and military leaders, replacing them with his cronies. The result of this shortsighted, politically motivated juggling, which was being passed off as leadership by Obama, resulted in the radical al-Qa'ida-backed Sunni rebels from ISIS/L fighting in Syria to be inspired to move whole hog into Iraq and set up their Islamic state because they saw a weakened Iraqi government.

These days we seem to start and execute wars with twenty-first-century thinking—applying roaring, immediate force, beating back our adversary conclusively; but then our politicians end wars with thinking from nearly half a century ago. Our nation was so hammered by the 1960s and '70s peace movement that we're often still applying thinking from the Vietnam era, and as a result, we haven't moved ahead politically or as a nation when it comes to our thinking on how to finish a war. If the military were allowed to go gloves-off, it'd be a different story—we'd hammer every enemy we faced. But politicians can't stomach the poll numbers long enough to see it through. But the flip side was that if the president did help the Libyans, he didn't want the accusation that he had aided terrorists by supplying the wrong rebel group. But to fix that, you have to get info on who's who, and as of yet, the administration hadn't given the CIA authorization to go in and figure out who the terrorists and rebels even were.

To me, the realities of what could be gained from engaging the rebels was in danger of being overlooked for political reasons. I always thought I was just an operator and a business owner, but now I had to be more: diplomacy and politics that lay behind the decisions now affected my every move. This is the reality now and I had to learn that game quickly because half the battle takes place behind the scenes and there is no training course except OJT, in other words, on the job. You have to learn the landscape and, to me, political maneuvering disgusted me almost as much as the things we'd see in Tripoli.

"I don't mean that you pay for it—we'll take care of that," I told them in her office, "but to do this right, I'll need to go. I'll need to take a small team—two of us. But I need permission to be there. Can you do it? Can you get me in with Shalgham? He hasn't defected, but he has denounced Qadhafi. He's a start and I think it's best to start there. I'll get on the next train to New York this afternoon." Ambassador Shalgham was the Libyan representative to the UN Security Council in

New York and I'd volunteered that my company foot the bill; I thought it could also be an opportunity for business development once I got boots on the ground.

Congresswoman Myrick raised her eyebrows. "You sure don't waste any time."

"No, ma'am," I said with a grin.

AS I WALKED DOWN THE STEPS of the Cannon House Office Building into the crisp winter air, worlds were colliding—America's and Africa's—along with my own and people a world away. This was not just a fact-finding project. Helping overthrow a dictator would impact millions—maybe become part of history. This could reverberate for generations in hundreds of ways I could never foresee and possibly be studied the world over. I had started with the CIA back in 1990 and worked in and around the intelligence and special operations community for more than twenty years. But this was a promotion I never saw coming.

CHAPTER 2

Meeting Ambassadors

Late February 2011
New York City/Cairo, Egypt

SECURITY ON THE STREET of Ambassador Abdel Rahman Shalgham's building was tight. NYPD's finest stood bundled up in their dark winter coats along the sidewalk or hidden back in the shadows within the ever-present warren of construction scaffolding that obscured the lower part of the building. Qadhafi's Jamahiriya Security Organization, or JSO, had thugs all over the world, assassination teams primed to hit those a lot less threatening than the man I was booked to meet.

This was my first contact with the Libyans and I wanted it to go right. I had to assume that there were still Qadhafi loyalists or at least a few riding the fence on the ambassador's staff, and that if they heard my name or got wind of my mission, I'd be dead as soon as my feet touched North African soil. The faster I could get in and out anonymously, the better.

The ambassador's office, high above the street, was long and narrow with lots of wood paneling and bookshelves on the left, opposite large picture windows on the right. Despite those long windows overlooking the Manhattan streets, the office seemed dark—or maybe it was the mood brought on by the slaughter happening back in his home country? An oil painting hung facing his desk from a square column oddly placed in the center of the room—it depicted a beach scene in Libya. An imposing desk faced the door I'd just entered. An older, diminutive man in a neatly pressed dark suit rose to meet me, shook my hand, and gestured that I sit.

Ambassador Shalgham was a balding man in his mid-sixties with a broad face and large, haunted eyes. He'd been Libya's foreign minister until 2009, when he was made Qadhafi's representative at the UN Security Council. His break with his lifelong friend and the regime on February 25, when he denounced Qadhafi before the council, had been public and bitter. A short time later, the Libyan dictator's prime minister, Al-Baghdadi al-Mahmoudi, had been overheard on a cell phone intercept threatening to burn Ambassador Shalgham's family in retaliation.

Tea was brought in on a tray, but I didn't delay; time was of the essence and I got straight to the point. "Mr. Ambassador, I come on behalf of Congresswoman Myrick, but understand that I do not represent the U.S. government in any way. I must be clear on that—I am not here as a U.S. government official. The congresswoman is interested in the situation in your home country and that of the Libyan people."

The leather of his chair groaned as he sat back with hands clasped just under his chin and steepled his fingers, nodding slightly as I spoke. He reminded me of a master chess player contemplating his next move. Silence filled the air, competing only with the muffled sounds from the air-conditioning vent above. He realized the power of silence and was using it . . . or he just didn't know how to respond.

"Sir, she desires to know more about the situation and what, if anything, is needed. She is not promising you anything, as she doesn't set foreign policy. Her only goal is to see that the killing of innocent citizens by Qadhafi stops."

Finally, he spoke.

"Thank you for coming, sir," he said calmly, "but I am not sure your government *is* willing to help. We have asked, but no one has responded." I could see that the last weeks had taken their toll; he seemed weary to his very core.

His skepticism was understandable. President Obama was talking about aid to Libya but nothing substantive had happened. Many saw the delay as political; they mentioned the president's doubts about getting involved in another war in that part of the world, his reluctance to invade a sovereign nation, his fear of tarnishing his reputation as a transformer of American policies abroad, his concern over his reelection bid and whether his left-leaning base would be offended. But civilians were dying, and my friends and contacts at the CIA were complaining about the lack of a presidential finding that would have allowed their organization to even start intelligence operations; and there had certainly been nothing said about covert operations to support the rebels in battle—that wasn't even on the drawing board, let alone the table for discussion . . . but perceptions and elections were. A presidential finding is a written directive issued by the president that gives an agency its marching orders to carry out a particular job. Answering to the executive branch, U.S. intelligence can't move until the president, its *prime customer*, clears the path by such a written order.

At the time, if you'd asked someone in the administration about the rebels in Libya, the conversation probably would have gone like this:

Question: *Who are the rebels?*

Administration: *We don't know.*

Question: *Who's their leader?*

Administration: *We don't know.*

Question: *Where are they based?*

Administration: *We don't know that, either.*

Question: *So, if I stood up in the back of a pickup with a pair of binos and looked east, I'd be as informed as I am now?*

Administration: *Probably so.*

I don't think that is the proper use of an intelligence apparatus.

BECAUSE OF CONCERNS about the Libyan rebels' disorganization, internal politics, and limited capabilities, the early days of ▇▇▇▇ U.S. ground support never went much beyond limited intelligence collection and scant diplomatic overtures from the State Department.

Chris Stevens would arrive the next year as ambassador. But faster, more purposeful support and leadership from the United States could endear us to the rebels and strengthen the hand of the rebel leadership in the National Transitional Council (NTC)—the civil government trying to position itself as successor to Qadhafi. It could open the way for tighter diplomatic relations and intelligence opportunities, subduing the influence of our meddling geopolitical competitors, namely Iran, China, and Russia. But all of that was way down the road.

I TRIED TO REASSURE SHALGHAM. "Sir," I began, "there are elements who might wish to take a wait-and-see approach, but Congresswoman Myrick is a powerful member of Congress and perhaps she can convince her colleagues and the administration to help stop the killing. If she knew more . . ." I let the sentence hang in the air.

I understood the power of silence, too.

I was anxious—not nervous, but anxious: I had never been in the position of having to persuade someone on a matter of such a monumental, history-making importance. Millions of lives were potentially in the mix here. I was trying to convince him to give me a shot at going into the fray immediately, before the situation deteriorated further and our chances to meet, greet, and help the rebels evaporated. It was a crucial trip and I had to make it happen.

On the train ride up from D.C., I'd come up with five objectives: First, deliver solid, fast, accurate information to the chairwoman about conditions in-country. Second, locate rebel leadership and secure a contract with them to provide strategic consulting services to them. Third, organize teams of veteran U.S. Special Operations personnel to deploy to the country to fulfill the contract. Fourth, use that contract to fund operations to gather *atmospherics* and push that vital information to the U.S. intelligence community.

The final goal was a long shot, but worth keeping as a high priority. I hoped to offer U.S. intelligence agencies the opportunity to even place

CIA officers in NOC (non-official cover) jobs in our company working under our Libyan contract. With agency officers in place with rock-solid "cover for status"—that's the lie that explains who you are pretending to be—and "cover for action"—that's the lie that explains what you're doing while you're there—the United States would have direct access to people in the seedy, murky underside of Libya, people whose motives and alliances were now unclear. The goals were a tall order, but don't tell me the sky's the limit when there are footprints on the moon, because as my dad would say, you never hit high aiming low. Sure, my plan needed to be thought through in more detail, and of course my guys would tear it apart operationally using a technique we called "red-teaming." But those five goals composed my overall intent, and I needed an answer now.

The ambassador reached forward and picked up his tea, then sat back and slowly sipped it, saucer in one hand, cup in the other. Then he broke the silence. "We are working now to pass Resolution 1973, which will hopefully create a no-fly zone over the country. The vote is coming soon," he said.

"Yes, sir, I know it's in the works. Do you think you have the support?"

"Yes, I think we do—if Russia and China don't go against us"; then he paused and shifted his gaze to the painting of the Libyan beach scene hanging on his wall. "You realize this is my home and Qadhafi and I went to school together? He was my friend, so this is all very difficult for me. But what he is doing—it is not right and it cannot be allowed to continue. We need the help of the West—we want it. But no one is speaking with us about that. I am very glad to hear of the congresswoman's interest. Tell me what you propose?"

This was the fork in the road. I leaned forward and took it.

"Mr. Ambassador, I need to go to Libya now and speak with the commanders of the rebels. I need to see the situation on the ground, in order to understand their needs logistically and strategically. I need you to authorize my travel and draft a letter in both Arabic and English stating that I am there to help and to give me all assistance that I require."

"You want to go to Libya, knowing the hell that it is?" he asked with an amazed look on his face.

"Yes, sir," I said. "I am aware of the dangers there, and I am not a staff member of Congress. I have experience in conflict zones, and you will not be held responsible for my safety. Nor will any friendly Libyans."

I didn't want him to kill the project because he was afraid something was going to happen to me and arouse the U.S. government's fears about intervening. I needed him to understand that the government had no interest in the fate of a nonofficial.

Ambassador Shalgham thought for a moment and then responded: "Tell me what you need and I will make the necessary contacts for your trip."

I couldn't have asked for more. Shalgham was willing to make the necessary connections in both Washington and Benghazi.

He looked at me for a few minutes. "You will have the letter before you leave," he promised.

"For my safety, please keep the knowledge of my trip restricted to yourself, Washington, and your secretary." I didn't want someone to find the letter in his copying machine and then send it to Qadhafi's people.

He nodded. "Yes, that is a good idea and I will do that," he answered. It was a go.

WE MOVED BEFORE ANYONE on either side could have second thoughts. Two days later, I'd said good-bye to my family and was in the air with my colleague Dion, or D, as we called him. D was a pro, a restrained, yet lethal man whom we called the human hand grenade—in an emergency, just pull the pin and stand back. He was a guy to whom I entrusted my life on a regular basis. We were bonded like Gorilla Glue. Dion DeLarancio had been with our company for nearly five years. He'd taken a hard time for his name ever since one of the guys heard the story of how SEAL Master Chief Hershel Davis, trying his best to pronounce D's surname, got frustrated and finally just started calling him Dion De-La-Dago, a dig at his Italian ancestry. The story stuck.

Dion came to us at thirty-four, with a huge grin and tattoos covering both arms. He'd already been overseas, working pretty hairy personal security details in Haiti back when that place was getting on its feet after the 2010 earthquake. He was a dependable, loyal man who could take down a rhinoceros as long as he didn't have to engage electronic devices to do it. The boy had a very limited capacity for gadgets and gave our IT division fits. Give him a BlackBerry and you'd have it back, as a brick-berry, in a few short weeks, needing replacement.

We were, for now, strictly a two-man team, backed up by personnel at the Ops Center in North Carolina, run by Colonel Rick Cantwell, a bearded, fit, hawk-eyed retired U.S. Army Special Forces officer, West Point graduate with a master's degree, a combat veteran who'd served in a Tier 1 Special Mission Unit, and who commanded a battalion of troops along the 38th parallel with North Korea. There'd be no one better to track our every move. We wanted it all to go down fast; we moved like our hair was on fire, trying to stitch together a flexible plan to get into Libya as fast as we could and develop the situation from there. We figured that speed was our security for now. If we linked up quickly in Cairo with our contact—Qadhafi's former representative to a European city—and then slipped away to Benghazi to meet the rebel leaders, perhaps we could leave anyone following us in the dust.

D and I flew on the same plane but apart. He sat a few rows ahead of me, both of us in aisle seats with belts unbuckled. We didn't talk in the ticket line, at the departure gate, or on board—nothing to indicate we were together, in case there had been a leak and Qadhafi's JSO men were tracking us. What better way to assassinate leaders of a rebel movement in hiding than to follow us to them?

We traveled using a principle taught at the CIA and to intelligence officers the world over—be the Gray Man. Blend in, don't stick out, don't be obvious. It's easy to spot the security contractors and the wannabes on airplanes—we even made a game of it. You look for the brand-new cargo pants with more pockets than stripes on a zebra, all held up by a massive OD green rigger's belt; clean, unscuffed hiking boots; digital watches with a compass strapped to the watchband the size of sand dollars; a tan ball-cap with the blood type scrawled somewhere on it; wraparound shades the size of welder's goggles; a shiny, brand-new, never-been-used three-day pack without a bit of sand, dust, or dirt visible on it anywhere, and all covered with patches Velcroed to it. But being a professional in this work means not sticking out like that. Not announcing you're a tough guy to the world. The toughest guys, the lethal men, are the ones you'll never notice—unless they decide. One of the most lethal men I know drives a Chrysler convertible, wears flip-flops, golf shirts, and faded jeans and listens to the Grateful Dead. Being gray provides the opportunity for sensitive work to be done privately, professionally, and, hopefully, unnoticed.

But we did have SOPs (standard operating procedures) that we adopted on board commercial aircraft just after 9/11. I'd been contracted to help revamp the U.S. Federal Air Marshal program out in Artesia, New Mexico. We changed the way they shot and fought, and the tactics they used on board the planes. Then, a few years later at our company shoot house in Mississippi, my people built a full-size aircraft cabin complete with overhead luggage compartment, a galley, toilets, and a cockpit. We burned through countless drills to defend the cockpit. We had a simple plan of in-flight action if someone tried another 9/11 and no air marshals showed up—collapse on the cockpit and defend the door with seat cushions, tray tables, seat belt extenders, and anything else we could get our hands on. The only other options were to let the air force blow us out of the sky or the bad guys crash the plane. I'd take our chances in a fight over those one-way tickets.

Separately, we deplaned in the busy Cairo airport, bought our entry visas from the Egyptian desk clerk, trudged through passport control, collected our rucks (backpacks) from the baggage carousel, and made our own ways through the airport. We'd each flown with rucksacks hidden inside large, colorful, touristy-looking REI duffel bags. The actual rucks we used were designed with a hidden sleeve between the frame and the pack where you could hide a rifle and retrieve it on the move with one hand. Hopefully, we wouldn't need rifles, but if we acquired them, this would hide them from anyone observing us from a distance; our goal was to make a small footprint—if any at all.

Cairo, the thousand-year-old city whose Arabic name translates to "the city victorious," is the largest city in Africa and is arguably the hub of the Arab world. Split down the middle by the Nile River, the country is, as a nineteenth-century writer once put it, a place where "splendid things gleam in the dust" and you simply have to submit yourself to the chaos in order to grasp it all. Chaos in traffic, chaos in politics, and even chaos inside chaos reigns, such as during the protests in Tahrir Square, where cotton candy vendors sold to families who'd brought their kids out for the day like it was a big carnival. The city is a blend of Africa, Asia, and Europe, where Cleopatra cigarettes are sold by street vendors on the corner in front of a restaurant offering stuffed pigeon for patrons who, in the regional pastime of the Middle East, sit outdoors puffing away on hookah pipes, discussing politics along with conspiracy theories. To the east in this vast urban sprawl lie the labyrinthine streets of Islamic Cairo; to the south is the Coptic Christian community; downtown houses the city's business center and the five-star hotels; and to the west is the isle in the Nile, the Zamalek District, where we were heading.

IN THE CAIRO AIRPORT, D and I moved independently, sweating from heat that hits you like opening an oven; it never quits, radiating down, pounding you, despite the time of year. I stopped and bought a local phone and SIM card with cash before I left the airport, then made my way to the taxi stand. If a government group has your phone in their database, just buying a new SIM won't help; they still have your phone's IMEI—the unique number hardwired into each phone. Come up on a net using a different SIM and your IMEI gives you away. You need to get a totally new phone and SIM, and then don't call anyone you ever called from the old phone. You also need to remove the battery from your usual phone so you're not tracked to your new location; that proves hard for iPhone users, but wrap them a few times in aluminum foil—that'll kill the signal. Before our departure, we'd done preliminary map studies and found our hotel, the airport, and a few other places we thought might be useful. One was the Fairmont hotel in Heliopolis, just a few miles down the road from the airport, along our direction of travel.

I asked the cabbie to pull over there, and I left a message in an envelope at the desk with D's last name on it. Inside the envelope was my new local phone number. Then, back in my cab, I wound my way yet again through the crammed, smog-laden streets of Cairo, asking the driver to take me through the souks and get us off the main roads. We popped out at Tahrir Square toward Gezira Island and the Zamalek District, crossing the 6th October Bridge and passing the burned-out buildings left from the recent revolution, finally arriving at the Marriott Casino, right in the middle of the Nile River.

Meanwhile, D loitered around the airport, buying a phone, a power adapter, a local SIM, and other tourist bullcrap to kill time. He was about ten or fifteen minutes behind me. He also stopped at the Fairmont, ordered a Coke at the bar, then wandered over to the reservations desk and inquired about any messages for him and picked up my envelope. It was a rudimentary drop to make sure our new phone numbers were clean, but it worked for our purposes. From his local phone, he sent a text to me confirming it was working and I responded. Then he headed in my direction to our hotel and also checked into his room.

Upstairs, I sent D another text advising him of my room number and confirming that I'd be making contact with the Libyans to set up a meet later in the day. He said he was going down to scout the hotel grounds, looking for quick ways off the property, places to conduct meetings nearby, and the location of security cameras. My next text was to Ambassador Abdel Bey, the Cairo contact given to me by Shalgham. I sent him my number and told him that I wanted to meet in three hours at the hotel.

This Libyan diplomat, recently named by Qadhafi as his ambassadorial representative to a European city, had instead refused the assignment and, in the coming weeks, would be my key link in Egypt and Libya, a liaison to military and political leaders within the highest levels of the NTC.

D and I planned to meet the ambassador at the hotel—it was large, with an outdoor café or two and numerous restaurants inside. A lot of people were coming and going for meetings and lunch, a wedding party was checking in, and a few individuals were apparently there to just get away from chaotic Cairo. The Marriott was like any other hotel—clean rooms, with satellite TV and Wi-Fi that worked most of the time; it had room service and even a gym, but as the place struggled to make you forget the hostile region beyond the gates, it just took one glance at the front door's metal detectors and bag X-ray machines to wake you up and remind you otherwise. The machines and the guards who ran them were about as sharp as a marble, but at least it gave the impression of security, which was better than none at all.

SPEED WAS STILL OUR GOAL. It was our security: we were trying to get inside the OODA loop of any possible pursuers. That term stood for *observe*, *orient*, *decide*, *act*, and was something we taught in our shooting and tactics classes, but it applied to adversarial situations of all types. In business settings, the OODA loop could take days or even weeks to cycle around. But in a fight, it happens in seconds.

The human reaction to stimulus—the time it takes to react to something the average person notices—is roughly one-quarter of a second. Take this example: my opponent has to observe me, orient himself to me, take a decision about what I'm doing, and finally act on that decision—run, attack me, or cower and die. A bad guy intent on killing and robbing me with a knife from twenty feet away can cover that distance within about two seconds on foot, completing that OODA loop from thought to finish—the knife sticking out of my chest. My job is to close my loop tighter, quicker than my opponent—in other words, to react faster. This means that I have to complete my mental loop in fewer than two seconds, which is why we trained on the shooting ranges to observe, react, and fire on targets in less than 1.5 seconds—which was our relaxed standard. Most of us did it way faster than that, with subsecond shots and the ability to dump at least half a magazine into a target in two seconds, all while moving laterally off line of the direction of the bad guy's travel. Result? Bad guy gets halfway to me and drops after being filled with bullets in his face and neck—and I don't have a knife sticking out of my chest.

In Cairo we weren't dealing with direct, head-on combat—we hoped. But the principle was the same: we had to move quickly, before any possible adversary could act against us. Benghazi, where the rebel leaders were headquartered and which was our ultimate destination, had been hot since Qadhafi's men had killed fourteen demonstrators, then shot up their funeral procession. Two days later, the rebels, with the help of a defector, had stormed an arms depot and fought Qadhafi's forces until there were only a handful of loyalists left in the city, holed up in a government compound called Katiba. The position of the rebels was stable, but that could change at any moment.

My cell vibrated—the ambassador replied, agreeing to the meeting, but adjusted the time by two hours. I agreed, asked him what he'd be wearing, and told him where to go once he was inside the hotel. Then D and I began setting up.

I would do the meeting and D would pull countersurveillance and act as my security. If things went sideways, he'd come in hard and hurt as many people as fast as possible to create confusion, then together we'd beat feet for the main exit and hit the escape routes we'd worked out earlier in the day. After falling back to our rally point—the Fairmont—we'd camp out at the airport until we could catch the next flight home.

THE ART OF SURVEILLANCE is a sophisticated one that breaks into three major pieces. The *offensive* portion is actually called surveillance and involves following a target and cataloging his routes, his stops, and his contacts along the way. You record the time, day, weather, and other things related to that target's movements. There are two types of surveillance—close, or discreet. *Discreet* is where the target never sees you or your team and there's a chance that you'll lose the target to maintain that invisibility. That's the risk. On the other hand, *close* surveillance is where you follow the target and don't care if he sees you. You practically bumper-lock his car with your own, much like the Soviets would do during the Cold War to someone they feared was going to defect. Both types of offensive surveillance are time-consuming and expensive if you field a proper team, because you need people and vehicles available continuously so you can swap them out and prevent the target from seeing the same face, car, or license plate enough to uncover the operation.

The second component to the art of surveillance is surveillance *detection*. That involves preventive and defensive actions taken by you to detect an enemy team and, sometimes, prevent it from following you. The primary tactic is a surveillance detection route (SDR), literally a route designed to force pursuers on foot or in a vehicle to make mistakes, to expose themselves, all while allowing you, the intelligence officer (IO), to maintain your cover and not appear to actually be craning your neck to see them.

Consider the following very compressed example of an IO in Rome heading out to meet an agent. He might take a taxi for a few blocks, then get out and walk down a one-way street against the flow of traffic to a shaved-ice shop. Inside he might buy a few scoops, then turn and eat while standing in the storefront window gazing out at the street he'd just used to get there. To the average observer, he looks like a tourist taking a break and getting a snack. But in actuality, taking the taxi forced anyone following him on foot to have to get into cars to catch up. Then walking down the one-way street against the flow of traffic stripped off those and any other cars that might have followed him down the road in the taxi. Standing in the window gave him a chance to see foot surveillance standing around in the street or on the sidewalks, trying to find something to do. But if the IO chose the shaved-ice shop carefully, there would be no bus stops to loiter near; no newspaper stands to read next to; no phone booths for pretend calls. In such a situation, it's harder for an enemy surveillance team to look like normal people: they stand out like dog's balls, and thus the SDR fulfills its function in detecting surveillance because it forces the team to commit errors of cover for status and action, as well as errors of correlation. An error of correlation is when the movement of the enemy surveillance team mirrors that of the IO. He turns left; they turn left. He stops; they stop.

The challenge to the IO, though, is to pull this surveillance detection route off without looking like he's checking for surveillance. It's easy to spot someone walking down the street obsessed with looking over his shoulder—you know he's guilty of something, or else why would he be looking? As an IO, you don't want to be that guy—you want to be relaxed and natural. The only way to accomplish that is to assume you are always under surveillance and let the route uncover surveillance, not your neck. That's the rule.

The third basic component of the art of surveillance is *countersurveillance*, or CS. Today, D would be my CS for the meeting. He'd watch my back to see if anybody was following me when I arrived and when I left. If the people and resources are available, the IO will set up a team who actually watch his back when he is going operational—when he's on his SDR. Using the IO in Rome again as an example, his CS team might take up positions at certain points along his route. As he passes these points, he might perform some action, such as stopping at a bench to sit down and drink something. After finishing the drink, he might stuff a napkin into the bottle and leave the bottle on the ground next to the bench and walk away. His CS team would stay in place watching that bottle to see if anyone moved in after he left. Did anyone try to retrieve or check it? If that happened, then it's one of two things—a trash collector or a surveillance team checking to see if the IO left a secret message in the bottle for his agent. If the IO's team sees that sort of activity, they then alert the officer that he has surveillance on him, at which point he'll probably abort.

THE SUN WAS BLAZING downstairs at the outdoor café, but I spotted the table and kept walking. It was shielded by plants from the other patrons and was a good spot. D would be at another table close by and able to watch me approach and to keep an eye on our surroundings during the meeting. He'd set up a video camera hidden in a bag to catch the events. We were set, and I was armed with a cover for action story to explain, in case anyone challenged why the ambassador and I were talking.

Today, D and I had no weapons and, to be honest, we didn't know what these guys looked like aside from the image of Abdel I had pulled off Google. We didn't know whether the guys showing up really were loyal to the rebellion or whether they were Qadhafi's feared and ruthless JSO hit men.

Qadhafi's men were barbarians who infiltrated groups suspected of plotting military coups such as the one currently in progress, and D and I understood we were definitely potential targets.

As I took a seat down the walk from the intended meeting site, D took his position under an umbrella. The Cairo sun was blistering as we noticed two unknowns slide into position a few yards away. Both appeared to be Libyans and wore loose clothing that concealed their waistlines. In our line of work, we generally put people who conceal their waistlines into one of three categories—they're either out of shape and hiding it, are too lazy to tuck in their shirts, or are hiding a weapon. In this area of the world, it was best to assume the latter.

The ambassador arrived right on time, dressed as promised. D's eyes, hidden behind sunglasses, tracked him. We let things simmer for a minute, watching for any signs that others were getting in place to observe things or for the ambassador to do something odd like signal to someone else. It's a good idea not to rush in, and instead to wait and see how the environment has changed before you expose yourself.

After a few minutes, D took his ball cap off—a signal to me that all looked good from his angle. I waited a little longer . . . then I moved.

Just a few steps from his table, I turned and entered the private patio area where the ambassador sat. I smiled and extended my hand, "Hi," I said. D's table was visible in my peripheral vision. The ambassador's back was to the entrance and I was glad—it gave me the seat with the view of the entrance to our little private spot. It was also good tradecraft to get to the meeting first and grab the seat, set the environment, and control what you could. We got there first but didn't want to expose ourselves and so decided to let him move, while we watched. If it didn't look good, we would have just calmly pulled out and slipped back to our rooms and no one would have known who we were.

The ambassador rose slightly, a big grin on his wide, round face, and shook my hand. "Mr. Jamie?" he said. "I am Abdel. Please have a seat." The ambassador sported a small, thin mustache like those worn by actors in the 1930s; he wore thick glasses that shielded sleepy eyes and so that's what we nicknamed him—Sleepy.

As we exchanged pleasantries and ordered drinks, I asked him to call Ambassador Shalgham back in New York to confirm we'd linked up—but also to reassure myself that he was actually the right guy. He dialed the number, got him on the phone, and handed it to me. It was Shalgham, and he said that I should show Abdel the letters I carried with me from Shalgham and the congresswoman. That set my mind somewhat at ease, as only Shalgham's and Myrick's offices knew the letters existed.

I took off my cap and put it on the table, my signal to D that we were good to go, and then got right to business. In every PM—personal meeting—we did what we called the "mad minute" as soon as we established the linkup, the bona fides, of the other party. The mad minute was a gunshot of information we dumped to the other person, telling them why we were meeting and what we were discussing, should anyone ask later. We also covered where we'd meet again if the meeting ended prematurely. All this precaution and deception protected us both and gave us a fallback plan if the meeting were to end up compromised.

Sleepy said there were others whom I needed to meet. One was the unofficial public relations adviser to the NTC, which was the political face of the revolution. Another was a finance guy for the rebels. I agreed and he started making calls, while I sent D a text jokingly telling him not to kill the next two guys who came into the area and sat with us. He sent me back a photo of his middle finger, ambushing me in the middle of the meet. Nice.

The other two arrived after about five minutes—they turned out to be the two unknowns we'd spotted earlier during our recon with their shirts covering their waistlines . . . and not because they were armed. One guy was in his early thirties, short, bald, and stocky; and he was smart enough to make the best of what he had by wearing high-end designer clothing. He was introduced as the rebels' PR guy. We nicknamed him Cue Ball.

The other guy had thinning hair, spoke very good English, was taller and thin but with a lazy man's paunch, and had ties to the old Libyan royal family—he was the money guy. His eyes, surrounded by dark circles, were magnified by the lenses of his glasses and looked bugged out slightly, earning him the nickname Rango, after the lizard character in the movie of that name.

I explained yet again that I wasn't coming representing the U.S. administration, but that Congressman Myrick's influence could definitely go a long way to help their cause, if all checked out satisfactorily. I went on to say we could discuss the possibilities of providing consultants and humanitarian support.

Finally, they said, it appeared that the United States was interested in doing something. They said they'd had zero contact with any Americans to date, except for two staffers from Senator John McCain's office who had just flown in a few days ago—we'd apparently just missed them.

Over the next hour they discussed their needs and I asked them specifics about how they were funded, how they managed to supply their troops, how their communications systems worked, where they were getting their weapons, ammunition, and medical supplies, and they couldn't answer anything.

These weren't military men, explaining why they couldn't answer most of my questions when it came to operational or logistical matters of warfare. I wanted to know who was supplying them, how was it getting to them, who funded it, and what they needed. Of particular interest were the questions of their lack of supplies and how their comms were holding up. Did they have adequate medical supplies?

I also wanted to get an idea of their overall strategic plan, their concept of operations, to defeat Qadhafi. Were they planning to pick off towns along the coast, secure the oil production facilities, and then divide Libya into east and west, separated by the Gulf of Sidra? The east had the oil—the major revenue source. The west had desert and mountains but no real economic power. Did they plan to take the east and cut their losses, leaving Qadhafi the other side of the Gulf? Or did they want the whole thing?

Did they have a plan to hunt down and kill Qadhafi himself, or would they be content to let him retire to Algeria or Niger, countries with which he had at least decent relations? It was hard to imagine they'd let him go; he'd engendered plenty of hatred. I grasped one thing for certain—they had to kill him or capture him or else they would lack credibility when they eventually assumed power. Everyone in the country would be afraid that he'd reappear.

These guys were the diplomats and financiers, not the warriors or operational planners. I'd need to see the generals to get military information. I asked them to set up a meeting for me with whoever was in charge of operations out of Benghazi. I told them I'd go to Benghazi and could leave anytime. They said the route was through Egypt—a thirteen-hour drive westward. I think they thought that would deter me. Fine, I said, "Set it up." Sleepy, apparently caught by surprise, said he would make the calls, and we all agreed to meet again the next day.

I slipped my ball cap back on, signaling to D that the meeting was wrapping up, said my good-byes, and left them all at the table. It's better to leave a meeting first; otherwise you take the risk that they go out, watch you exit, follow you, or worse, finger you to someone else who snatches or kills you. I wasn't worried about being abducted on the hotel grounds, but I did want to keep the habits of good tradecraft consistent. The plans all seemed to be moving in our direction—we'd linked up successfully, gotten past the first hurdle, and now were negotiating for the second objective, Benghazi. But I'd have done well to remember that when everything seems to be going your way, you're probably in the wrong lane.

CHAPTER 3

Cairo

March 2011
Cairo, Egypt

WHOEVER SAID THAT IF YOU WANT to make God laugh just tell him your plans was probably right. The good Lord must have enjoyed a nice, long chuckle when it came to me. The day after our rendezvous, Sleepy rang. The Benghazi trip was on hold, but the general in charge of all military operations wanted to meet. But even before that, Sleepy said, there was someone else with whom I needed to sit down.

I told Sleepy that first we needed to talk about it—I needed to get control of the situation with him.

Starting like this wasn't good—you don't plan something and then let your contact take over the scheduling. You don't do that unless there is a really good reason—like a security reason. But you still have to walk that tightrope between being flexible and effective.

I arranged a meeting with him the next day at the hotel. We sat and talked inside a coffee shop in the lower level with D right across the hall in a café pulling CS/S (countersurveillance and security) for me. I pressed Sleepy hard on the reasons for the changes. First, he was indignant, but then he caved from that position and said it was a matter of our safety, which he said neither he nor anyone in Benghazi could guarantee.

"That's shit. I'm responsible for that, not you. You've got specific orders to get me to Benghazi and assist my mission—period," I said. I needed to make him think I was angry. It was for dramatic effect and I was playing a part. After nearly twenty years, I wasn't half bad.

Sleepy was the kind of guy who communicated mainly by blush: his neck reddened up through his cheeks, and he pursed his lips in frustration just as his eyebrows shot upward for a fraction of a second. He swallowed and cleared his throat a few times, and I noticed his feet—they were angled toward the exit. Then came the verbal backpedaling, as he muttered about creating divisions among the tribes. Sleepy's body had just unconsciously betrayed him in about a half dozen ways.

The human face can make forty-three distinctive muscular movements, called "action units," and when you put three AUs together, there are three thousand different possible facial configurations that actually mean something. A liar breathes faster, drying the throat out, and thus the person swallows to lubricate the throat. But lying also increases adrenaline production, which gets a liar's saliva flowing so the person gulps, swallowing spit. But then the saliva production quickly tapers off and the person starts to clear his throat again, because it's now dry. Sleepy's quick lift of the eyebrows signaled momentary distress when I challenged him. His pursed lips suggested aggravation that he wasn't being believed, and the feet—those feet were pointing to where he wanted to go right now, to the exit—out of this conversation. But lying is a cooperative act, and people believe a lie because they are hungry for something—usually the thing the liar is peddling. If I chose not to cooperate, his lie held no power.

He was boxed in and I suspected that the real issue was the fear that I would report to D.C. the presence of radical Islamists in the rebel army, thus torpedoing the chances of U.S. support. But that was what Myrick wanted—the truth on the ground. She certainly wouldn't back people who might turn against the United States.

"I'll take the meeting with the general, but don't you ever tell me you'll do something and then back out again. If I did that with your military support one day, I don't think you'd appreciate it," I said. You have to take control, to dominate the relationship, and I hoped to do it by making him think I could turn his military support on and off with a phone call. Of course, I couldn't, but he didn't know that. What I didn't say was that I planned to work the general to get D and me to Benghazi anyway. "Who is this other person you want me to meet?" I asked.

"He is from the intelligence department—the Mukhabarat, but now he's with us now," he said.

My antenna went up—the Mukhabarat infiltrated coup plotters. They killed them—this guy was former JSO. "Why do you think he's not still with them?" I asked.

"His father works in the army," he said, "and he helped us take Benghazi, defecting, opening up the arms stores—how do you say—the armory, to us. His son fled, too, and they have nothing left for Qadhafi. He can be trusted."

If I was working for the CIA during all of this, I could have cabled headquarters (HQS) to run a trace on the army guy's son. I was slightly uneasy. Although the guy knew about me, I said I'd see him in an hour, hitting hard the fact that I'd name the place and that Sleepy had to come to ID the guy. I got up and left him there.

I passed D's position and texted him to get to my room. Moments later, we were laying down plans. D suggested we convene down by the pool. Likely due to the recent Egyptian violence, tourism was a trickle and the pool was isolated. I called Sleepy, gave him a time, and said I'd call with the place. No need to trust too much—not right now. Then D and I went down to double-check the area.

The pool sat in a depression of sorts surrounded by a high retaining wall with shrubbery. A guy was swimming laps but that was it. I chose a set of pool chairs in the corner near the deep end where I could eyeball the steps and keep my back to the main hotel building's balconies. D got in place under an umbrella roughly twenty yards away and pulled out a book. Because of the glare of sun on the water he was basically out of sight from where I sat. I sent a text to Sleepy telling him where to meet.

Moments later, Sleepy and a well-dressed man walked down the brick steps with a tall, thick man with no facial hair and a touch of gray at his temples. I signaled to D that this was the guy.

When I asked what he did before he defected, he said he had worked for Kataeb al-Amn, the security battalions who provided and maintained security for the regime along with supporting units in the major cities. He had worked out of Tripoli and Misrata. His father had indeed defected. Strangers lie at least three times within the first three minutes of meeting someone new and men tend to lie eight times more about themselves than others—I wasn't taking what this guy said at face value.

But at the same time, I couldn't have asked for better access. If his story was true, this guy grasped the inner workings of Qadhafi's security organs, and he likely knew others who worked in other towns and cities who either had defected or, better yet, were still in place.

Politely, I asked Sleepy to give us a few minutes. Understanding, he nodded, pulled out a cigarette, and walked away.

Typically, recruiting someone takes time. You spot your target and make a determination about whether he has value. The person might have direct access to information or, if not, then perhaps he has access to someone who does. Once you get that basic box checked, then you go through a lengthy process of establishing that the individual isn't a bad guy in disguise—a double agent or crackpot—and then you run deep background on him. All this helps you get to the *pitch*—making the approach, offering him the job. It's taught by the acronym MICE, which is short for money, ideology, compromise, ego, and as an officer later suggested, revenge. You get a sense whether your contact is motivated by money or ideology—he likes what you believe in; or maybe you've discovered that he's compromised himself, allowing you to figuratively twist an arm to help your cause. Or it could be that he just wants to be on the winning team for his ego's sake; or maybe he's just pissed-off and wants to get back at somebody and you're the instrument to make that happen for him. In truth, I think using compromise—figuratively twisting the target's arm—should really be the last option, because he'll always be looking for a way out of the deal from the beginning.

Today, though, I didn't have the time for all that. I took a calculated risk and banked on looking for cues of deception—those microexpressions—while trying to corroborate what he said with what Sleepy told me earlier; then I'd test him by giving him something to do. I hit the guy straight on and asked if he was helping the rebels right now and was he willing to do more? He said yes to both. Nothing about his body language caused me alarm. This guy was either honestly committed and telling the truth or he was going to get people killed. Everyone in the spy business lies; I just hoped his falsehoods weren't life-threatening to our side.

So although I was leery, I plowed ahead. Could he seek out like-minded people, rebel sympathizers in key cities—specifically Tripoli,

Misrata, Bani Walid, and, finally, in Qadhafi's hometown of Sirte? Could he develop a small network of trusted cooperators? Could he organize a cellular structure with him as the proxy—the cutout? Could he act as the interface with the network, instead of us? This did a few things—it provided security by insulating us from direct contact. It also provided security for the informants in the network. If it was properly organized and each cell was isolated from the others, then, in the event anyone were to be compromised, Qadhafi's people could identify only a few. This guy said he could do these things, and he knew people who were ready to help; they just needed organization and leadership.

Could he collect information about the workings of militant groups and tribal structures? Did he have access or information on troop movements, areas of towns or villages that weren't covered by soldiers in case supplies or people needed to be moved in or out? Finally, did he think he would have access to any information about Qadhafi or his family's whereabouts?

To fully answer the questions posed by Washington, we needed this type of information. To be clear, Congresswoman Myrick was not sanctioning or requesting that we collect intelligence—that wasn't in her power to do even if she had wanted to. She was asking for clarity—information that could be used as a litmus test against what she was being formally shoveled by the administration. Our information would provide context and the backstory to help better grasp the events on the ground.

The guy was conscious of the fact that he was likely going to be the point man on this—he would be the proxy for this network. I expressed my confidence in him and in his professional instincts when it came to choosing his people, but I reminded him of Qadhafi's technical capability and to stick with the old-fashioned way of doing things, using technology sparingly. He gave me his local mobile number. I gave him a webmail account that we'd created in the hotel's business center before the meeting. I put my ball cap back on, signaling to D it was over, stood, shook the man's hand, and left.

D stayed behind watching. The man made a call and shortly Sleepy returned. They sat for a few minutes talking and smoking and then left. D left shortly afterward. He and I circled back together in my room, where I shared the conversation with him. We decided to give the tall, thick Libyan with graying temples a call sign. From now on, he was Silverback, just like the African gorilla.

LATE THAT AFTERNOON, the general arrived. Sleepy would make the preliminary introductions, but for some reason he said that neither he, nor Cue Ball, nor Rango would be at the meeting. I was fine with that since they didn't seem too keen on us going to Benghazi anyway. D and I had found a large, empty dance hall in a section of the hotel without any security cameras and barely any guests and decided to meet the general there.

The first guests to arrive were four Libyans in black leather jackets and blue jeans, with tanned, weathered faces covered with black beards and hard stares. In their late twenties to early thirties, they looked to be tough characters—a Libyan version of the Bowery Boys.

Behind them came Sleepy and Brigadier General Abdulsalam al-Hasi. Based in Benghazi, he was the chief of operations for the rebel military. Standing nearly six feet tall and in good shape except for a potbelly, he was probably in his sixties. His lantern jaw was framed by a thick shock of gray hair, and a pair of reading glasses rested on the tip of his nose, together giving him the air of a professor.

The younger men were his security team. They fanned out into the room as I shook the general's massive hands, which was like shaking a bunch of bananas. His security guys kept watch on the hall. D moved to cover the stairs as Sleepy bailed out of the room completely.

The general spoke through an interpreter, saying that he'd served in the Libyan military for forty years and was the former commander of their special forces. I asked him about how the Libyan army—Qadhafi's forces—were holding up in terms of equipment, since he had the most recent exposure to it before he defected.

He said that though the army had a large quantity of fighting equipment, the vast majority was bought from the Soviet Union in the 1970s and '80s and was largely obsolete. A high percentage remained in storage, and a large quantity had also been sold to various African countries over the years. He said that no major purchases of equipment had been made in recent years, largely due to a sluggish economy and foreign sanctions.

This and other internal factors seriously decayed the strength of the whole of the Libyan armed forces, which has lagged behind its major neighbors in terms of its true war-fighting capability.

I asked if he had any indication of the enemy's order of battle; what the plans and intentions were of neighboring nations; and what he thought about the impact local Muslim religious leaders might have on operations. We talked about the tribal structures, and the militias and what, if any, tensions existed between them and rebel military leadership. I asked about their intelligence collection capabilities and, finally, what he felt they needed militarily. That's when he essentially produced from memory a shopping list of equipment, arms, and munitions.

He wanted fifty jeeps, fifteen central communications systems, five vehicle and handheld field radio sets, ten thousand uniforms, thirty armored personnel carriers, an unspecified quantity of light antitank weapons, surface-to-air MANPADS, three thousand NODs (night observation devices), two hundred rangefinders, updated maps that he could print off, and live "Google Earth"–type capability. Finally, he wanted one large UAV—an unmanned aerial vehicle, a drone—and an unspecified quantity of smaller UAVs. Not much. I was surprised he hadn't asked for a nuclear sub or stealth fighter while he was at it.

I told him that we might know someone who could legally supply his army with the nonlethal things on their list, but certainly not all he was requesting. These rebels were unknown commodities at this point.

But arms weren't my real concern—we didn't sell weapons anyway. He'd get those from the governments of Italy, France, or Qatar, if he got them. I wanted to push into the subject of putting my men on the ground—that was how we'd get solid information and turn a corporate profit. They would have to pay our way, with no loss to the U.S. taxpayer, and we could then dig up information that could save Libyan and, perhaps, American lives.

I told him that I wanted to put a team of fifty-two *consultants* inside Libya, all special operators, all Arabic speakers, with experience training insurgent guerrilla forces. We had the men, an incredibly able cohort of warriors. I reminded him of the successes in Afghanistan in 2001 and 2002, accomplished with men just like that.

Split into ten teams of five, each with a team leader and an assistant team leader, our men would infiltrate the country overland from Egypt or by sea, staging out of Malta. Then they would scatter, attaching themselves to all the major fighting divisions within the rebel army, as directed by the general. D would be the in-country project manager; Jana would run the Maltese forward-staging base. A study in contrasts, Jana was a former marketing major, fashion designer, and model with pale blue eyes and long blond hair, who was described by one of the guys as the personification of the old definition of curves—the prettiest distance between two points. But her good looks were deceiving—she was smart, had common sense, and could shoot the Glock like not many other women around. She came to the company originally to head up public relations with our spokesman, Steve Honig of Los Angeles. However, she soon showed interest and aptitude for other work and began taking surveillance, HUMINT, and weapons courses, migrating into the operational logistics field.

As far as the scope of our work was concerned, we'd been asked by the rebels in writing for assistance and had congressional backing in the form of Myrick's letter to poke around and dig up answers to questions for a report we'd produce. But if it were deemed acceptable by the U.S. government, we would take our work to the next level and provide training to the rebels, showing them how to break things and kill bad guys more efficiently, how to improve their communications, how to set up efficient combat medical systems, and so on.

This wasn't new territory. My guys were experts at training foreign nationals in their home countries, and when I was at the CIA, we did exactly this against Saddam Hussein. We devised a plan to teach Iraqis shooting, demolitions, sabotage, and other hard skills—*kinetic* operations, as they were known.

While the teams worked with the rebels in Libya, they would be performing another key service, pumping intel back to Washington. If everything went well, we would quickly be in position to advise U.S. intelligence agencies about where Qadhafi's loyalists—the bad guys—were encamped, what was happening in key cities and other areas on the battlefield, whether the atmospherics were stabilizing, and whether the rebellion was significantly allied with al-Qa'ida or other radicals, or if not, then we'd be in a solid position to hear rumblings if they tried. It was standard fare for an IO, and it was all stuff that the Obama administration should have been interested to know. If things worked out, the plan to put agency NOCs in our teams operating with the rebels would give the CIA people on the ground, embedded, using us for cover.

On the entrepreneurial side, the figures weren't chump change, either. One month of operations was going to cost the Libyans over $200,000. The money was flowing in to the rebels from external sources—namely the Qataris, who were instrumental in harnessing Arab support for the UN Security Council resolution. They had also sent troops into Libya and funneled money to the rebels for equipment and supplies. They'd even delivered air support. The tiny kingdom of Qatar is one of the richest in the world and has pursued an activist foreign policy for years, championed by its satellite TV news channel Al Jazeera, which recently bought out Al Gore's drowning, left-wing Current TV network—which was circling the drain.

Unfortunately, the Qataris supported the more radical Libyan elements, as we would later learn, who would turn out to be very deadly and eventually become enemies of the United States. Many thought the Saudis would jump to help the rebels, since King Abdullah had no love for Qadhafi, after he sent four of his JSO operatives to Mecca to murder him. But the House of Saud demurred; they had their own internal problems and set about putting down the protesters fanning the flames of rebellion at home. The Saudis used a simple solution—they bought them off.

Qadhafi hadn't just made enemies in Saudi Arabia. He'd been accused of subversion by a host of Arab and Berber countries—Morocco, Jordan, Sudan, Egypt, and Tunisia, to name a few. So often had he screwed others in the region that in 1986, when the United States bombed Libya, hardly anyone complained.

Among Libya's possible benefactors, there was a particular wild card: the Iranians. Though they were Persians and not Arabs, they were offering their support to the Arab rebels to foster their own agenda. They sought to recharacterize the rebellion as part of a regionwide *Islamic* awakening, when in fact it was a regionwide *democratic* awakening. The Iranians wanted to empower the oppressed Shiites around the region, giving Iran even more influence throughout the Middle East and North Africa.

So with all the funding sources at play and the need on the ground, I laid out the plan to the general, but he pushed back. He was very focused on getting the arms for his rebels, but he vetoed Western advisers in-country. He was concerned about his ability to control the fight and was downright paranoid that foreign forces might appear to be directing the battle. But the key problem was our skin color and home country. The Libyan rebels were happy to have Western pilots in the air, and our special forces training them out in the western mountains out of sight, but they didn't want us on the ground, up close to the fighting, where journalists hung out.

After another hour or so, I told him I'd take his list of the nonlethal gear—the medical supplies, uniforms, trucks, maps, laptops, and boots—with me to Washington. I needed to make sure the U.S. government had no problem with us supplying the gear and only then would I have my team start sourcing suppliers. But first I needed to get to Benghazi to look around myself. It was then I showed the general the letter from Shalgham. He blinked, read it again, and looked up at me over the top of his reading glasses in surprise. He didn't want us to go, but I could tell he felt the heat. Then, just as I'd planned, I showed him the letter from Congresswoman Myrick and said, "General, if we go to Benghazi, help might come to your army faster, based on the report we file. But if we don't, I feel very sure that it won't."

He blinked again, looked back at both letters, and then at me, saying, "Okay, we leave in the morning before dawn"—in perfectly accented English.

D AND I LEFT THE MEETING WITH THE GENERAL FIRST, and headed straight for positions we'd scouted earlier. We wanted video of the general that we could shoot back to D.C. We'd done the same with Sleepy and all the guys we'd met so far.

One of the gaps in knowledge back in Washington was over exactly who these rebels were. Who was in charge? Were they defectors? If they were claiming to be defectors, were they true defectors or were they actually known to be strong, loyal Qadhafi supporters who might be double agents? Were they al-Qa'ida infiltrators? Were they from another terror group, like the Libyan Islamic Fighting Group—the LIFG?

I headed to a table in the outdoor café that sat just off the main path leading back to the meeting site. I'd hidden my tiny video camera in a shoulder bag lying on the table and ordered coffee, which I never drink. The lens was pushed back and had a clear line of sight back up the path toward the door. The viewer screen was flipped out and I could control the zoom with my fingertips while appearing to look over the menu.

The general came strolling down the path, and then Rango came into the picture. He'd been walking from the other direction. The two stopped and talked, then broke and went their separate directions.

Upstairs, we got out laptops and began selecting still frames from the video for the report, which we then sent by secure e-mail to the Ops Center, in North Carolina. The Ops Center kept track of our location and travel schedule, received reports from us, and also pushed information out that we might need. In an emergency, Colonel Cantwell's team would coordinate everything from medical care to transportation for us. Today, they would be relaying our stuff to the Pentagon, the U.S. Special Operations Command (SOCOM), and the CIA.

Early the next morning D and I would be loading up and slipping over the border with Libyan rebel fighters and heading into the battlefield of Benghazi, the capital of the rebel resistance. Truth is, we didn't know who they truly were. They could have been Qadhafi's men, al-Qa'ida, or any number of other possibilities—we just didn't know.

CHAPTER 4

Travel to Benghazi

March 26, 2011
Cairo, heading to Benghazi

EARLY THE NEXT MORNING after our meeting with the general, Sleepy called to say the vehicles and drivers were waiting at the rear of the hotel. D and I went out the back into the dark and met three SUVs filled to the nostrils with luggage and bottled water. There was a slight chill in the air as we threw our rucks into the middle one and loaded into the backseat, which smelled of years of cigarette smoke and stifling body odor. I pulled out my GPS and turned on the track feature to save our route in case we had to come this way again. Or, more important, in case we had to turn and run back to Cairo on our own.

The night before, D and I had discussed what we would do if this turned into an attempted abduction, something always a possibility in this part of the world. The basic plan wasn't all that complicated—we were in the backseat and they were in the front. We'd kill them, take the truck, turn around, and haul ass back the way we'd come. If the other two trucks wanted to follow, they'd have to catch us first. It was better not to get caught than have to rely on a rescue after the fact and we both knew that getting a kidnapped person back home was complicated.

But now, leaving Cairo, our small convoy headed west through the early morning traffic. Orange light from the streetlamps slipped through trees here and there. People were out, but not many. A donkey pulled a battered, faded wooden cart carrying loaves of bread, as the ubiquitous taxis rushed about. We pushed to the suburbs in the direction of Giza as we angled toward Alexandria. In the early morning haze I could just make out the tips of the Great Pyramids while the Libyans up front yammered away in Arabic to each other or sent text messages.

As the sun started to rise, I noticed the interior of this ridiculous four-wheeled contraption as we sped along. Front and center on the dashboard was a hodgepodge of electronic gadgets that looked like they were purchased from a Radio Shack closeout sale. They stood atop one another thanks to Velcro, tape, and superglue, all leaning like a poor imitation of the Tower of Pisa, nearly reaching the dangling rearview mirror, which wobbled with every bump in the road, causing anyone reflecting in it to resemble a bobblehead doll. The gadgets dated back to the mid-1990s and allowed the driver to play everything from cassette tapes to CDs and, through a Rube Goldberg–type device screwed into where the air conditioner vent used to be, MP3s—after he plugged into the cigarette lighter and slipped in an old DCIM memory card (like those used in cameras) that the driver no doubt had loaded with Arab Top 40 song files from his home computer.

Every surface in the cab was covered with yards of adhesive tape painted to look like oak wood grain. From the turn signal to the door handles, dashboard, glove box, steering wheel, and even the visors overhead—all had a faded pathetic resemblance to a dilapidated tree, long since dead, but authentic enough to give a termite a happy heart attack on sight. Rounding out the odd décor was an animal skin, complete with fur, adorning the top of the dash; tassels dangled from the headliner and windows; and a miniature teddy bear hung from a suction cup stuck to the windshield just above the silver beads draped over the incense ball, all of which swung precariously from the bobblehead mirror. It was all evidence of a niggardly attempt of one man trying very hard to make you forget you were in a simple 1990s SUV filled with sweating, stinking humans squeezed together in a small space, jostling over pothole-filled roads. He failed.

The general was in the truck in front of ours, which was a shame because having access to him for thirteen hours straight would have been good. I tried twice to switch to his truck when we stopped for a piss break, but was rejected each time. I thought about installing a listening device in his truck—a bug. We had at least a couple with us. But I never did.

I REMEMBER MY VERY FIRST technical covert operation. Just before Christmas holidays I'd gone to a Radio Shack in Oxford, Mississippi, to buy an RF transmitter that worked on the FM band and cost nineteen bucks. The size of half a pack of Wrigley's chewing gum, it had a one-foot-long black antenna wire attached to it. Every Christmas, like clockwork, our family did four things—woke up to see what Santa Claus brought; ate an orange ring pastry and country-fried ham for breakfast that Mom had made; drove five miles to my dad's parents to open presents; and then, after a huge family lunch there with Mema and Granddaddy, packed it all up again and drove an hour to my mom's parents for Christmas dinner, where we stayed until late that night with cousins, aunts, uncles, and everyone in between.

Granny and Granddaddy's house, as we called it, was a warm, loving place where everyone from Mom's side of the family gathered. Granny, quick with a smile, a laugh, and a hug, but also a wit sharp as any razor, was the matriarch of the family on that side. She was a strong-willed woman—she had to be; she had dozens of children, grandchildren, and great-grandchildren to contend with and keep in line. We all would cram in with cousins, aunts, and uncles, food, and laughter. The men clustered around the den TV watching an old action movie, while the women talked and prepared food. The kids could be heard out back shooting fireworks at one another, playing hide-and-seek or chase around the house, or wrestling in one of the back bedrooms. Sometimes we had more than fifty people in their small country home and it was wonderful. So on this particular Christmas, knowing we'd all drive an hour to my mom's parents' house, I'd decided to bug Mom and Dad's car with the RF transmitter from Radio Shack.

I hooked it to my dad's seat belt with black electrical tape, concealing the long antenna along the underside of the seat belt itself with more tape. Christmas morning came, we opened presents, and then little sister Ellen, Mom, and Dad piled into the family car and pulled out while my brother, Todd, and I followed in our car. We dialed in the car radio to the frequency of the bug and suddenly we were listening to the conversation in the other vehicle and to my little sister humming her head off in the backseat. It was magic. Todd and I rode along, laughing and listening to them for at least ten miles, proud of the accomplishment . . . then we had total mission failure.

"Honey, what is that on your seat belt?" Mom said to Dad, over the muted sounds of Andy Williams Christmas music playing on their radio and Ellen's angelic voice as she sang to her dolls in the backseat above the hum of the road noise.

"I don't know . . ." Then came the muffled sounds of a microphone being jostled and tape being ripped loose. "What in the world?" Dad could be heard saying, and then an inaudible noise came through our radio as the device was ripped from its perch. We watched as their brake lights came on and the car veered to the right shoulder of the road, gravel and dust flying in all directions. Dad's door came open, he got out, and then he flung my first bug as far as he could, out into the pasture off the side of the highway.

He gave us one look, got back in the warmth of the family car, and took off . . . we both thought we were sunk. Dad was strong, really strong. When I was a young kid, I once saw one of our horses bite him as he was trimming his hoof and Dad reacted, punching that horse straight in the forehead, knocking the animal out. The only consolation Todd and I had was that at least we had another forty-five minutes of travel remaining and a whole family waiting for us. If we were lucky, he'd forget about it. We were right, he never said another word, but we all laugh about it to this day. (The horse was just fine, too.)

ON THE ROAD TO Benghazi riding with the Libyan rebels, I thought back to that day and wished we could have bugged the general's truck. But, if that had been discovered, we wouldn't have gotten off as lightly as I did on that Mississippi back road; not by any stretch.

Hours passed. Eventually we skirted south of Alexandria, and then, more than six hours and 340 miles from Cairo, we came into the coastal Mediterranean town of Marsa Matruh, a beautiful little place. Ancient buildings dotted the coast while a white sandy beach hugged the crystal-clear bay in a gentle crescent.

I checked the Garmin—we looked to be just about two hours away from the Libyan border crossing.

D was on his computer, watching episodes of a big-boy cartoon he enjoyed called *Archer*. I caught his attention and rolled my eyes. He lifted his middle finger, smiled behind his Oakleys, and went back to his entertainment.

AFTER D ENROLLED IN OUR OPERATOR SELECTION COURSE, which was conducted at our company's Mississippi training center, he took nearly everything we offered, from close quarters battle (CQB) and pistol and carbine courses, to surveillance operations, tactical HUMINT, and our nearly monthlong high-threat protection course. I watched him, liked his work ethic, and saw he could put up with a lot of stress. Our courses were designed to do that and I used them to spot potentially good people whom we might want to work one day.

D proved he could get along with a fence post and had a solid fighting background in grappling and combatives, and the guy could shoot, too. Just over six feet tall, an East Coaster who weighed in at 220 pounds, D had been—in one of his many former lives—a skinny, professional bike racer who raced against Tour de France podium finishers such as Lance Armstrong and Bobby Julich. When D decided to make this line of work his career, we saw a good fit.

One evening following his second class, I invited him to go for a ride and we stopped at Oakland Catfish, off Interstate 55, to grab a bite. I asked him about his plans for the future and then offered him a job with us. He accepted, asking if he had to move, and we talked about what he'd do. We let him stay on the East Coast for a while, but then as the training center grew he went down to Mississippi to help run things day to day.

We bought an old antebellum house and renovated it. We put in a big-screen television, repainted the walls, and installed surveillance cameras and an alarm system. We put bunk beds for the instructors in one end of the house, created a bedroom solely for D to use, and then on the other end of the place had a room for when I came to town. D lived at the house rent-free, had a company vehicle, and was paid to shoot—not a bad job.

He ran courses, reached out to local law enforcement in surrounding counties and states, and promoted the training center. Whenever we got a job outside the continental United States (OCONUS), he always had his hand in the air to go. He was the perfect guy to have with me now on the road to Libya.

THE FINAL MILES PASSED and soon we came to the border village of El Salloum. A massive cream-colored concrete-and-stone gate adorned with an Egyptian flag snapping sharply in the breeze, under a sign that read WELCOME TO SALLOUM, marked the entrance to the village. On the right was a huge red banner ad for Vodafone cellular service. Gray emergency vehicles with blue lights sat near the gate. A man guided a donkey burdened with bundles of green grass and reeds tied on either side. Another beast of burden pulled a cart—that seemed to be the taxi system in this town. The village was like most in North Africa—low one- or two-story plaster-and-block buildings, tan and dusty. Trash of all sorts lined the edges of the streets. Compared to the semi-resort town we'd left awhile back, this place was a mess; it was filled with a flood of refugees from Libya. Everywhere there were people, packages, donkeys, mopeds, luggage, cars, vans, trucks—and misery. In front of us was a ridge overlooking a harbor; there the border checkpoint stood, extending into the desert and protected by mines. Beyond that ridge was Libya. We stopped, refueled, drained our bladders, rehydrated, and stretched our legs.

Then we all reloaded and pushed on up the ridge to the border itself—the Salloum Land Port—a massive concrete gated entry with four channels for passage, above which the golden eagle of Saladin from the Egyptian national flag stared down on all who came and went. From here those who thought they were seeing light at the end of the tunnel realized that it was most likely just a train. But as the saying goes, if you can't see the bright side, polish the dull side, and that's just what these folks seemed to be doing as this madhouse of Libyan refugees tried to get out of the country, carrying massive bundles on their heads. Egyptians loaded down with suitcases were there to cross back into their homeland, while members of the press were trying to go the other way, into Libya. In the air hung the stench of human misery—smoke, feces, diesel exhaust, body odors of all sorts. Vehicles crowded the roads and people were screaming at one another; drivers yelled at potential passengers, and refugees crowded the streets carrying boxes and pushing along carts filled well beyond their intended load limit. Trucks, vans, and cars were loaded to three times their height, as everyone seemed to be dragging their life's belongings behind them in a massive North African version of *The Grapes of Wrath.*

Out in the distance, as far as the eye could see beyond the huge concrete gates that formed the barrier with Libya, there was nothing but flat desert dotted with hapless refugees trying to get away.

We kept our heads down as we inched slowly through the crowds, moving toward the checkpoint up ahead. At the border, our traveling companions requested our passports, and one of them left the truck to work his magic, which likely involved a bit of *baksheesh*—a Persian word that essentially means a bribe. As I waited, I noticed a plump, older Egyptian guard in faded camouflage, an AK-47 hanging lazily from his neck, wearing a helmet two sizes too small for his enormous head. He glared at our convoy for only a moment before his attention was pulled away to other drama taking place in this seemingly endless debacle. Our trucks rolled forward a few more yards, officially signaling we'd crossed out of Egypt, and our passports were handed back to us.

Americans now had boots on the ground, as the politicians are so fond of saying, in Libya—a country with whom our nation had been in conflict on and off since I was a child. Now we were on their soil, infiltrating overland with the leader of a rebel army to a military camp to discuss the destabilization of the regime of Muammar Abu Minyar al-Qadhafi.

CHAPTER 5

Meeting the Rebels

March 26, 2011
Benghazi, Libya

IT WAS ANOTHER FIVE HUNDRED MILES, or just over eight hundred kilometers, to Benghazi, but our driver spared no boot leather as he mashed the accelerator to the floor. I nicknamed him "the Stig" after a character on my favorite BBC program, *Top Gear*, who was the show's "tame racing driver" but really drove like a madman. The coastal desert road offered snatches of the Mediterranean Sea if you were paying attention, but mostly it was sand dunes, scrub brush, and only a village here and there to break up the monotony.

The trip had been long, but aside from the guys chain-smoking up front and constantly popping in cassettes of the Arabic Top 40 music equivalent of Rick Dees, it had been tolerable. I compensated by slamming 5-hour Energy shots, keeping the windows down for fresh air, and many miles ago had engaged the miraculous creations of Steve Jobs to get something into my skull that I recognized as entertainment, while D watched his precious *Archer* cartoon, laughing every now and then in fits and spurts, startling our traveling companions up front.

We were heading into a landscape that would soon be littered with the dead and haunted by the cries of those who survived them. But I was trying to think about other things: my family, my children at home. You can never be 100 percent confident that you will make it out of a place like this. I've seen war zones for more than twenty years and I know what's sometimes required in order to survive in these decaying, desperate places. Life was cheap here, anyone with a gun could extinguish it, but D and I were determined to go home—to get back to those we loved—and we'd kill anyone who tried to stop us.

CASUAL ENTERTAINMENT—that's the impression of killing given by novels, movies, video games, and television. But it's not. It's something so powerful at first that you have to put it away, into a box in your brain where you can't feel it, where your kids won't find it, where it won't trip you up in a way you don't expect. But sometimes it finds its way out and visits you while you sleep. But I'm not one of those screaming at his family or throwing down too many vodka shots and swallowing handfuls of Zoloft because he can't deal with life and death. I'm no different from any other American who's served his country—killing is done in defense of yourself, your teammates or for your country, but I don't lie around pondering it. Bad guys are dead and if they weren't they might have slaughtered more innocent souls, readily killing me or my teammates in the process. But killing someone with a gun is a lot different than doing it up close. A gun usually puts distance between you and the target, a separation to some degree. It's like the silly statement about something being easier said than done—what isn't easier to say than do? It's easier to shoot someone than stab them, just like it's easier for a pilot to drop a bomb on bad guys than shoot them—it's all relative.

General Norman Schwarzkopf once said, "a professional . . . understands that war means killing people, war means maiming people, war means families left without fathers and mothers." But there are things worth fighting for, no matter how much we hate war . . . and that means someone is going to get killed. After that it just comes down to who wants to live the most. It boils down to this—you've got to accept that you're going to die one day. The only thing to choose is whether you do it on your feet or on your knees.

AS WE CLOSED IN ON BENGHAZI and the congestion increased, we began encountering checkpoints manned by rebel militia carrying rifles of all makes and models, wearing old camouflaged army field jackets, an assortment of T-shirts, and every now and then, a pair of camouflage BDU pants. I took a Garmin hit to get our GPS coordinates, punched D, and we started videoing the scenes as covertly as we could. We'd decided to do this at each checkpoint. Sometime later, it might be good to review it so we could see the layouts and the professionalism of the guards. It could also be instructive for any future predeployment mission briefings for our own guys.

The more elaborate checkpoints had huge shipping containers sitting on each side of the road, two stories high, with other containers spanning the gaps between them like massive entrance gates. The hasty ones were nothing but rocks set in the road to make you swerve and slow down while a couple of armed guys checked IDs.

I've navigated many checkpoints—alone, in pairs, and with a team. Sometimes we'd hit multiple checkpoints in a single day. Leaving a base, we'd go through a military checkpoint, then a local government checkpoint manned by some sod with an itchy trigger finger and a weapon pointed through the window demanding our paperwork. Down the road and out past the Green Zone could be simple crooks looking to make a buck—so we'd pay them; and then another one farther on when we'd get into the badlands controlled by bandits or terrorist groups. But at each one we'd have to understand that engaging in a gunfight at the checkpoint wasn't the objective—it's just another obstacle we have to move through. So we'd do what's necessary to deescalate the situation and quietly pass through. Guns overseas are a fact of this life and the bottom line is that you have to learn to be observant—assess what's going on—and talk or bribe first, and then ram or shoot your way through only when absolutely necessary. But if we had to shoot, we were prepared to set a new tone in that area and kill them wholesale.

We flew through, with the Stig honking his horn as all three trucks were allowed to pass with no holdups. We were riding with the equivalent of one of the Joint Chiefs of Staff for the Libyan rebel army, apparently.

Inside Benghazi the press corps was staying at the Noran and Uzu hotels, guarded by rebel militia. We definitely didn't want to go there, and our hosts completely agreed, taking us to their seafront headquarters instead, where we finally stopped. It was so quiet I felt I could hear my blood fighting its way through my veins as the sun retired over the horizon—and then would come sporadic gunfire. If you strained your imagination slightly, got past the black char marks on most of the large buildings, the destroyed vehicles, the rubble from cratered buildings in heaps everywhere, the gut-wrenching stench, the bullet-riddled walls and shot-up concrete and steel power poles, you could just about picture Benghazi as a once-beautiful seaside city. In other words, if you closed your eyes, held your breath, and stopped up your ears and pretended you were anyplace else, it was great.

We found a corner in a barren, concrete room with one window high on the wall and put down our gear. Stepping out into the cool, humid evening air, I stretched my legs, taking in the faint smell of the sea as it too fought its way through the diesel exhaust and smoke from the burning trash. I replaced batteries and tried to get a GPS fix and mark our position on the Garmin while D swapped out the satphone's stubby fixed antenna that we used when traveling with a wire antenna and threaded it out the window, taping it in place. Once he got reception in the building he began typing up a SITREP to send to Rick, letting them know we'd arrived with our heads still attached to our bodies.

The second battle for Benghazi had been over for a few days now; the signing of UN Resolution 1973, on March 17, which Ambassador Shalgham and I had discussed in his office and he'd managed to get pushed through, had turned the tide by opening the door for NATO air strikes. Now the war front was south of us by a few miles.

During the first battle for Benghazi, Qadhafi realized that the fight was going to the rebels and flew in a few hundred foreign fighters—mercenaries, many paid close to a thousand dollars a day—from neighboring African countries, including Chad, Niger, Mali, as well as from other places. The townspeople had responded by attacking them, driving them into a police station that was then burned to the ground.

The town of Katiba fell when rebels commandeered bulldozers and abandoned tanks and rammed the walls. Hundreds died on both sides in four days of fighting for control of that city.

Nearly one month to the day, the second battle of Benghazi had started. Qadhafi's forces shelled the city for nearly two hours with rockets and artillery. Then armor rolled into town and blasted anything and everything in sight. Bombs were dropped on the citizens—one during prayer time—killing women and children. People began jamming the roads out of town, trying to get clear before the city was locked down, because they knew what would follow. That was no mystery—it would be extermination.

The fighting raged for hours until the rumor began to circulate about the arrival of Western airpower. That spark of optimism was fanned when an old, rusting rebel tank opened fire on the lead Qadhafi tank in the attack, damaging it enough to make the crew bail out. The tank crews behind it panicked and began to retreat, and the first wave of the attack was beaten back to the city limits. Around this time, a rebel MiG-23 jet crashed, prompting the rebels to use loudspeakers to caution the people not to shoot down their own aircraft. Images from the crash, caught on film, were broadcast around the world at the time.

Within two hours of that, French jets arrived on the scene and, with the help of British and American cruise missiles launched from ships offshore, began laying waste to Qadhafi's bottled-up army. These attacks continued throughout the night and into the early morning hours. The two-day battle was over and once again the city was saved.

SLEEPY AND HIS FAMILY HAILED FROM TRIPOLI, which I guess accounted for his reluctance to travel to Benghazi with us that day in March 2011. It was the first hint of the animus between the rebels from eastern and western Libya; I was a neophyte when it came to this country. I imagined that if I asked someone to explain it, I'd receive a T-shirt with the Libyan equivalent of "It's a tribal thing. You wouldn't understand," stamped across the front. With more than 140 tribes, they'd be right.

Benghazi and Tripoli, I would later learn, are worlds apart. With its tribal influence and conservative, almost fundamentalist Muslim nature, Benghazi deeply offended Qadhafi. That partly explains why he came after it with a vengeance when the war started. Despite the trauma the city suffered, Benghazi seemed very undeveloped; but from what I could gather, the residents liked it that way. There was tremendous pride in this place. You could feel it in conversations with those few who actually spoke English. There was also a tremendous affection for the United States there at the time, too. But then I've seen that all over the world where people are being slaughtered and the United States offers help. They love you, but once the fighting's over, they usually couldn't give two craps about America.

The rebels we encountered were young people for the most part. There was a plumber, aged twenty-three; a taxi driver, twenty; and a cell phone salesman in his late teens. Mostly, the older folks were defectors from Qadhafi's regime or were expatriates who'd come back home to fight for their homeland. The young made up the fighting force of the revolution, and the old decided when and where these kids would die. But then that's how every war is fought—old men deciding a younger man's fate on the battlefield. But it doesn't take a hero to order men into battle—the hero is the one who goes, because courage isn't something you take with you, it's something you find once you're there.

These people were standing up to a dictator who'd ruled them with an iron fist for four decades. He wouldn't hesitate to torture, maim, murder, or use any other means to root out dissent. Failure to these townspeople meant death—and that was the best thing they'd get out of any defeat. Attack helicopters, fighter jets, tanks, and artillery were coming after them. They had a professional army attacking them. They had a ruthless intelligence service hunting them and the minute they joined the rebellion, they had indeed burned their boats at the beach, as the saying goes. There was nowhere for them to go but to Tripoli and to victory. We should have tried to help them earlier and with more force than we did.

Senator McCain and Congresswoman Myrick had it right—we should have been providing the rebels with intelligence to help defeat Qadhafi, technical assistance such as secure communications and ISR (intelligence, surveillance, and reconnaissance) platforms via our UAVs and piloted aircraft—and humanitarian help should have been increased. We should have sent in teams of CIA officers and Special Forces to link with the rebels, as we did in Afghanistan—basically to do what my team was trying to do for them privately. The Obama administration was simply leading from behind, pushing a noodle uphill—getting nowhere and doing little.

I hoped that if our private effort showed results by weakening the tower from which Qadhafi wreaked havoc and destruction, then perhaps our president would decide he ought to get on the side of the winners in this struggle and do more than talk. The rebels needed to figure out how to communicate securely and to properly organize and resupply themselves. If they could afford our help and Washington didn't object, we might be able to give them advice on improving in those areas.

ONE OF GENERAL HASI'S AIDES showed us to another empty room, which would be our quarters during our time in the city. I got the feeling that we weren't the first people to call this room home, as there were wrappers, crushed yogurt cartons, and empty water bottles lying around everywhere.

A skinny Libyan kid no more than fifteen came running up with a big smile, revealing a few missing front teeth, and handed us two thin, foam mattresses on which we stretched out our Therm-a-Rest pads and sleeping bags. I broke out two Quest protein bars for dinner. I always carried Quest bars and 5-hour Energy with me—no local food for this redneck. I had to work and I intimately understood the limitations of my belly—one bite of goat head, swig of tap water, or handful of rice and I'd be wrapped around the local porcelain like a starving Somali pirate's hand on a chicken leg.

Making friends in foreign countries usually involves eating with them, and many times that meant going to their homes and sitting with a tribal leader while looking at piles of rice, grilled ram testicles, kebabs, and lamb brain stew. You can tell me it tastes like chicken all you want, but having experienced food poisoning more than twice while working overseas, I'm quite content to pack protein bars, eat nuts, and stick to what I know.

ONE DECEMBER I WAS IN A VILLAGE in eastern Afghanistan meeting with a local tribal leader in his walled, guarded compound. I sat as the lone American, cross-legged at the far end of a long, rectangular room of mud and stone with the musky smell of animal skins mixed with wood smoke. We all sat on carpets rolled across the floor from their usual storage place against the edges of the walls. Eighteen others joined me—all men, all Afghans from the village and members of the local Pashtun clan. It was dark out but kerosene lanterns lighted the room with a flickering orange glow. Despite the subzero temperature, the lofty elevation, and the snow coming down in a horizontal blur and collecting in massive drifts, we were all toasty warm due to fires built under the raised floor of the room—it was Stone Age radiant heat all night long. In front of me were piles of rice and chunks of mystery meat; the men dug into it with their dirty, bare hands—straight to their mouths, then back into the communal pile, time after time. I sat at the far end of the food spread from the main man—the chief. I'd squirreled away a protein bar between my crossed legs hoping to pretend to eat their food, but in reality pinching off pieces of the protein bar. It worked for about ten minutes.

The tribal leader, a man who had total control over this region of the country and could have someone killed with the snap of his fingers and buried by morning, got up and came over to sit next to me—a very uncharacteristic thing to do. The room fell deathly silent. He asked why I wasn't eating the food they'd prepared. I couldn't believe he'd seen what I was doing, at his age from that far away in such a dimly lit room. I said I had a medical condition and the food I was eating was special. I'll never forget what he said next: "You realize you're my prisoner now?" *Is he joking? Is this a test?* I thought. His dark, deep-set eyes, surrounded by a scraggly gray unibrow badly in need of a trim, were impassive; his gray beard revealed no hint of a grin under the glow of the lanterns hanging from the ceiling.

This situation could now go one of two ways—depending on the next words from my mouth. At times like this the brain does amazingly quick calculations and mine was busier than a two-dollar hooker on nickel night. I became acutely aware of the kerosene lanterns hanging from hooks in the ceiling, of my Glock pistol underneath my shirts, the two spare magazines on my left hip, totaling forty-five rounds of ammo if you counted the gun. I took stock of the eighteen potential targets and that all their rifles were stacked by the door at the far end of the room, and that the closest guy to them was seated, legs crossed, leaned over and eating . . . and roughly ten feet away. I know I can accurately empty a Glock in less than three seconds and reload in under two. No man in this room was more than fifteen feet away from me. If this old man meant me harm, I'd kill them all and burn this place to the ground. That might sound crazy, impossible, or even ridiculous, but you have no idea what you can do when properly motivated, your back is to the wall and your other option is to end up on YouTube losing your head. No thanks—I'll strike a match instead.

But then I recalled the twenty-foot-tall walls, the massive gate that took two men to open, the snowstorm, and the fact that I was basically in the Himalayan Mountains, miles away from friendlies . . . yeah, those variables definitely affected what came out of my mouth next.

"Sir, I could not have been captured by a more honorable man," I said. He looked at me for a long, long second, and then a grin broke across his hairy, wrinkled, tanned, weather-beaten face and he laughed long and hard as he slapped me on the shoulder and went back to his seat. Needless to say, for the rest of the night I ate anything and everything that was passed by me—it could have been goat, dog, cow tongue, or donkey dick for all I knew, it didn't matter—I was eating and that was that. After dinner I rolled up in a bundle of blankets just like the other men, only I slept with one eye open and a Glock under my rolled-up sweater I was using as a pillow, doubled over in pain.

But the trouble really kicked into high gear the next morning when I started throwing up every last scrap of anything I'd consumed the past day. That devolved into the sharts—flatulence that morphs into crapping your pants. Quick good-byes, rushed handshakes, and thanks for the hospitality were offered amid a flurry of mind-numbing lower gut pain and a valiant struggle to keep things together. Soon my Toyota was bouncing and sliding fast over the rocks, potholes, and snow-covered roads heading back down the mountain. The sharts became terrible—literally. I thought at the time that nothing could be worse than having to ride over icy mountainous roads with those noxious odors in the cab and residue swirling around, all while hurling out the door and freezing to death as snow was driven sideways through my window—which had to remain open if for no other reason than to have fresh air to breathe.

This strategy worked until things took a turn for the obscene with full-blown, ground-hugging, dig-a-hole-and-clamp-your-nose diarrhea that locked on to me so badly I could've crapped through a screen door and never hit a wire. I couldn't drive any farther and just locked up the brakes, stopped on the side of the mountain road, opened my door, and hugged the truck seat until my stomach muscles were in spasms and my backside felt like I'd been wiping with ten-grit sandpaper, all as flaky, cold, wet snow covered my back.

Thanks to that drive, I pack my food with me if I can—even to family reunions.

BACK IN BENGHAZI, no sooner had I begun eating than the same buck-toothed kid came back in with a tray of hot tea and two cups. Then he returned with a platter of mystery meat, nuts, and dates on a bed of rice. D was in heaven—the boy could eat carrots grown at Chernobyl and sleep soundly. Me? I dragged out bottled water from my ruck and kept on plowing into my protein bars. We stuffed ourselves and rolled into our bags. Unable to sleep, I thought of home—my family, my children. I had not planned to live a life away from them; had tried hard, in fact, to guard against it, even changing my career at one point, because next to God, nothing meant more to me than home.

CHAPTER 6

How Much Is This Going to Cost Us?

March 27, 2011
Benghazi, Libya

THE NEXT MORNING we sent a SITREP to Colonel Cantwell to let them know we hadn't been killed in our sleep, then set about packing up and stepped out to stretch and see what was going on. General Hasi's aide told us we had a meeting in one hour with the general and other leaders.

When we joined them, he was out of uniform, as were the other men in the room. They explained to us that they feared the tribal groups would notice us, foreigners, together with the NTC leadership, and then break with the rebel army. Personally I didn't see it. We had seen and heard too many pleas for Western help to think we wouldn't be welcomed. Regardless, it was a stated concern of our hosts and so we had to do our best to deal with it.

Libya is a land of tribes and clans, linked by networks and subdivided into multiple branches. Often you can identify a person's tribe simply by knowing his last name. Qadhafi is a good example—he came from the Qadhadfa tribe, an Arabized Berber tribe from a western Libyan region now known as Sirte.

"Gentlemen, thank you for coming here," the oldest of the men began, in English. He never told us his name, nor did any of the others. Dressed in slacks and a nicely pressed shirt that hung untucked, he was reclined on his side against a pillow in the traditional way. An interpreter spoke in the background, turning his words into Arabic for those who didn't speak my mother's tongue.

"You honor us with your presence and I trust your night was restful?" His English was perfect, with perhaps a hint of south London. The terp droned on in the background.

"Sir, yes, we rested very comfortably and we appreciate your hospitality. The honor is ours that you would see us," I replied, waiting for the terp to finish.

People make the mistake when using an interpreter of speaking to him and telling him to say X, Y, and Z to the intended recipient. It's far more effective and thus more advantageous to your cause if you speak to your host and don't acknowledge the interpreter, but allow him to do his job in the background. It makes the conversation more personal to your target.

"We come on behalf of Congresswoman Myrick from Washington, D.C. She is very interested in learning what you need. Understand this, however—we are not representing the U.S. government. But your fight against the dictator Qadhafi is being watched by the world, and many want to see you succeed and to help you," I continued, trying to make eye contact with each man in the room as I spoke.

"General Hasi and I spoke at length back in Cairo," I said, looking in the general's direction. "He told me in great detail what you seek in terms of equipment and weapons."

The men looked at Hasi and nodded. Hasi sat impassive, listening.

"I want you to know that I did not come to bargain with you over the sale of lethal equipment. I know that is what you want more than anything. But I did not come to talk about that. That may be a discussion in the future, but that is not something I have any authority to discuss with you today. Things must be done in steps," I said.

"I can discuss the supply of nonlethal equipment, but even more valuable to you, I can bring advisers," I went on. I noticed men leaning into one another and whispering. I let that die down before continuing.

"As you all know well, these things are as needed to fight a war against a professional army as the bullets and guns."

Certainly, that was true, but I still appreciated their position. If I were in their shoes, I'd want the bullets and guns, too. Because without those you die, no matter how many trucks, boots, and advisers you might have. In war, it's far less important who starts it than who finishes it.

Still, I wasn't going to step across a line and start bargaining over things I didn't even have, never mind the fact that I didn't have permission to sell them even if I did have them. My highest priority was to get the rebels to trust me, if even in a small way. Then to send information back to Washington.

A gray-bearded old man reclining a few seats to my right spoke up in Arabic. "How soon could you have this equipment delivered to us and how would you get it here?"

He was testing me, wanting to see if we had the horsepower to deliver on a promise. Luckily, D had sent General Hasi's request back to Colonel Cantwell when we were in Cairo.

He spoke up and said, "Sir, we could have it delivered to you into the port of Benghazi. We can source the equipment from southern European providers, which would shorten the time frame for delivery. But I cannot tell you exactly how soon it would arrive. That depends upon the supplier's inventory. It would come from many different places because we will shop for the best prices for you."

As we finished I noticed a puzzled look on their faces, followed by beards turning and mumbling to one another. The older man then spoke up after a few minutes.

"What do you mean when you say best prices for us?"

"Well, sir, the equipment is not free and must be purchased before it can be sent to you," I said.

"Why does the United States government not simply give it to us, as you did with the Afghans and the Iraqis?"

"Sir, as I explained to the ambassador and to General Hasi, I do not work for the United States government. I am here on behalf of Congresswoman Myrick only to gather information for a report that will be submitted to her. But she is not offering to supply you with anything, either. I am offering to provide you a quote for nonlethal equipment and military advisers on a private basis, unconnected to the U.S. government. This would have to be paid for from either NTC funds or from external assistance, such as the Qataris or the House of Saud," I told the group.

The men again looked at one another. They appeared surprised that I was even aware of support coming in from Qatar and Saudi Arabia. My friend Bob Baer, former CIA counterterrorism officer, author of *The Perfect Kill*, and the guy George Clooney played in the movie *Syriana*, had been working his sources and passed those angles to me.

"The United States will not give us these small things that we ask for?" he said, still apparently confused. I cleared it up for him.

"Sir, again, I don't speak for the U.S. government. But as a taxpaying U.S. citizen let me say that my government has spent quite a lot of money already—hundreds of millions—flying over and attacking Qadhafi's forces at the risk of our pilots' lives and costing our citizens directly. To my knowledge, no one has asked you to repay that. It comes from the U.S. people because they are a kind people. Don't you think that if you want supplies that you should pay for them? Someone has to pay—it's your revolution; we already won ours," I said.

Honestly, the more people I met, the more I liked my dog. This guy had just pissed me off and what I'd said was bold and something I regretted not long after it came out of my mouth. But it was the truth; it was out and that was that. Whatever they said next, I couldn't change. Seconds of uncomfortable silence ticked by. I wouldn't have been surprised to hear crickets chirping in the background. I glanced at D, who sat stone-faced. He was with me no matter what happened and I knew what was going through his head. We had an inside joke that was truer than we ever acknowledged—be polite, be professional, but have a plan to kill everyone you meet. He was thinking about how to get out of this room and to a working vehicle if things went ugly. That's how our teams worked. While one guy was doing something necessary, the other was figuring out the next move.

"Tell me about these advisers," said the old man, breaking the silence.

"Sir, I propose to offer you fifty-two men, all with backgrounds in U.S. Special Operations, who work for us and will help your army win the fight against Qadhafi by offering services related to strategic and tactical operations. They are all combat veterans, they all speak Arabic to some degree or another, and they are all very familiar with considerations of culture and religion for your area."

"But that is too many," he said. "The problem is not with your men, for many of us here believe they would be very helpful. The problem is that if too many of them come, the newspeople would start to say that it is a Western-led revolt, run by the Americans or the English. Qadhafi has already said that our revolution is a colonial plot. We cannot afford to have the people believe that."

I explained my plan: to sort my men into smaller teams and have them go out to rebel units and work with their commanders. They'd be out of sight; they'd dress like the rebels, grow beards, and blend right in.

"How much will this cost us?" he asked.

I told him and he didn't blink, and no one else blinked, either.

As I read the room and felt the energy turning in our favor, a thought occurred to me for the first time. *This is crazy, but this just might work.*

CHAPTER 7

Spying on the State Department?

1991

Virginia

SOMEONE WAS BEATING ON MY WALL, HARD. I sat up in the bed of the small hotel room. In the hall, men were raging. One sounded drunk; the other was screaming, pissed-off, in a language I didn't recognize.

Lights off, I felt under my pillow and my hand hit the wood and metal of my gun, and I wrapped my fist around the grip. I didn't turn on the bedside lamp—the light might spill out under my door and draw their attention. The area I was in was considered a nonpermissive environment, hostile—think Iraq.

The shouting grew louder; I heard a scuffle, as someone was slammed into a wall close by. We'd been told by our CIA bosses that the local intelligence service was good, so maybe this was all just to get me to open my door so these guys would have a reason to grab me. I had gone to bed fully dressed, boots and all. My room guarded the corner of a four-way intersecting hall and, unlike any hotel or motel room I'd ever been in, this one had two doors to the hallways. Inside, it was spartan—no curtains because there were no windows. The floor was plywood worn to a shine. The broken television with its bent rabbit-ear antenna sitting on the dilapidated dresser was fit for a pawnshop. About ten feet from the foot of my bed I could see light shining under one of the doors; on the wall to my right, also about ten feet away, was more light from the other door. I wouldn't be getting any sleep.

Abruptly the door on the right of the room broke open and spilling in with the light from the hall I saw the silhouette of a large, thick bald man with a bottle in one hand and a stick in the other staggering in. Then the other door crashed open, letting in more light and another guy. Things were still for a split second and then the doorknob came loose, fell apart, and hit the floor. A man in dark blue coveralls stood there swaying with what looked like a logging chain swinging from his right hand. Then they both started yelling, screaming, and threatening each other . . . and then Blue Coveralls flipped on the lights . . . and they saw me.

My hand tightened around the grip of the pistol still hidden under my pillow. I didn't want to bring a weapon into this if I didn't have to—they were illegal, and that would blow my cover. Raising my left hand and scooting back up the bed toward the wall, I tried to calmly tell them to stop, playing the part of the scared rabbit, but the bald guy staggered forward, raising the stick, while the guy in the coveralls started yelling at me in English. I repeated the command to get out, then reached for the phone, my eyes glued to both men. Blue Coveralls started to back away—he seemed to have a few brain cells still functioning.

But Baldy advanced, raising the stick like he was about to cave my head in. I slid the pistol out, rolled back onto the bed, and gripped it with both hands, kept both eyes open, and placed the front sight post over the silhouette of his face and fired three quick shots. He dropped. I tracked his body with the sights as he fell and then shifted the sights left onto Blue Coveralls—he stared in disbelief at the guy on the ground and then his hands went up immediately.

But I thought he was raising his chain, and my pistol bucked three more times in quick succession. His body went limp and he collapsed where he stood.

I was up and off the bed as quickly as I could move, heading to the door with the broken knob. I pushed it closed, leaning a chair against it to keep it from opening. Then I moved to the door on the right, got next to the wall, holding my weapon tightly to my chest, and looked through the crack at an angle up the hall. Stepping to the other side of the door, I looked down the hall the other way—it was empty, clear . . . for now, anyway.

I wanted out. I needed to get clear of this room, get a vehicle, and get moving. Giving the near-empty room a fast visual pass, I flipped open the cylinder, reloaded, and tucked the now-hot weapon down the back of my pants, took a deep breath, and stepped out into the poorly lit hallway. Closing the door behind me, I tried to calmly but briskly move to the nearest exit to hit the parking lot and my car.

"Endex! Endex!" I heard my instructor, Red, say, ending the training exercise. The lights came on and Baldy and Blue Coveralls resurrected. Red took the training pistol from me. One more exercise had just wrapped up at the Farm, the CIA's mammoth facility where U.S. federal employees learn the arts of breaking the law in other countries.

The Farm is where gray work of covert operations and espionage is taught. At one end of the national spectrum is white, shining peace—that city-on-a-hill concept. At the other end is black, raging, savage war at the foot of that hill. The space between is the gray zone where the haze of diplomacy and combat meet and bleed into one another. That's where the CIA works. That's where men and women carry out covert operations and practice the art of espionage secretly, clandestinely around the globe. The Farm is ground zero for learning the trade, and that's exactly what I was doing.

I had been at the CIA ██████████ stationed in Washington, but at the Farm, I was finally getting what I wanted, the craft of a spy, drilled into me with the zeal that separates life from death. I think people who do this work, not unlike athletes, are driven, from the beginning, by the desire for excellence and the need to test themselves against the finest. There is a drive, an intensity necessary to do this job, a determination absolutely essential to surviving the trials along the way. As long as I'd been old enough to know what it was, I had wanted to serve my country, be the best shot I could be, beat myself into solid physical shape, learn how to fight, study tactics and try to grasp strategy, and be the guy who raised his hand to try and help.

I WAS BORN amid the majestic, dark green magnolias and sweet, fragrant honeysuckle in the rolling hills of north Mississippi. I was blessed to grow up in a warm, loving family of five, where Mom and Dad taught us to believe in God, Jesus, the Holy Spirit, and the right to bear arms, to serve our country, and help our neighbors. With cane poles and worms we caught catfish, watched *Happy Days* and *The Waltons* together in the family den, went to church every time the doors were open, and prayed together every night before bed. Early in the mornings before the sun was up, I'd head out with an old man, a family friend, Mr. Calvin Mangrum, through the woods and creeks checking traps, learning how to track and catch animals. My dad worked hard six days a week and even found time to build—by hand, in secret—the first car my brother and I shared together, giving it to us on Christmas morning. Dad, Granddaddy, my younger brother, Todd, and I hunted deer, squirrel, and dove and that was my whole world—God, family, church, riding horses, hunting, and playing in the woods. So when I first walked through the doors of CIA headquarters in 1990, everything felt surreal. I was entering a realm of moral ambiguities in one sense, a landscape where the world's harsh realities would be laid bare. But I wanted it—I wanted to see how things really worked. History strongly suggested there'd be war in my lifetime, and I'd have to go as did my forefathers before me. So who better to go with than the best trained? It seemed to me that you have a better chance of living through it than being a self-propelled sandbag on a beach somewhere. Now home was behind me, and a new world was ahead.

That was my foundation, but my training might have started when I was a young teenager. My much older cousin Doug was home from the navy. At six foot two, over two hundred pounds, with sandy blond hair and a bushy, walrus-style handlebar mustache, he'd been a diver and EOD (Explosive Ordnance Disposal) tech and was an avid student of Chinese martial arts. He'd even interviewed with Commander Richard Marcinko out in San Diego when he was forming SEAL Team 6. One of the first white guys accepted into a Chinese kung fu monastery in Hawaii, Doug trained there as much as he could, and then moved on to study Jeet Kune Do from one of Bruce Lee's direct students. It sounds like the story of the Karate Kid, but I literally went to his house and raked leaves and did chores until he agreed after many months to teach me, my younger brother and best friend on earth, Todd, another bespectacled boy two years younger named George, and two younger fellas named Tripp and Justin. We five amigos got more than we bargained for . . . before the movie ever came out.

Doug's cabin was in the wooded hills on the outskirts of town. He hung a thick rope in a tree with a bell on it, and we had to climb the rope before and after each class and whenever we took water breaks. Thirsty? Ring the bell. Gotta pee? Ring the bell. Hungry? Ring the bell. We fought with no pads on our hands, feet, face, or groin, and he expected that whatever he taught us during the last class we would have committed to memory by the next one. We fought one-on-one, two-on-one, and even three or four on one, but Doug's program turned out success. Todd went on to join the Army and became one of the brightest network engineers I've ever known. For a while, he came to work with me when I eventually started my own company. Justin studied at Harvard, and then returned to our hometown of Batesville to help disadvantaged young people. George, in his John Lennon glasses, became a successful investment banker and ladies' man extraordinaire in Memphis, while Tripp became an active-duty Special Forces officer (a lieutenant colonel as of this writing), served with distinction in Iraq, and moved over to the black side—the covert side—where he still works today.

We went at it. Doug would swing full force and we stopped the blow, ducked it, moved, or got hit—hard. He pulled no punches. Once, on his porch after a long Saturday of training, he stood with a spotlight hanging from the roof behind him, shining right in my eyes. Earlier in the day, he'd been teaching us how to defend against someone swinging a weapon like a bat, stick, or chain. When night fell, he raised the stakes. Without warning, he went inside, returning with a four-foot-long stick with a two-foot curved blade fixed to the end of it. Down south we called it a Joe blade; others called it a kaiser blade, it's used to cut down small trees, brush, and such. Doug brought it out, warned, "Get ready," then hauled it back and swung it my direction.

Exhausted from a full day of training already, I couldn't see crap with that porch spotlight blasting into my eyes, except for his hulking form moving vaguely like a baseball batter at Mach 4, but I moved in fast, rushing him, closing the distance like we'd worked on all day. My hands came together and my forearms formed a triangle, slamming all at once into the shoulder joint, bicep, and chest of the arm holding the weapon, blocking its forward momentum. The force of my movement colliding with his incoming arm was so hard that the weapon went flying out of his grasp, landing somewhere behind me in the dark woods.

The principle when fighting a swinging weapon is getting inside its danger zone—inside its arc. Whether a chain, stick, or bat, the weapon can't hurt you if you're standing face-to-face with the guy swinging it, breathing his air . . . then you just have to deal with the man—and then it's all head butts, elbows, and knees.

Fighting skills have always been an important part of any operator's tool kit, and I've continued to learn, hone, and develop them over the years. They're perishable skills—gone if you don't train, refine, and sharpen them. When I started out as a teen, I was kicking high, punching, doing backflips and crazy, fancy moves like I saw in the movies. But as I've matured, I've painfully figured out that it's about what works—keeping your feet below your waist, kicking in knees, crushing arches in the foot, and attacking common peroneal nerves on the side of the legs. Then if it gets closer, you bring elbows to the temple, side of the neck, or throat, or head butts to the face, fingers to the eyes; if it goes to the ground, it's choking the guy out, dislocating elbows or knees. It's about tearing off ears, and hooking eyes, cheeks, and anything you can grab. It's more efficient and quick and not fancy or even pretty to watch, but it's not a show; it's about what works—it's about winning.

Whether shooting, clearing a room, going to the driving track, or working on fighting—combatives—you have to always push harder than your adversary. The idea is to be first in the fight—first to read the intentions, and first to strike. As an older Delta operator said once, "I don't train to be in a gunfight; I'd much rather be in a shooting—there's a difference. A gunfight means he's shooting back at me. In a shooting, I'm doing all the work." There are no second-place finishers—you don't take silver, you simply lose gold. Second place is nothing but the best loser—nobody lost better than the guy in second place. But on the battlefield that guy usually winds up dead.

But I was also learning something else of great importance—a new way of thinking. Anyone could hit, kick, and shoot, but Doug showed us that the guy who could manipulate events to prevent the fight or turn things in your favor by seeing two and three moves ahead was the better warrior. Dad taught me that as well during the hours and hours my brother and I spent trying to beat him in chess. To this day, I don't ever remember winning a single match against him, even when Mom would urge him to let us win. But those lessons of observing, anticipating your opponent's moves, and letting the situation play itself out were what nearly two decades later we'd call "developing the situation."

Later, as my ambitions turned toward the CIA, I had to come to a new level of understanding of the world and its actors, the clandestine reality behind the conflicts that threaten us every day. I wanted badly to understand these things—to look behind the curtain. If you don't want it like that, it'll be hard to make it in the long run.

BY THE DAY I first stepped into CIA headquarters in Northern Virginia as a sworn officer, in early August 1990, I felt as though I had survived more tests than a PhD student in physics. My chassis had been primed and endlessly inspected by the agency's doctors. My psychological state had been plumbed for depths I didn't know I had, and my superiors pronounced that I was just the right kind of crazy. I realized I had to push myself every minute from day one and never settle for second place, never accept being the first-best loser. I wouldn't win all the time, but I had to have that attitude.

On that first day, my royal blue plastic ID badge was still shiny and without a scratch. Hanging around my neck from a dog-tag-style chain, it made me proud. The badge didn't have a logo or the letters *CIA* or my name on it anywhere, just a reddish orange five-digit alphanumeric, my picture, and a D.C. mailing address on the back in case I lost it. As the hot August sun hammered me, I was sweating in my starched shirt, and it wasn't even eight o'clock yet. But this day was important to me. I had no idea, however, what was going to happen to my country before I even had lunch.

As I walked the long pathway from the huge west parking lot, where my roommate and I had carpooled from our agency-rented apartment, I saw the SPOs (security and protective officers) in their black Smokey the Bear drill sergeant hats, white shirts, and dark sunglasses watching everyone pass through. Entering the spotless New Headquarters Building, or simply NHB, I saw former director William Casey's plaque in my periphery. I walked in as proud as I could be, the son of a small business owner from the poorest state in the nation, who now worked for the single remaining superpower's most potent intelligence organization.

I'd been studying the CIA for years and I knew its history from the beginning, when it was started as the Office of Strategic Services—the OSS—in World War II. Then in 1947 it became the Central Intelligence Agency. Back then it was divided into four major sections called directorates.

Staff in the Directorate of Intelligence (DI) analyzed incoming raw information from all sources and prepared reports for clients across the U.S. government, but the main customer was the president, in the form of the President's Daily Brief (the PDB) and the National Intelligence Estimate.

The Directorate of Administration (DA) was tasked with security functions, logistical supply needs for stations and personnel, as well as accounting and payroll worldwide. If the agency needed pens, payroll, or personnel, the DA provided it. It was renamed the Directorate of Support in the years following 9/11.

The Directorate of Science and Technology (DS&T) was where engineers with forty-pound brains created technical collection systems, made disguises, encrypted communications systems, and created covert listening devices and other things that would make James Bond drool. These were the folks who engineered the miniature drones smaller than dragonflies, as well as the fake rocks designed to conceal gadgets used to listen in on enemy cell phone calls.

Finally, if James Bond existed in America, he'd be found working in the Directorate of Operations (DO), which in 2005 became the National Clandestine Service, or simply NCS. This was where the case officers and paramilitary officers hung out. Contrary to movies, novels, and news reports, a CIA agent is not a U.S. citizen, but a foreigner recruited, run, and handled by a case officer. The agents do the majority of the actual spying and deliver information to the case officer, who is always a U.S. citizen and full-time employee of the CIA—a blue-badger, in agency parlance. Blue badges denoted full-time federal employees, and green badges were for contractors. The DO collected this HUMINT—short for HUMan INTelligence—worldwide and passed it along to the DI, who tried to make sense of it in light of the president's policies and the nation's security interests. It wasn't so much about connecting the dots, but figuring out what were really dots that needed connecting, to quote my friend and former CIA officer Bob Baer.

I remember on that first day going over from the cafeteria to the front entrance of OHB—or Old Headquarters Building—and staring at the sixteen-foot-large seal of the CIA in the floor that I'd seen in books and movies back home. To the left of the great seal, the memorial wall stood framed between the U.S. and CIA flags. Carved into the wall were rows of stars representing CIA officers killed in the line of duty, and beneath the stars, jutting out from the wall about waist high, hung a book under glass listing a few of their names; other stars had no names at all—those officers were still classified. Across the lobby on the south wall, a statue of Major General William Donovan, recipient of the Medal of Honor, National Security Medal, Distinguished Service Cross, and leader of the OSS during World War II, kept silent watch as the father of modern U.S. intelligence. To his side on that wall, an American flag hung, and a single star could be seen etched into place in dedication to our forefathers of the OSS.

I'll always recall my first walk that day down the marbled hall with its narrow, tall windows on one side and paintings of all the former directors hanging on the other. I remember moving toward the tunnel that led to the Bubble, a large, seven-thousand-square-foot domed auditorium sitting just in front of OHB under large shade trees. Minutes later, all of us were all standing, shoulder to shoulder, in a small room in front of an American flag, raising our right hands and swearing to protect the United States of America against all enemies. My chest swelled with pride; my thoughts turned to my dad, who served in the U.S. Army National Guard as a tank commander during the 1960s and into the '70s, and to both of my grandfathers, who served during World War II, one in Europe who crossed the Rhine in General Patton's Third Army and the other in the Pacific under Admiral Nimitz. I was carrying on this lineage of service holding a top-secret clearance in the employ of the top spy agency in the world. I was one of only a few dozen others who'd been selected, vetted, recruited, tested, and hired from tens of thousands of other applicants who applied—less than half of 1 percent; they kept reminding us of that, that we were the cream of the crop, the best this nation had to offer. For a young guy like me, it made me feel special . . . and I guess that was their point.

The DO, as it was called then, was organized into geographic divisions such as the Near East Division (NE), which handled the Middle East; SE division, which existed at the time of my employment to handle Soviet–East Europe; AF division, which handled Africa; and CE division, which handled Central Eurasia, to name a few. Once I was told to go over to LA Division to pick up reports and I asked why we had a division devoted to Los Angeles. Through fits of laughter the case officer told me what an idiot I was, that LA Division handled Latin America, not the Southern California metropolis. So much for being the cream of the crop; I felt more like the dregs of the barrel that day.

The DO was also divided up by centers—such as the CTC, short for the Counter Terrorism Center; the CNC—Counter Narcotics Center; and the CIC—Counter Intelligence Center, where the spies spied on the spies and tried to keep out the likes of traitors such as Aldrich Ames or Edward Lee Howard. Inside the divisions and centers were the desks that handled various regional or specific targets. For example, in the NE Division was a desk that handled Near Eastern issues, involving countries like Iraq, and in CTC there was a desk called RASHIA, which worked the RAdical SHIite target.

I had been assigned to the Near East Division—hotbed of terrorism, crazy dictators, and oil money. It wasn't that I had specific expertise in the Middle East—quite the opposite, in fact. It was simply that it was crisis time there and the division needed bodies, so mine was aimed that way. They were swamped, and as it turned out, I didn't get a briefing. I got a war.

ABOUT THE TIME I was walking into Langley (another name for CIA headquarters, after the area in McLean, Virginia, where it was built) in August 1990, a cable from the U.S. Embassy in Kuwait was flashing into the Operations Center at the State Department with urgent information—Iraq, under the leadership of dictator Saddam Hussein, had invaded Kuwait, the tiny country to its south, and surrounded the U.S. Embassy. Two of our embassies actually—one in Baghdad, one in Kuwait City—were surrounded. In other words, on my first day in service, history was being made; this was a major fork in the twisting road that would lead to America's invasion of Iraq twice, the bloody downfall of the vicious Hussein and his evil sons, a monumental shift in the reality of the Middle East, and a massive task for the administration of George W. Bush, whose father—George Herbert Walker Bush—was then president.

Washington, D.C., was in shock at the news of Saddam's invasion.

Earlier, in April 1990, a delegation of Republican senators—including Republicans Bob Dole of Kansas and Alan Simpson of Wyoming—had visited with Hussein to deliver a message from President George H. W. Bush—abandon your chemical and biological weapons programs and stockpiles and, in return, the United States would continue working to improve relations between the two countries.

Senator Howard Metzenbaum, a Democrat from Ohio, also with the delegation, told Saddam, "Mr. President, I can tell you're an honorable man."* The dictator—an honorable man? The same man who rained poison gas on the Kurdish village of Halabja just two years earlier in 1988, killing an estimated five thousand of his own citizens and wounding ten thousand more just because he thought they were disloyal? The same man who once sentenced his elder son, Uday, to be executed after he beat the dictator's food taster to death in front of scores of horrified party guests, but later rescinded the order? He wasn't an honorable man. He was a tyrannical dictator described by Robert Kaplan as being "in a category all his own, somewhere north of al-Assad and south of Stalin," when it came to brutal cruelty. Calling him an honorable man was simply a ridiculous, political obscenity from a U.S. senator who should have been given a dictionary with the word *honorable* highlighted in it—or who should have just stayed home.

Just three months earlier, America had still been sharing intelligence with Hussein in his war against the Iranians. In July 1990, when the dictator had begun to amass forces along the Kuwaiti border, most in the American intelligence community saw the suggestion of aggression as a bluff by the Iraqi leader to gain leverage in the ongoing OPEC talks. On July 25, U.S. ambassador April Glaspie met with Hussein and was asked about Washington's position on Iraq's dispute with Kuwait over the oil fields. She couldn't get anyone in Washington to answer the phone since it was night back on the East Coast; she wasn't prepared for that specific question and so she just stuck with talking points from earlier—the United States had no opinion on Arab-Arab disputes. Hussein apparently took that as tacit approval, and eight days later he invaded.

None of the experts at the CIA or State Department believed that

---

* http://memory.loc.gov/service/mss/mssmisc/mfdip/2007%20txt%20files/2007wil04.txt.

Hussein would risk a confrontation with the United States by actually invading Kuwait, despite the presence on the border of the dictator's elite Republican Guards, who had been called "the very guarantors of his rule." In other words, we had been blindsided.

More than one hundred Americans were trapped in the U.S. Embassy in Kuwait City. Perhaps two thousand Americans were hiding from Iraqi soldiers throughout the capital city, and at least 115 were already in Iraqi custody, essentially hostages—human shields against a U.S. military response. Iraqi forces were hauling a number of Americans, mostly oil workers, to Baghdad, where they were put up at local hotels. The Iraqis would not allow the "freed" Americans to leave the hotels or even meet with embassy officials. It was clear that although the Iraqis called them "guests," they were hostages. Iraqi officials later dropped the ruse and announced that their forces would hold the citizens from any country threatening Iraq as hostages until the threats ended.

Deputy Chief of Mission to Baghdad Joseph Wilson, the ranking U.S. diplomat at the embassy in Iraq at the time, understood what he was up against: Saddam—and Washington. He got the fact that, if he waited for D.C. to act, which could take weeks, he would be sharing his Christmas turkey with a smelly dictator with food in his mustache. He and the Diplomatic Security Staff were also smart enough to know that securing the building was the first objective, so they performed a thorough review of security procedures, getting the windows painted over to foil snipers, destroying classified files and documents, and preparing for the remaining files to be incinerated in a heartbeat, if necessary; they also instigated the creation of evacuation strategies and a plan to get nonessential staff out as quickly as possible. On that first day of my career, I learned from those trapped men and women an essential lesson: *Do something.* Many times the big guns won't move because they're scared to get blamed for making a mistake and they'll point blame at whatever you do or they'll run in to take the credit if it works out well. But sometimes you just can't wait: you do what you, the one actually on the ground, know to be right and you don't wait for the desk jockeys to get up off their hands.

AS WORLD EVENTS SEEMED to be hitting fever pitch, I was hustled down the sixth-floor corridor of the Old Headquarters Building. It was under renovation that year, its long halls lined in places with plastic sheeting over walls or doors, as green-badged carpenters and painters dressed in stained overalls with tool belts hanging on their hips intermingled with intelligence officers, commandos, secretaries, and suits of all flavors. Everywhere I looked, someone seemed to be moving with a purpose in a suit or uniform, carrying files under an arm, or pushing a cart—seemingly all heading to do something important. I stepped out of that stream of humanity and focused confusion and into the office where I was to work, checking in with the head secretary. She took my name and picked up the phone, and suddenly a short, thick, red-faced guy who, it seemed, was my boss, kicked open his office door and stormed toward me with a stack of papers. Then he said to go see the chief.

So out into the stream I went once again, weaving my way through one of the busiest halls at CIA, thanks to the turbulent Middle East. A few seconds later, I stepped into the chief's office, checking in with yet another secretary. The chief had a reputation—an intimidating one. A thick man with dark curly hair, he was predisposed to fits of profane screaming at subordinates. The secretary hit her intercom and was greeted by a man yelling to get me through his closed door into his office.

"Shut the damn door," he said, as if I should have known to do it. "You're the new guy, right?" *Yessir.* "I need you to go to State. You'll be working in the task force every day until I call you back here, got it?" *Yessir.*

"The ambassador running the task force will be the only one there who'll know you're CIA, so don't f*#$ yourself." *Yessir.* "You're my eyes and ears over there—those a**holes aren't telling us anything that's going on, and I want you to damn well change that for me—understand? Get me cables—bring 'em back every day.

Clear?" *Yessir, clear.* "Good—now get the hell out of my office."

Surely, he knew I had zero training at that point. It was hard to believe. The chief had just asked me to basically spy on another government agency. Did they really not know what was going on at State or was it just a test for me as part of training? Maybe it was better to spy at home among friends before trying it out overseas? Surely not. Looking back, when we first were hired, a lot of us had crazy, conspiratorial notions about the agency and why they asked us to do the things we did. In hindsight, much of it was routine and pragmatic, with no Orwellian plot behind it at all. Regardless, I had direct orders from the CIA equivalent of a two-star general.

As I was headed over to State, Secretary of Defense Dick Cheney was already pressing Bush 41 to go to war, arguing that the president needed no congressional authority. But on the other side of the Atlantic, Hussein was telling Joe Wilson that if the United States reacted militarily to the invasion of Kuwait, America would be responsible for "spilling of the blood of ten thousand soldiers in the Arabian Desert."

CHAPTER 8

Escaping Saddam

August 1990
Washington, D.C.

MY BOSS JUST ORDERED ME TO SPY on the State Department, my country looked to be going to war, and it was basically my first day on the job.

The Iraq-Kuwait Task Force was located at the U.S. Department of State and was housed in a maze of glass. As you might expect, it lay behind additional security layers—namely an old man in a navy blazer sitting at the entrance who checked to see if you had the bright canary-yellow badge clipped along with your State Department badge. Once you got past that lethal instrument, it was a warren of conference rooms and tiny phone banks literally no larger than a phone booth. Diplomatic specialists were frenetically handling crises exploding in their regions all over the globe. I reached a glass door, poked my head in, and found I was in the right spot. I introduced myself to a secretary who said the former ambassador to Iraq, April Glaspie, would be out to meet me in just a moment. The ambassador had been called back to Washington after her meeting with Hussein that many blamed for his decision to invade Kuwait. Her second in command, Joe Wilson—who eight years later would marry Valerie Plame, who rose to fame when syndicated columnist Robert Novak publicly identified her as a CIA officer—was acting in the ambassador's stead back in Baghdad.

I walked into the second room, with the officers around the conference table. On the floor, in boxes, were stacks and stacks of printed communication cables from embassies around the world relating to the Iraqi invasion. They were all classified at one level or another—Confidential, Secret—even a few Top Secret—all just lying around in cardboard boxes that used to hold printer paper. Now I understood what my chief was experiencing. This place was overwhelmed; they were doing well just to field the mounting problems, and reporting to the CIA wasn't their priority. I saw a copier against the wall and set about following my orders.

The task force ran twenty-four hours a day, seven days a week. It was led by an ambassador and was assigned foreign service officers from the bureaus of POL/MIL (Political- Military Affairs), Near Eastern Affairs, Economic and Business Affairs, and Consular Affairs; the Department of Foreign Affairs; and Legal. Everyone worked in shifts. These were the folks I'd noticed around the conference table as I'd tried to find my way around earlier. The two tiny phone-booth-size rooms I saw were crammed with a chair and a large, encrypted telephone unit called a STU-III, short for secure telephone unit, third generation. It was squeezed onto a tiny shelf and looked much like an office reception telephone, but you had to insert a crypto-key into the right side of it and dial a phone number, then a display would tell you whether your call was nonsecure or secure. If the other party had a STU, you just hit the "secure" button and started talking. These were the only open links to the besieged embassies—they were direct, secure telephone lines from the State Department to the embassies in Baghdad and Kuwait. I could not imagine what the long-distance bills for that would look like.

The place was frantic, but when the ambassador came out, she graciously and calmly introduced herself as April Glaspie. She was unruffled, determined, and I remember her fondly. Her long brown hair had a few streaks of gray in it and was pulled back into a ponytail. She wore little makeup and reminded me of someone more at home at Woodstock than at the seat of our nation's diplomatic corps. But because she'd met with Hussein before the invasion and hadn't told him not to invade Kuwait, she was about to take the fall and I think she knew it.

Before the invasion, she had delivered a letter from the president to Hussein, informing the dictator of Bush's pleasure at hearing of his willingness to negotiate with leaders from Kuwait to ease the tensions between the two nations. Iraq and Kuwait were at each other's throats over a debt Iraq owed Kuwait to the tune of $14 billion, which Kuwait had loaned to help them fight the Iranians in the 1980s; they also argued over claims by the Iraqis that Kuwait was slant-drilling for oil into Iraq's Rumaila oil field; and they bickered over Iraq's claim to part of Kuwait dating back to a 1913 treaty enforced by the British. But that's the nature of the Middle East—old rivalries and long memories.

According to Joe Wilson, the Iraqi leadership was "startled by the positive tone of the letter,"[*] which they interpreted as being overtly conciliatory toward Iraq and its dispute with Kuwait. Iraqi Undersecretary of Foreign Affairs Nizar Hamdun would recall that the letter left the impression America was more concerned about good relations than Iraqi military moves.[†] He also believed that the letter "sent the wrong signal to Saddam by not explicitly warning him." Wilson concluded that "this letter, much more than any other United States statement, appeared to have influenced Saddam's thinking"[‡] prior to the invasion. Couple that with Ambassador Glaspie's unexpected meeting with Hussein, and it was an unintended recipe for invasion.

The ambassador told me she wanted me to operate one of the communication lines to our embassies—the literal secure phones units in those two tiny rooms connecting Washington to the embassies in Baghdad and Kuwait. I said I'd get right on it, but I also suggested that I go in and organize the printouts of the communications cables, putting them up on clipboards so they could be seen more clearly and getting them up off the floor. These cables were not literal cables, such as wires or cords, but was a name for encrypted text communications between an embassy and its parent country. The term cable came from the time when underwater submarine communication cables were used to transmit these messages and it's still in use today. So I suggested I organize them, suggesting not only would they be more secure than lying around in printer boxes, but they would be more accessible to the officers working in the task force. When she agreed, I got right to it, because it also gave me cover for action—and I had gotten a seat next to the copying machine. I was in business.

In the next few weeks, Glaspie's experience would be as instructive

---

* http://www.historycommons.org/context.jsp?item=a072790bushletter#a072790bushletter.

† Ibid.

‡ Ibid.

to me as Joe Wilson's. She was about to get scapegoated and was treated by many in the press as the person who green-lighted Saddam's invasion; practically no one at the top but Joe Wilson came to her defense.

I organized the cables by date, with the most recent on top, grouping them by classification. I used one clipboard for those classified Confidential, one for Secret, and another for Top Secret, the contents of which I concealed with blank sheets on top. These clipboards went up on the back wall of the task force working room so that the officers didn't have to go searching through the boxes scattered on the floor when they needed something.

As I did this, I was also copying specific documents in those piles—except those labeled Top Secret—and putting them into a separate box, which I slid under a small desk against the wall. Later, I'd gather them up for delivery to CIA. If anyone saw me copying them, I would simply say I was making backup copies in case we lost any from the clipboards.

That evening when my shift was over, I stuffed as many of the copied non–Top Secret documents into my book bag as I could manage and caught the CIA's blue shuttle bus back to HQS, where I delivered my first batch to the chief.

He was ecstatic. Score one for Mississippi.

Back in the Middle East, Joe Wilson was summoned to see Saddam. Wilson, determined not to let Hussein get the better of him with Iraqi photographers, refused to do anything that could be construed as bowing to Hussein, which was an effect Hussein liked to achieve in photos with important visitors; Wilson dared not so much as chuckle for fear that a photo might be manipulated by the dictator's propagandists.

At the meeting, Hussein proposed a solution to the Iraq-Kuwait problem—if the United States blessed Iraq's annexation of Kuwait, he promised cheap oil for America and vowed not to carry his aggression farther to Saudi Arabia. If the United States did intervene, there would be blood, the dictator promised, a great deal of it. When Wilson pressed for foreign citizens to be allowed to leave Iraq, Hussein asked if he should take the request as an indicator of a U.S. military response. So no progress was made at the meeting. As a side note, it's instructive that when offered cheap oil—the thing America is always accused of trying to take—we didn't. Instead, our nation stood up for human rights and freedom and we liberated Kuwait.

On August 8, 1990, Wilson and others in Baghdad learned that the Iraqis were placing about 115 American hostages at strategic sites they considered most likely to be targeted by U.S. air and ground strikes—in essence using them as human shields. Two thousand Americans still remained trapped in Kuwait City, where Iraqis were, as Wilson would write, "terrorizing the population."* After I arrived at the State Department, our days got longer and more and more grim. One thing I learned was that a bureaucrat will throw you under a bus and then back over you and spin out to get a promotion or to make a score with his boss. But when American lives are at stake, Washington becomes a different world, a community where the players are transformed back into human beings who will do anything to get their people safely back to their families and to protect our country. The situation I was witnessing showed me the national security establishment at its best, with caring, brave, patriotic people going all out, working long hours, to any lengths, to rescue our own. This was real; this was genuine. I was proud to be there.

ONE AFTERNOON AS I WALKED INTO THE TASK FORCE ROOM, I noticed the receptionist was shaking like a hound dog passing a peach pit. Looking around, I saw a roomful of people near hysteria. "Secretary Baker is on his way down here—he wants to talk to the embassy in Baghdad," she said over the top of her reading glasses. *Okay, big deal,* I thought, as I walked back to my post. *Secretary Baker's not my boss, and he's coming to do what I've been doing for months. It's not hard—pick up the phone; it's lying right there on the desk.* The line to the embassy was open and running and had been for weeks. We checked in with them every fifteen minutes; plus, they were trapped, so it's not like you would get an answering machine.

A few minutes later, from my tiny phone booth, I realized that the larger room beyond my door had gone completely silent. I looked out to see U.S. Secretary of State James Addison Baker III, in a dark gray suit

---

* http://books.google.co.ma/books?id=diVDOY7LPlEC&pg=PT140&lpg=PT140&dq=joe+wilson+%22terrorizing+the+population%22&source=bl&ots=dFREwsudHw&sig=8cHIYiwbtsAzqFxiXHvCvN4t0lw&hl=en&sa=X&ei=WNHbUuntJ8nG0QXK44GIBQ&redir_esc=y#v=onepage&q=joe%20wilson%20%22terrorizing%20the%20population%22&f=false.

with a green-and-blue-striped tie, standing unaccompanied in our little office—no entourage in sight. That alone was odd—people at his level always had "step-and-fetch-its" around them. He was here and was expecting to speak to our people in Kuwait or Baghdad. I reached to check the comm link, but when I lifted the receiver and started to raise Baghdad, the line was dead. No background noise, no feedback, and no white noise—nothing. Dead silence. That had happened probably three times since the invasion. If stupidity were a capital offense in Iraq back then, there would have been a massive population drop. But on this day the Iraqis managed to cut the connection—sometimes that brain trust actually succeeded at something.

I had two options: I could get the embassy staff back online, which would take a few minutes, or I could run down to the Ops Center and they could bring them back up in a few seconds. Nobody was saying anything to Secretary Baker—they all seemed to be stunned he was even in the room. So I walked over to him, extended my hand, and said, "Sir, the line to Baghdad just went down, but if you'd still like to talk to them, I can take you to the Operations Center and we can—"

Just then a round, fat-bodied, pompous, bow-tie-wearing aide showed up and interrupted, saying, "We know where the Operations Center is!" Secretary Baker seemed embarrassed by the guy, shook my hand, thanked me for my service to the State Department, then walked out, following the aide back toward the Ops Center. I'll never forget the look on his face. He wore the expression of a man in control, a decent man and way beyond caring about protocol or rank. I know he wouldn't remember that day, but his extraordinary gravitas and seemingly confident mood changed a day that was almost ordinary.

BY NOW I'D DELIVERED an untold number of documents over to CIA—but nothing top secret. There were special handling rules for those, and violating them would have put me in a serious jam. The chief was pleased with what I'd done and told me I could stop my paper route—he'd apparently worked out something with somebody higher up the food chain at State and was getting what he wanted through more conventional channels now.

IN DECEMBER 1990, I called my little sister to wish her a happy fifteenth birthday. This was the day that the last charter flight picked up a group of U.S. Embassy personnel and other Americans who had been hiding in Kuwait for four months. Not everyone was leaving: more than two thousand American were still incarcerated by Saddam and in danger of being used as human shields. Hussein, however, would ultimately attempt to win credit with the international community by letting them go—after long, complicated diplomatic efforts by the United States, United Kingdom, and Canada. Five months earlier, on August 24, Saddam had ordered the closing of the American embassy in Kuwait City, but Ambassador Nathaniel Howell, his deputy, and two other members of this skeleton crew had kept the place open in defiance of Saddam's order—reminding me of General McAuliffe's famous response to the Nazis' demand for surrender at the Battle of the Bulge: "Nuts!" For three months, the embassy staff had gone without electricity and municipal water. They slept out in the heat, surrounded by flies and the entire Iraqi army, surviving on canned tuna and rice, planting gardens, and drinking from the swimming pool.

Now, in December, I bent over the secure telephone unit in my tiny office in Washington. "Kuwait, Kuwait, this is State, comm check, over," I said, as I'd been saying for months. The embassy worker responded, "State, State, this is Kuwait—this will be our final comm check, over."

"Roger, Kuwait, I understand this will be your final comm check—you are closing down comms, is that correct? Over," I said. He answered, "You are correct, State.

"State, State . . . thank you for all you've done. Everyone here really appreciates your professionalism; what's your name? You're not DOS, are you?" He knew I wasn't a diplomat. I used words like *roger*, *wilco*, and *negative* when we spoke. I spelled things using the phonetic alphabet and allowed time for the encrypted messages to be sent through the satellites to him before trying to speak again, preventing us from talking over each other. My predecessors didn't, and most State folks, aside from security and comm officers, didn't, either. They just talked like they were on a standard office phone line in the United States and that resulted in garbled transmissions that stepped on each other, frustrating on both ends of the line. I figured those guys had enough problems on their end; the least we could do was communicate effectively with them.

How did I answer that question, though? I'd been talking to this guy for weeks on end, months, multiple times every day. Many times we thought the Iraqis were going to raid them, take them captive. He and I had formed a professional bond, and I didn't even know his name. But I couldn't reveal my true employer and I didn't want to—especially not on a phone line where the National Security Agency (NSA) or even foreign governments were certainly listening and recording every word spoken. That would end my career before it even started.

"Kuwait, Kuwait, I am not at liberty to answer your last—and there's no need to thank me. You guys just have a safe flight home. That's thanks enough," I said.

"State, State, I didn't think so. [redacted] See you soon, brother. Kuwait out."

"Roger that, brother—safe travels. State out." I listened for him to hang up his STU-III for the first time in months, permanently closing the connection that had remained open since August. The line went dead, and for the first time I placed the receiver in its cradle, killing the connection on our end.

The U.S. Embassy in Kuwait was now unoccupied after being barricaded for 132 days—they were coming home and I was heading out. My chief had finally sent word that it was time to get back to the CIA. My training at the Farm was about to begin and soon I'd start a strange and exciting life where men in blue coveralls broke into my room waving chains and threatened my life while veterans like Red showed me who it was I would become.

CHAPTER 9

Plan B

Spring 2011
Benghazi, Libya

WHEN GENERAL HASI CAME TO SEE ME, I was sitting cross-legged on the floor, starting in on a protein bar and updating my notes. The seconds seemed to drag by as I awaited his verdict on our plan to support his rebel teams. But this was how it worked when you're trying to integrate into a tribal culture to help them—hurry up, get ready, and . . . well, wait. It was almost like working for the federal government. For this job, our men would grow beards, wear local clothes over their gear, and interact with the rebels at every level, becoming what U.S. Army Special Forces Major Jim Gant called "American tribesmen."* We would train rebels to fight, help them with strategic targeting decisions, and report the *ground truth* intelligence to the U.S. government—which translated into what was actually happening on the ground by giving visibility on leaders, potential problems, emerging leaders, munitions, how their logistical systems worked, and anything else that appeared noteworthy or was requested. But to get into this position we first had to build rapport with the rebels and establish trust. So far we were moving in the right direction—they'd brought us into their world, their headquarters. Now it was up to the tribal bigwigs.

---

* http://agora.stevenpressfield.com/2009/09/one-tribe-at-a-time-1/.

Across the world, in Washington, the uproar over Libya built to a crescendo. It was a fire that seemed to sear the brush, but it never got hot enough to light a fire under the politicians who built up the blaze to warm themselves, then ran to the hills when it came time to burn the dictator. Qadhafi, calling his people "rats," was far from any kind of surrender; he was threatening to "cleanse" his nation "house by house." Obama's efforts seemed tentative and political.

"We have discussed your proposal," the general told me. His look suggested we weren't going to be playing on the same team.

Never underestimate the power of people to make seemingly insane decisions when they shield themselves within large groups. U.S. politicians were handing over Obama's apparent halfhearted efforts to a broad coalition of NATO forces who would move to solidify the maritime blockade and no-fly zone. I hoped the Libyan general wasn't counting on them to be the cavalry. Deadlock would dull their impact and I didn't think they would ever be able to ensure the people's safety, partially because of the UN's unwillingness to unleash the kind of firepower that would risk civilian lives. I didn't want civilians hurt, either, but at the same time, there's really no such thing as surgical war—innocent people are going to die—and refusing to engage the enemy simply hands over victory. The American public assumes surgical strikes make no mistakes because they saw the clean, pinpoint hits during the first Gulf War and the complete victory over Saddam's army that followed, not understanding that it was not the norm. You fight the U.S. either stupidly or asymmetrically, as one general put it. Saddam simply placed his army on a golf tee and the United States walked up with a nine iron, as General Stanley McChrystal once said. But the concept of surgical strikes comes from medicine, where surgeons carry out their profession with such precision. Yet surgeons make altogether between 1,300 and 2,700 operational errors annually, cutting the wrong places on the patient.* Mistakes are going to happen; nothing is perfect—not even surgeons. Collateral damage is part of war. The U.S. media and politicians must wrap their collective brain around the idea that war is violence, and that has universal value and is

---

* http://well.blogs.nytimes.com/2007/11/28/when-surgeons-cut-the-wrong-body-part/.

a language everyone understands. Stop the hand-wringing and embrace the war hammer because if we don't, someone else will.

The Libyan opposition was still limited, and its ability to protect population centers was doubtful; the proximity of the dictator's forces, facilities, and equipment to civilian infrastructure was a threat. But at the very heart of the problem, the question of who the rebels were still complicated everything. That was where we could help—if we could get in. I waited for the general to continue.

"We do not want that many of your men," he said. "But we do want some. We think too many will not be good. We also want to know how much the equipment will cost and when it will be delivered."

I was elated. This was not a complete rejection and we could work with this. If we got a few of us on the ground, we could show them our benefits, gain their confidence, and the teams would grow. Already, we had Silverback on board, with his knowledge of Qadhafi's security. He would soon be setting up networks, recruiting informants, and pushing information to us. You combine Western butt-kick with reliable on-the-ground intelligence about enemy movement and the only thing you'll need after that are two pallbearers at the funeral, since garbage cans only have two handles.

WE MOVED. D AND I GOT OUT OF LIBYA, not letting what little grass there was grow under our feet. We had a job and it couldn't wait. After flying back to the States, landing at Dulles, we headed to our homes, repacked, and agreed to link back up at the training center. There was a ton of work to do, and the staff was already cranking on it before we even had wheels down.

The operations order (OpOrder) was being drafted at our company headquarters by a small team led by Kendrick, a former U.S. Marine Corps major. This document would govern how we would operate the teams at every level, how we would resupply ourselves, what we'd do in case of emergency, and on and on. It was a comprehensive document that we drafted every time we deployed a team anywhere. Whether it was providing security for the Motion Picture & Television Fund during the Emmys or sending teams into the Middle East, we always worked from an OpOrder and our teams would then execute those orders. Concurrently, we would report to CIA and the Defense Department that we were on the ground, asking them what essential elements of intelligence (EEIs) they desired, then pushing those questions down to the teams who'd collect it during the course of their work.

Reports from Silverback were trickling in nearly every day about developments on the ground, as well as on how our fledgling network was growing. It seemed to be spidering out all over the place. From my GMC truck back in Virginia, I burned up my iPhone, e-mailing and giving orders as we hurtled forward on this huge undertaking. I watched my youngest daughter's gymnastics competition from the top of the bleachers as I covered the microphone above the din of the cheering crowd to brief Myrick's office by phone; I took my oldest daughter to her driving test as I sat on the phone with Colonel Cantwell to figure out the best way to purchase medical supplies. As my son and I fished on the creek bank, I was e-mailing an old Vietnam-era POW contact in Virginia who had commercial shipping links into Libya that might be able to help with smuggling in the equipment past Qadhafi's coastal defenses. We didn't stop—the kids seemed to think I was always on the phone—and I was. We were helping coordinate a war and the road to success is always under construction.

Colonel Cantwell had a list of the rebels' logistical needs and his team was running on all cylinders. In Europe, Jana was scouting property to set up a safe house, making trips to London to meet with property agents. We needed a place to bring in personnel for the trip into Libya and while Malta was our first choice, giving the teams a place to stay while avoiding having to check in to hotels as they waited for the boat, Egypt was a remote and last-resort option. Since the land border was rumored to be closing soon and the trip was far too long a drive, it was a very long shot, but one we at least wanted to consider.

Malta is an island about twice the size of Washington, D.C., lying about fifty miles off the southern coast of Sicily in the Mediterranean Sea, roughly two hundred miles north of Libya. For decades drug smugglers have pushed hashish and cocaine into Europe through Malta, and now those same routes were being used by the rebels to illegally bring in weapons and fighters, while legally bringing in medical supplies and reporters on the same boats. The reality of things is that espionage requires dealing with liars, smugglers, traitors, and criminals of all sorts—because honest, trustworthy, upstanding citizens don't traitor against their own country. So we used the criminal underbelly of the world, but to accomplish a noble goal.

We secured a place overlooking the port in the Maltese village of Birzebbuga, with an office down the street. A local law firm would do the leases and keep us anonymous on paper by having everything in the name of the firm, with us paying them to pay the rent. Using attorneys in this way, both in the United States and abroad, helped nongovernmental organizations remain covert. It was all relatively simple when it came down to it—just like the foolproof method for defeating a listening device from picking up your voice in a room, vehicle, or elsewhere: just get close to your listener, cover your mouth, and . . . whisper. Simple worked quite often.

D beat me to Mississippi, linking up with Todd, who ran that office and the training center. Together with Deputy Art Watts and my childhood friend Deputy Clint Roberson, both solid law enforcement officers who were part-time instructors for us, our southern staff began vetting candidates and inhaling résumés for predeployment workups that would get the men ready to operate in Libya.

TWO DAYS AFTER GETTING BACK FROM NORTH AFRICA, I kissed the kids in Virginia, grabbed my pack, drove out to a private airfield in Suffolk, and boarded the company jet for the two-hour flight to Mississippi. The plane was a twin-engine passenger jet that seated nine and could get us from the East Coast to Colorado Springs on one fill-up. Rich, a great guy, former naval aviator, and veteran A-6 Intruder pilot, had a unique way of landing. He kept the nose in the air for nearly the entire time, with just the rear wheels touching the ground. It looked like we were doing a wheelie coming in; it saved the brakes by using the air to slow us. "A private jet has advantages, I have to admit. Once I took my family to my parents' hometown for Christmas. When we left a few days later and were somewhere over Alabama, I realized that I'd forgotten my laptop back in the tiny airport. Rich turned the plane around and went back to get it—try that on Southwest.

Todd met me at the airstrip in one of the company Suburbans and we headed north up Highway 7 to the training center in Holly Springs, stopping just long enough to pick up a rack of the best BBQ ribs at the BP Station on South Lamar. We barreled on the rest of the way, with sauce on our fingers, laughing like we were kids. There is no one I am closer to than Todd. An army veteran, Todd power-lifted at Mississippi State, once putting up 373 pounds on the bench, and he only weighed 185.

He started working for the company as the IT guy—he could fix and install anything. I eventually began relying on him for more and more as I went overseas. Our company's facility was a place for our personnel to train, and it was where we offered instruction to law enforcement, military, and select private clientele.

I FOUNDED MY ORIGINAL company, SCG, LLC, in 2002 after things went north at Blackwater. A true southerner won't say something went south, since going south isn't derogatory at all, in our opinion. Blackwater wound up in the news in 2007 for killing civilians. And the shooters were convicted in 2014. Over the years, its owner was hauled in front of Congress, it had numerous employees up on charges, was being sued repeatedly, was being chased by one federal investigative agency after another, and changed its name multiple times. That was a development that should have been no surprise, given the political winds blowing at the time, plus what I experienced with the petty rivalry when I was there. Blackwater Security Company wasn't going the way I'd originally envisioned. Outstanding patriots and real heroes worked there with remarkable skills, but we grew too fast in the beginning and as a result we began taking on a few guys who were not of the caliber I'd originally intended. I was also concerned that making money was overtaking the quality of the predeployment training. One example is a former SEAL who was shipped over to Site 1, our Kabul posting, and negligently discharged his sidearm inside the CIA's compound. No one was hurt, but I sacked him and he was shipped home on the first flight out. I wanted professionals there and we were being paid top dollar. Most SEALs are pros, but our men were supposed to be above normal, above negligence of that sort. The guy told me later that when he'd shown up at Blackwater for the workup, he'd been given a box of fifty bullets and a Glock and told to go out and shoot. The problem was that this guy had never shot a Glock in his life, just the navy-issued SIG P-226, and he wasn't used to the trigger on the Glock. According to him, when he was removing his weapon from his vest one evening it somehow snagged and his finger slipped onto the trigger and launched a round down into the dirt. In my opinion, standards were dropping and that put everything I had been trying to build at risk.

But while at Blackwater I had completed projects in Afghanistan, Pakistan, and Uzbekistan. I had set up and was the director of a multimillion-dollar, multiyear U.S. Navy contract that we won to train thousands of sailors from across the country to protect ships in port and prevent another USS *Cole* attack. As vice president of Blackwater USA and director of Blackwater Security at the same time, I helped build one successful enterprise from scratch and make the other profitable for Erik, Gary, and Blackwater, but it wasn't working for any of us—me especially. The last shoe to fall was when I learned of activities taking place between the owner of Blackwater and his former nanny, who'd been shipped there from Northern Virginia to work as my secretary. I had concerns about what I now knew and its implications for the company and overall morale. Not wanting to be the senior man with a secret, I brought it to the attention of my boss, who just put his hands over his ears, closed his eyes, and started making babbling noises, saying he couldn't hear me. Clearly, he didn't want to know what the woman shared with me about her relationship with Erik, something Erik would ultimately admit thirteen years later in his book. I went back out to the range to shoot and to think.

By the end of the first magazine I had decided to resign. As I walked back to the office to tell Gary, he beat me to the punch, saying that he'd already called Erik, and they were firing me. I left that day with no job, none waiting in the wings, and with two men who didn't like me very much—and one was a billionaire. But I had skills that not too many possessed. I'd been allowed to create a company from thin air and an idea; built it into a respected, multimillion-dollar powerhouse in a few short months; and recruited, trained, and deployed teams to war zones around the globe. But there was bad blood, and I later heard folks making up crazy stories about me to hurt my chances of starting over. I wasn't a threat to that behemoth. But I knew the business—I'd seen what worked and what didn't. I knew people in the industry now, and I was just in my early thirties. Our family of four was living in a small rental house just up from our favorite pizza joint—Pungo Pizza—surviving off our savings, but I had those contacts, a doctoral degree in law, and an idea. So on a milk crate upstairs in a converted attic office, I broke open my Rolodex—kids, that's a list of contacts. I knew that if I could make money for someone else, I could do it for myself. I decided to ignore the rumors coming out of Blackwater and get to work—founding Virginia-based SCG, LLC.

I really had no other option. I too was like the explorer who'd burned his boats at the beach, because that fall we made another trip to the hospital and our third child—a sweet, blond baby girl named Mallory—entered our lives. At the time, I wondered whether it was possible to love more than I loved Morgan and Cole, but somehow the capacity of a parent's heart just grows and grows, and her birth brought me profound joy.

But in 2002, I saw the strategy: Attack al-Qa'ida everywhere. Disrupt its plots. Penetrate its cells. Capture or kill its members. That's what President Bush said after the three-pronged hit on 9/11 and it had not stopped. He'd embraced the war hammer.

Terrorists were being killed or captured from Bangladesh to Beirut and all points in between—nowhere was it safe to be a bad guy opposed to the United States. Before the attacks, there was talk of whether we even needed intelligence agencies anymore, but all that chatter was now outdated and out of style. Covert operations were being executed worldwide with precision and lethal effectiveness. Tactics had changed. Clandestine meetings were conducted quickly, sometimes on the fly with high security, but newer technology was pushing espionage in different directions, allowing safer transfers of information between the intelligence officer and agent than ever before—many times eliminating the need for face-to-face contact.

The first wave of this change was when the CIA, not the Pentagon, led the war that defeated the Taliban in Afghanistan and drove al-Qa'ida out. The CIA also pioneered the use of armed drones that were smoking Hellfire missiles into camps, homes, and vehicles, ████████ killing with accuracy without risk to human pilots. Assaults and raids on terrorist hideouts started off in helicopters, with fast-roping onto targets, doors blown, flash-bangs tossed into rooms. Now warriors were even better; they used stealthier movement with suppressed weapons and NODs (night observation devices—night vision). They came in trucks, or did long foot marches to reach their targets to keep from tipping off the bad guys by arriving in a helicopter. They engaged and moved, keeping the enemy blind until the last minute just as death was visited upon them in the dark without them ever getting a shot off . . . that's a shooting, not a gunfight.

I witnessed this tactical evolution firsthand and had taught the latest changes to sailors, airmen, soldiers, IOs, and marines. It was all part of the way a superpower stays one up—by seeing threats and changing to meet them.

Then came phase two of the evolution of warfare, when Joint Special Operations Command (JSOC) merged intelligence collection resources and the CIA's paramilitary teams into a killing machine like none that has ever existed on this planet.

I knew how the private military business worked, too—from the public and the private side. I would fund the business from work we did, set up a clean, efficient website, work from a cell phone, and, as the business grew, I'd think about renting space in an office park. Within three months in 2003, without borrowing a dime from anybody, I was teaching small classes across the country nonstop. Word spread and soon SCG was booked for the majority of that year. The former director of training at CIA e-mailed, asking if he could buy the rights to an online surveillance-detection program I'd created. It was about the time CIA was taking their case officer training online. I sold it to him for five thousand dollars. I soon got a call from a Marine Corps officer in charge of a unit from the Fourth Marine Expeditionary Brigade out of Camp Lejeune. He said they had received an order to protect marine officers O-6 (colonels) and up who were going into Iraq, Afghanistan, or the Horn of Africa (HOA). He'd heard about my training courses and wanted to know if I could price it out for him.

I sent him a quote that night, and within days we had a no-bid contract to begin training U.S. Marines. I wrote the curriculum and started teaching the courses with Todd. It soon grew and we hired instructors; together we eventually trained hundreds of marines and created a new high-risk protection curriculum that is still used more than a decade later.

The marine contract led to our next growth spurt. One of the marines was related by marriage to a retired CIA officer who was helping one of the largest American defense contractors vet and source a security company to protect its people in Afghanistan. Todd and I drove up to Northern Virginia to meet him and then met their vice president for security. He said they'd looked at Blackwater and a few other companies, but he really wanted someone without all the baggage—somebody lower profile. He awarded SCG the job, and we had our first private paying protection gig—PSD (protective services detail) missions to Kabul.

We started running lots of PSD teams into Afghanistan and Pakistan for them, which grew into a larger opportunity in 2005, when one of the largest defense contractors in the world, that I'll call ADC, asked us to protect a new U.S. Army facility that they were charged with running. The kicker was that we'd be under contract to a small freight-forwarding company that I'll call SKM. We agreed to this structure of working for the freight company, which turned out to be a mistake; we didn't have much choice, but it was my fault for agreeing to those terms. Either we accepted the contract terms or we didn't get the job. It was lucrative—$15.5 million for five years of work.

I soon realized that it was time to hire solid, full-time people. So I stuck to the standards that I created for my first Blackwater team and made them tighter, even more stringent. All my guys were veterans, all either spec-ops or CIA paramilitary, and American, British, or Canadian citizens, none of them with less than five years of experience in a Tier 1 or 2 unit, have finished at least one combat tour, and have no marital issues, which meant be either happily married, happily divorced, or happily single.

I also needed a solid manager who could be head of operations when I was away. I made an offer to a great friend and solid, God-fearing man whom I admired immensely—Dick Roten. A colonel in the marines who was up for promotion to general, he was finishing up a tour as the second in command at Marine Corps Base Kaneohe in Hawaii. Dick came on to handle details of things like organization, hiring administrative staff, and generally setting things up to run efficiently for our training and operational work. We also brought on a secretary, an accountant, a full-time instructor, and an IT guy to give Todd a much-needed break. Dick set up the Operations Center and, along with another former marine, made sure it ran like a Swiss watch.

We bid for and won a massive U.S. Navy contract and opened branch offices in Ventura County, California, and Gulfport, Mississippi, to support the work. When Hurricane Katrina hit in 2005, SCG trucked relief supplies down free of charge and were soon hired by the state of Mississippi to provide security, food, potable water, transportation, and communication services to their staff all across the state so they could get small businesses back on their feet and moving again.

We won an FBI job gathering intelligence overseas for them. Then we were hired by a democratically elected leader of an African country to gather intelligence on his opponents and help him regain his position, from which he'd been illegally ousted during a coup. Following that, SCG won a massive multiyear, multimillion-dollar U.S. Air Force contract under which we grew yet again, opened another office in New Jersey, another in Hawaii, and a shipping and logistics office in Moyock, North Carolina—right in Blackwater's backyard. We trained thousands of air force personnel in combat gunfighting, emergency driving, and combat medicine and gave classes on Middle Eastern and Central Asian culture, as well as Dari and Pashtun languages.

We hired Mike Rush, a former SEAL warrant officer from ST6 with twenty-three years in Special Operations, as vice president of operations in January 2009. He'd started out with the notable Commander Dick Marcinko, founder of SEAL Team 6, and stuck with it through all the changes. We called Mike "Captain Coathanger." He was tall and thin as wire—and was one of the best snipers to come out of ST6. Mike would eventually go on to become president of SCG, LLC when I stepped out to start another project. I'd eventually have his employment contract terminated by our attorney. Mike was responsible for delivering a multimillion-dollar proposal across town to the navy—his old base. He waited until the last minute, was too late, and we lost out—after thousands of dollars and man-hours.

We had another top SEAL, a lieutenant commander, also named Mike and also from ST6, who came on board in the early spring of 2009. He spoke French fluently, had served in Somalia, had an easygoing manner, and was always willing to help. We called him M-2, since he was the second Mike to come aboard. Things became even more complicated when we hired a third SEAL named Mike, but instead of calling him M-3, we called him "Ski"—a takeoff on his last name. In fact, nearly everyone had nicknames—call signs—and most were based on something they'd done or some characteristic. Another SEAL was DirtDice because he was extremely educated and it was a gamble when he got into an argument as to whether he'd talk his way out of it or take the guy to the ground and choke him out. Mine was RamRod—given to me actually by DirtDice because whenever something got stuck or we were at an impasse he said I managed to ram things through and get it moving again . . . at least that's what he said it meant.

We had a solid team, solid work history under our belt, and honest, patriotic projects on our plate. We were receiving calls to do everything from securing foreign heads of African countries and escorting gold shipments to Swiss, Israeli, and Hong Kong banks, to protecting Hollywood VIPs. Once I was at our house in Hawaii and saw a couple and their two kids standing near our back gate by a coconut palm. A third guy with them started climbing my coconut tree. Fearing he'd fall and get hurt, I came out, asked what they were doing, and was introduced to supermodel Heidi Klum, her husband, Seal, and their two kids. I gave the kids a coconut and told the couple I'd see them at the Emmys. They laughed, probably thinking I was just talking, but that September, as Heidi walked into a party that my team was securing, I came up and reintroduced myself, to which she said, "Oh, hey, it's the coconut guy!"

At our property in Mississippi we expanded our training facility and built a firing range one hundred yards square for doing anything from pistol and shotgun to carbine and light machine gun work. Next to that were two smaller, fifty-yard ranges. Each range had steel targets, and the large range had a moving target system, electronically controlled and moving at varying speeds by remote command. Surrounding everything—all our ranges, the shoot houses, and urban areas—were massive dirt berms that prevented bullets from leaving the range by accident.

Elsewhere on the property was a five-thousand-square-foot shoot house. Unlike other shoot houses, ours wasn't just a giant maze, but was broken into venues—similar in concept to the one I'd trained in years earlier at CIA. It was wired for sound and lighting so that we could pump sound effects of foreign cities, battle noises, or screams all while controlling the lighting for low-light or no-light training. There was a prison section with three cells, a mock-up of a drug lab, and a room that replicated a hotel room for practicing clandestine intelligence meetings, complete with two beds, a dresser, and even a busted TV. Another room simulated a schoolroom, another a full-size commercial aircraft cabin with overheard luggage bins, and still another room simulated a terrorist hideout with computer equipment to give shooters training in target exploitation, the collecting of intelligence from a target after it's been assaulted—basically ripping hard drives out and collecting thumb drives and other files.

ALL IN ALL, IT WAS STATE OF THE ART, perfect for the training of candidates for the team heading to Libya in 2011. As the summer heat built in Holly Springs, the staff managed to run two classes of guys through selection and training programs in preparation for our return to Libya. "Success trains and failure complains"—and we didn't complain. Silverback was still pushing atmospherics from the network that was growing beyond my expectations back to us, and we pushed hard to get that information to the proper people in the U.S. administration. Colonel Cantwell's team had the medical equipment prepared. In short, we were ready to pull the trigger and get moving.

But the rebels weren't.

The Libyan NTC leaders said they were finding it difficult to fund any operations. The NTC, the head of the government for the rebels, had continually asked the world community to release frozen Libyan funds, but that hadn't happened. Then they changed tactics and asked to keep the funds frozen and just give them a line of credit. That wasn't working out so well, either. More radical elements went to the Qataris for funding, which they provided. We found out later that major politicking was taking place inside the rebel hierarchy, as well as armed groups jockeying for power and control, anticipating Qadhafi's fall. One militia in particular, 17 February Brigade, run by known terrorists, was going directly to the Qataris with the support of Ali al-Sallabi, an influential Libyan Islamist cleric with close ties to Yusuf al-Qaradawi, the spiritual head of the international terror group the Muslim Brotherhood. While these militant Islamic radicals got the money, moderates and others who challenged their radical views received little support.

This is where my job gets tricky; no one trained me for this combination of finance, diplomacy, and negotiation. I was an operator with a doctoral degree, but suddenly that included being Donald Trump mixed with a little Donald Rumsfeld. Welcome to the brave new world where you better get your butt in gear because if something is important to you, you'll find a way to make it work and if it's not, you'll find an excuse. This was important, so we tried to help the rebel leadership—represented by the ambassadors back in the United States—by finding alternative sources to fund our operations. Our people went to the Middle East, Africa, New York, London, and elsewhere, but no businessman wanted to take a chance on the Libyans winning. They all asked, "What's in it for us?" All we were hearing were excuses—it just wasn't important enough to people.

But the potential backers did have a point: this did not constitute an investment in the traditional sense. It was basically a charitable donation to a Libyan aid agency that would then hire us. Our emissaries tried to convince potential donors that the rebels would not forget those who came to their aid during their struggle and that an investment now would ensure future access to Libya. But few could imagine the nation without the dictator. Although Qadhafi—who loved to adopt the pose of statesman-philosopher—had pretended to step down in 1977, camouflaging himself as just a symbolic figure, he actually ruled for an astonishing forty-one years.

So we got even more creative, relying on the example of the strategies of the U.S. government when dealing with small nations. Our company's finance department came up with a concept where we would donate our services for no up-front payment at all. We were cash flush from our previous contracts and could float operations for a while. The catch was that the rebels had to agree to a deal allowing us access to natural resources. We knew the Libyan southern oil fields had great potential for petroleum development. Our concept was that the Libyans grant us exploratory rights in their southern fields for a period of years. We would then leverage those to a private American fund in exchange for cash, while keeping a few parcels for ourselves, for making the arrangements. The cash generated would then be used to fund our project for the Libyans.

The complicating factor was that the Libyans didn't want to give up their exploratory rights. To them, the choice we offered meant them releasing long-term rights to a potential moneymaking resource (portions of their oil fields) for a certain amount of years, during which the money those fields would generate could be as much as ten or twenty times what we would be charging them for our services.

For example, our work for the NTC might total up to $20 million for one year's work, but the oil fields might generate $200 million over five years. They would be giving up all that income to us. To them, it wasn't worth it to engage a team of Western consultants whom some of their leaders didn't want anyway. When the NTC did the math, they figured it was better to let the war take a little longer than to give away that much money—it was less expensive to send a few more boys to die and let things drag on than to pay us. It's harsh, but that's the world's calculus quite often.

I was pissed. I could definitely see the profit potential in this for our company—we'd earned millions on similar projects from Afghanistan to Madagascar. But I could also see that missing out on the opportunity meant bidding farewell to potential intelligence that could benefit the United States in a multitude of ways in the region for years to come. I could also see the wheels grinding ever more slowly on the rebels' side.

One major area where we could help the rebels was their deficit in strategic planning and preparation. This should have been no surprise: they were civilians for the most part—students, doctors, businessmen, and defectors from the Libyan military. They just didn't grasp the concept of taking and holding ground. Before the no-fly zone was instigated, the rebels would dash out across the desert, run up on a village or town abandoned by Qadhafi's forces, move in, and claim victory and hold a photo shoot. But they didn't have the supply systems to develop their conquests as strongholds. They couldn't fortify their defenses in the new area. Instead, they'd bring up the press corps, boast, and then, emboldened, race out even farther into the desert. Sooner or later, they would run into a heavily armed column of Qadhafi's tanks that would pound them with rockets and airpower, handing them their butts and driving them back to where they started.

Rebel discipline was also abysmal in many places. If you gave many of them a penny for their thoughts, you'd get change back. Everyone wanted to be on the front lines fighting, to be the lions of the desert. They didn't grasp the concept that not every man was meant to be—or could be—a fighter. They needed mechanics to keep their ridiculous Mad Max contraptions moving; they needed medical technicians; they needed cooks and drivers to supply the troops with food and equipment; they needed operators for their communications equipment. A body that works is made up of more than just one organ or one limb, and the rebels needed every available molecule to make their tattered body function, let alone fight. Most of the rebels couldn't operate anything more complex than a walkie-talkie and most of the time resorted to traceable and penetrable cell phones, if a signal could even be obtained.

Leadership was sketchy in places, while in others they had solid men at the helm. But our guys were experts at managing this sort of thing and working with shoddy, unprofessional armies. Collectively, our people were not theoreticians, but practitioners of covert operations, intelligence, and guerrilla warfare with hundreds of years of combined experience in planning and executing covert missions and combat operations around the globe.

But getting the Libyans to understand the benefit of bringing our expertise to the table was like a used car salesman trying to sell a guy a warranty extension when the guy was looking at a set of custom forty-inch gold-plated rims for the same price. One was intangible but had long-term benefits, but the rebels wanted shiny objects—guns and trucks. They really wanted guns, guns, and more guns. What we tried to convey to them over the course of that summer was that guns don't get you much without proper application of strategy and intelligence. It doesn't take a genius to spot a camel in a flock of sheep; why didn't the Libyans just open their eyes and look around? You just had to look at the militant morons running operations in Somalia to see that. They had all the rifles and rockets they could carry, but it was a failed state with starving people and open sewage in the streets.

WE DECIDED INTERNALLY that the Libyans needed our help even if they couldn't afford it yet. Out of all the problems they had, opening their eyes seemed to be the one solution they needed most. We had a fledgling intelligence network in place that we intended to use for our own benefit, so we decided to turn it wide open for theirs. Silverback was on. We had to move, despite the accelerating risks.

• • • • • • • • • • •

CHAPTER 10

• • • • • • • • • • •

To the Shores of Tripoli

Late July 2011
Libya

WE CAUGHT A BREAK a short time later from within our ever growing network—an informant had intel about an important, strategic target—the city of Tripoli. Earlier, Silverback sent a text message to the uncle of the young man named Muhammed, telling him where to be and when so they could have a covert meeting inside Qadhafi's capital city—right under the dictator's nose. The informant would be picked up for a quick drive with a family friend to discuss family business—that was the cover for action. Muhammed, still inside Qadhafi's army, had been targeted when his uncle, a rebel sympathizer friendly with Silverback's family, told us of his nephew's disillusionment. Immediately, we tried to recruit him.

In Tripoli, Muhammed knelt in the alley behind a beaten blue-and-green metal garbage bin. His rifle hung loosely from a sling. Glancing at his phone, he saw he was right on time. He was nervous. He was right to be.

Above him, in the sky, he heard the omnipresent beating of helo blades, antiaircraft fire, and rockets, the current soundtrack of the war.

Alaeddin, another informant who answered to Silverback, rode his beat-up Jawa moped through the streets. After passing the Safeer Hotel with a minute to spare, he parked his vehicle against the sheet metal fence, chaining it to an olive tree. Removing his aviator-style sunglasses, he ducked into the darkened tangle of alleys and pathways snaking through tiny shops selling everything imaginable.

Heading to the spices, he turned left at the shop of an old man who sold vegetables and bananas. A few more yards and he reached a leather shop whose owner was secretly aligned with the rebels and he ducked inside. He was in an enemy-held city where Qadhafi's spies and security worked round the clock. If he was captured, they'd torture him and kill him and his entire family, and our other informants would scatter in the wind.

BY THIS POINT IN THE SUMMER OF 2011, NATO had beaten back Qadhafi, bringing in Apache attack helicopters that hit with more precision than high-flying jets. They reduced the risk of civilian casualties, but given their vulnerability to ground fire, their deployment also increased the risks to Western forces, who were suffering their first casualties.

Through a series of clandestine meetings and contacts fostered by Silverback during this time, our informants began to gather information, convinced others to defect, and set up cells inside Tripoli to do everything from housing fighters and storing weapons to coordinating beach landing sites for reinforcements from other towns by boat. Preparations for the final conflict there had begun: the battle for Tripoli.

Silverback worked his sources to infiltrate Qadhafi's troops and turn his soldiers into our spies. But the hard part was actually finding a way to meet with them in the first place. That kind of work was still likely to get a guy killed.

Dozens of militias—united by the NTC, but divided by faction, tribe, and the subtle nuances of Islam—were raging against Qadhafi yet warring among themselves. The question was whether the dictator, a master at tactical maneuvering, could exploit the divisions. His larger forces were weak; always fearful of a coup, he'd kept them poorly armed and untrained. But his most dangerous were four crack brigades of decently equipped and trained soldiers, composed of members of his tribe or those loyal to him. One, the Khamis Brigade, was led by his son of the same name.

The eastern rebels had moved into strategically important areas and even managed to hold a few. To the west, they had support from NATO helicopters. Allied forces also dropped leaflets urging Qadhafi's people to lay down their arms. Coalition leaders had used airpower to foster a link to the moderate/centrist who led the NTC and was essentially Libya's acting prime minister. They were pressing Mahmoud Jibril—a former economic minister in the Qadhafi regime and an economic adviser to several Arab countries—to shake up his leadership and eliminate the more extremist elements. "The problem is not with Sharia or Islam," Jibril would later say; "the problem is with the interpretation of Sharia. When we turn Islam into some ritual, into a box, when we say 'You do this, you are an atheist' or 'You do this and you are a believer,' this is not helpful to Islam."* His was the kind of voice we needed to encourage, but if we did not understand who his opponents were, our hopes of developing our influence were just pipe dreams. But the reality was that we were assisting an insurgency, just the opposite of what we'd been helping to defeat in Afghanistan. There the Taliban were the insurgents, and here it was the Libyan rebels. I knew from the Afghan conflict that time is on the side of the insurgents—all they have to do is not lose. But to do that you have to start small, while thinking big, and that's where our spies and informants came into the picture.

INSIDE THE SHOP, our informant Alaeddin stepped behind a curtain and quickly pulled on a tan suriyah from his tattered pack, yanking it over his head. The traditional tunic covered up his stylish, faded blue jeans and CSI: MIAMI T-shirt. He left the backpack, stuffed his baseball cap in his pocket, and stepped back out into the souk.

Alaeddin, now a different man, wormed his way through the women trying to buy the staple goods of flour and sugar, which were in short supply. He moved smoothly; his life depended on it. So did the man he was to meet—Muhammed's.

Alaeddin meandered through the twists and turns, stopping in a shop here and there to sample a date or pop an almond in his mouth from the bins set up along the way. Each time he stopped, he made sure to casually turn back and face the vendor, allowing him a look back for anyone stopping or following him.

---

* http://berkleycenter.georgetown.edu/resources/quotes/mahmoud-jibril-on-sharia-law.

Satisfied, Alaeddin moved until he came out of the souk on the opposite side from where he'd left his moped. A few feet down the street, he spotted the tiny, beat-up, green 2004 Daewoo Matiz with tinted windows that sat on the curb, just where he'd been told it would be. Reaching the car, he knelt down by the front tire, as if tying his shoe. His left hand searched under the fender for the key.

Key in hand, he cranked up the golf-cart-size, four-door Korean-built attempt at a car and headed slowly down the street. He was still on schedule; it was 11:12 A.M.

As he turned left at a four-way intersection a shopkeeper was opening his store. Another, on the other side of the road, rolled up the protective door to his locksmith shop. As he drove, Alaeddin reached down and slid the passenger's seat back as far he could. Two more left turns, and then he took a right into an alley. There he spotted the beaten blue and green metal garbage bin. He checked the time; it was 11:19 A.M.

He rolled toward the garbage bin and pulled up slightly on the car's handbrake to slow it and keep the rear brake lights from coming on. Reaching over, he opened the passenger door. In clambered Muhammed and his rifle, crouching down in the tiny space out of sight onto the floorboard as Alaeddin kept the car moving.

Alaeddin started in on the mad minute, just as he'd been trained, "How much time do you have?"

"A few minutes. My friend is to pick me up just down the street to go in to work," Muhammed said. Alaeddin then gave him the cover story for their meeting, what they were talking about and when they'd meet next.

Muhammed, it turned out, was very well placed—better than we realized. He served with the security brigade in Qadhafi's Thirty-Second Reinforced Brigade of the Armed People, the Khamis Brigade, named after their commander, Khamis Qadhafi, the seventh and youngest son of the dictator. It was reputed to be the best-trained and equipped force in the Libyan military and one of the most important military and security elements of the regime, with headquarters roughly sixteen miles west of Tripoli.

"Thank you for meeting me, my brother," said Alaeddin. Muhammed nodded and slouched down, his rifle sticking up uncomfortably by the gearshift lever.

For the next several blocks, Alaeddin explained the strategic situation to the young man, painting a bleak picture for those who stuck with Qadhafi's forces. He mentioned war crimes, trials in Libya, and executions.

"We are told by your uncle you will work with us. Is this true?"

"Yes, I will do whatever I can to help, *inshallah*," he said, the last part meaning he'd help if it was Allah's will. Muhammed knew he was on the losing side. He'd also been to Misrata and Zawiya and witnessed firsthand the slaughter of his countrymen by his fellow soldiers. It turned his stomach and he'd said so to his uncle—the man who'd raised him. But we already knew this—the uncle had passed this along to Silverback. Now our network had someone deep inside the security apparatus of Qadhafi.

Throughout this book I've oversimplified the process of recruiting people—from Silverback to Muhammed and everyone in between. It's not that easy and it's not an exact science, because every person is unique, everyone's motivations are different, and each situation is one of a kind. It's a process of constant refinement, experimentation, and adjustment with every new attempt. You have to realize that while you have your own goals, they do too, and understanding those goals is immeasurably important. On top of these obstacles, you also need to worry about what you're getting from them—the product itself, the actual intelligence information they are providing. How did they get it? Did they have continuing access to it? If caught with it, how could they justify having it? Did he have an agenda for giving it to you in the first place? In other words, was he trying to influence and thus control you, and if so, why? Granted, in Libya the rebels were in need of help and we offered it, and it didn't take a PhD in psychotherapy to persuade them to accept it. They'd already made the break mentally from their country; we weren't asking them to betray anything that they didn't already hate—Qadhafi's regime. But it's by no means a cakewalk to get people on board.

ON AUGUST 21, JUST A FEW WEEKS LATER, the Khamis Brigade headquarters was overrun by rebels as they made a major push. Muhammed's assistance from the inside helped achieve this victory. Then another victory as our network of informants inside the city worked in coordination with the Libyan military, NATO aircraft and rebel factions from across the western Gulf area who took Tripoli, the capital city, and liberated it.

With that major strategic goal in the rearview mirror, it was time to enter the ninth circle of hell.

II

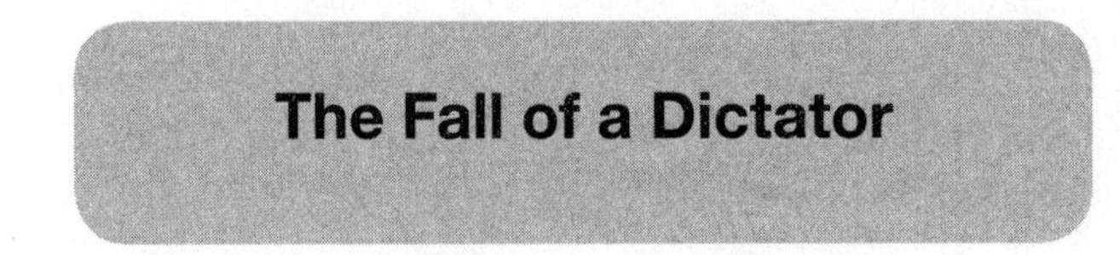

The Fall of a Dictator

CHAPTER 11

Inside the Militia

August 22, 2011
Cairo, Egypt

THE FALL OF TRIPOLI brought remarkable scenes. As hundreds of sweating, bearded rebels stormed into Qadhafi's Bab al-Aziziya fortress, the bombardment was furious. The mortars, rockets, and small arms fire were, in the words of a *Guardian* reporter, "a dark, rolling, continuous symphony."* Across the city, screams of triumph brought cheering citizens from their houses, as the rebels in Qadhafi's compound tore apart a gilded bronze head of the despot and set fire to the famous Bedouin-style tent where the dictator was said to sleep. In a crazed audio address, the fallen leader urged his supporters to "comb" Tripoli for "devils." Moussa Ibrahim, his spokesman, vowed that the battle for Tripoli would go on and that they had the ability to fight "not only for months, but for years."† Pro-Qadhafi strongholds remained in the southern desert city of Sabha and in the coastal town of Sirte, his birthplace. This was also the place where rumors circulated of the dictator's secret caches of chemical weapons, and from which a rocket with mustard gas was said to have been launched.

Amid the melee in the days after Tripoli fell, Silverback said there

---

* http://www.theguardian.com/world/2011/aug/23/gaddafi-tripoli-compound-libya-rebels.

† http://www.theguardian.com/world/middle-east-live/2011/aug/24/libya-rebels-take-gaddafi-compound-live-updates.

was someone else I had to meet, and I sensed we were about to hit pay dirt. The battle for Tripoli had been relatively light, compared to Benghazi and the surrounding cities. It was basically over within twenty-four hours. But it could have been far bloodier if not for the recruited spies, defectors, and informants inside Qadhafi's regime. They betrayed him and allowed the covert operations that supported and facilitated the victory to be carried off in spectacular fashion. The brigade of our defector-informant Muhammed had folded like a tent in a hurricane. The rebels now controlled the seaport, the airport, and the main military bases, striking at the heart of the regime. But there were disconcerting rumors; an Egyptian news agency would report a convoy of six Mercedes vehicles crossing into Algeria. Speculation was that senior Libyan officials, perhaps even Qadhafi and his sons, had fled Libya.

At the time of Silverback's call I was back in Cairo working on another project and took the next flight to Malta. I cleared passport control and stepped out into the sweltering humidity and brilliant sunlight that is the Maltese airport.

Sleepy approached me in the lobby, glasses askew, wrinkled, navy blue short-sleeve polo shirt hanging out of his pants and barely covering his growing paunch. He took his glasses off and wiped the sweat that was beading up on his brow like a cold glass of tea on a hot summer day. He smiled and we did the "bro hug." I noticed a tall Maltese white guy with short blond hair with him. Sleepy introduced him as Timmy, his driver.

"We have to hurry. The boat is waiting for us," said Sleepy. Timmy may have been an asset to Sleepy, but his micro-size European two-door car wasn't and I wished then that I'd told our Maltese office to meet me with a vehicle. Timmy's car became an immediate issue for me since my rucksack was nearly as large as the entire backseat. I crammed it into the box of matches on wheels and then managed to contort myself on top of it in a manner that might have convinced Cirque du Soleil to offer me a job.

Sweating and trying hard to breathe with my gear pressing from all sides, we set off for the port at dashboard-gripping speed through the twisting, turning, narrow streets for which his car was apparently designed. It was rush hour. Sleepy kept squawking into his mobile phone in Arabic. From what I could make out from the backseat, he was telling someone to keep the boat waiting for us. The ride was rough, and Timmy's car seemed to feature a pothole magnet option he'd thoughtfully purchased.

When we finally skidded into the dock area, Sleepy said for me to hand up my passport, which he hurriedly passed through the window to another Libyan who seemed to have materialized out of thin air, and who promptly ran off with it. I could only hope he was coming back or didn't drop it into the water along the way.

Off we roared just when I thought I was going to be able to unfold and work out the kinks in my body. Then again, we stopped after only a few hundred yards next to a large fishing boat straight out of the TV show *Deadliest Catch*, except for one small Arabic name on the bow—*Al-Entisar*—and a white flag for the aid group i-GO flying from the mast.

Anyone wanting into Tripoli now, or anywhere west of Benghazi, had to go in by boat or overland through Tunisia. It was just too far to drive from Egypt; plus the border was being sealed randomly—not to mention that you could get killed along the way by any number of groups.

I stood looking at the massive white ship whose name in English meant "the victory" as the grayish green water of the Maltese harbor made a sound against the hull like dogs lapping. It was big, with the bridge located in the middle of the ship two decks above with windows spanning its width. Atop the bridge were two large lime-green spotlights and radar enclosed in a white dome. An orange crane for handling cargo sat bolted to the foredeck. The captain was a weathered Korean who spoke an infinitesimal amount of Arabic, and as I found out later—next to zero intelligible English. His number two was a Libyan who spoke almost no Korean. It was crewed by a mix of bedraggled Filipino and Korean deckhands who scampered across the ship in flip-flops and shorts with cigarettes dangling from their lips, dragging refueling lines and hauling various pieces of ship gear around while babbling incoherently.

A narrow, wobbly, wooden gangplank rattled as it spanned the short distance from ship to shore, with crewmen loaded with equipment scooting up and down it like it was the boardwalk in Santa Monica, when in fact it was just two simple weather-beaten boards that looked like they could fall into the murky water of the marina at any minute. Also loading things onto the boat were a few Libyan aid workers, Westerners from Doctors Without Borders, and a handful of journalists who'd talked their way on board. This was fantastic—I was about to be on this floating Tower of Babel for at least a twenty-four-hour ride across the Mediterranean straight into the war-torn port of Tripoli—the first boat to enter since the rebellion had started.

Enter Kamel Fakroun, a large Libyan in his mid-forties wearing an i-GO baseball cap, tan photographer's vest over a white T-shirt, and tan cargo pants tucked into combat boots. Sleepy had told me a bit about him on the ride—the guy was a senior leader in one of the Libyan rebel militias as well as financier of the i-GO Aid Foundation, which funded this boat. The boat was supposed to be used to provide humanitarian aid to the Libyans in besieged coastal towns, but it was also used by the rebels to ferry in weapons and munitions and, at times, to smuggle in fighters. I didn't know this at the time, but I suspected the ship had a secondary use other than just as an aid vessel. After all, how was it that Sleepy, a senior defector from Qadhafi's regime, and Kamel were able to command a spot on the boat at the last minute and bring me—a U.S. citizen and former CIA officer—on board with them?

No, this ship was doing more than making food runs to needy families.

Sleepy spoke to one of the crew and he showed me to my cabin. A cabin? This boat was packed with people and no one else had a cabin—none of the aid workers, none of the journalists. How did I get this premium real estate at the last minute? The nameplate on the door of my quarters said "Engineer." I hoped I didn't meet that guy later, as I'd apparently been given his room. I unlocked the door and was greeted by two things: the musty onion-stink of whoever occupied it before me and the fact that it was small—no, make that tiny. Two steps opposite the door were two bunks and a tiny privacy curtain clinging desperately to the few chipped plastic clips remaining in the ceiling track to give the sleeper some concealment. My visual link to the world beyond was a stained brass porthole a few inches above the top bunk with enough marks on the Plexiglas to make you wonder if a blind cat had confused it with a scratch post. A tiny locker of splintering laminated wood stood on the right bulkhead (nautical-speak for a wall). Faded, peeling stickers from indecipherable soccer teams pretended to be wallpaper here and there, while graffiti in Indonesian and Korean was scrawled above the bunk on the ceiling, and a faded, well-used adult magazine was stuffed on a rickety shelf—all the residue exposing the life of the civilian sailor—spartan, desperate, and makeshift. Above the bunk a fluorescent bulb clung to the wall by loose screws and wires. I flipped the switch and it sputtered to life with a hum. Blessedly, there were also two power outlets—both 110 volt, so I didn't have to dig around for my adapters. The whole room was just big enough to allow me to stand up straight, but it was certainly better than sleeping on the hard deck, exposed to the elements. I stowed my ruck on the top bunk, plugged in the satphone and my spare BlackBerry to keep them charged, locked the room and headed topside down the slippery linoleum floor just as I heard the low, deep rumbling of the engines throttling up and felt the ship shudder as it slowly began pulling away from the dock.

I grabbed a thin mattress from the dozen or so that were piled in a bin on the foredeck for those unfortunate souls without a cabin, and I climbed to the top of the ship—literally on top of the bridge amid stacked orange fishing buoys. High on my perch, I spread out on top of the buoys and watched things below. Down there, a celebration began pierside as Libyan supporters waved the flag of the rebels, honked car horns, and cheered for those heading back to their homeland across the sea. Libyans knew the importance of this journey—it was to be the first time a ship had entered Tripoli's port since the war started. On board our ship one old man with a long white beard wearing an i-GO Aid ball cap and green T-shirt three sizes too big was screaming "Allah Akhbar!" or "God is great!" from the forward deck, and soon a chorus of the chant was being repeated, bellowing from ship to shore; one Libyan ran to the mast and hoisted the unofficial Libyan rebel flag alongside the aid group's flag. It was surreal to be a fly on the wall watching this historical trip begin as the big ship eased out of the protected port and pointed its nose south.

As I watched from my perch, a fine mist settled on me as the ship's bow turned seaward and gently rose and fell, crashing through the waves as we picked up speed. The crew was busy doing what ship's crews do; the sun was settling below the horizon off to my right and a purplish pink hue mixed with the lingering clouds to flood the sky. A yellow and green ambulance donated from Germany sat strapped in the deck's hold amid gurneys; another was secured next to the orange crane on the foredeck. Crates of medical supplies, water, food, and other needed things for a rebel army opposing a dictator's regime were secreted in every nook and cranny of this old fishing boat.

The journalists on board hovered over everything the Libyans did like flies at a family picnic, taking pictures and running around for better and better shots. Staying up here I felt immune from it all, an observer, yet a participant in ways my fellow Westerners below couldn't imagine.

Only Sleepy and Kamel knew who I really was—knew that I was an American, knew I was a former CIA officer, knew I was here at the request of the chairwoman of the United States House Intelligence Subcommittee on Terrorism, HUMINT, Analysis and Counterintelligence. Only they knew I was on a secret mission on board this boat, knew that I'd already been to Libya, and knew that I was working to help dethrone the dictator. I glanced once more back toward shore, where the lights of the city, harbor, and boats flickered to life as the sun faded, reminding me of lightning bugs back home in the pasture on a summer evening.

I watched as the Libyans all began to congregate at the bow. They took off their flip-flops; others brought out large crates of boxed milk, juice, and food. They spread mattresses and blankets up near the massive shiny, painted black anchor chains. I saw Sleepy and Kamel walk under my perch, around the railing, and up to the bow. They sat cross-legged and then Sleepy glanced up and caught sight of me, smiled through his Coke-bottle-thick glasses, and gestured for me to come join them. He looked like a man off the clock, resting for a second from his duties. I smiled, waved, and gave him a nod, then made my way down.

I sat on the bow among twenty or thirty Libyans; we broke bread together as they celebrated the end of the Ramadan fast for that day. Ramadan is the monthlong fasting period where Muslims deny themselves food, drink, smoking, sex, masturbation, applying medicine to the anus, or performing any medical tests on women where any instrument is inserted internally. They can't accidentally swallow a morsel that becomes dislodged from the teeth, or saliva that gets mingled with blood, or apply medicine drops to the nostrils, or deliberately make themselves throw up. This fasting period is to go from sunrise to sunset, with the goal to help Muslims focus on cleansing their bodies to become closer to their god.

But they don't truly go without food or drink for a month—no one can do that and survive. They sleep late into the morning, get up, and then fast until around 7 P.M., then they break out the food and drink, eating until late into the night, go to sleep, and repeat the cycle until Ramadan ends with the celebration of Eid al-Fitr, or just Eid (pronounced "eed").

A fellow American who'd hitched a ride on the boat was the young man I'd dubbed "Sumo the Journalist." He and the news crew from PBS *Frontline* and Doctors Without Borders were all watching this feast from a discreet distance. I got a funny look from one of the *Frontline* journos, as we referred to journalists, as well as Sumo. I think they were genuinely curious as to why I'd be invited to break bread with them, and why I'd been given my own private room on board a boat with dozens of people sleeping exposed on the decks.

Don't misunderstand, I'm a follower of Jesus Christ. In fact, I'm an ordained minister and have even performed a marriage or two, but joining my Muslim travelers on that day was a time I won't forget. Sleepy and his companions showed hospitality and graciousness to me, but the scene also highlighted the ridiculousness of our world.

We fight and battle one another, we collect intelligence against enemies and friends alike; we struggle against tyrants and terrorist groups—and for what? So that someone else can harness power in some dark corner of the world. In my humble opinion, it's the search and lust for power that has made the world such a mess. The Bible says it plainly—the love of money is the root of evil. Power and money go hand in hand.

But when you boil it down, we are all the same on this planet and death is hereditary. We should treat each other better and love our neighbor. In fact, Jesus was asked what was the greatest commandment issued by God and He said to love God with everything you've got—your heart, your soul, and your mind. The second greatest? To love your neighbor as you love yourself. The last one is something that I've found nonradical, nonmilitant Muslims to be always willing to do—to be gracious hosts, regardless of your beliefs . . . unless of course you're Jewish; then it seems all bets are off.

Sleepy, ever the professional diplomat seeking to defuse a problem, also saw the situation developing with the Westerners and he waved them over, inviting everyone to join in. Like teenagers at their first dance, they reluctantly stepped over the line, taking a nervous seat. First the Doctors Without Borders people, then a journalist, and then another, until finally everyone was eating, drinking, and smiling.

After the sun set over the horizon and darkness began to envelop the boat, I slipped away, leaving them to their food and drink, and made my way to my cabin, where I crawled up into my rickety bunk and fell asleep to the gentle, rhythmic rise and fall of the boat and the deep rumble of its engine as we plowed ahead into war.

THE NEXT MORNING I AWOKE to the sun's rays reflecting off the calm, flat sea visible through the marred porthole as the *Al-Entisar* continued its southern trek through the Mediterranean. I wandered topside to my perch above the bridge after doing some pull-ups off the stern. From there I spotted Kamel Fakroun moving about, and it soon became obvious from the way others deferred to him that he had a lot of pull. As the sun rose higher, I saw him watching me, perhaps considering the level of trust he was willing to commit.

By now, NATO forces had flown more than twenty thousand air sorties. Without the West, which would expect payback—in oil and commercial deals, political support, and perhaps even the return of Western military bases—the rebels could never have accomplished what they had. But the fight was turning, and the brigades were about to go to war against each other to see who would run that country. I had a hunch that Kamel was part of all that.

I was on a boat surrounded by people whose alliances I couldn't be sure of, and I had no assurance that, for whatever reason, they wouldn't turn on me once we hit Libya. But I had committed; the boat wasn't turning back and I'd just have to see how the situation developed.

I took Sleepy to the back of the ship and had a heart-to-heart talk with him. He told me that Kamel was the fund-raiser and right-hand man for the leader of one of the most powerful militias running Tripoli. Prior to the war, Kamel's family had run a construction business and an export company that worked with another company out of Malta. Sleepy, looking furtively around to make sure that the stern area was clear, then got Kamel and brought him over. That's when they told me the reason for asking me to come on this trip. Kamel and Sleepy had arranged for me to meet Mahdi al-Harati, the leader of the Tripoli Revolutionary Brigade, arguably the most powerful brigade in the country.

Five "brigades" were vying for the right to govern Libya after the dictator's removal. These brigades weren't formal military units but were essentially militias, all with leaders hoping to take power in some form or another. Sharia law under their thumb seemed inevitable, but the makeup of the Islamic government—the extent of its commitment to fundamentalist principles—was in play, along with the character of the new Libya. The grab for power was going to be brutal. The militia with the biggest guns would win control; it was about firepower.

Two brigades were destined to emerge as rivals. The Martyrs of 17 February Brigade was good-sized with approximately twelve battalions and a large arsenal of light and heavy weapons. The group carried out various security and law-and-order tasks in eastern Libya and Kufra in the south. The second, the Tripoli Revolutionary Brigade, supported, it seemed, by Sleepy and Kamel, was led by Mahdi al-Harati, a hero after the fall of Tripoli, where he had helped drive the assault. A unit of the National Liberation Army, the Tripoli Revolutionary Brigade (TRB) had originally been formed in April 2011 by fifteen men in Benghazi, then relocated to the Nafusa Mountains, the closest front line to Tripoli—where the brigade had recruited most of its other members before advancing into the city with an increasing number of fighters. It included four sub-brigades. Without a doubt, Harati was one of the most important rebel commanders of the war when it came to Tripoli. He was also second in command of the newly formed Tripoli Military Council.

Fundamentalist Muslim groups, ranging from the Muslim Brotherhood (MB) to al-Qa'ida, were part of all five brigades, but the extent to which the radicals dominated each was uncertain. Sleepy emphasized the terrorist connections of the 17 February Brigade, led by Hakim Belhaj—a confirmed militant Islamist and former fighter in the Soviet-Afghan war; I knew his name well. He said that 17 February had about six hundred members and was composed of ex-military, Muslim Brotherhood, and fundamentalist elements. Headquartered on the front side of Wheelus Air Base, the old U.S. air base in Tripoli, just across the highway from the sea, the group was, Sleepy said, backed financially by Qatar, and the eldest son of the emir was involved.

Sleepy's assessment of the fundamentalist loyalties of 17 February Brigade was hitting all the terror trigger points and made me wonder if he was intentionally trying to influence my opinion. Clearly he and Kamel were attempting to direct my loyalties toward Harati's Tripoli Revolutionary Brigade, which had fifteen hundred men under arms and, according to my traveling companions, had reinforcements coming. Sleepy and Kamel made no mention of the group having any ties to al-Qa'ida, the Muslim Brotherhood, or radicals of any other kind. I noted this convenient omission. None of the groups were that clean. Somehow I needed to get more information on Harati, but do it in a way that wasn't alarming to him or anyone around him. I imagined that he wasn't a saint and I needed more background on him.

"We want you to meet with Mahdi al-Harati," Sleepy said, interpreting for Kamel. "Talk to him. He is also in need of protection and we need to improve things in the brigade."

They kept mentioning how he was second in command at the Tripoli Military Council, which was not a brigade, but a group claiming to be aimed toward unifying all of Libya's armed militias. I saw it as a power-grab opportunity rigged by somebody and Mahdi al-Harati just might be that guy, although he was deputy, or second in command, under Belhaj—the known terrorist. So the guy led an entire brigade and was second in charge of this unifying council being formed—he sounded to me like a plum asset to try to get to know.

"Okay, I'll meet with him," I said as Kamel's wide mouth curled into a smile that I couldn't quite read. It was a red carpet into a place where no Westerner had gone, and possibly I could play it, use it as leverage to get the terrorist Belhaj to sit down, too. What was he thinking? What were his alliances and goals? What did he need that the United States could use as leverage to get him to cooperate? Or find out if he was hostile to the United States, get a fix on him, and let good old Uncle Sam send a Reaper over to rearrange his backyard from fifty-thousand feet.

AFTER WE'D ARRIVED IN TRIPOLI, Sleepy, Sumo, Kamel, our young driver, and I lit out of the port in a Toyota SUV, turned right, and headed southwest along Gergarish, paralleling the coast. A short, stocky, bespectacled Asian kid wearing a dark blue T-shirt and a dark ball cap, Sumo was an independent photographer traveling solo from the States. I'd met him back on the docks in Malta, where he told me he'd spent his own money to get here, hoping to get into Tripoli, although he had never been to Libya or the Middle East. He was doing this thing on a shoestring budget with only the clothes on his back and a small camera bag that housed his gear. I had to respect his courage, even if I did think he was swinging without a net. He thought I was a logistics producer—a position we made up as my cover—for a major news network. So when he had asked if he could tag along, I told him we'd see what we could do to help him out.

The meeting with Harati wasn't quite scheduled yet; I would have to wait—as usual. As we rumbled through the twists and turns on the way to Sleepy's house, I started putting together a SITREP and shot it over to the Ops Center from the backseat as we drove. Kamel reached back and handed me a folding-stock AK-47. I took the gun, popped the magazine out, checked the ammo, grabbed the rifle's front sight, and yanked on it to see if it was loose. Running the charging handle to the rear, I inspected the chamber, then reinserted the mag, charged a round, placed the weapon on safe, and dropped it, muzzle-down between my legs—all this earning me an odd look from Sumo. As we drove, the streets were hot and gunfire rumbled in various places across the city.

We wound our way into an area of nice homes surrounded by high walls, a few with video surveillance cameras long since out of service, but all with scars of war: bullet holes, scorched walls, burned-out vehicles, and downed power lines. We stopped at what seemed to be Sleepy's house—a three-story white building surrounded by a wall. Kamel dropped us off and pulled away, saying he'd come back later, as Sleepy opened the gate. He'd not seen his house since the start of the war. His wife and children had fled to another country and today, as he went into their house for the first time in a long while, I could tell it was emotional for him. Fortunately, it hadn't been looted, as had so many others in this neighborhood.

A bit later, after a shower to blow off the sweat, ocean grime, and dirt from the past few days, I went up to find Sleepy, who said we needed to go down to his friend's house a few blocks away. Hakin, a balding, middle-aged man, greeted us warmly. Dressed in his man-jammies, he introduced himself and spoke fairly good English. He and Sleepy hugged, having not seen each other for months. Their two families were very close and when they parted at the start of the rebellion, they honestly didn't know if they would ever see each other alive again.

We sat on the patio and Hakin's young son offered Sumo and me tea and water—the rest didn't get the offer, as it was Ramadan. I declined out of respect for my hosts. Once darkness fell, the firing across the city seemed to flare up more. A machine gun here, a distant explosion there, streaks of tracer fire across the night sky danced wildly. We all moved inside and found places to sleep. "Sumo, don't get too comfortable," I warned the young photographer. "Keep things packed up in case we need to move." My ruck and emergency bag were right by the couch I'd be sleeping on that night. The AK-47 was lying on the floor at my fingertips and I kept my boots on.

That next night, we got the call warning us that Qadhafi's men were heading our way to kill us; after our flight through the night lit by tracer fire from Hakin's house to his father's, I sat awake, keeping watch on the street while the others slept. When the dawn broke, the sun's rays shone through the trees and spilled over onto the rooftop, warming me and waking the rest of the group. As it happened, we got through the second night safely. I wondered if our luck would hold, at least long enough to meet Mahdi. We left the rooftop, making our way back to Hakin's house, where we had been sleeping before the incident.

SPEEDING THROUGH TRIPOLI, I thought about how it seemed that every Libyan we rode with had this delusion that he was actually testing a Bugatti Veyron through the Hammerhead turn on *Top Gear*'s racetrack just beyond London. Somehow we reached the rotary in one piece, turned left onto the coastal road, and made our way to Wheelus Air Base, the new headquarters for the 17 February Brigade and the Tripoli Revolutionary Brigade.

At the gate, we were turned away by 17 February forces who had no interest in admitting a truck from the Tripoli Brigade, an indication that my instinct about a pending battle for militia supremacy was on target. We entered the backside of the base, winding our way into an area that looked out over the water near the runway. I noticed Qadhafi's jet sitting out back—it had recently been featured on a CNN segment by Nic Robertson I'd watched from my Cairo hotel just days earlier.

Sleepy took me into a one-story concrete structure to wait. It was dark inside and everywhere men were sprawled about, lying spent from battle. Some slept or ate, some fiddled with their rifles, while others whispered to their comrades.

I stepped out to get a sense of things and take a Garmin hit—32°53'42" north by 13°16'49" east. Men milled about outdoors smoking. Up a small incline a young Libyan struggled to repair one of their gun trucks. As I looked around I noticed a slim, blond-haired white guy in dirty pants with a scarf tied just under his reddish beard. He was squinting in the bright sunlight making notes, squatting under the porch of a building to my left. My first thought was that he was an intelligence officer—which would have been a surprise, but a good one. I walked over and he introduced himself as a correspondent for an Irish newspaper. He said he'd been embedded with the Tripoli Brigade for a few weeks, even accompanying them as they'd pushed into Tripoli. He was sharp, smart, and apparently knew his way around war zones. When he asked what I was doing there, I stuck with my cover, telling him I was a logistics producer for a news network and was waiting on a meeting with Harati. Astonished, he expressed his frustration at being unable to speak with Mahdi, on or off the record lately despite being embedded with them. He said he'd been there when Mahdi was hit in the ankle by a sniper and that he himself had actually taken a round to his helmet during a firefight, but apparently Mahdi wasn't ready to give an interview yet, despite promises to the contrary.

An idea began to form. I had questions about Mahdi; this reporter needed access and I needed to offload Sumo so I could get on with my work. If I could arrange an interview for him, get Sumo in on it to shoot pictures for his first big break, and salt the interview beforehand with my questions, then manage to sit in on it, I might get what I needed to fulfill my own RFIs (requests for information) and kill three birds with one well-aimed rock. "Hey, I think I can get you an interview with Mahdi today," I said.

"Could you truly do that? That would be fantastic," he said.

"I'm pretty solid I can handle that for you. Let me introduce you to this freelance photographer who just got here. He should be in on this with you—he's new, but he's a good guy and needs the work." We walked to meet Sumo in the other room. As we sat waiting for Sleepy, I pinged the journalist about what he planned to ask. If I could manipulate things so that he asked my questions for me, it would keep me from having to press Mahdi too hard, which could raise his guard with me and throw cold water on things before they ever got off the ground.

"Well, I thought about asking what his plans were now, since he's taken Tripoli," he said.

"Well, that's not bad, but here's another angle to supplement that. What if you did a piece on him—on his background? Where he came from, who his family is, what brought him here and things like that?" I said.

"Hey, that's a good idea," he replied and started scribbling down questions.

"Ask him about this new council that he's a part of and the other guy who's in charge—Belhaj. Get him to talk about that guy."

The U.S. government didn't have anyone on the ground collecting this stuff. Here was a huge opportunity to gain access to the leadership of Libya's most powerful paramilitary forces and possibly to people who might one day run the country—or be a threat to those who would. I spent the next fifteen or twenty minutes suggesting questions, all of which he wrote down—and all of which he would later ask.

Sleepy finally poked his head in and motioned for me to come, alone. We walked through a large room full of armed guys toward a closed door guarded by a phalanx of security. Sleepy spoke a few words to them; they parted and one opened the door, ushering us inside. In the room among the knot of men was a Libyan in his mid-thirties, thickset and roughly my height, wearing old British-style desert camo from the nineties; a pistol sat in a holster on his right hip; a cheap laminated badge was clipped to his left breast pocket; a stylish watch and silver ring were on his right hand. He stood to shake hands. He had a wide face, spoke very little English ,and had a brown beard that wrapped under his jaw but barely reached his chin or lip, reminding me of an Amish guy. On his head sat a crumpled military-style garrison cap matching the rest of his uniform. This was the famed Mahdi al-Harati.

Also present was Youssef Ben Hamad, Mahdi's political officer, who looked more like a college professor with his glasses, civilian clothes and neatly trimmed salt-and-pepper beard. He was from Birmingham, England, as were many of the men in the brigades, and had originally been a business manager in another life. A thin fellow with a jet-black beard in full military garb sat in the back and was vaguely introduced as Mahdi's intelligence officer. I made a mental note to get to know that guy.

We arranged chairs in a tight circle away from Mahdi's huge, ornate desk and Sleepy kicked things off, explaining my connection to Congresswoman Myrick of the Intelligence Committee, and my experience in training, security, and such things. Then out of the blue he dropped a bomb that nearly made me fall out of my chair when he spoke the letters *C*, *I*, and *A* and looked my direction. I never expected him to use that to establish my bona fides. I had no real idea who Mahdi was or whether he'd had good or bad experiences with the agency. For all I knew, I was about to be shot—or worse. I placed my hand on Sleepy's forearm and tried to take control of the conversation.

"Commander, first let me be clear," I said. "I am no longer with CIA, nor am I representing the U.S. government in an official capacity."

"Thank you for coming so far to see me," Mahdi said, smiling, as Sleepy translated. Inwardly, I breathed a sigh of relief. At least for now, I wasn't going to be shot.

The meeting continued for at least an hour, with Mahdi and I peppering each other with questions. One in particular was whether I thought he should keep his headquarters here at the old U.S. air base or at the port. His Tripoli Brigade and the 17 February Brigade shared control of both places. He said that his group also controlled the hotel where the journalists stayed exclusively.

I told him that I'd keep them all, but especially the airfield. If coalition forces agreed to send them supplies, they most certainly would want to do it by air as opposed to water—it was faster getting in and getting out. Mahdi held the rear of the airfield where the runways were; he'd have control over what came in—that gave him leverage and, as Archimedes the Greek engineer said, "give me a lever long and a fulcrum on which to place it, and I shall move the world." The 17 February Brigade held only the front of the airfield, which had no serviceable runways.

I advised him to have a security survey conducted on the parts of the base that he held, to determine how to strengthen his position. That was what I was hoping we'd get hired to do first, giving me our opening. He liked that, and I saw Sleepy's face relax. I guess I was making him look good.

I suggested that he consider allowing someone to assess and then train his personal security detail. My intent with that was to get a small team of our guys embedded by offering the training. Provided the U.S. government gave us permission, it would be a great way to develop relationships inside his brigade. I had no illusions that I'd be best buddies with Mahdi, so who better to develop than those guarding him? You'd hear their gripes, know plans for where he was going, know whom he met and when—it would be a great opportunity to offer to our government so they could collect intelligence and recruit sources. With that, he had someone step out and bring in the leader of his security detail—a young white guy who looked like he could have been from the United States, British, or Canadian military. He had reddish hair and looked as though he'd flipped through and bought everything in the Blackhawk catalog—assault vest atop his desert fatigues, gloves with the fingers cut out, and a pistol strapped to his thigh. His trousers were bloused into his boots paratrooper style.

Taking off his glove, he extended his hand, "Hi, I'm Mohammad but you can call me Matt," he said in English with a strong Irish accent. I noticed a tooth missing when he spoke. "I'm in charge of Mahdi's security," he said.

"Your English is great; where are you from?" I asked.

"Ireland—Dublin. Mahdi is from the same area, but his English isn't so good; and you, you're from the States?" he asked, confirming that he had been given a data dump on me and also giving me a location for Mahdi's hometown.

"Yep, I'm from the States, and we might be working together soon," I said, testing those waters. Many in leadership positions hate someone coming in to help, no matter whether they need it or not. It can be seen as a challenge to their manhood, their warrior skills, or other silly crap. This didn't seem to be an issue with him. Nor with Mahdi, who appeared inclined to accept me. Leaning over, I asked Sleepy if we were basically done. He said we were. Now it was time to work in the reporter and Sumo to hopefully fill in the gaps in my ever-expanding profile on this man. Addressing Mahdi directly and putting my hand on Youssef's shoulder, I said, "Mahdi, I have an idea. Would you grant an interview to an Irish newspaper team today? You know the reporter.

He looked at Youssef, then looked at me, and said, "Na'am," for yes, in Arabic.

I stood up from the circle of chairs, slipped over to Mahdi's big wooden desk, and took a seat in his massive, studded leather chair in front of the window overlooking the runway and pulled out my Moleskine notebook and stubby pencil. The journalist and Sumo came into the office and shook the hands of the half dozen men present, all beaming. Taking a seat next to Mahdi in the circle of chairs, he started asking questions. To his credit, he began with his own, but shortly mine began showing up—every last one of them. I couldn't have been happier as I sat there with my phone recording it all and taking notes in my lap. Meanwhile Sumo fluttered around the room, taking photo after photo with his massive digital camera. Once he looked my way and raised his camera, but I raised a finger and wagged it back and forth, smiling, and he moved along. Toward the end however, I did ask Sumo to take a photo of me and Mahdi just to record the event.

I learned that Mahdi was born in April 1973 and had left Tripoli for Ireland eighteen years ago, after Qadhafi's agents arrested him because members of his family had been preaching antiregime rhetoric. He briefly lived in Manchester, England, where he ran a produce stand, then he returned to Ireland. While there, he volunteered teaching Muslims to speak English and was heavily involved with "free Gaza" efforts. He added that he had been arrested and held in Israel for five days for his part of the "Gaza Freedom Flotilla," back in 2010. I recalled that story being in the news.

On May 31, 2010, thirteen Israeli naval commandos had pursued the flotilla with speedboats and helicopters to force the ships to the Israeli port of Ashdod for inspection. But, on one of the ships—the Turkish passenger ship MV *Mavi Marmara*—teams of prepared, trained, and uniformed activists, armed with metal rods cut from the ship's rails and dressed in protective clothing, prevented Israeli boats from advancing by throwing broken plates and metal chains at them. Commandos attempting to land on the top deck were attacked with knives. Two commandos had been thrown to the lower deck, one of them headfirst, and were abducted along with a third. Nine activists had been killed and dozens wounded. Seven Israeli commandos were wounded, one seriously. The five other ships in the flotilla reportedly employed passive resistance, which was suppressed without major incident. The ships were towed to Israel, where everyone aboard was detained and eventually deported.

When the reporter got into his medical condition, I learned that Mahdi claimed to be diabetic and have a heart condition. He went on to say that he had wounds on his lower right leg from the Tripoli fighting and other scars from being shot by the Israelis in the flotilla incident. He lifted his pant legs and showed off his wounds.

Then the reporter started digging into his family life. Mahdi was married to a woman named Eftaima, who lived with his four children back in Dublin. As the interview continued, I confirmed that Mahdi's chief rival was indeed Belhaj, commander of the council that governed all the militias and his immediate boss on that council. That sounded to me like a recipe for trouble for Mahdi.

Mahdi stressed to the reporter and Sumo that his group, unlike 17 February, was not filled with fundamentalists, but represented a cross section of Libya—exactly the line that Sleepy and Kamel had fed me on the ship. He went on to explain that he was seeking financial support in order to counter the money 17 February had been receiving from Qatar, so that his group could remain a viable alternative. Another motive for recruitment—money.

So there was dissension between Mahdi and his boss on the council, and money was the way to exploit that division—he needed it to keep from being overtaken by Belhaj. If I could get this information back to Colonel Cantwell, and to the seventh floor back at CIA, perhaps we could introduce one of their officers to Mahdi and let them take over. The CIA had the money and with it they could burrow into the good graces of the Tripoli Brigade like a tick on a hound dog and use that to gain upstream access to what was going on in the new Tripoli Military Council, which would give access to all the brigades in one form or another. Not a bad idea.

Once the guys finished up their interview and the good-byes were said, Youssef came up to me and asked, "How soon can you come back and get started with the security assessments of the airfield and the other bases?"

I told him I'd return to the States, get the permissions, hopefully, and be back within a week or two. Out in the sunlight, as the reporter and Sumo expressed their appreciation through squinted eyes, I executed phase three of my plan for the day—dumping Sumo. I broached the subject about Sumo tagging along with the reporter. Sumo loved the idea and, to the reporter's credit, he agreed, though I'm not sure how long that union lasted. As Sleepy and I were saying our good-byes to Sumo, he pulled me to the side and said, "I don't know exactly who you are or what you're doing here, but I want to thank you for all the help. Be safe."

The old saying "Never miss a good chance to shut up" wandered through my mind for a second. Mostly I was preoccupied with the thought of getting out of there. Sleepy drove me back to the docks, where I loaded myself back onto the *Al-Entisar*, hoping for a tranquil overnight ride back across the sea to Malta, where I'd check in to a hotel, get a good bath, and enjoy a steak dinner. But that, just like everything else in Libya, wasn't going to happen, either. Halfway across the Mediterranean in the middle of the night, the ship ran into a massive storm, with lightning, thunder, and wind-driven rain tossing us on waves so large it made walking down the passageways nearly impossible. On more than one occasion I prayed that Jesus would just show up and do a New Testament miracle and calm the storm. It was so bad that I found it a challenge to simply sit up on my top bunk without being thrown to the floor or against the walls. But even more problematic was walking down the passageway to the latrine—which is a generous description for the hole cut in the deck of the broom-closet-size space. Once I had made it inside and was trying to take care of business with one hand while holding onto the hook in the ceiling, the waves hammering the ship managed to launch me straight up into that ceiling, bringing to a startling, wet conclusion what was already an omnidirectional experience. I ricocheted off the walls until I got back to my cabin, crawled up into my bunk, swallowed an Ambien, snatched my privacy curtain closed, said a prayer, and hoped for the best.

CHAPTER 12

Shoot 'Em in the Teeth While They Sleep

September 5, 2011
Virginia Beach, Virginia

BACK IN WASHINGTON, LIBYA already felt like old news; the end of the Qadhafi regime was in sight, but it seemed that few could be bothered to consider who would replace him. The talk now was about Syria and its despotic president, Bashar al-Assad, a dictator on par with Qadhafi when it came to murder and mercilessness. In January 2011, a month when it was cold enough to freeze your shadow to the ground in Old Damascus, a Syrian police officer had brutally beaten an old man on al-Hareeka Street with his baton. He was relentless as he kicked his victim's head and back with his steel-toed boot. People walking the street nearby stopped and stared, but only for a second because this was Syria, the home of iron-fisted rule by one of the most vicious regimes in the Middle East.

The man lay unconscious, broken and bloody, on the cold concrete sidewalk until the police arrived to arrest him, gathering his near-lifeless body by the arms and legs, tossing him into a van and taking him off to an unknown fate in prison. This was the winter day that the Arab Spring burned its way into Syria, but hardly anyone seemed to be paying attention to the sparks.

While all the work was going on in Libya that summer, the smoldering in Syria caught fire. As we were moving in and around Tripoli, Colonel Cantwell and Fred Burton at Stratfor forwarded daily SITREPs on the growing rebellion in Homs, Damascus, Aleppo, and many other cities and towns, as Syrian intelligence was hunting down, torturing, and executing protesters and rebels. As I read these reports I began to see yet another opportunity—not only to try to help bring freedom, but also to generate another business opportunity. In fact, the two projects were overlapping quite by happenstance as Silverback's team had picked up that Qadhafi was making calls to Syria's al-Assad. Did he need a sympathetic ear, or was he trying to line up a safety net that he could jump into? We had no idea, but quite honestly on this day I had other things way more important to think about—my son Cole's birthday.

BUT ON THE DAY OF THE PARTY, as I was heading to pick up Cole's cake from Farm Fresh, my phone sparked to life: it was Silverback with the latest SITREP—Qadhafi had fled with his son Khamis and his daughter. When rebels started to surround the place, the dictator had disappeared fast in a massive convoy of Land Cruisers. He was next spotted in Bani Walid, about a hundred miles southeast of Tripoli. If the rebels chased them there—where only the Warfalla tribe lived—it would be the start of a massive tribal war. We all suspected that his flight from Tripoli to that area appeared to be an attempt to draw the rebels into hostile tribal territory and to split them into fighting the tribes, too.

But the rebels had managed to place scouts ahead of Qadhafi's convoy, ambushed it, and killed more than a dozen people . . . yet Qadhafi escaped. Silverback's spies said that on that same night, a quick funeral had been held for someone very important. He suspected that the dead man was either Khamis or the son of the regime's intelligence chief. Silverback's people reported a large troop presence the next morning in Bani Walid and surrounding villages. Since then Qadhafi had been spotted heading in the direction of Sabha, more than three hundred miles south, in the direction of the border with Chad and Niger. We'd find him though, I knew it—every slug leaves a trail and the spotter network of informants that we'd built had eyes out watching, listening.

I knew that D and I had to go back. I returned to the house and brought in the cake and had a great time with the kids. But often I'd catch myself sitting alone, watching everyone having fun, but feeling remote from it all—knowing I'd be leaving again and wondering if this would be the last time I would see them this side of eternity. General Robert E. Lee once said, "Get correct views of life, and learn to see the world in its true light. It will enable you to live pleasantly, to do good, and, when summoned away, to leave without regret." But death caresses you at times like this—when you know you're not just leaving on a business trip to Memphis. Your mind fills with regret, superstition, confusion, rage, denial, happiness, and acceptance, all in a big, merciless wad . . . and then you shake it from your mind as you try to soak up every last memory, every detail, every last precious hug and moment with those you love.

Days earlier, when I'd gotten back to D.C. after my meeting with Mahdi in Tripoli, I stopped into BLT Steak for a filet and to see my friends Will and Marcel. That place is the best in the city and if God made anything better, he saved it for himself. As I plowed through my meal, I reached out to Colonel Cantwell and Bob Baer and touched base with Fred over at Stratfor. Then I headed over to Capitol Hill and briefed Congresswoman Myrick's staff, telling them about Mahdi and the militia infighting. I explained my concern that Libya was going to be the scene of a battle for control between the civilian NTC and the guys with the guns—in other words, the militias, many of which were run by radical Islamists. I reiterated, over and over, that the guys with the biggest guns would be making the rules. It was the militias that had them, including Belhaj—a known terrorist—especially, and that the United States needed badly to penetrate those groups so we could know what they were up to. If Belhaj managed to unify all the militia into one group, he would be the dominant military power in that country—effectively running the show.

Belhaj was listed as an "emir" in the Libyan Islamic Fighting Group (LIFG), which was included on the State Department's list of terrorist organizations. At one point he had fled Libya for Afghanistan, where he joined the Taliban and developed close relations with al-Qa'ida. He was arrested in 2001 inside Pakistan and handed over to the United States, then repatriated to Libya. He fled Libya again, but again the United States caught him—this time at Kuala Lumpur International Airport in Malaysia in 2004. He was again returned to Libya, where he was held this time for six years. But in March 2010, Saif Qadhafi, in a massive display of ineptitude released him and 170 Islamists in what he called a "deradicalization" program. It didn't work.

Now in 2011, even though Congresswoman Myrick and I tried to get colleagues and the administration to listen, we just couldn't seem to get any traction with anybody on that issue—Washington had basically missed the Arab Spring. A few days later, I followed up my oral briefing with a report that went not only to the House, but SOCOM and to the director of the CIA as well.

The report provided a detailed breakdown of each brigade and then all the details I'd learned about Mahdi, the threat posed to the fledgling Libyan civilian-led government by the militias, and opportunities for SOF (Special Operations Forces) and intelligence involvement. We explained that Belhaj was, in short, the personification of what the West feared would happen after Qadhafi: terrorist infiltration and takeover of the government. We warned American leaders of this through every channel we had, with the exception of the national news. We did everything we could short of publishing it in the *Washington Post* to alert them to the need to engage these militias in order to get some traction with them. We needed to recruit spies in all of them—not just those militias we wanted as our allies, or those we needed to help guard our embassy or consulates.

We needed to have spies buried deep, as a barometer to measure the growth of radicals in the country, to know where the weapons were, to know when attacks were being considered, to learn when new bad guys came to town . . . basically, to grow our intelligence network in North Africa. If we didn't, we warned over and over, we'd pay for it later. Unfortunately, that prediction came true in September 2012 when U.S. ambassador Chris Stevens, another embassy staff member, and two CIA contractors were killed. There's simply no way to know whether our information could have changed this outcome, but we had a lot of information on the leaders, the boat used to smuggle in weapons and fighters, the infighting, the politics, backgrounds—we knew quite a lot.

I also had access to Mahdi, a much more palatable ally than Belhaj, and he trusted me. Surely someone would see the opportunity to use what we'd developed to get inside his organization and develop that situation. No one did. I was stuck in the trenches while the guys in politics played power games.

IN MY BUSINESS, if you don't see exactly where you figure in the big picture, you're going to wind up making the wrong move or dying of frustration. Part of what I have to do is to appreciate that, so that I can be effective for my country—but also to my company. You have to learn to look for the larger games being played and do your best to figure out how to fit in or whether the circumstances suggest a tactical withdrawal.

Whether viewed as a blessing or a curse, I've been allowed to look behind the curtain to see how the world operates in a few different corners. One theme seems to run through it all, whether the leaders function in the public or private sector: it's about the pursuit of power, as in, control, influence, and the ability to get what you want. Power controls: you can have a great salary, but you can get the ax. But if you're the boss, you can wield both the carrot and the cleaver.

A few may claim I'm depriving some village of its idiot, and I certainly don't claim to be a scholar of diplomacy or international relations, but I do watch, listen, and try to learn. What I have seen lying behind so many of our problems, what compromises our attempts to get things done, are power games, careers, and too much focus on getting elected at the expense of getting things done.

Governments all have a basic goal of protecting what they have—their lands, their people, their independence—essentially their way of life. Threats to America from beyond our borders result in escalations of force, not unlike the process police officers instigate with unruly suspects. First, the officer uses a verbal challenge—that's diplomacy on the world stage. If that doesn't work, the officer calls for backup—as a government would summon the support of other nations or organizations, such as the UN—to intimidate the suspect. If that fails, the police officer or the government might use nonlethal force, such as—in the case of the cops—pepper spray or a Taser. You might see these as the rough equivalents of the sanctions and blockades that governments use to intimidate the bad guys into compliance. But when that fails and the suspect yells, "Don't Tase me, man!" and pulls out his knife or gun, that's when the officer's Colt .45 comes out. That is also, one might say, the point when the government turns to warfare.

But people misunderstand warfare and think it is an end unto itself. But on the international stage, war is nothing more than another tool of diplomacy. If your country doesn't have a credible, powerful military force capable of bringing pain, death, and destruction to an enemy, then your diplomats can't get much done, because you simply aren't powerful—there's no threat of pain they can wield. That's why the western Pacific island nation of Nauru doesn't have a seat on the UN Security Council. Not recognizing this principle is shortsighted (no disrespect intended to the fine people of Nauru).

But warfare is a last-ditch diplomatic tool to force the opponent to give in, give up, and go along. Spying or covert operations can postpone wars—and alter their outcomes if already under way. To give diplomats the best chance to succeed, leaders must know what their opponents' weaknesses are and what will influence negotiation; and quite simply, sometimes you just have to steal this information. Espionage essentially boils down to stealing usable facts—on military forces, strategies, and technology, on leaders and what makes them tick, or on an enemy nation's goals and plans. It's of course a direct threat to the enemy nation's ability to remain powerful, because information is power.

This theft is accomplished in a hundred different ways. In its basic form you hire, coerce, entice, or threaten someone who works in your target's backyard to pass secrets to you. Or you tunnel through their computer networks until you find that sweet pot of gold they're trying so desperately to hide. If they have it air-gapped from a network—meaning unconnected to the Internet—then you go in and physically steal the equipment, trick someone to stick a USB in it, or clone it. You can set out passive equipment to relay phone conversations to recording devices; you can scope someone's computer in their office from a van parked on the street and see everything on their screen, or load malicious software that tells you every keystroke they make. Or you can do what the United States does and simply hack everything in sight—from mobile phones and mainframes to webcams and Bluetooth devices.

But espionage is also about getting inside the mind of your target, and you can't fully do that with electronics or signals equipment. You must know the target's intentions, and that's only uncovered by having human beings involved, conducting personal meetings in cars, hotels, and back alleys, in desert wadis, or on dirt runways in airplanes. You meet your contact, go through the mad minute, telling him or her the cover story for why you're talking together in case you're busted, get what they have for you, ask them questions to make sure you understand what they're giving you, then task them with the next project and set up the next meeting.

Then, after diplomacy, but before warfare, your government might use that stolen information, and that's where covert action might come into play. It's a tool, perhaps just below conventional warfare on the scale of aggression, and is basically anything from calculated violence to political shenanigans, all manipulated to reduce the power of your adversary to the point of them giving up or coming to the negotiating table. Power for your side grows when the other side doesn't know your intentions; when they don't know what you're doing they end up pouring resources into ineffective defenses. This is what helped bring the Soviet Union down when President Reagan caused them to believe the United States was building antiballistic missile defense capability. Concerned they'd be strategically lacking, they went "whole hog" on their defense budget and bankrupted themselves.

Once again, if I don't grasp my place in this larger picture, I'm likely to wind up as confused as a baby in a topless bar. You've got to learn to see the big game, of which you are only a small part. If you don't get it, it'll get you.

Money is what makes diplomacy, military, and covert action possible, though. Whoever controls the money controls the action, and this is a truth that the population of Washington understands better than most.

In a grossly oversimplified example, America might desire a base in Mali to deter the growth of al-Qa'ida in the Islamic Maghreb (AQIM). Mali might not want a U.S. base, but needs to act, because intruders they can't keep at bay are overrunning the nation. So, keeping our national intentions to ourselves, American diplomats offer Mali U.S. trainers and advisers. The Malian leaders want the help, but they can't afford to pay for it. America already knows this thanks to our intelligence officers working the African target, and the United States offers to send the trainers and advisers in exchange for something else, in the case of Mali, perhaps gold-mining rights. The Malians agree. The United States keeps half the mining rights and sells the other half on the open market, benefiting the U.S. Treasury.

Later, after the American advisers are successfully at work, the United States goes back to the Malians and offers more help, perhaps even military hardware. The Malians give up more natural resources in exchange. But the hardware requires more American crews for support, maintenance, and training. Our diplomats make the case that these Americans need a place to live, so they are granted a section of land where a camp is created. This might become a U.S. base from which missions can be launched against AQIM. Over time, as aid increases, the Malians get hooked on the ██████ benefits and come to enjoy the prestige stemming from their relationships with the Americans, which their neighbors might not have. They've developed a dependency on us. Gradually, we expand our base even further.

This very simplistic scenario has been played out again and again for hundreds, if not thousands, of years around the globe, in one country, tribe, or empire after another. But to continue to use it effectively, the United States must maintain our reputation and military reach.

Similar power games are played out between government agencies inside nations. I saw this happening between the CIA and the Defense Department as our initial actions in Afghanistan began to pay off. In various Washington circles, the success in Afghanistan was too often seen not as a success for American interests in general, but as a score for the CIA over the Pentagon. It was as if the budget and Beltway power were more important than one simple fact—we won the fight. No matter who was in charge—the CIA, the Pentagon, or the Social Security Administration—we blasted bin Laden's flip-flop warriors and the Taliban back to the Stone Age.

Cofer Black, then chief of the Counterterrorism Center at CIA, and Hank Crumpton, a senior officer who authored a great book on intelligence, were selected to lead the effort at CIA. Then Cofer successfully lobbied President George W. Bush to trust the agency to lead the entire Afghan war. This happened, basically, because the agency could put men on the ground there just nine days after 9/11—they were faster. The Pentagon had been too risk-averse and too large to respond that fast. But these days it seemed that the CIA was behaving in a similar fashion, perhaps through no fault of its own, and we in the private sector were now the ones responding quicker.

Throughout the Afghan war, the infighting between the CIA and the Pentagon continued. That conflict—not in the best interests of post-9/11 America—lay behind a good bit of the decision making, resulting in Secretary of Defense Donald Rumsfeld vowing never again to allow the Pentagon's role to be diminished. Internal politics, infighting, and power struggles raged around his efforts to take back control of the conflict from the CIA.

It seemed that Washington didn't grasp that it was a new day, didn't see what the operators and specialists were now capable of, or understand the wave of the future. One CIA friend of mine said, "It was stupid to invade Iraq and Afghanistan with uniformed forces. Rumsfeld managed to get the CIA pulled out, put big army in, and the rest of this shit storm followed. We should have let the agency quietly send in more kill teams to wipe out bin Laden and the rest." I personally admire Rumsfeld immensely and respect his long, distinguished service to America, and, whether right or not, I feel sure that his disagreements were because he felt the U.S. military should do the killing and the CIA the collecting.

But this is where General Stanley A. McChrystal and his intelligence chief, Major General Michael Flynn, made their mark by blending the two. They set about transforming the way the military units acted on intelligence. McChrystal was a tough-minded, lean West Point grad, Special Forces soldier, Ranger, and commander of Joint Special Operations Command (JSOC)—and he saw that the enemy was benefiting from our slow decision-making cycle. So he and Flynn cut through the bureaucracy and introduced the idea of the "fusion cell," where JSOC elements skilled in killing people partnered with CIA's intelligence gathering and paramilitary prowess to create a battlespace where the stakeholders had true situational awareness. General McChrystal ultimately developed and implemented a strategy in Afghanistan and a comprehensive counterterrorism organization that revolutionized the way the military and intelligence agencies interacted and operated.

A simplified example: CIA gets word from a HUMINT source or perhaps an NSA cell phone intercept that a bad guy is going to be at a certain house. That intel would be sent to the JSOC planners at the fusion cell, who would spin up a Delta or ███ team: shortly after, lethal

Americans would be slipping into a village by truck or on foot and shooting bad guys in the teeth as they slept in their mud hut. Again, that's a shooting—not a gunfight—and that's preferable.

Once the shooters bag or tag the occupants, their biometric info is logged into the SEEK Avenger device, the Secure Electronic Enrollment Kit and Multimodal Identification Platform—the same type of device that helped the CIA operation identify bin Laden on the raid that killed that worthless oxygen thief. Then the sensitive site exploitation (SSE) technicians would arrive to collect thumb drives, rip open computers, and take out the hard drives, and start to exploit and analyze any data recovered at the site, using the government's various biometric, facial-recognition, and voiceprint databases. This information would be relayed in real time back to the fusion cell where analysts located in CONUS (CONtinental United States) and OCONUS would come up with links, then new assaults and raids would be set in motion before the first assault team even RTB'd (returned to base). That process might be repeated a half dozen times or more in one night, in just one region—and that was happening all across the entire target country. This is the way it's going to happen in the future, only at a faster and faster clip, if the turf warriors in Washington don't get in the way.

IT ALL SOUNDS SIMPLE, but the barrier of distrust between the CIA and Pentagon still prevents cooperation and delays progress at times. I often get stuck in this kind of frustrating loop. That was what was happening in Libya in 2011. We had information and passed it to Director David Petraeus's office at the CIA and offered it to Defense, but because the information wasn't coming from a government source, it died somewhere in the system. Plus, the American elections were coming and everyone wanted to be the hero; everyone wanted the others to get it wrong.

On the one hand, I realized what was going on politically, but on the other hand, I was as baffled as Adam and Eve on Mother's Day. Why didn't anyone care to even hear the information we'd collected in Libya or to use the access we'd managed to develop? I reached out to a few friends who were former and current agency staff. I called Bob Baer first—he was great for general sanity checks and always gave sage advice drawn from his decades of experience across the globe.

When he picked up the phone and I asked how he was, then we got down to brass tacks.

"Who in the national security establishment can we reach out to who gives a crap about Libya? The radicals hate us, and they're going to be running this place if we're not careful," I said.

"Really," he said emphatically, "no one is going to give two shits about anything you guys are doing—because they didn't come up with it on their own. If they didn't dredge up the intel themselves, they won't touch it. But I've got a name or two I'll send over that might be able to help." Bob was right, but in the end asking advice from anyone is usually something you do when you already know the answer but wish you didn't, and I knew the answer, too.

We took our information—Libya's new leadership, Mahdi, Belhaj, militia and rebel operations, goals, aspirations, key figures, points of contact, and estimates on their future plans—to nearly everyone: Defense, SOCOM, the Defense Intelligence Agency (DIA), the Office of National Intelligence (ONI). Nothing. A black hole. It sounded like the split second after a fart in a boardroom—silence.

But it appeared that someone up there did leak the information about Mahdi and his contact with us, because just two weeks later he was gone. According to Silverback and Sleepy he was out, labeled a hand of the West. When I reached out to Youssef—Mahdi's political officer, who was visiting his family in the United Kingdom—he confirmed it all. Belhaj had triumphed. That meant trouble for the United States from radicals for decades to come. Even if Belhaj stepped aside, radicals were clearly controlling things in the militias.

We didn't know if someone inside Mahdi's staff had betrayed him or if it was someone on this side of the Atlantic, but according to Sleepy, Belhaj learned that Mahdi, his deputy and rival, had been talking to an American and relieved him of his position as deputy with the Tripoli Military Council. Mahdi was paid more than two hundred thousand euros. Reports were that he went back to Dublin for a while, but then he showed up in Syria in that fight. Following Mahdi's departure, Belhaj managed to consolidate his power by combining the radical Islamist 17 February Brigade and Mahdi's more moderate Tripoli Revolutionary Brigade into one militia, which he then controlled. But in the years that have followed, Belhaj has faded into the background and Mahdi has returned to Tripoli like a windstorm, being elected as mayor of Tripoli in August 2014. Animosity is reportedly simmering in the background between the two men and time will tell how this turns out.

ON THE PLANE RIDE TO NORTH AFRICA I was preoccupied. In my head, I had already written off Qadhafi—the man was finished. I scanned the SITREPs I was getting from Fred and Rick. More Syria: it was looking more and more like that was our next destination. If Assad, the dictator there, fell and stable leadership could be instituted before the radicals could move in, the Middle East would change for the better in that place—plain and simple. But again, it all depended on moving quickly.

For decades, Syria had been a thorn in the side of both the United States and Israel, along with many Western interests. Syria helped facilitate attacks on Israel and allowed Iran to funnel supplies, men, money, and ammo to Hizbollah right across their borders in a sort of protected land bridge of terrorism. Cracking Assad's regime could cripple operations for both groups.

But cracking Syria wouldn't be easy at all. The al-Assad family had ruled since 1970, when Defense Minister Hafez al-Assad took over in a bloodless coup—ironically, almost exactly one year after Qadhafi took over in Libya. Assad aligned Syria with the Soviet Union and took arms, advisers, and training from the communists. Although three-quarters of the Syrian population were Sunni Muslim, the Assads were Alawites, members of a small Islamic sect that made up just 11 percent of the population. The Alawites were aligned with the Shiites and had been recognized by the Iranian (Shiite) ayatollahs and by Lebanese Shiite leaders.

The confidence of Hafez al-Assad didn't extend far beyond his fellow Alawites, whom he had placed throughout his military in positions of strategic importance. It was in this fashion that he had coup-proofed his country. The Alawites were in charge of everything important—intelligence services, military units, government agencies. This didn't sit well with the Sunnis, but it suited Assad just fine.

His other methods of ensuring he stayed in charge were more brutal. Assad was a man who destroyed, through any means necessary, anyone who spoke out against his government. He'd crushed many who had tried to usurp his power, including the Muslim Brotherhood—themselves dangerous opponents who exported terrorism across the region. Their founder was a cleric named Hassan al-Banna, who believed like all fundamentalists that Islam was destined to dominate the world and impose its law on all nations. It was the Brotherhood who assassinated Egyptian prime minister Mahmoud Nokrashy in 1948, tried to assassinate Egyptian president Gamal Abdel Nasser in 1954, and succeeded in assassinating Egyptian president Anwar Sadat in 1981. The Brotherhood saw these men as secular Muslims not following the true faith and catering to the infidels, in Egypt's case the Soviets. To them, Assad was just as unsavory. He was, after all, an Alawite.

Now the Brotherhood, whose leaders took power in Egypt in the summer of 2012, were certainly part of the mix in Libya and were attempting to elevate its position, downplay its terrorist origins and radical fundamentalism, and rebrand its leaders as diplomats and statesmen worthy of governing nations and acting on the world stage. Just like the terrorist Yasser Arafat did in the Palestine Liberation Organization.

In Syria back in 2001, the Brotherhood was experiencing a resurgence of strength, despite the country's peaceful change of leadership from the old man to the son. In the summer of 2000, the old man Hafez al-Assad died of a heart attack. His successor and son, Bashar al-Assad—an equally determined opponent of the Brotherhood—took over just seven days later. A reserved but erratic man, the new dictator had been trained as a medical doctor in Damascus and had gone on to specialize in ophthalmology at the Western Eye Hospital in London. Now more than ten years later, despite his expertise in the field of vision, there was much he overlooked, particularly the looming wave of reform that was sweeping the region and destabilizing his own country.

Gradually, the assaults against the regime's enemies were growing more and more bloody and repugnant. But again, for Americans, it was a question of who the regime's opponents were—potential allies or Islamic terrorists? We had to attempt to find out the character and intentions of those who would assume power if Assad were ousted.

The conflict built: By the time I began my journey into Sirte, Libya, dozens of Syrian citizens were being killed on a daily basis by the government. Children were being tortured and families murdered by the hundreds. The world demanded that the killing stop, but Assad did not.

I knew what the growing influence of the Muslim Brotherhood meant—they would step into the vacuum of power if the dictator fell, just as they had in Egypt.

Congresswoman Myrick and I had discussed Syria during our briefings. I had offered to do what we did in Libya: find out who the players were and report back the stated needs of the opposition. Once again I received an official letter authorizing us to generate a report on the uprising and the rebel groups, which meant that D and I would need to get on the ground and meet them eyeball-to-eyeball.

My main concern was getting in and out unscathed. In Libya we contended against one enemy—Qadhafi's forces. But in Syria we'd be up against Assad's men; Hizbollah, whose organization included a truly professional intelligence service; and against the Iranians. This was going to be a different enemy, an extremely complex situation where finding trustworthy allies would present a complicated challenge.

As those around me concentrated on Qadhafi, I had already mentally turned the page.

CHAPTER 13

Building a Spy: The Foundations

[redacted] 1991
CIA Training Facility

FINALLY, I WAS WHERE I WANTED TO BE, TRAINING. I had done Washington and I wanted to see if I could cut the real stuff, the meat of being a CIA operator. I relished the thought of banging my head up against the best when I got to the Farm in 1991 as a twenty-one-year-old and still working my way through college at the same time.

The Gulf War had blown up that year and, like millions, I watched as the F-117 stealth strike aircraft hit Baghdad with an astonishing display of high-tech bombs and missiles. There were Hail Mary movements across the desert and an air war like none seen before. We vanquished the Iraqi navy and crippled the Iraqi air force and in that short time frame the world saw what the United States of America was now capable of accomplishing. It was a war that vividly demonstrated the changing technology. There were two ways to fight the United States—stupidly and asymmetrically. Saddam chose to put his military on the battlefield with the only superpower in the world and go toe-to-toe; he fought stupidly and we put boot to ass. But the cost of conventional warfare was escalating. Americans were less willing to commit to engagements where troops would lose their lives.

The era of drone warfare was on the horizon, as was a new breed of fighting specialists so highly trained and equipped that each one was as explosive in the field as the most destructive weapons of my grandfather's generation. The increasing reliance on this new kind of operator would mark the course of my career. These were men trained for covert, strategically devastating missions that advanced our cause against our nation's enemies quickly and efficiently without the movement of huge numbers of troops and the risk of thousands of lives. By the time I got back to the Farm, the first war with Iraq was officially over, but the bombings and killings raged on. Bad guys of all stripes were flowing into Baghdad, and because I was now submerged and isolated from the rest of the world during training, I lost track of it all.

I was entering a world of its own, the kind of place that, for many, existed only on the big screen, on TV, or in novels. For me it was all becoming real. I was focused and wanted to know everything the CIA could teach me.

Reaching the near-empty parking lot circled on my map by the SPO (security protective officer) at the front gate, I checked in to my quarters—a dorm-style room, twin beds, a desk, a chair, and a bathroom connecting to the room next door. The dorm rooms had no locks—integrity and honesty were expected. Rumors suggested another reason for the lack of security: we could be kidnapped at will during the SERE (survival, evasion, resistance, and escape) phase of training . . . but again, rumors abounded.

Located in Virginia and surrounded by what has to be the longest single chain-link, barbed-wire-topped fence on the East Coast, this unique facility teaches breaking laws—not U.S. laws, but those of every foreign government in the world. Espionage—spying—is illegal in every country on the planet, and this place was spycraft's Harvard.

To the left of the dorm sat the gym, with its massive free-weight section, basketball court, speed bag, and heavy bags. Across the grass was the cafeteria, where I walked in to find the milk machine and got the coldest, best-tasting chocolate milk I ever had. Inside, I also noticed a large accordion-style wall pushed back. This separated the main dining hall from a separate space where students going through immersion language training on the post could eat with people speaking their language and thus stay focused and not be distracted by English during meals. There was also a simple bar at the Student Recreation Building. It felt like a sports bar out in the real world, except it was self-serve—not a waitress in sight, just a bartender.

Classes on the Farm ranged from the Basic Operations and Paramilitary courses, to the Countering Terrorist Tactics class, affectionately known as the crash-and-bang course, along with foreign-weapons training, explosives, tradecraft, driving, parachute jump training, surveillance, and a lot more. The system designed and churned out fully trained, certified case and paramilitary officers in about ████████ months.

Every small arms weapon, foreign or domestic, could be found in the armory. On the road to the ranges, hidden underneath two decades of vines and deer-infested weeds, a sharp-eyed observer could catch a glimpse of what we were told was the mock-up of the old U.S. Embassy in Tehran. According to legend, Delta Force trained here to rescue the hostages taken in 1979. Still visible were marks in the concrete at the top of the walls where the ropes were thrown over, as well as spike marks where the assaulters climbed up.

If you knew what to look for, you might see students from the Farm ████████████████████████ practicing surveillance detection runs, brush passes, dead drops, and other esoteric skills needed for espionage in nearby cities and towns. Training in advanced paramilitary skills is the responsibility of several other secret locations, ████████████████████████████ Here courses such as █████ Explosives █████ were taught, where students learned not only to make improvised explosives, but also to use conventional explosives to destroy unique targets like fixed missile sites.

Our class was bused to a large warehouse near an old, abandoned set of train tracks. Inside we lined up and gave our sizes to a group of old ladies behind large tables piled high with cardboard boxes brimming with combat jungle boots, pants, caps, and shirts. They tossed me new U.S. Army camouflage BDUs, short for battle dress uniforms, and a pair of jungle combat boots one size too large. There were no name tags, no ranks—just the uniforms, and I'd spend the next part of my life in them.

The Farm creates intelligence officers and other operators for the future, but it retains a foot in the past. Most of what is cutting-edge derives from what has been: if you're going to fire a Stinger missile, it would be a good idea to already know how to shoot a gun, and whether you're in Normandy or Bamako, you absolutely had better not get lost. Thus our training started with learning how to navigate on land using a compass, protractor, and topographic map, or "topo." The handheld GPS was a thing of the future in 1990, so we learned how to do it old-school—which back then was simply just school.

The concept was simple enough. For example, one method to figure out where you are is by looking around for hills or other terrain features and then finding those same hills on your map. Once you've found two of them, you point your compass at each one, read the degrees off the compass—that's called an "azimuth"—and then do a simple bit of math to get what's called a "back azimuth." Once you've got your back azimuth, you place your protractor on the map and draw a line from the hill back along the back azimuth, then do the same to the other hill and where those two lines intersect is your location.

Don't have a map or compass and it's nighttime? If you can see a crescent moon, take the two points and draw an imaginary line toward the horizon and it will generally point to the south if you're in the Northern Hemisphere, and just the opposite if you're down under. If you're above the equator in the Northern Hemisphere you can also locate the Big Dipper (Ursa Major)—it of course looks like a big cup with seven stars creating a long handle. The two outer stars of the cup are the pointers—think of it as that part of the "cup" you'd clink if toasting someone. If you drew an imaginary line between them roughly five times their combined distance from each other, you'd be right on the North Star (Polaris). Once you find it, stretch out your arms to find east and west, and south will be directly behind you. Then, if you can see the horizon, stick your fist out in front of you and count how many fists are between it and the North Star. Each fist is roughly 10 degrees, so if you counted four you'd be at about 40 degrees latitude, about the same latitude as Denver, Colorado. If you're south of the equator, you look for the Southern Cross; it's a bit more complicated, but doable. In an urban area? Most television satellites orbit around the equator, so check rooftops for satellite TV dishes to tell north or south. In the daytime we learned how to take two sticks and use the sun to find direction, and even an analog wristwatch—aim the hour hand at the sun, find the center point of the angle between the hour hand and the number 12 on the watch—that's the north–south line.

The instructors gave us eight- and ten-digit grid coordinates that we would have to locate on the map and then go find them on our own. We ran land navigation on foot with a compass and map both day and night—it was great, sweaty, exhausting, mosquito-bitten fun. For the final exercise, we were given a ton of points and told to find them—wearing fifty-pound rucksacks. They were miles apart through swamps, hills, pine forests, bramble bushes, and thickets, and it took all day and into the night. A lean marine captain from Force Recon, named Jake, became my training partner. At least ten years older than me, he sported a ragged-looking scar on his left bicep, which he said had been chopped in half during a parachuting accident. We became fast friends, and if we had the time and energy, we'd run the back roads together on the infrequent days off.

I learned to field-strip U.S. and foreign weapons in the daylight, then with a blindfold. Once, as an impromptu competition, our instructors broke us up into teams of two and took an ███ machine gun, an ███ rifle, and a ███ pistol and laid them on a poncho liner. It didn't take long to figure out what came next. Jake and I were a team and he was first up. On the whistle, he ran twenty-five yards to the poncho, where another instructor shoved a black pillowcase over his head and he had to disassemble all three weapons as fast he could. I watched intently, until I saw his hand shoot up. Then I took off. When a black hood was forced over my head, I started to reassemble the mass of gun parts.

Sweat dripped into my eyes and I could hear my two competitors, on my right and left, running and sliding into position to start on their piles. I started with the large M60 pieces because they were easier to locate in the mass of springs and tubes. Finished, I did a functions check on the big gun, laid it aside, and started in on the M16 rifle as I heard Jake urging me on.

Again I started with the big pieces, setting the plastic hand guards in place, then finding the T-shaped charging handle and laying it into the upper receiver upside down in my lap. I searched for the bolt, popped it into the bolt carrier, dropped in the firing pin, pushed the cam into place, and shoved in the cotter pin that held the firing pin. Then I gave the whole assembly a sling downward to seat it all. I felt the cam. Somehow I'd gotten it oriented correctly. Just then an instructor blew an air horn as another threw dirt and shot us all with a water hose. I wasn't going to be distracted—I just had to set these pieces in place, check that they worked, then finish the pistol and I'd be done.

The point of the competition was to get us working under pressure without using our eyes. You had to be able to strip a weapon down in total darkness, whether to fix it during a fight or just to maintain it. Unlike a military unit, we would often be on our own with no one to rely on but ourselves. Jake and I came in first place.

Years later we coated our weapons externally with green OD Teflon, but the inner working parts were coated in black Teflon. Teflon protects the weapon but keeps it lubricated in dry, sandy places without needing as much gun oil, which attracts grit and dust. The colors were for a reason, too. OD green didn't absorb heat energy from the sun as much as black, so it wouldn't show up if the enemy looked at you with night vision. Black soaked it up like crazy and glowed white-hot under NVGs. So coating the internal parts with black helped us when cleaning weapons and stripping the guns in the dark because we could do it with NVGs and see them all very well, but the green kept us hidden from view when moving around. Any advantage we could get, we took.

The CIA has a paramilitary capability, certainly. But the primary job is to collect intelligence. In fact, before 9/11, most IOs never carried a gun unless they were in a war zone or a high-risk area of the world. Before you can carry a weapon, you have to get qualified. What happens at the Farm is similar to army basic weapons training, but the CIA goes way beyond just shooting at targets three hundred yards out with an M16. Our class eventually worked up to shooting on the move, from moving vehicles, into other vehicles, and while seated, standing, kneeling, prone, and even running. This was just the warm-up act where we got to know the weapons and the seven fundamentals of shooting—grip, stance, sight alignment, sight picture, trigger control, breathing, and follow-through. If a shooter follows and applies them correctly, he can only blame his gun or the ammo for failing to hit the target.

We spent another week learning the agency's method for hand-to-hand combat. It was simple, concise, and effective. The system was focused on immediate stop techniques: strikes to the three main systems that would end a fight—walking, breathing, and seeing. If you took out anyone of these, you ended the fight immediately. It was the same concept that Doug had taught me years earlier. Kick a guy's knee in and he can't chase you. Ram your fingers into his eyes and he gets myopically focused on whether his eyes will ever work again. Slam your elbow into a man's windpipe and his world shrinks down to his primary focus—breathing. By now we were shooting fast, lifting heavy, running long, and fighting hard. Like Red said once, "Suck it up now and you won't have to suck it in later."

EXPLOSIVES AND BREACHING

Our first day of explosives training started off by walking down to a small building overlooking a large, blackened, sunken dirt pit with a few wrecked cars and vans at the bottom. We passed through the door and as soon as our first classmate stepped inside, a small explosive charge went off right above his head near the ceiling. The instructors had set up a booby trap. Inside, stadium-like bleachers overlooked a large angled picture window made of plastic. From this perch we had a ringside view of the pit with the mangled vehicles in it. We all gingerly looked under our seats, though, just to make sure we weren't going to get our pants blown off.

The thickly muscled instructor, who looked like he was missing a neck, came up front wearing a navy blue T-shirt that read LIE, DENY, AND MAKE COUNTERACCUSATIONS. He looked like he could probably have bench-pressed the van in the pit. He talked about explosives, what they could do, and how they could be used. Then he started the show—he blew up the van with C-4 plastic explosives, then he set off a claymore mine, and then another charge took out the car. I was hooked—explosives were awesome.

Eventually, we were bused ████████████ for more intensive explosive work. We learned how to make field-expedient charges out of products easily found in a pharmacy or home swimming pool, and much more.

Many years later, I would add to my knowledge of explosives by learning ██ ██ ███████████████ I also learned the difference between electrical and nonelectrical firing devices. ████████████████████████ ██████████████████████████████████████

We learned to breach door hinges, locks, and knobs with a shotgun and how to do quick assessments of target doors. Which way did it open? If you could see the hinges, it opened toward you; if not then it went away from you. Was the knob on the right or left side of the door? Doors inside a structure, like bedroom doors, usually opened into their room, so the hinges weren't visible. If you could see them, it was likely a closet too small to allow the door to open inward. Those things mattered if you were breaking into a place, breaching and entering the room—you didn't want the door opening back into your face or to have your team rush into a broom closet.

If you want to kick open a door, you had better think long and hard about it. Is it metal or solid wood? If so, and you kick it, you'll likely just hurt yourself. But if it's not, then kick it right next to the doorknob, with the goal of having the plunger tear through the thin wood holding it in the door itself. When you do decide to kick it, turn around and kick it like a mule—you get more power that way and if it caves in, you won't have your leg stuck through a hole in the door, getting shot to shreds on the other side.

SHOOTING

I really enjoy shooting, whether rifles, shotguns, or pistols—it was something I grew up doing. We killed birds, squirrel, rabbits, and anything else we could shoot with our BB guns. Once, my dad told me to stop shooting the birds because there were basically none left on our entire farm—I'd killed them all and no more would come around. Then, when I was old enough, Todd and I took our .22 rifle, which we'd saved up to buy from Flint's Hardware, and headed a few miles down the gravel road to the trash dump—it was the best place to shoot rats, lots of them. Down below us in the gulley they were running around everywhere; we'd tear them up.

But now I was learning how to *really* shoot from the greatest combat shooting instructors in the world, and Red was one of the best. He had a no-nonsense manner and was able to diagnose a shooter's problems after watching you pull the trigger only two or three times. He was a large man with close-cropped red hair and I'd heard he was a marine prior to joining CIA. Red was a veteran of the paramilitary staff, serving since way before I was born, and he knew his business. He and his cadre taught us how to operate all sorts of foreign and U.S.-made weapons.

The weapons we'd initially be qualified to carry were those the station would likely have in the armory for use in case the place was ever attacked, like what happened in Iran and Vietnam. These included the Browning Hi-Power 9 mm pistol and the Winchester pump-action twelve-gauge shotgun. Many locations, Red admitted, would still have the old revolver, which was why I'd been shooting that in the hotel room exercise earlier.

We shot on outdoor firing ranges rain or shine, but it was under a covering that, we were told, was to keep enemy spy satellites at bay. The training initially taught shooting a Modified Weaver stance, where the shooting arm is straight and the support arm bent—the same way Jason Bourne shoots in the movies. When firing, they wanted us to push forward with our shooting arm and pull back with the other, all while standing with our bodies turned at a 45-degree angle to our targets and our heads bent slightly to align the gun sight. This push-pull concept was supposed to create a more stable shooting platform. The technique was soon replaced by the Modified Isosceles, which features both arms outstretched, the weapon gripped with pressure from both hands and no push-pull going on. It's a much more natural and effective way to shoot, especially under stress—Jason Bourne was wrong.

Techniques like these, as well as equipment, are studied, analyzed, and tweaked constantly. You ask three questions of any tactic, technique, or process, whether in shooting, in business, or even mowing your grass. First, will it work? In other words, will the way I'm doing it get the job done? Second, is it necessary? In other words, is there a better, more efficient way to do it? Finally, can I do it under stress? A negative answer to any of these questions means you toss that technique until you find a way to do it that leads to three yes answers.

Will it work? Is it necessary? Can I do it under stress?

Here's how you might apply it: People argued and even fought over which stance was better—the Jason Bourne way or the Modified Isosceles. Most of the debate came from guys who'd argue over whether professional wrestling was real and who'd never been shot at, nor shot at someone else. Regardless, passions on the subject ran high in the shooting world. To resolve it, apply the three questions. The Weaver stance was created out of a desire to give the shooter a solid grip—the straight arm was supposed to replicate the stock of a rifle and the push-and-pull action was to help keep the gun stable. On top of that, people have been shooting people using the Weaver stance for years. So yes, it worked, and yes, and it could be done under stress. But was it necessary to do it that way? No.

Why? Weaver says you have to have the push-pull to steady the gun—to hit, in other words. Therefore, by default, that must mean that you can't shoot with one hand, because there's nothing pulling back. But you can shoot one-handed; it's been done for ages. So no, the push-pull wasn't necessary—meaning the Weaver failed this part of the analysis. Another problem with the technique was that they wanted us to lower our heads to line up with the gun sights. That's a waste of critical microseconds—you bring the gun to your face, not your face to the gun. That eliminates one more moving part in the shooting equation. So that part of the technique was also unnecessary—it was another failure under the analysis. Yet another failure was turning 45 degrees to your target—that just exposed the shooter's armpit—a deadly area to take a bullet. But standing square to the target, the Modified Isosceles way, made maximum use of the shooter's body armor and didn't expose the armpits. So that was a third failure under the analysis.

Examining processes, techniques, and tactics forces real answers to serious questions—all in an effort to make things better, more efficient, and faster. But the crux is that if you could hit, whether shooting Weaver, Isosceles, or carrying five red balloons in one hand while riding a unicycle, then do not change what you're doing if you're hitting, because the goal is to win the fight—you don't get points for style.

To practice shooting, we started off on a range with wooden frames built out of two-by-fours in the shape of a lowercase *h*. The long side of the h allowed us to practice shooting from behind cover—such as from a door on both the left and right sides. The horizontal part of the h provided a kneeling horizontal barricade, like the hood of a car, and the bottom of the h was covered plywood with just a shoe-box-size hole cut in it. This let us practice shooting through something like the vent in an office door. We had to make a certain number of shots in the kill zone on the paper targets within a set time frame. We shot kneeling, and prone, and graduated to shooting from behind real doors and through real windows and over car hoods. We learned that when shooting over a car hood, you don't lean over the top of the hood and rest on it, like Starsky and Hutch. You backed away from it, because incoming fire might strike the engine block, which slopes upward, then hit and deflect off the engine up through the hood, throwing lead and engine frag into your face, arms, and chest.

That's all part of terminal ballistics—what a bullet does when it hits something. When a bullet hits a wall, it doesn't necessarily ricochet off at an angle opposite the one it came in on, like a cue ball on a pool table. It can actually hug the surface of the wall or ground for a while and travel along that surface. The principle didn't apply just to vertical surfaces, either—we applied it to shooting under cars. If the enemy was using a vehicle for cover, we could fire at the concrete or asphalt in front of the car, about where the shadow line would be on the ground at midday. Our incoming rounds would chew underneath, sending bullet, asphalt, and gravel into the legs and ankles of the enemy shooters. Then you did it again to send the same thing back into their bodies after they fell from having their legs chewed up.

We learned to shoot not only under cars, but into them, studying the effects of the glass and doors on the bullet—more application of terminal ballistics. If I were facing a vehicle and shot into the windshield with my 9 mm pistol, aiming at the chest of the guy in the front seat, the bullet would actually hit him somewhere in the lower abdomen, depending on how far away I was. The reason is that the underside of the cone-shaped bullet would make first contact with the glass, dragging the bullet down slightly. So, to hit a target sitting in a car in the chest when you're shooting at him while facing his car, you aim at his face. That worked for nearly all pistol rounds. If you're shooting a rifle like an M4, whose bullets travels a lot faster, the bullet won't drop that much, and it was basically point of aim, point of impact—where you aimed was where he'd get hit.

We trained to fight from a vehicle, as well. Our first choice when faced with a threat is to escape or run him over. But there were times when a car might not move fast enough, or it might not work at all—it could be shot up, broken down, boxed in by other vehicles or roadblocks, or just out of gas. In those cases, we needed to know how to fight from a vehicle quickly, then to get away from it and to another position of cover.

If faced with a threat coming at you from the front of the car, most law enforcement officers were taught to crack the door open and fire through the V-notch created by the open door and the frame of the car.

But that takes extra time—drawing the weapon from a seated position, opening the door, positioning the weapon in the V-notch, aiming, taking the shot—and time is opportunity for the bad guy. Instead, we fired straight through the windshield, right over the top of the steering wheel. The first round punched a hole in the glass and we'd dump a hailstorm of bullets through it. We did it with handguns, but the most fun was having two of us with the German ■■■ submachine guns throwing a maelstrom of lead through the windshield at simulated attackers from the front at the same time. You didn't want to be the guy in the right seat—that little submachine gun spews out hot brass at an amazing rate. But the windows were wrecked, as were the targets downrange.

Yet again, terminal ballistics comes into play when shooting from inside the vehicle. The glass affected that bullet in ways you couldn't anticipate without testing it first. It was just the opposite of how a bullet reacted when firing into the car. This time the top of the bullet's nose would come into first contact with the windshield, due to the angle of the window. That would drag the bullet upward, which meant that to hit a man in the chest with a pistol I had to place my front sight on his belt and fire. This would result in the bullet landing in his chest area, depending on how far away he was. The reason was the same as before, just inverted. If you didn't understand the effects of these materials on bullets, you could get yourself or your teammate killed.

Jake grew up in the South, like I did, and we were regularly the top shots in the class, competing for first place nearly every day. He beat me by one point on the final shooting. Not bad for a guy still too young to take a legal drink.

We studied legal and illegal vehicle checkpoints and how roadblocks were laid out with chase cars and blocking cars—we called them VCPs and IVCPs. We were taught tactics for running them and fighting from them—all worst-case scenarios. One method was the ■■■-gun technique. The assumption was that we were in hostile territory, had pistols, and also had a rifle or shotgun hidden in the vehicle ■■■.

It went like this—assume you're driving a left-side steering wheel vehicle and are stopped and approached from the driver's window. Your window goes down and your hands immediately go up in the surrender pose right into the face of the road guard and you're putting on the show of your life—acting scared, intimidated. This hopefully makes him see you as no threat. He asks for your papers, and you say you're going to unbuckle your seat belt to get your papers from your pocket. Slowly, as you maintain eye contact and keep talking to the guard at your window, you move both hands toward the seat belt release. Your left hand is a distraction for the road guard, giving him something to look at as it goes for the buckle release, while your right grabs the pistol from under your thigh. All this happens in one motion. Then, quickly, you bring both hands back up to the window in a double-hand grip on the weapon and dump the entire magazine into him at point-blank range. What you've also just done is to release your seat belt so you can get out quickly. We sometimes even wore our seat belts under our armpit to keep from getting our arm tangled in it on a hasty exit. So after you've shot the crap out of the guy you throw the gun into the floorboard if you can't bring it with you: there is no sense giving the bad guys another gun to use right away.

Then you'd either stomp the gas and drive off, or if the way ahead was blocked, you would yell, "Bail! Bail! Bail!" to everyone else in the car. Often we'd run it with four people in the car and that was great, chaotic fun. Everyone would start bailing out through the doors on the opposite side from the road guard and begin firing on any target with a gun while moving to covered positions around the car. The two in the backseat went out the same rear door, while the two up front went out the passenger's door. One went to the rear fender and started firing, another to the front fender; the third man got down behind the now-open rear door and tossed smoke grenades over the car to conceal our movements, while the fourth was turned around facing away from the action—or outboard, as we called it—searching for a place for the group to run to next.

Once he found it, he'd yell the direction and distance and we'd bound in groups of two, kick in a door if it was a structure, take over the space inside, turn around, and set up new shooting positions to cover the other two so they could run back to us. When they heard us shooting, they'd turn and run toward us through the open door and file past, taking up other positions or searching for a way out the back so we could continue to bound away from the fight and escape. It was mad, organized, lethal chaos that relied on speed, surprise, and overwhelming, accurate fire-power at the outset to gain the tactical advantage on the folks manning the roadblocks. We weren't prepared to fight a sustained battle—we just didn't have that much firepower. But when you take four of our guys who can shoot, move, and communicate, then give us the edge of surprise and overwhelming, instant violence, you should place your money on us.

Once we were proficient and qualified on the various weapons, the training moved into the agency's kill house—or shoot house, as it would be called later, just in case someone got the wrong idea about the intent of the training. Personally, "kill house" was probably the best name for it. The house was covered—but was large, a truly huge group of rooms contained in the largest tire house I'd ever seen. The whole exterior was covered in stacked car tires filled with sand and dirt. That's what kept the bullets from coming through the walls. Inside there was a bar, hotel rooms, den, office, school—all were replicated. This was the place I found myself after finishing up the hotel room exercise for Red with Baldy and Blue Coveralls.

Red and I entered the classroom a few yards from the shoot house, and he told me to take a seat. Another instructor, a former Special Forces lieutenant colonel, flipped on a TV, killed the lights, and told us we were going to watch my little Jerry Springer session in the No-Comfort-Inn on video.

I watched as the guys broke into the room and flipped the lights on. There was lots of yelling, three shots, then another three. Just as I was moving toward the first door, the instructor paused the VCR. The colonel noted that my first three shots looked good; they hit the guy in a vital spot. But he pointed out that I shot a guy armed with a rolled-up newspaper—not a stick. Then he said that the second guy, the one I thought was attacking me with the chain, was actually surrendering and that I shouldn't have shot him, either—and when looking at the video playback I could see it all very clearly. Basically, the only thing he did like was my shot placement—shooting them both in the face, instead of the body.

The logic was simple—you shoot a person in order to stop him from doing something. The goal was to stop their actions as quickly as possible. Shooting someone in the torso—even a heart shot—simply meant that you were bleeding him to death, and that took precious time. During those moments a person can do a lot of damage. I'd witnessed this principle hunting white-tailed deer. You can blow a deer's heart out and they'll run for hundreds of yards, even miles, trailing blood the whole time until they die from blood loss—a sort of natural loss of hydraulic pressure.

Similarly, an attacker can keep functioning before he dies from blood loss. Sure, it depends on where he's been hit—hit an artery and it gets pumped out faster; give him a head wound but miss the critical part of the brain and it will take longer because of the smaller, spread-out capillaries, which don't carry a ton of blood volume. He could continue firing, set off a bomb, run you over in a car, stab you, or even beat you to death with your own gun—all of which has happened before. To make matters worse, if he is wearing body armor and you've just shot him in the body, you will now have one pissed-off attacker moving with even more of a purpose—a much harder shot to make.

But if you shoot someone in the teeth or the nose, the bullet goes straight back, basically unhindered, except for a few teeth and soft tissue in the back of the throat, into the brain stem—the medulla oblongata, as the medical professionals call it. That's the critical, essential area that controls motor functions. If that's hit, all activity stops. It's like pulling the power cord. Blood loss isn't a factor because you've just made a CNS hit—the central nervous system. In other words, that guy's CPU just took a bullet and his computer just shut down. From the side? Shoot them in the earlobe. From the back? Hit the base of the skull. All this is called proper shot placement. You can kill someone with a .22-caliber, a twelve-gauge, a .50-cal, a BB, your fist, or even theoretically with a needle if you hit this spot precisely and with the right amount of velocity behind it.

The next point the instructor focused our attention on was that the hands and then the waistline of the threat—not the face, the voice, or anything else—are what kills. When you're in a shooting, it happens in seconds and can be over in less. It's violent and fast, and the results are obviously designed to be fatal. Split-second decisions about whether to shoot somebody have to be simplified because the brain can only take in so much in a compressed amount of time.

So you come into the room taking the path of least resistance, your teammate goes in the opposite direction, and you both clear your corners scanning for threats. Once you locate them, your eyes drive straight to the hands and waistline of anyone you see to determine if they're armed, whether with gun, knife, stick, grenade, or detonator. If you see one, your gun sight tracks to their faces, the trigger gets pressed until they aren't there anymore, and they get dropped as hard and fast as possible. It doesn't matter if they're men or women, old or young—they all can kill you. You shoot them in the teeth, the base of the head, the upper chest and throat or the earlobe—depending on how you find them—pressing the trigger until they aren't there anymore. It's not like TV or Hollywood, where Steven Seagal comes in, shoots twice, and moves on. You shoot until they go away. If that means emptying a magazine into them, reloading, and shooting them again, then you do that. The goal is to shoot them until they stop doing what you shot them for in the first place.

A team of the best shooters in the world, in a hostile country, moving quietly through a building from multiple directions, in the inky blackness of the night, under the highest stress you can imagine, all while making decisions on who lives and dies in milliseconds upon seeing that person, and then consistently nailing threats in the teeth with precise gunfire, isn't magic or about being superhuman; it's about training, rules, and rehearsals.

Training is shooting, moving, communicating over and over until your hands bleed, feet blister, and body gives out. Rehearsals are conducted on mock-ups of the target until it can be done in your sleep, time permitting. Rules are kept simple. For example, rules of engagement for the CIA's shooters on the bin Laden hit allowed shooting anyone with a weapon, anyone displaying hostile intent, and for UBL himself, he was a status-based target [redacted]

[redacted].

In the real world, the hit rate for police officers is less than 20 percent, which means that more than four of every five bullets miss and go somewhere else. It's not necessarily the individual police officer's fault, either. I have many friends who work in law enforcement and they are solid men and women who do a terrific job. But the training opportunities at most departments are not what they should be, because many times the budget is spent on shiny objects like cruisers with new paint schemes so the chief can point to something that he spent taxpayer money on when asked by the city council. But it'd be far better to spend that money on training now than on settlements to lawsuits later.

During training at the Farm, we shot until our hands bled—in fact, I've got a scar to this very day from it. We trained hard and long on shoot/no-shoot situations in buildings and in cars, and in low light, no light, and daylight. Hands, waist, weapon, front sight, press-press-press, and move—we repeated that over and over, then watched it on video. At first we spoke to one another during an assault, calling out that we were moving, or that we needed a breacher, or that we had an open door here or there. But then we progressed to saying nothing at all—just moving, shooting, and hand signals; but most of the time everyone knew what was needed without comms at all because everyone was doing what we called "looking for work." Besides, if you were in a foreign country conducting a clandestine raid, speaking American English would be what those in law enforcement call a clue about who was behind it.

Long gone was the instruction on instinctive shooting, also called "point shooting," which promoted being able to fire without using the sights—just basically pointing the weapon in the direction of the threat and firing.

Pulling my hand from a hot pot—that's instinct; moving away from a snake—that's definitely in my DNA somewhere. But nothing is instinctive about drawing a mechanical device from a concealed holster, raising it to your head, lining up the rear sight, front sight, and the target all while you and your target are moving in different directions over uneven terrain, and then pulling a trigger and causing an explosion to launch a chunk of metal to intersect that moving object many yards away from you all in under 1.5 seconds; that is decidedly not instinctive to human beings. So the agency worked hard on training us to find the target, find the hands, find the waist, use the sights, and eliminate the threat.

Delta, ST6, and ■ worked this like no one else. It all became second nature, to the point that when I walked around in public, whether a mall, on the sidewalk, or even in church, I'd scan the hands and waistline of everyone coming my way looking for anything that could be a weapon. It just became a way of living—hands and waistline first, everything else second.

TRAINING WAS NONSTOP AND VOLUMINOUS, with no concept of eating the elephant one bite at a time—we basically had a feeding tube shoved down our throats and were force-fed the entire pachyderm. It was like drinking water from a fire hose—you retained a bit; you lost more. Or, as my fellow classmates described it, "like throwing crap at a wall—some's gonna stick, some won't." We just hoped the right crap stuck, because we were tested all the time—written tests, oral exams, and practical exercises. All were graded, and we lived and died by the results. I came in wondering if I could handle it—if I could make the grade. I started off keeping to myself, not talking to anyone, mainly because I had more self-doubt than I would have admitted and didn't want anyone to know. The training was hard and sometimes my progress was slow, but quitting wouldn't speed it up.

CHAPTER 14

The Battle for Sirte

September 26, 2011
Sirte, Libya

THE SKY WAS A SOMBER SLATE GRAY, and sand dunes and date palms dotted the road on all sides, but the bright spot in the day was news that Benghazi and Tripoli were in rebel hands, Qadhafi and his family were on the run, and we were managing a network of informants supplying good information on where the rats were running. D and I were here to eyeball the battle and report back on its development to Washington. We suited up in our Crye Precision CAGE body armor getting ready to go to work. It's the best I've worn; it hugged like a turtle's shell and had a slim profile allowing me to wear local clothing on top of it without looking like the Michelin guy. Today, we use their AirLite plate carriers that can be rolled up and stuffed in a pocket for travel—an amazing design.

Our plates were top-of-the-line ceramic composite that could stop an AK round. I had three rifle-mag pouches built into the carrier and three more attached to the front of those; my radio was hooked up and my pistol was locked into place. I preferred having it on my chest rig. I could get to it easier in a vehicle, plus it wouldn't scrape and bang into things when I was running around or crawling over pavement, rocks, or concrete. Underneath and behind my front plate was a slim trauma kit that could be yanked out from the bottom of my carrier to stop bleeding. On my back was a sleeve holding my CamelBak water bladder, with the drinking tube running over my left shoulder, buried into the shoulder straps. I had my Medford TS-1 knife threaded into the MOLLE strips on my right side of the plate carrier.

"Radio check, radio check," I heard through my earpiece. "Lima Charlie, how me?" I said back to D, short for "I hear you loud and clear, how do you hear me?" "Good to go, boss," he said. We wrapped keffiyehs around our heads and lower faces to hopefully help us blend at a distance, not to mention keeping out the sun and sand.

It was the start of a busy day—a day the end of which neither D nor I could have imagined. We knew what we expected to see: we were back in Libya, heading into Sirte, where the war with Qadhafi was at its ugliest and perhaps bloodiest moment.

A huge Libyan we had started calling Goliath held his massive PK machine gun, bipod attached, in his right hand, Rambo-style. His partner, nicknamed Beckham for his love of soccer, was also ready to roll with his AK and a 9 mm pistol. He had on a cheap black tactical vest, sans body armor. Both men were rebel combat veterans whom we'd started referring to as the Brothers Grimm—both were out, having left to visit a friend of theirs at the local hospital.

I powered-up the Panasonic Toughbook, pulled up Google Earth, loaded our GPS coordinates into it, and zoomed in on our current location.

D and I had been back in North Africa for only thirty-six hours, arriving in the seaside town of Misrata—yet again with no passport stamps and aboard the *Al-Entisar*. Misrata, specifically Tripoli Street, was a scene of postapocalyptic destruction after a long, hard-fought battle that started in February and lasted until the rebels finally took the seaport four months later. Two thousand rebels and civilians had died, with nearly a thousand others wounded.

Silverback walked into the room as we were getting ready to go. He said that part of the dictator's family had made it into Algeria and Niger, both safe havens, and that the dictator's son Saif had escaped Tripoli and that he believed father and son were hiding and regrouping. Everything we knew, and what everyone believed, was that Qadhafi had returned to Sirte, the base of his tribal support.

Suddenly we all heard the squeal of brakes and an engine getting cut off; then the Brothers Grimm rushed in. From a wounded man they had heard that the rebels in Sirte had the enemy surrounded and were sending rockets into their positions. Their source had been running forward when a truck blew up next to him. Small arms fire hit others and they basically withdrew.

Silverback shifted slightly as he sat on the carpet, legs folded. "There is a big battle going on right now in Sirte," he explained. "The fighters have made good progress and if we can beat them there, we will win this—it will basically all be over except for a few small pockets of resistance."

Then Silverback asked, "Would you come speak to a commander there?"

D and I looked at each other briefly—we both knew we were going—and I nodded yes. As we piled our gear into a two-tone Mitsubishi L200 pickup truck, I wondered if I was about to get the crap shot out of me again.

ARRIVING IN THE CITY OF SIRTE, which sits halfway between Tripoli and Benghazi, I saw plumes of thick black smoke rising from across the horizon to the northeast. As we drew closer, the muffled thuds and crumps from ordnance being sent downrange transformed into massive, ear-splitting explosions as we both stuffed ear plugs into our ears. We passed artillery pieces lined up among rows and rows of palm trees, their long gun tubes aimed skyward toward the city, belching out orange balls of fire and smoke, shaking the ground and slinging palm fronds against their moorings as the gunners turned away, plugging their ears with their fingers with each pull of the firing lanyard.

Muammar Qadhafi's hometown was about 155 miles east of Misrata. It had taken us nearly four hours to get there. The city was under rebel siege from both the east and west, pinning Qadhafi's forces in with their backs to the Gulf of Sidra. They had nowhere to go. The town of Bani Walid, to the west, also would be addressed, but Sirte was the main goal and the real holdout. The day before, the rebels had launched a surprise attack using rockets, artillery, the crazy, hand-painted Mad Max truck-mounted weapon platforms, tanks, and a ragged-looking batch of infantry, all supported by NATO jets overhead. They almost reached the city center, with rebel armor pounding shells right into the middle of town to pave the way for the advancing ground troops. From the east came the rebel version of the cavalry—pickup trucks with men hanging from the rails wearing wife-beater shirts, bandannas, baseball caps, and flip-flops, and all carrying rifles and RPGs. They launched themselves forward to try to clear outlying farms and buildings as they too advanced on the enemy forces.

The advance had stalled in one section of the city today, though. Qadhafi's artillery, rockets, and sniper fire were raining down on the rebels from somewhere near the coastal road where the spotters and pockets of resistance remained.

Our group began a slow, circuitous route south—there was no more fast driving. Silverback, who had gone ahead earlier, was there with the commander we were to meet. I double-checked on my Garmin for the exact location and showed Beckham the tiny onscreen map as he drove. He nodded. We could hear rockets screaming as they left firing tubes and the soft crump of explosions and the crackle of automatic weapons fire echoing across the city. We had to thread carefully through the fluid, shifting western lines, diverting south enough to not get hit by incoming artillery, and somehow pass through the front line of the eastern advancing troops without them thinking we were Qadhafi's fighters or mercenaries.

Sirte was vibrant with color. Dark green palms framed the skyline. A mosque with a yellowish gold tip drew the eye. Orange and red buildings mixed among the white and tan against the sky. Only upon close inspection would you notice the black blast marks surrounding a dark hole in the base of the mosque and bullet pockmarks on almost every building in sight. The sky seemed angry, too, as it billowed with thick, dark rain clouds and was streaked with contrails from fighter jets as well as billowing smoke from smoldering fires in the city center.

The Brothers' phone rang; they answered and were apparently being given directions on new areas to avoid as we looked for a safer place to enter the city and link up with Silverback. Progress was slow.

Beckham put his phone to his ear yet again, and then leaned back toward us and excitedly screamed above the noise, "We have the port! We just took the port!" He was beaming with pride. Goliath was hooting and yelling, punching the dashboard, and slapping the roof with sheer excitement.

D pushed out a SITREP on his BlackBerry to Colonel Cantwell to let him know about this strategically important victory, which cut Qadhafi supporters off from seaborne supplies and prevented them from fleeing over the water. Qadhafi's men couldn't go anywhere or do anything except fight or give up. But, from the way it looked, it seemed surrender wouldn't save them.

We passed a half-naked body on the side of the road lying facedown in the debris. A carpet had been partially thrown over it; a shoe was missing from one foot. We wound through a turn where the street was literally covered in empty shell casings. Virtually nothing had escaped the battle, as even the light poles had been shot to pieces, some were bent while others had completely given up and were lying across the road with holes the size of coffee cans punched in them from the big guns of the tanks. Buildings had lost their exterior walls, exposing the naked rooms inside and the remnants of the lives of those who used to live in them. Shells had torn holes in everything. I'd been in Afghanistan, the Balkans, Pakistan, Northern Ireland, and Iraq, and I'd never seen such destruction. It was a no-man's-land—just smoke, rubble, and the dead.

Beckham quickly made a tight turn, driving the truck into what looked like a beat-up old storage shed made of concrete blocks. We all squeezed out and left the shed, with Beckham rolling down the protective door and padlocking it. It was afternoon. As we made our way slowly up the alley in a staggered foot formation, Beckham was on point on the left; Goliath was about five yards behind him with the belt-fed weapon. Following them, D and I were spread out about the same distance apart but on the opposite side up near the buildings.

Rule number one in urban movement is to avoid open areas like the plague—don't move down the center of a street, alley, or brown zone, such as a Libyan park. If you can get into buildings and move through them, that's better. But we couldn't so we stuck to the edges of the road. The way we were moving allowed each two-man group to cover the other two across the road.

Rule number two is to try to move rapidly from one covered and concealed position to the next. But in reality, you either moved as slow as a snail so the bad guys didn't see you, or you moved as fast as humanly possible, so they couldn't shoot you if they did. The Brothers Grimm wanted to run all the time. It was like holding back greyhounds. If you rush around too much, you draw attention and get shot at—if the shooters are good, then you get hit.

The equation is simple—slow down. When you need to move fast, do it with all you've got, but know when the time is right to run. Otherwise, stay low, and move slow.

Every corner we reached worked the same way. We'd advance on a corner and everyone would stop. Goliath would do a slow turn to our rear to check that area. D would edge up on our side to get a look across the road around Beckham's upcoming turn and clear it for him, keeping his sights on the area. I'd then motion for Beckham to move up. He would ease up slowly, look across the road toward our corner, and clear it for us just like he'd watched D do. With Goliath still covering our rear, and once both corners were cleared, I'd motion for Beckham to move on out. He'd then scoot up and around into the next road or alleyway, with Goliath hearing him and following. After they did it a few times, we moved like clockwork and I didn't have to signal them to move; they just knew when to go.

There wasn't a person anywhere. It was as if everyone had just vanished in the last few days. It was eerie.

Beckham pointed to a building, saying we needed to move in that direction, toward the blown-out market and a concrete structure with a hole in the wall.

Rule number three: Know where you're going before you move from where you are; visually check out the place you're moving to—don't just run blindly from one spot to another. Think it through.

We slowly worked our way over toward the burned-out concrete thing that was once a building, each of our sights slowing tracking high, low, left, right. Perhaps it housed condos before the war, but now it was just full of holes, burned to a crisp with not one pane of glass in any of the windows. Beckham eased up to a hole in the wall and peeked inside.

Rule number four: Don't silhouette yourself, whether in an alley, a door, a window, or a rooftop. Come up to take a look from unexpected places—the corners of windows or using a periscope or mirror—but don't stick your skull up in the center of it.

While the rest of us took a knee and watched the streets in every direction for movement, Beckham motioned to follow, and he started into the structure with Goliath right on his tail. D and I rose and, after checking our rear area, we followed. We'd just stepped into the dark space behind the Brothers when someone shouted and opened fire . . . we heard shooting and screaming.

Someone opened fire from a room down a short hallway. "Contact front!" D and I both yelled out at almost the same time. Pieces of the ceiling showered down on all of us and we poured into the space. D went left, along the wall we came in on, weapon up. Behind him, my rifle to my cheek, I went opposite to the right.

The noise was deafening in the concrete room as guns roared from my front and right. Head up, gun up, elbows in, I swept my iron sights to the right, looking for threats, and then back toward the center of the room, my feet moving forward over rocks and debris, as I moved to the source of the noise. Goliath was flat in front of me and his PK machine gun was roaring as it spewed shell casings into the air; I stepped over his tree trunk legs. My brain briefly registered Beckham's shape off to my right, where he'd fallen down behind a flipped-over table, one hand up, his eyes squeezed shut as he blasted blindly toward the open area ahead.

The world seemed to slow down, like when they showed the bionic man running in the seventies TV series. I caught movement to the front and saw three unknowns, three shooters. One was down on the ground; then movement left caught my eye. My sights tracked over to blue jeans and a black T-shirt, scrambling with a rifle in his hand. As I brought my front sight post up through his torso, I continued to move forward, my brain talking to my body and making minute adjustments like a hawk as it dives on a mouse. My sights settled on him and the world tunneled down to just my rifle sights and the guy in front of me—I pressed the trigger four times. It felt like I could literally see the rounds leaving my muzzle and slamming into my target. I was vaguely aware of D cranking off rounds from his direction. My guy, Blue Jeans, dropped like a broken tombstone. Nearly at the same time the sound returned and my vision was back to taking in the world around me again as I looked around to find D and the Brothers.

What happened is common to police officers and soldiers the world over. The heart rate shoots up as an adrenaline-laced chemical cocktail is dumped into the bloodstream. Blood is shunted from the limbs to the core, making fine motor skills hard to execute, but the brain does an amazing thing—it shifts to what seems most important and blocks out the rest. If you need to see to shoot, you'll see that target in front of you while your hearing goes out the window. We train our students to break this tunnel vision after a shooting drill by simply forcing them to look left, right, and rear—literally making them turn their heads—until they find an instructor holding up his fingers. Students have to yell out how many fingers they see.

I stayed on my sights, moving forward, scanning for number three, and found him in a camouflage field jacket, red bandanna tied to his head; he was on the floor twitching, an AK lying next to him. He'd been in D's line of sight and he'd engaged him just as I shot my guy. That made all three down. Fire continued to pour from Goliath's machine gun in the direction of the two we'd just shot—he was putting security rounds into them, I guess.

D and I were trying to advance to make sure no one else was in that room.

"Goliath, *bess*! *Bess!* Stop! Knock it off!" I yelled out, making a cutting motion across my throat at the same time. He stopped shooting.

"Moving!" I yelled, letting D know I was about to continue to head forward. He moved with me down the short hall and we swept into the small room, me right, him left.

"Clear left!" he yelled back, shifting his sights across on the area I was moving into. "Clear right!" I said, bringing mine over to his.

The three guys we'd shot were bleeding out. "Got three down," I said. One black guy and two Arabs.

"Everybody all right?"

"I'm good here, boss—you?" asked D.

"I'm good—set security and search 'em!" I yelled, my ears still ringing.

Goliath got up and ran over to the hole we'd come through, looking out for more.

Beckham had concrete in his eyes and was trying to wipe them clear.

D and I moved the weapons from the bodies and searched—no ID, just two beat-up cell phones, loose cigarettes, matches, and other pocket litter. Two men wore flip-flops, and one had on a tired pair of black loafers. The phones had no calls coming or going, no text messages. They were probably African mercenaries brought in by Qadhafi. Beckham and Goliath came over, both breathing like they'd just run a marathon. Everyone's adrenaline and heart rate was through the roof.

"Mercenaries. Qadhafi's mercenaries!" yelled Goliath at the top of his lungs. All our hearing had been shut down for the moment by the avalanche of weapons fired in such a small, hard space. Normally I'll wear one earplug so I'll have at least one good ear working, but I hadn't put them back in and heard nothing but a high-pitched whine that seemed to eat into my brain.

We'd stumbled in on these men and their hide site, apparently. The whole place reeked of urine and feces and I could see why—it was everywhere in the corners of the other rooms. They had clothes on the floor, bottles of water, mats for sleeping, and a cooking pot—they did it all right here—eat, sleep, and crap. We just added die to that list. We had surprised them and they just started shooting.

The first guy to die was the tall, thin black fellow in dark trousers and a tan hoodie and wearing flip-flops. He had to have been facing Beckham when we came in because Hoodie fired on him almost as soon as he yelled out. Luckily, the guy had been sitting or squatting down and his shots went high into the plaster ceiling above Beckham's head, throwing debris and crap into Beckham's eyes instead of full-metal-jacketed bullets.

To his credit, Goliath, seeing this, had dropped flat on his stomach and blasted fire at a distance of just under ten meters with a 7.62 mm belt-fed machine gun down the hall, killing the guy almost immediately and nearly cutting him in half. I'd been working in this world for more than two decades, had countless hours of training and years of real-world experience, and had taught hundreds, if not thousands, of students how to kill another human being, and this wasn't the first time I'd looked at a body—they're the same. D, too, had countless hours as a student, instructor, and operator under his belt, and neither of us sat around and cried for the guys lying in that room. They shot at us, they rolled the dice, they lost.

It's as reactive to see the threat and attack it as it is to reflexively reload a magazine when it runs dry—you do it because you have burned those actions into your procedural memory. D and I had both hit the two Arabs at basically the same time in their necks and heads. The whole gunfight took place in a concrete space just over thirty feet long, counting the hallway, and was over faster than a knife fight in a phone booth, with no one injured on our side, but for a few chunks of dirt in Beckham's eyes, cuts on Goliath's elbows and knees from glass on the floor, and a gash on D's neck from flying debris. The other side had gotten off one burst, but the other two never even fired their weapons. It's a good thing, too. No gunfight in that sort of space works out well.

"Your friend is just a few blocks from here; we should go!" yelled Beckham, putting down his cell phone and pointing off toward the east. Like ours, his hearing was destroyed. To this day, the hearing in my left ear still suffers somewhat. Goliath was still looking out a hole in the wall toward the sea, to the north. D and I were straining to listen to Beckham's update. The rounds from the rebels' tanks were landing to our left, toward the water. The government's loyalists were responding with artillery fire—and we were sitting in the middle of the impact zone.

CHAPTER 15

Dogs, Cans, and Dead Snipers

September 26, 2011
Sirte, Libya

AN EXPLOSION DETONATED WAY TOO CLOSE TO US, shaking the building's foundations and sending dirt, plaster, and pieces of the building down on us. We ducked and flinched. D and I moved to the corners. It was the safest place to be in case the roof came down—at least we might have air if the roof pancaked in on us.

"They are coming, we stay right here!" Beckham yelled, after talking to Silverback by phone. "We stay here now." They were coming to get us. If they could get here. We all took up spots in the place covering every direction and waited in a place that neither D nor I thought was the best.

I caught motion coming from my right. D saw it, too, and we turned to see three teenage fighters poking their heads into the room. They were staring into our front sight posts, my finger already putting pressure on my trigger. Two wore camouflage; one was in jeans and had a headscarf tied around his bushy black hair, which stuck out the top.

Beckham yelled, "*La! La!* They are with us! They are ours!" *La* was Arabic for no. He was afraid we'd shoot these fellas, and he was right—we would have. We lowered our guns . . . but just a little.

While D watched them and I shifted my attention back to the potential entry points, these new interlopers came up and hugged the Brothers Grimm while keeping a concerned eye on us, then darted back toward the way they'd come. Goliath motioned us to follow, explaining they had been sent to get us; we threaded our way through another sandy parking lot and a group of burned-out single-level storefronts until we finally reached a dusty open area lined with a partially completed concrete wall about nine or ten feet high. Rebel trucks with rocket pods and huge antiaircraft machine guns bolted to their beds sat on our side of the wall.

There was Silverback, grinning. We bro-hugged and did the traditional two-cheek pretend kiss common there and he introduced us to a guy he called Commander. I wasn't sure if he was the commander or just a guy in charge of this group of people, or whether he just renamed himself commander for the fun of it. I covered my ears quickly as I watched a lanky Libyan in a camouflage sleeveless T-shirt with a dark green helmet hanging lopsidedly off his head set off a rocket from his truck using a remote control box with wires running back to the rocket pod. The whole vehicle shook back and forth as the orange-flamed rocket streaked off to visit destruction on some other part of the city.

Before I could say hello properly to the guy called commander, a hand-painted desert camouflage tan truck filled with injured rebels roared up in a cloud of choking, talcum-like dust. One rebel, unconscious, had been shot in the stomach, and another was wounded in his leg. Another had been shot through the hand. One after another, they came in with bloody shirts, keffiyehs, or anything else they had been able to find to wrap the wounds and stop bleeding.

Surrounded by the noise of rockets screaming from their launch tubes in the background, machine guns ripping bursts loose from trucks, and the thudding impact of artillery striking nearby, the medical personnel, such as were available, darted from one to the other, bandaging wounds and cutting off blood-soaked clothing. The dark, cloudy sky above set a somber tone as I looked at the blood covering the bed of that truck in ever-widening pools. Somebody said that a helo was being called in from Misrata to pick these poor guys up, while other rebels were out trying to find a spot suitable to use as a landing zone. They just needed a flat place with no power lines—a soccer field, a big assembly area, a park; anything like that would do.

Silverback was talking with the commander, who wore desert BDUs, a baseball cap, a flak jacket from the Vietnam era, and black combat boots. There was a pistol on his hip, too, and he had a radio in his hand.

He slapped us both on the shoulder, saying, "*Shukran, shukran*," Arabic for "thank you, thank you." Then he was back on the radio, yelling again.

"The commander is having a very difficult time with the snipers," Silverback said. I guess the commander thought we might have a neat idea or cool weapon or could even call in bombs to help him out. Unfortunately for him, we didn't have any of that.

"Let's get a look at the area where the shots are coming from," I told the commander through Silverback, thinking we could at least find these snipers. What to do about them was another problem, though. He hit the radio. A few minutes later, a truck pulled up with two guys inside and we headed back into town, turning onto a flooded road with trash floating everywhere. We dismounted and started moving through stinking, ankle-deep water, headed into a destroyed building. Considering what we'd just experienced in the previous supposedly abandoned building, D and I entered with even more caution. The guys we were with saw our concern and kept trying to reassure us that they controlled this part of the city and not to worry.

The two escorts took us deeper inside. Rubble and evidence of humanity trying to scratch out an existence from desolation were everywhere. We moved up some broken, partial stairs to the second floor, which put us moving parallel to the road. We crawled below blasted-out holes where windows used to be; when we reached an interior wall, we simply hopped through a hole blown through it so we could move without exposing ourselves to enemy snipers.

At what we judged to be close to the T intersection, we got back down on our bellies and inched forward to a small hole at ground level. The older of the men with us pointed up toward the intersection, saying, "sniper." This intersection was the place the rebels were trying to clear, but the effective fire by the hidden marksmen was preventing it. Through the tiny hole in the wall, just slightly larger than a golf ball, was a view of the road. I pulled out my little 8x monocular and saw they were facing the southern side of what used to be a four-story terra-cotta-colored apartment block overlooking the intersection. The space between the intersection and that building was essentially clear and open, as was the entire block in front of the thing. That structure was in a position that dominated the area and all in front of it, covering nearly 270 degrees. Anytime someone moved, they got zapped—and in daylight it's nearly impossible to see where the shot came from if the shooter is hidden well.

Qadhafi's snipers were doing what snipers did—hiding deep inside the buildings, concealing their muzzle blasts, and shooting from cracks, holes, or any other openings they could see through. The rebels' momentum was faltering because of them. Every time the rebels sent people out in this area they had to dive for cover in the maze of buildings—or else they were dropped in their tracks. One lone truck in the road with a body still in the front seat, head listing to the left, was a testament to this.

Snipers are a unique breed of warrior. In the United States, military snipers are considered strategic assets because they wear on the enemy's psyche, provide intelligence on the battlefield, and are extremely cost-effective. The Defense Department found that in the Vietnam War it cost roughly $23,000 in bullets for the average soldier to kill one person, while a sniper cost seventeen cents.

The training is rough and long. The army's basic sniper school is five weeks. The marines take eleven weeks; SEALs spend three months. In relative comparison, these Libyans weren't real snipers, but more like guys hiding in rubble with a scoped rifle firing off a shot or two and getting lucky. They had neither the training nor the equipment. They lacked top-of-the-line precision optics and weapon systems, range finders, or Kestrel wind meters. They had no formal schooling in stalking, building hide sites, in terminal ballistics, calculating adjustments for windage and elevation, or making high-angle shots. Sure, a few were decent rifle shots, but many were simply told to go kill somebody and learned by trial and error what worked and what didn't—it was strictly OJT here. We'd seen a few of them with the Dragunov SVD rifles and others with Heckler & Koch (HK) G3s with scopes, but not many.

We also knew Qadhafi's Libyans didn't fight at night, so D whispered, "Send your people over tonight and kill 'em in their sleep."

"No, we don't fight at night," Silverback said quietly as we all began backing away and starting the return journey through the rubble. Neither side fought at night much and it wasn't due to manners—they didn't have night-vision equipment and simply didn't train to do that. Back on the street, D and I took a knee next to the truck and huddled for a minute, kicking around options. We were here to check on the intelligence network and help coordinate the search for the dictator, not get bogged down in trying to clear snipers at the tactical level. This made the second time I'd been caught up in this little racket over here.

"Boss, I know these guys have scoped rifles, but they'll never be able to hit anything from back there. Plus, God didn't make enough time to wait that long. They just don't have the skills."

"You're right. They're wanting us to do it for 'em, but we ain't gonna be doing that."

"Roger that. But how about rocking their world through the proper application of ordnance?" he said with a grin. A smile crept through his beard so wide that it thinned his eyes.

I knew what he was talking about instantly—just hammer them off the map with overwhelming firepower. That required good intel and a reasonable chance of avoiding collateral damage. We had a general idea of which buildings they were in and every civilian had fled days before.

We drove back to brief the commander. He liked the plan and we set to work.

"Goliath, I need cans to make noise and some raw meat. Doesn't matter what kind," I told him.

D pointed to two soldiers, "You and you, get your trucks and move them back to where you can fire your rockets at the building where the snipers have been." Those fellas had the BM-21 Grad launchers bolted into their truck beds. Beckham translated and they set to work. Why hadn't they done this already? They certainly had blown snipers out of buildings—there were cratered buildings all up and down the Gulf of Sidra that pointed to this. But that was when they could identify where the snipers had been hiding. It was getting dark and they couldn't find them, which meant yet another day stuck here.

D went over and gave the heads-up to a few more truck crews with Russian DShK and NSV heavy machine guns mounted in the beds. These massive guns shot 12.7 mm rounds and could knock planes and helos out of the sky. They all started to crank up and move out.

"Silverback, tell them all to move up as quietly as they can, but not to go around the corner," I told him. I probably didn't need to add that last part—they knew what would happen if they did. He ran off to catch the trucks before they got away.

"You, find a stray dog," I said, as a rebel ran off. It was getting near dusk now and the end of the fighting for the day, or so they thought.

One guy returned with a tan and brown stray dog on a rope; it was one of the million dogs that seemed to be everywhere in North Africa. Goliath showed with the meat—it looked like a goat's ankle. Taking 550 cord from my vest pouch, I told the other kid, via Beckham, to tie the tuna and Coke cans to the tail of the stray.

"Tell the rest of your people to carefully get to the corner of those buildings and pay attention. As soon as they hear fire from them, they'll need to push around and open up on it."

With that, we grabbed the dog and the meat, got in a truck, made sure the headlights were off, and headed back down to the T intersection. The Mad Max trucks were already there, just back from the corner with their engines and lights also off, waiting. Goliath held the squirming, growling mongrel in his huge arms and followed me as we crept down the right side of the flooded road to the corner. D was right behind him. The suspect building was around on our right. It was getting seriously hard to see now.

Goliath put the dog on the ground, still holding him by the rope. He was a skinny thing who probably hadn't eaten anything worthwhile in days. I counted seven vertebrae rising through his skin, and at least as many ribs were visible. When I put the meat in front of the dog's snout, he tried to devour it, snapping and snarling as Goliath held him back. Then, stepping out as much as I dared in the darkening night, I threw the goat part as far up the road as I could in the direction of no-man's-land and then jumped back behind the corner with Goliath, who released the dog. Then all three of us bolted for the trucks. Nothing happened—no one shot at us from the building down the road. Either they couldn't see us, they weren't watching, or they weren't there.

But when the dog took off after the meat, dragging a bouquet of steel and aluminum that clanged, banged, and made more racket than a redneck wedding in a bowling alley, all hell broke loose. Within a few seconds, the enemy opened up, shooting in the direction of the dog. We could see the flashes of orange and white light flickering across the walls of the adjacent buildings in the darkening skies. They were just spraying and praying—likely fooled by the dog's noise into thinking some rebels were advancing on them.

Go time. When the other side started shooting, the Mad Max trucks raced up the final few yards through the flooded street, water jetting up in rooster tails behind them as they sped to the intersection. The men with the BM-21 Grad rockets in the bed of the pickup truck poured everything they had into the face of the building from where the muzzle flashes were coming. The DShK and NVS heavy machine guns mounted to the beds of the trucks roared long, orange flames like fire-breathing dragons, sending shell casings flying in every direction and shaking their tiny four-wheeled platforms back and forth. Soon it seemed that all the rebels, whether with rifles, pistols, machine guns, or RPGs, were shooting something in what became one enormous, continuous roar.

Once the shooting stopped, the rebels hauled away from the spot like they'd just robbed a 7-Eleven. They feared a response from artillery, but none came. A silence settled like fog over the charred, broken battlefield for the first few minutes, as if the city itself took a huge sigh. Then you could hear things pick up again with a dog barking here and there, sporadic fire, and the response from another gun somewhere else across town. Jets shrieked overhead once in a while and things returned . . . to normal. No snipers used that spot again, to my knowledge, and stray dogs soon became scarce in Sirte. I think they got the notion that it wasn't a fun place to hang out anymore. Yes, the dog was fine.

CHAPTER 16

Creating an Operator

1991
CIA Training Facility

AT THE FARM, my excitement had been replaced by a persistent fatigue. The humidity was baking the dirt and sweat into my pores as I sat, idling, in a big four-wheel drive truck with zero AC, parked on the side of a gravel road winding deep into the Virginia forest. My crash helmet, which was way too small for my head, made it all worse and was stiflingly hot. Jake said I looked like a human microphone—others chided that I just had a big head and they felt sorry for my mother.

Red gave me the thumbs-up, I did a radio check—it worked—and he responded, "Move out!" I pulled the big diesel into gear and headed off down the road, expecting something, but not quite knowing what it would be.

CIA officers spend a lot of time in cars, whether driving to meetings or holding them in the vehicles themselves; moving is part of the life. You have to learn to squeeze every bit of potential from what you drive. So far, we had shot into and out of cars, but there was much more: vehicles are in some ways the ultimate ground guy's weapon. In one package, you have a lethal ramming device that protects you from bullets, gives privacy for espionage, and a means of escape. I don't know of a gun, grenade, or anything short of a tank or helicopter that does the same thing. The current lesson was about ramming roadblocks, using vehicles as weapons, and handling them with precision in emergencies and bad weather.

We had lectures on vehicle dynamics, braking, the path to take through corners, and how to drive over rough terrain. We practiced driving armored vehicles, which was a challenge because of their weight and the difficulty of handling them at high speeds. We covered how to load out a vehicle for different missions—how to black out the lights, dashboard displays, and interior lights for surveillance or clandestine meetings, as well as how and where to place weapons, medical kits, and extra ammo for hostile environments.

We learned how ████████ to change the lights at night to throw off surveillance. We studied types of skids and how to counter them in rain, ice, or snow. Our instructors showed us a video of a late-eighties land-barge four-door sedan being shot to pieces by a group of a dozen or so guys using every conceivable handgun, shotgun, or rifle known to man. After the shooting finally stopped, one of the guys climbed carefully over the broken glass into the driver's seat, cranked it up, and drove off. The vehicle certainly wouldn't have passed a DMV inspection, but it showed just how tough vehicles really are: you should think long and hard before ever giving up on them.

Then came the test I was going through today: As I came over the rise of a hill and started down the other side, the gravel road turned left. I was used to driving on gravel—I grew up with it. But I still took the turn a little fast and the bed fishtailed behind me just like *The Dukes of Hazzard*. Rounding another corner, I caught a glimpse of a forklift backing into the woods away from a gray, damaged four-door car now blocking the road in front of me. Apparently, I wasn't supposed to see the forklift, but I was moving fast and caught him in the middle of setting up the scenario—a roadblock. This part of the course was all about ramming roadblocks. Since we'd actually be ramming them, there obviously weren't any role players foolish enough to stand behind them and we had to imagine that part. But this was just to get us used to making contact—that is, slamming our vehicles into another one. The ramming training covered how to push through walls and fences, as well as through roadblocks set up by parked cars or trucks, and a guy couldn't have asked for a better day. Have a wreck, on purpose, don't get hurt, and don't worry about the police or State Farm. Awesome.

Just as we'd been taught, I eased off the gas and pretended to slow to a rolling stop. I played it to the hilt and, smiling, hooked my thumbs into the top of the steering wheel to keep control, but raised my fingers to signal the imaginary bad guys at the roadblock that I wasn't a threat. But creeping along, ever closer to the barricade, I planned my attack. I had to make contact with the car at its lightest point—the opposite end of the engine—to hopefully spin the thing out of my way. It wasn't supposed to be a hard hit—that would damage my ride and me—but rather more of a shove.

No more than twenty or thirty yards away by this point, I gripped the wheel, rolled my thumbs out to keep from having them broken, and pushed the throttle to the floor, aiming the iron bumper of the big truck at the trunk of the car. The impact wasn't too bad, though it was definitely noticeable. Metal screeched and gravel scraped beneath the tires as my truck shoved the car out of the way, pivoting on its engine—the heaviest point. It was a good thing the old truck didn't have air bags. With today's vehicles, students are taught to hold the wheel not at 2 and 10, but at 4 and 8, in the lower hemisphere of the wheel, so that if the bag deploys, it doesn't slam the driver's arms into his face and break them and his pearly whites.

We practiced high-speed turnarounds going forward, called J-turns, as well as going backward—reverse 180s. We learned how to take out another vehicle using our own in a PIT (precision immobilization technique) maneuver. We executed the PIT on other cars going forward and backward and spent days fending off moving attacks on our vehicles from instructors. We drove through a maze of other junked cars, only to have the instructors ambush us from the roadside. Or they would drive up next to us firing shotguns and pistols with blanks from the rear, left, and right; they tried running us off the road using one, two, and three vehicles at a time and we had to solve all these problems and escape.

The vehicle portion of training also covered what to do when you're alone, on the ground, needing to escape hostile territory. We needed to know how to steal a car, formally called "vehicle commandeering," and were taught how to quickly acquire one without a key. We'd learn to improvise the tools we'd need, how to select the best car in the circumstances, how to defeat certain alarms and locks, and how to find the right electrical circuit, both inside the car and under the hood, to start the thing. We even learned how to steal fuel from other cars by siphoning or—if there was time and a concealed spot to work in—making off with an entire fuel tank, which we could throw into our trunk, plugging the holes with rags or whatever was on hand.

We learned stealthy ways to break in through glass windows and doors. Oddly enough, hammers didn't work on car glass because of the way glass spreads the force of the blow. Instead, we learned to use the crushed-up white enamel of a spark plug and throw it at the tempered glass like that of car windows as well as sliding patio doors, to shatter them in near-total silence. Just toss a broken BB-size piece of spark plug ceramic at a tempered window with no more force than you'd use to flick a cigarette and the glass appears to freeze for a second, then millions of pieces of glass start raining down, barely making a sound.

Club steering wheel locks didn't stop us. We just sawed the steering wheel in one place and then slid the Club out through the slit. Two minutes later—no more Club. The Honda Accord, the most stolen car on earth, can be opened with a tennis ball. Punch a hole in the ball and place the hole against the key slot, ram your hip into the ball, and the air will shoot out with enough force to activate the pneumatic locking system, blowing it open. Just don't let your friends see you trying it—it looks like you're trying to hump your car. This was all great training and we were becoming the best drivers and car thieves around.

DETECTING SURVEILLANCE

Late summer, and it was shaping up to be a long day. Jake and I were both slumped at our desks, heads down, muscles sore, shins bruised, and nearly asleep in the back of the darkened classroom. The window air conditioner unit rattled away full blast trying to cool off a room full of exhausted men. We'd all come in from PT, which had consisted of a run through the obstacle course and then a hot, five-mile run at a pace worthy of a white-tailed deer. Our BDUs were soaked with sweat and after gulping down nearly a gallon of water, we'd practically fallen into our chairs. The suffocating heat and humidity had pressed down on us, day after day. Our energy was fading but now, we were told, it was time for something new, something crucial, something the instructors never seemed to stop talking about: surveillance detection.

As he cut the lights, an instructor told us he wanted us to spot the surveillance in the video that was starting up on the screen at the front of the room. I fumbled through my cargo pocket and grabbed my green, government-issued notebook and my ballpoint pen from my BDU top, and got ready to jot down what I saw—then he said put it all away and do it from memory.

Fade into a tight urban street view looking up a small curving incline in a far-off country. Multistory buildings lined the road; people milled between cars parked curbside. Judging by the license plates and the architecture, you'd guess it was Europe somewhere. The parked cars on the right were pointed away from me, which meant they likely drove on the right side of the road, ruling out at least England, Ireland, and Malta. A man walked out of a building from the left carrying a briefcase, moving through pedestrians. Cars pulled up and parked as others left. Then the video clip ended.

"Who saw surveillance?" the instructor asked. Keefer's hand went up to say that he did. Thick like a fireplug and just a shade above five foot six, the guy sported a bald head and had been nicknamed Special K after we had taped a cereal box to his back. He had an army background as a captain in the Chemical Corps, was always seated in the front of the class, and tried to answer everything, whether he actually knew what he was talking about or not. He was obnoxious to the point where we all joked that his mom probably wished she'd given him a toaster and radio as bath toys.

Today, as usual, he had the wrong answer. I didn't have a clue, so I kept my mouth shut, as did Jake. A few more classmates tried to point out where they thought surveillance was in the film, but ultimately the instructor disclosed there was none. He made his point—surveillance could be anyone, anywhere, at any time and we had no better idea on how to spot it than did any civilian on the street.

It wasn't always about blowing up cars, running roadblocks, or shooting your way out of problems—that's part of ■■■ job, but there's another part, espionage. The art of espionage is that the practitioner carries out the task and no one realizes it's even been done—at least until it's too late to reverse it. To do that you had to *go black*, the term used when the operator is out of the enemy's sight. That meant that we had to know if we were under surveillance, which was a tall order if the surveillance team knew what they were doing.

Detecting surveillance wasn't haphazard, but a planned and

extremely subtle thing. You started with the foundation—the surveillance detection route, or SDR. All stops along the SDR are executed to make surveillance personnel reveal themselves without you appearing to be looking for them. The instructors said for us to let the route expose surveillance, not our necks. In other words, don't have your head on a visible swivel looking over your shoulder and *don't, don't, don't* look suspicious. An IO obviously doesn't want to be identified, but even if he or she has been pegged by the host country's security service, he wants something like the following written about him in the logbook of the enemy team if they follow him:

> *Subject departed residence 0930 hrs. Drove to the same shopping centers he has frequented previously on Saturdays. Subject returned to residence at 1645 hrs. No operational activity noted.*

That's what you want recorded, even though, in reality, you may have passed a message or received one from your agent along the way—when you were *in the black* to the surveillance team . . . when you were out of their view for just a few seconds.

At the beginning, we started out riding with the instructors as observers. On a two-way radio, we'd listen to the surveillance team's chatter as they tailed the "rabbit," as the IO under surveillance was called. (The IO was another instructor.) In our observation van, we had maps just like the one the IO used that showed us all his preplanned stops, allowing us to see how his choices affected the surveillance team's movements.

As the IO drove his car down a long stretch of straight highway with two lanes, the surveillance teams surrounded him, front and rear. Our van cruised way back, watching it all play out. After the IO signaled a turn, he shifted to the right lane. His reasoning was clear: there was an exit ramp, an opportunity for him, on the right. The surveillance team leader had to direct the rear car following the IO to also change lanes—in case the rabbit exited. That decision was considered a "tell," an indicator that informed the IO that he had a possible tail. Officially, the opposition had committed an "error of correlation"—that movement of the surveillance team correlated to that of the IO. That was one strike against them.

The surveillance teams were using two of the main three surveillance techniques—the floating box, the ambush method, and the cast of thousands, also called the waterfall technique. The floating box is just that—a box of cars or people who surround the target on all sides—such as on parallel streets left and right, a few cars behind and a few ahead, so that if he makes a turn there's always someone to take over the "eye." The ambush method is where you set out a picket of observers in static positions who report when the target goes by. The last one, the waterfall, is used by the Chinese and Indians quite a bit because they have a large body pool available and it's where the teams are sent directly toward the target, one after another, a different person each time, reporting on his movements as opposed to following behind him, and it is extremely difficult to detect surveillance done this way—but not impossible.

Skipping the exit, the IO stopped a few miles down the road, changing lanes when it seemed natural, attempting to flush out any more pursuers. Because the weatherman was forecasting rain, our man got out, took his umbrella, and walked toward an arched entrance that funneled all foot traffic onto one tiny brick sidewalk shielded on all sides by hedges, trees, and a white picket fence, leading straight to a dead end at a park bench overlooking a body of water. At the end of the walkway stood a huge block of granite, a memorial to cancer survivors. Nothing more. If you weren't actually on that walkway there was no way to see what he was doing; it was a terrific spot, not to go *operational* necessarily, but to draw out surveillance, again because they had no idea whether he was meeting someone, dropping something, or picking up.

The surveillance team that was set up around the rabbit's parked car had to decide whether to push one or more of their members in to get an eye on the IO. If they did, that was another error of correlation and strike two against them. Worse, the IO—walking out just as the surveillant walked in—would be able to get a look at his possible pursuer and note everything about him or her. But there was yet another problem: the team now had a man who couldn't alert the IO by just running back out to pursue him. The car team had a choice—let the IO drive off, leaving the surveillance team with one car there to pick up their man, or leave the man behind. Either way, the team just got smaller by the well-planned route.

The IO then drove on into town, making a series of normal-looking left-hand turns. These were calculated. When turning across an opposing lane of traffic, it's natural to look back to make sure you aren't about to be broadsided—but it is an opportunity for the IO to get an eye on the vehicles behind him without doing something abnormal. A right-hand turn didn't offer that chance; it would be too fast, too tight for him to grab a look before a building blocked his view. A left turn gave the IO a chance to see if the vehicle that changed lanes with him earlier was still behind him, a few cars back in traffic.

The IO eventually stopped at a fast-food joint and started walking again—now in the drizzle, umbrella up—toward a coffee shop on the corner of the street a few blocks away. He stopped to speak to a young man putting up umbrellas in front of a restaurant as they got ready for the lunch crowd. The two chatted for a few seconds, and the IO handed him something. The boy smiled and then went back to his damp work.

Our instructor explained that move was called a "dangle" and was designed to confuse those tailing the IO and to once again reduce their number. They wouldn't know whether the boy was the IO's contact or not. Had he just passed a covert message or instructions? They didn't know and couldn't risk missing a message drop: one or two people from the team would now have to peel off and snatch up the kid for questioning. In this case, the clever IO had simply asked the kid when the restaurant opened and given him a business card for the owner, telling the kid that his company might be interested in renting the place for a party and to pass the card to his boss. It might take hours to obtain these details from the boy and the longer it took, the longer the team had to do without vital members. Yet again, the team got smaller thanks to proper route selection.

At the coffee shop, the IO bought a cup, turned to the window as he drank, and surveyed the street and the path he had taken to the shop. We scrutinized him as he took in his pursuers—one walking down the sidewalk he'd just come down and the other across the street. Another had paused across the intersection under the awning of a store, ostensibly to keep the rain off. All were visible to the trained eye of the IO, who had a dry, ringside seat.

The coffee joint was the only place on the street that was open. There were no bus stops, no phone booths. All this was planned: the situation gave the surveillance team nowhere to go. The IO had chosen well. His opponents had a few, not-so-great choices: either they sent someone inside the store with him, posted a man in the rain, or simply left. They'd just been forced to commit yet another an error of correlation, as well as an "error of cover for status" and an "error of cover for action"—all three mortal errors for a surveillance team. Three strikes now—all at the same time.

The rule clearly stated that once could be an accident, twice might be coincidence, but three times was enemy action. The IO could not have escaped the fact that he was under surveillance unless he was blind. He'd made them and never broken his cover, never craned his neck around, and never did anything out of the ordinary. An SDR should go like that. But there was one thing left for us to observe—the "brush pass."

The instructors told us that the IO would complete his mission—passing something to an agent. They pointed out the obvious: in the real world, he'd abort the pass because of the heavy, obvious surveillance on him. But for training purposes today, despite the teams on him, he would still accomplish his mission, and he bragged that neither they, nor we, would see the IO do it. We were all skeptical, to say the least. How could this guy hand something to another person in broad daylight in front of our eyes and those of a professional national-level surveillance team following him without anyone seeing him do it? We were all about to throw the BS flag when the instructor told us to pay attention.

The IO left the shop, checked his watch, cut through a hotel lobby, and sauntered up the sidewalk for a few blocks. He made his way over to an outdoor pavilion with a stage. The radio sparked up as the teams called out, identifying who had the "eye" on the rabbit. The old spook cut across the grass, heading to the right of the stage, where a small opening—a door—led backstage. He stopped, turned, and leaned against the wall with the door to his left now. He shook the umbrella in his right hand, causing water to run from it. His left hand looked to be in his pocket. Then, after only a brief moment at rest, he pushed off the wall and started walking back the way he'd come. We heard the chatter from the surveillance team—they'd never had a chance to get anyone behind the stage, and now the IO was heading back into them, inverting their box, dragging the team's bubble away from the pavilion . . . just as he planned.

"There's the pass—did anybody see it?" asked the instructor in the van. No one had; we truly didn't believe he'd done anything. We all got out and walked over to the pavilion while the instructors all called "endex" over the radios. Everyone—the surveillance team members, the IO, the other instructors, and our class—all gathered by the backstage door. The lead instructor asked again who saw the pass—no one answered, not even Special K. The instructor then asked for a guy named Rico to step out. Rico was role-playing as the foreign agent, and he stepped through the door from behind the stage. He held out his fist and opened it, revealing a small plastic film container—the pass had been made.

The cadre then showed us what we'd missed. The IO had leaned against the wall, using his right hand to hold the umbrella, which he shook to distract observers—it was misdirection. This pulled the eyes of anyone watching away from what he was doing with his other hand. With that hand, his left, he had reached back through the doorway, palming the container into the hand of Rico, who had timed his appearance to exactly match the IO's and walked in the opposite direction, concealed—or screened, as it's called—from everyone by the huge stage. Once the IO felt Rico take it, he'd walked back the way he'd come, dragging the surveillance teams away from Rico, allowing him to escape in the other direction. These guys were better than Penn and Teller.

TRADECRAFT

In the clandestine service at the CIA, there are two broad worlds—that of the case officer and that of the paramilitary (PM) officer. The former gets heavy training in the tradecraft of recruiting and running agents, with light focus on shooting and martial skills in a course called the Special Operations Training Course, or SOTC (pronounced SOT-see). In SOTC, case officers become familiar with foreign weapons and receive enough direct training to qualify them to carry station weapons when needed, along with evasion and counterinterrogation training and survival skills, like building emergency shelters to hide from the enemy, how to signal search and rescue teams, or how to skin and cook a rabbit, all while on the run from an enemy coming for you with dogs, troops, armor, helicopters, and search planes.

Paramilitary officers, however, typically received heavy training in weapons, explosives, vehicles operations, and other kinetic, martial subjects with lighter focus on tradecraft, recruiting and running agents. That did change somewhat after 9/11, when the full-blown Field Tradecraft Course (FTC) was opened up to PM officers and even Defense Department folks.

At its heart, the FTC is about recruiting and handling agents. A CIA "agent" is the spy who is recruited by the officer and delivers the goods to that officer. FTC is about planning and executing a capital crime in a foreign country without being detected or caught. The set of skills that enable an IO to carry this off undetected falls under a broad heading of tradecraft and it's the heart of what makes the clandestine side of CIA the CIA. It is the core of the dark arts of espionage and there truly are none better at it.

That gray work—that tradecraft—is picking up messages from dead drops, running surveillance operations, and conducting clandestine meetings with agents in cars, apartments, hotels, or wadis. It is planning and executing SDRs; using clandestine photography; implementing disguises; spotting, assessing, and recruiting agents; and using a host of other skills and technology.

A close friend and mentor who retired as one of the most highly decorated CIA officers alive today, a living legend, once defined it for me this way: "Tradecraft is knowing your operation and situation in detail, integrating into the operation the political and cultural considerations, and practicing how to conduct oneself and your agent in those circumstances and using technology appropriately while thinking through the preparation for potential consequences."

His definition covers practically every aspect of espionage tradecraft. In broad strokes, you first need to understand the mission—What are your orders? What is your boss's goal? What are your red lines legally, ethically, and morally? Then you need to develop your operational course(s) of action, get it approved, and rehearse it over and over again. You game it out with realistic what-if scenarios where you plan for the most likely outcome, the best possible outcome, and the worst-case scenario, all in an effort to get the mission accomplished and, most important, keep your agent safe.

That too is an area that Hollywood and novelists misunderstand—the CIA officer and agent relationship. CIA officers are often portrayed as being callous to the well-being of foreign agents working for them, willing to let them twist in the wind. But the exact opposite is true—the agents are the lifeblood of CIA work, and during training it's hammered into your skull in no uncertain terms to protect them—at all costs. That is why FTC is so important and learning the material is critical to a CIA officer moving ahead. If you don't learn it and practice it properly, your agent suffers and so do you—they are the lifeblood of the Clandestine Service. Without the agents it's pointless.

Surjeet Singh is a prime example of how using poor tradecraft can screw you—and he paid for it with thirty years of his life. He left his home in India one cold winter night, telling his wife he'd be back soon. Thirty years later she saw him—after he'd spent all that time in a Pakistani prison because he was spying for India.

In the mid-1970s, he made more than eighty-five trips into Pakistan as an intelligence officer for India, bringing back documents for the Indian army. The trips were always one day long and trouble-free. But on his last trip, things went wrong—very wrong.

"I had gone across the border to recruit a Pakistani agent. When I returned with him, an Indian official on the border insulted him. He slapped the agent and wouldn't allow him in. The agent was upset so I had to escort him back to Pakistan. In Lahore, he revealed my identity to the Pakistani authorities." The agent, still fuming over the insult, then burned Singh like a moth in a candle.

Had Singh thought through his operation in enough detail? Had he taken steps to ensure that his home-country border officials knew he would be coming across with a Pakistani? Had he considered the cultural ramifications and practiced his actions at the border with his would-be-agent? It sounded like there was much that could have been done differently. A successful mission is the result of the best tradecraft, that is, the gray work that keeps the IO, the agent, and the operation alive. Fail to plan and you plan to fail, as the saying goes. You can't fail to plan when carrying out gray work.

THE CLASS SLOGGED THROUGH learning about agent operations, recruiting, and holding meetings at every hour of the day or night and in every imaginable venue, from hotels, apartments, and cars to forests, ditches, garbage dumps, restaurants, and even private aircraft. We covered how to signal agents covertly, and how to work satellite telephones and classified encryption and communications equipment; the instructors explained how to execute brush passes and service dead drops, which are covert ways to leave something for someone to pick up after you've left.

During the maritime phase, we worked with small boats and kayaks on infiltrating hostile coastlines. We learned how to make clandestine nighttime beach landings, how to read tidal patterns, and how to estimate the slope and shape of the bottom based on the waves hitting onshore. If the bottom is flat and wide, you'll see spilling breakers that seem to crumble as they move along. A steeper beach slope will have waves creating a plunging breaker—the kind surfers like. On the steepest bottom slopes the waves, called surging breakers, usually don't break before hitting shore at all. We covered how to plot courses in small boats and kayaks across large bodies of water using nautical charts, and four ways to navigate: piloting when close to markers or land; dead reckoning, which is starting from a known point and steering toward another; celestial navigation, which is using the stars; and finally, using electronic or radio navigation aids.

TONIGHT I SAT IN A ZODIAC RUBBER RAFT next to another boat crew of CIA trainees, bobbing up and down in the inky black waters of the Atlantic Ocean off the East Coast of the United States as we puttered along a predetermined heading. I listened to the motor, the waves, and the wind. The salt water sprayed my face and the familiar salty, clean air made me breathe deeply as our rigid inflatable Zodiac boats cut smoothly through the water, rising up a swell and crashing down the other side. The sky was pitch black—a front had rolled in, and clouds were blotting out any light that might come from the quarter moon or stars. We were pushing to our rendezvous with a nuclear submarine—we hoped.

We were in the final phases of learning how to signal, find, and then load ourselves into a submarine in the open ocean. The use of this skill might be for recovering an agent or defector from hostile territory like North Korea. The scenario might be to sneak ashore, link up with our agent, then take him or her offshore into the ocean in a boat where a submarine would be the quickest and most clandestine way to get the asset off the peninsula.

At a prearranged spot we cut the engines and there was nothing but the waves lapping against the boats and the gentle breeze. John, a kid from Kansas who'd never seen the ocean before joining CIA, was our assistant navigator tonight. He broke out the IR (infrared) strobe lights, double-checked his compass, and then began pointing the lights along a specific azimuth, hoping it would be viewed by the sub's periscope. We did that for a few minutes and waited—nothing. A guy from our sister boat named Mark, a former Army Ranger hailing from Brooklyn who'd been rolled back to our class after a medical injury prevented him from completing with his previous class, started to wonder aloud if we were in the right spot—and he was the primary nav guy for that boat. In our boat John ditched the IR lights and resorted to another technique that took advantage of the sub's sonar capability—banging two pipes together underwater. A few minutes later we saw and heard the signs of a sub—bingo.

Each of our boats had an IR light affixed to it so we could be seen by the sub, and as soon as we knew they had a fix on us, I threw a line over from my boat to Mark's crew—each was secured with D-rings. Then, like a phantom from the deep, the great black ship eerily became visible as white water started churning behind us. Ever so subtly, its mast broke the surface and we all watched mesmerized as that small trail of white water grew until it plowed a path straight toward our two boats, caught our line, and kept going, sending a gentle jolt through us all as we started moving once again but heard nothing but the water.

It was an amazing rush of adrenaline to go from dead silent, floating in the ocean, to having a nuclear-powered submarine rise noiselessly from the deep, catch your boat, and begin to quietly, powerfully, and rapidly tow you over the ocean to the horizon. We moved along with nothing but the sound of water breaking and the wind whistling over our boats for at least thirty minutes. When we were at a location safe, meaning OTH, or over the horizon and out of sight from the coast, the sub surfaced and we loaded ourselves aboard. The instructors told us if we ever had the misfortune to be on a sub in real life that we should forget trying to PT, expect no laundry or showers on board, and plan to be living in the torpedo room—he was correct. Through the years there have been a few times when I've been misidentified as a SEAL—once in a newspaper article, another by someone introducing me to speak—all likely due to my having worked at Blackwater or because a lot of SEALs worked with us. But my few times aboard claustrophobic submarines quickly reminded me of why I'd not joined the navy.

We also spent a short time on an aircraft carrier under way to learn the ins and outs of life on board those massive ships, in case we had to use one for any reason. Facing backward in the seats, wearing helmets, goggles, and life vests, we flew out from a U.S. naval air station on the East Coast on board an aircraft called a COD, for carrier onboard delivery. It was a twin-engine Grumman C-2 Greyhound designed to ferry people, cargo, mail, and other supplies to the ship at sea. We did a carrier landing—which was like taking a dump truck going 100 mph and bringing it to a full stop in around two seconds. I thought my eyes would never come back to the front of my skull. We ate in the mess hall, spent the night sleeping in crew berthing areas, toured the ship, were loaded back onto the COD, and were launched off the flight deck bound for shore. This time it was just the reverse as that steam-powered catapult slung the plane down the runway. I felt as though my teeth were coming out and I couldn't bring my head back to the headrest to save my life. Over two decades later I'd have the honor of visiting a carrier again, but as a VIP at the invitation of Admiral David Anderson, a close friend. That was a much, much better tour than what I received via Uncle Sam the first time.

DURING THE AIR PHASE, the training centered on all things having to do with covert operations from aircraft, whether rotary or fixed wing. We learned how to rig cargo for drops from aircraft; how to set up landing zones (LZs) for helicopters during the day and night; how to fire machine guns from moving helos; to hold our weapons with the muzzle pointed down so, in case someone accidentally cooked off a round, it wouldn't go through the roof and hit the blades; and how to board helos in formations called "chalks." A chalk was a throwback to World War II, when U.S. pilots of troop transport planes wrote their plane's number in chalk on the side so troops would know which one to board.

It was a blast to be in the back of the DHC-6 Twin Otter cargo plane, shoving a package out the port-side hatch, trying to hit the T-shaped pattern created by the bright orange VS-17 signaling panels set out by another student team on the ground at the designated drop zone. But even more difficult was doing it at night with nothing but night-vision goggles searching for tiny, blinking IR lights taped to nine-volt batteries, which we called "FireFlies," down on the ground. The Twin Otter was great for this type of operation. It was a short takeoff and landing (STOL) aircraft that had wings mounted high on the top of the airframe that allowed for packages or personnel to be dropped from the plane rather than flying back into the propellers.

We also were put through a two-week parachute program called "Jump Camp." The army's is three weeks long, but the whole thing could actually be run in one day—in the case of both the army and the agency. We learned how to do a PLF, or parachute landing fall, which transferred the energy of a landing through our feet and knees into the side of the body. We had to do five jumps, one of which was while carrying seventy-five pounds of gear on a ruck. Just before landing, we had to release the ruck so that it hit the ground before we did—otherwise we'd break our legs with the additional weight on our bodies. I hated jumping.

FINALLY MY TRAINING ENDED. Jake was the honor grad, if one existed, for our class. His schedule called for him to take a few more courses at another site because he was going to be an instructor for a few months first. He'd go on to a great career as a PM officer and would be instrumental in defeating the Taliban in Afghanistan. Keefer, Special K, made it too, much to the amazement of many, including me. He stayed with the agency for ten years and never did figure out who slapped the Special K box to his back. That covert operation remained secret . . . until now, anyway.

I finished just behind Jake, or so Red told me in my final evaluation. I was happy with that; Jake was my friend, a great guy, and an excellent operator. But I'll admit that I still hated being second. As I've said before, I'm competitive but I guess I could say that there was no one to whom I'd rather have lost.

I went straight from the course to a short five-day program called Tactical Locksmith, offered by a private company and only available to federal government and military personnel. They taught us methods to covertly defeat locks by picking, shimming, and using bump keys (a special key used to open pin tumbler locks; 95 percent of homes' and businesses' locks are vulnerable to this technique). We did a lot of offensive casing and surveys of target buildings and then came up with a plan to gain entry. Once inside the structure you had a mission to accomplish—like taking photographs, stealing documents, or planting devices. You learned to wear rubber gloves, hairnets, and the white face masks like those to ward off bird flu in Beijing, all to keep your DNA from being left behind. We took a picture of a desk before touching it in order to be sure everything was put back just right. We learned how to manipulate safes and padlocks and pushbutton locks, as well as how to create keys from stolen key codes, ladies' hairpins, photographs, or even impressions we managed to get of the key itself. We learned how to get out of double-locked handcuffs, plastic zip-ties, and even duct tape. But we also worked on observational skills once inside a structure—looking at the behavioral residue left behind by the occupant. Things like dirty laundry left out, scented candles for décor, diplomas hanging, or even decorative pillows on couches or beds can teach a lot about someone and how they want to be viewed. One glance at a private space could often be better than hours watching the person in public.

It was a lot of work—and a lot of fun. I came back with a complete lock pick kit and, for breaking into cars, a sweet tool kit called the Sully. I was now ready—I was tired, but in great shape, with a head full of knowledge about breaking things, breaking into things, stealing things, and killing bad guys. It was truly the best, most comprehensive training I've ever experienced. I thought back to when I started and Red told me, "If you're persistent you'll get it." When I was finished, he told me, "Now be consistent to keep it."

CHAPTER 17

Old Meat in the Locker

September 28, 2011
Sirte, Libya

FOR NEARLY THREE WEEKS, Muammar Qadhafi—dressed in loose-fitting gold-colored pants with a gold-encrusted Browning Hi-Power pistol hidden under his clothes—had moved from one abandoned house to another every three or four days. His guards scavenged for food, and they all lived with no electricity.

The room he lived in on this day in Sirte was dark and dim—sheets of metal to conceal the interior and stop bullets covered the windows. He didn't go outdoors and his personal chef cooked his meals in a make-shift kitchen in the yard that was also covered by a metal ceiling of roof-ing tin. His core of fighters started out at around 350 but their numbers had been significantly reduced—by getting killed, and others wounded or just quitting. Still, he had dozens of snipers stationed on rooftops guarding his shelter . . .

. . . and he had something else: a plan.

The morning after the dog barrage, Silverback called my cell phone, saying that he had someone else for us. A short time later, he drove up in an old, cream-colored Peugeot with the wizened old man in the passen-ger seat. I guessed him to be in his sixties. A man of small stature, he was a resident of Sirte and was part of our man's network in the city.

"Mister," said Silverback, "this is Abdel. He has worked for me for many weeks and is a trusted man." I reached out and shook his hand, then touched my right hand to my heart in the traditional way of that region, showing my honor in meeting him.

He was old, his long, tanned face wrinkled and worn; a white mustache clung desperately to his upper lip; dark eyebrows framed his deep-set eyes. On his head was wrapped a twisted white cloth that draped down onto his left shoulder.

"Mister, I believe that he is here in Sirte," Abdel said, referring to Qadhafi. Suddenly the day took on new meaning.

"Sir, why do you think that?" I asked.

"There are many troops, as you know, in District 2. There are also many vehicles—expensive vehicles—there. Many of them—over twenty that have not been here before this battle started," he answered.

"Exactly where have you seen this?"

"Northern Sirte, near Salahin Street. They have moved from the house numbered twenty-four this morning. They move from house to house every few days. Someone important is there—the soldiers are protecting someone in District 2. I think it can only be him," he said, pointing a bent, arthritic, bony finger in the direction of the sea.

"Have you told the commander about this?" I asked Abdel.

"No, I have been waiting for you," he said, shaking his head and touching his heart with his palm. He was loyal to Silverback, seeing himself as part of *our* network. I turned to Silverback and said that the commander had to be told. "If Qadhafi's here, if he's that close, your guys need to seal off that area to prevent him from getting out. Once he sees this place falling, he'll run for sure."

Moments later, the commander called Abdel over, talked to him for a few minutes, patted him on the shoulder, and then got on his radio.

AS TIME PASSED AND WE MOVED INTO OCTOBER, the rebels claimed more and more ground nearby, and NATO warplanes pounded the city. Perhaps to stay sane and keep busy, Qadhafi read from stacks of books he'd taken when he fled Tripoli. As the battle grew more intense and it became clear Sirte was going to fall, he devised his means of escape to the village of Jarif, his birthplace a few miles west.

He likely discussed the plan with his chief of security, Mansour Daou, who would caution him against trying it—saying it was too dangerous and that he was underestimating the rebels and NATO, who had surrounded them and were getting closer with each passing day.

But the dictator must have insisted and on October 20 he ordered the commencement of his escape attempt. He and Daou got in his Toyota Land Cruiser and the convoy of nearly one hundred SUVs and pickup trucks made a break for the west coastal highway and freedom, trying to escape District 2, Sirte, and the rebels.

But other eyes were watching them.

Qadhafi's convoy was speeding along and, as yet, had met no resistance. Their confidence built, though they had traveled only a mile or so. They were arrogant men who thought their luck would hold.

Then they turned down a sand-covered coastal street, passing the stark white wall of an electrical substation. They were just twenty yards from the main road when the first truck erupted in a fireball.

British Tornado fighter jets streaked into the airspace, followed by French fighters that came out of the patchy blue sky like angry wasps. Trucks and SUVs burned, smoked, and blew apart under their strafing runs, killing at least fifty of Qadhafi's men. Seconds later, all fifteen trucks in the dictator's convoy lay smoldering, many of the passengers still strapped, charred, dead in their seats.

But the dictator's luck held for a while longer, despite his SUV being hit hard—he was wounded but alive. He and Daou were both injured—Qadhafi in both legs. His bodyguards opened his door, pulling both men out and running toward a stand of low-hanging olive trees, perhaps hoping to escape the eyes of the aircraft above.

Salem Bakeer and his fellow rebels, nearby when the jets struck, watched the attack and spotted the group, then began racing after them in their battered trucks.

Fleeing through the trees, the bodyguards spotted large twin-hole drainage pipes about a hundred yards away. In they went, shoving the dictator inside. The pipes were less than three feet in diameter and, unknown to the fleeing group, were open at both ends. They seemed to believe they had not been spotted in their dash to the hiding spot.

Nothing, however, had escaped Bakeer's men, who were now speeding toward the pipes. Aiming their truck-mounted guns carefully, for the past, for the future, for everything that the people of Libya had suffered, they shot at the entrance to those pipes. No response. It was then that they decided they had to go in on foot.

What they saw was this: one of Qadhafi's men waving his rifle in the air and shouting surrender.

Was it a trick?

As soon as the bodyguard saw Bakeer's face, he opened fire. Then, inexplicably, he stopped and put his weapon down. "My master is here," he yelled. "My master is here! Muammar Qadhafi is here and he is wounded!"

Mohammed al-Abibi, a late-middle-aged Libyan with a neatly trimmed graying beard and a New York Yankees baseball cap, led the way into the pipe. Seconds later he and the rebels came out, dragging Qadhafi, his son, and their bodyguards into the daylight. Three bodyguards were killed immediately, their bodies left bleeding out in the sand nearby.

Mutassim Qadhafi, son of the dictator, and Libya's national security adviser, was dragged away. He would be filmed not long after, smoking his last cigarette. Cause of death: multiple gunshot wounds to the throat and upper body.

Abibi searched the dictator, finding the golden pistol and stuffed it into his own trousers. Qadhafi pleaded, "What is wrong? What is wrong? What have I done to you?" as he was dragged along the ground. Hands gripped him from all directions—there was no stopping this mob. Someone fired a 9 mm handgun at him, hitting him just below the rib cage.

His death was neither quick nor civil. He was beaten, slapped, and kicked, chunks of his hair yanked out at the roots. The rebels threw him into the bed of a truck, dozens of them clawing at him, taking his picture, and videoing his last minutes with their cell phones. He was flipped over and sodomized with an AK-47 bayonet. His hands were bound, and he was dragged behind a truck, and then he was shot again. Hands yanked him up and threw him onto the hood of another gaudily painted rebel truck, and he was driven around for show. Finally, a man walked up and placed a black Beretta 9 mm pistol to Muammar Qadhafi's left temple and shot him in the head, killing him.

He died a horrible, slow, painful, and ultimately a disgraceful death on YouTube. Again and again.

His body was driven in an ambulance from Sirte to Misrata. There it was taken to a city market and put on display in a meat freezer. Thousands of townspeople lined up to gawk and take pictures. A man whom they'd only seen on television or heard over the radio was now prostrate at their feet, reduced to a bloodstained corpse in a meat locker.

Just three days after the death of the dictator, the NTC declared Libya to be "liberated" and announced plans for a democratic state based on Islamic law.

EVERYTHING, NEARLY EVERY SKILL I had learned as an operator, came into play in Libya. The list was long—diplomacy; trying to determine intentions by body language, intonation, and voice inflection; land warfare; CQB; espionage; surveillance; tactical planning; negotiations and bargaining; evaluating sources; and dealing with the often mysterious and questionable people you must work with to be effective.

Being an operator is much more than being able to shoot, move, and communicate while wearing tan cargo pants, a big watch, and hiking boots. That may look cool on the gun range, but this sort of work requires more. It's the adult side of contracting. Standing guard at an embassy or annex requires certain skills and comfortable shoes—I've done it. Teaching shooting requires patience and a love of Groundhog Day, because it's the same day in and day out and I've done a lot of that, too. But what paramilitary contracting does is different every day and requires a wide range of skills and maturity. This is the future of warfare.

ON SEPTEMBER 11, 2012, just short of one year after Qadhafi's death, the American consulate in Benghazi was attacked. Four Americans died, and it didn't have to happen.

My team tried to warn of the threat posed by radical Islamists for more than a year after our experience in Libya. We told our U.S. leaders in countless reports that militias needed to be reined in, engaged, or penetrated because they were dangerous. In my opinion, more effort should have been made to get inside the militias, gain their trust, recruit agents, and use them to leverage insight into AQIM and perhaps into al-Qa'ida worldwide. We did it—we penetrated a brigade and had access to far, far more using just two men and zero governmental support, so imagine what could have been achieved, the lives that could have been saved, all in a shorter amount of time, with the might of the U.S. government.

I WATCHED THE NEWS of the embassy attack in Benghazi from North Africa in 2012. By that time, I transitioned to another war—in Syria, which was in full flame by the time of the downfall of Libya's despised dictator. The Arab Spring continued. Hundreds of thousands of demonstrators all over Syria were fired at with rifles, heavy machine guns, tanks, and armored units. In Talbisa, the regime randomly shelled residential areas as the citizens starved. In Homs, Shabbiha mercenaries—Assad's killers—prevented anyone under the age of forty from leaving their houses. The regime leaders unleashed their firepower at ordinary people in Deir Ba'alba, Khaldiyah, Inshaat, and Bab Sbaa. The wave of kidnappings and rapes of young girls and boys was staggering.

Espionage and covert operations are timeless, going back to biblical days, when Joshua sent two operators—his spies—into the fortified city of Jericho to assess their defenses and probe for a point of entry for his army. Once inside, a whore named Rahab provided them a safe house. The battle saw the defeat of Jericho and the operators rescued their agent, Rahab, who came to live in Israel until her death. This was perhaps the first covert operation where operators used a safe house and then rescued their agent from hostile enemy territory, all wrapped up in one event. It all began with the Bible, the defense of the defenseless, and then the ultimate rescue mission, well before ■■, Delta, and ST6, when Jesus came to infiltrate and rescue us—even me.

III

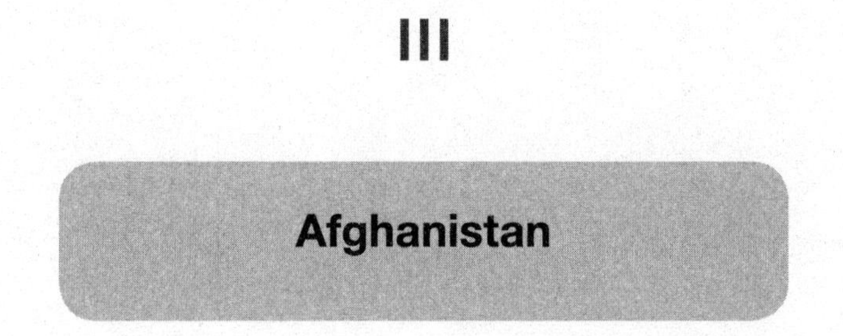

CHAPTER 18

Blackwater

September 11, 2001
Jackson, Mississippi

THE SUN WAS UP that Tuesday morning; the sky perfect, almost too perfect, it seemed later. Before 8 A.M., I was already in my office at the law firm, as was my custom; I liked to get in early and get quiet time to check my upcoming calendar, pray, read my Bible, and generally take a breath before the day started. My life had segued into something completely different after the CIA. I went to work now with a briefcase, not a rifle: I'd been in my new job at the law firm in Jackson, Mississippi, for a few months and studying for the bar whenever I could. Since starting at CIA more than a decade earlier, I'd been to the Middle East countless times, to India and Europe, and of course Washington, D.C. In 1996 I sought a doctoral degree, graduated in 2000 from law school in Virginia, then spent another year in postgraduate studies at Boston University. After much thought, and suggestions from my family that I find a less volatile line of work, I took a job in a law firm. At the same time, I was trying to be a husband and father. But I was bored by our life in the Deep South as a lawyer, where the most exciting thing to happen in a day might be an old widow dropping in to my office to ask whether she has to pay her deceased husband's Amex bill. It was hard to just be what society said was normal after what I'd experienced.

Attorneys were filing into the building; I could hear small talk being made as people greeted one another. The smell of the coffee as the receptionist's phone chirped. My extension buzzed—my wife, Alli, was on the line. Odd—she rarely called this early and always used my cell. I looked down at it as I picked up the office line—I'd forgotten to take it off silent the night before. I had three missed calls.

I answered, anticipating some kind of terrible news about her, the kids, or a relative. "Where have you been?" she asked, not angry, just curious, but there was something else in her tone that told me something wasn't right. I told her about the cell being on silent but she glossed right over that and asked, "Have you heard about the plane that hit the World Trade Center?" she asked. No, I told her.

"They think it was a small plane that ran off course." I flicked on the TV in my office. She wasn't panicked—she didn't get that way about much unless it was a snake in the house or one of the children was bleeding.

As she talked, though, a knot grew in my stomach. I knew this was no freak accident. I recalled the previous hit on the tower in 1993 and my shock, the year before, at the suicide attack on the U.S. Navy guided missile destroyer the USS *Cole* (DDG-67), during a refueling stop in the Yemeni port of Aden. Seventeen sailors, in line for their noon meal, died after a small craft pulled along the port side of the *Cole* next to the galley and detonated a seven-hundred-pound charge ripping a forty-by-forty-foot gash in the ship's hull. Thirty-nine had been injured in the deadliest attack on a U.S. naval vessel since Iraq hit the USS *Stark* in 1987. Not only did al-Qa'ida take credit; it boasted about it in recruitment videos. This was the first time that most Americans got wind of the existence of al-Qa'ida. Now they were up to something even more heinous.

At almost 9 A.M. in Mississippi, the first tower fell. My mind conjured the scene at CIA—people would be huddled around monitors watching it all unfold, some would be scrambling to reach out to every source on the planet to see what they knew. I had left that place earlier because I wanted a family and hoped to offer my loved ones more than a man always on a plane, bringing home nothing but secrets from a job I couldn't talk about.

"JUST WHEN I THOUGHT I was out," says Al Pacino's Michael Corleone in *The Godfather, Part III*, "they pulled me back in." Pop culture has created this idea that the CIA is like the mob—you can never quit. Not true; there are literally tens of thousands of former employees no longer receiving a paycheck who can vouch for the fact that you can leave whenever you want, despite the huge amount of money the agency spends recruiting, vetting, testing, training, and deploying you. They may try to talk you out of it, but when you boil it all down, it's a job. They get over it; replace you and you move on.

Life creates pressures that can be taxing when coupled with a job requiring a double life. I kept hearing stories about unhappy spouses leaving and marriages falling apart: I heard that more than two-thirds of the officers in the clandestine service were on their second or third marriage. That wasn't my family's way—who sets out saying, "I think I'll marry so I can get divorced"? I wanted what my parents had—a loving, stable, lasting relationship. Of course, I knew many officers who were happily married, but the vast majority of what I saw about that life didn't support it. I wanted to do everything I could to make a loving home and raise our children.

WHEN I MOVED TO WASHINGTON, D.C., to start at the agency in 1990, we tried the long-distance thing—she stayed in college at Ole Miss and I worked and trained while taking various courses by correspondence, as well as going back alternating semesters to finish my degree and take some ROTC classes. If I were doing it over again today, I'd still go to Ole Miss, but I'd study at the university's Center for Intelligence and Security Studies, run by a solid former FBI special agent and his able deputy. They've created a truly unique program that prepares students for work in the field—languages, immersion studies, foreign travel, and a massive real-world practical final exam.

I wrote her letters from D.C., but she was just starting college and the distance came between us and she started to date other guys. I was usually unavailable anyway, halfway across the world. Her family—on the upper side of middle class—lived in Houston and was close, conservative, and Christian; they went to church every time the doors opened. Her father was a renowned, respected architect. My life was an enigma, and she wasn't the type to sit by the phone wondering if her husband was dead in the tribal areas of Pakistan. It all sounded dangerous, foreign, and unpredictable to her; she wanted stability. Despite this, she did support and follow me for twenty years, putting up with quite a lot. She's a wonderful person, mother, and friend, and we are still close today as we raise our three children. But back then I made a choice—intelligence work or something else, and I wound up choosing something else.

But she wasn't the only one concerned about my occupation. My mom is a worrier—plain and simple. She loves her kids more than anyone I've ever seen. She is beautiful—like Elizabeth Taylor in her younger years, but without the drinking, smoking, and multiple husbands. Mom sings in the choir, and bakes a delicious pan of rolls; in short, she's the best mother ever. But my not being able to talk about my job or tell her where I was at times put a strain on her, too.

So all these things and more helped me decide to go to law school, though what I knew about that career had been picked up from John Grisham novels or television. Soon, I was back in my little red hatchback, driving with all my worldly possessions to Mississippi, to sweaty summers, fried catfish at Oakland's, a good read in a comfortable chair above Square Books, and smelling the sweet fragrance of magnolia blossoms in May.

Then my grandfather on my dad's side, the one we called Granddaddy, died. The man who taught me to whittle; the man with whom I'd walked acres of forested family land; the man who told me stories of his childhood; the man I'd hunted and fished with and stood next to in church as he sang with me through hymns while Mom and Dad sang in the choir; the man I loved almost like a second father left my world. They say that smell is the sense most linked to memory. I know this to be true. The unforgettably intoxicating fragrance of plumeria takes me to warm, breezy beaches of Hawaii, while the gently sweet aroma of a magnolia blossom transports me to a white metal swing in Batesville, back when I was all elbows, skinned knees, and teeth, sitting and listening to Granddaddy tell stories of when he was a boy. The memories of my childhood are bound up in a man whose name was Morris, yet in that hospital room, as his life was slipping away, most of those memories were now forgotten to him. Stolen by old age, I wondered where his memories went?

Shelling peas on his back porch . . .
Doting on my little sister, the first baby girl in our family . . .
His wrinkled hand tracing the lines of "Amazing Grace" in the hymnal as we stood and sang together in church . . .
His wife of more than fifty years, Doris, right there by his side . . .

All these precious moments of a life falling away, like petals in an autumn frost. Is God catching them as they escape Grandaddy's mind and holding them in His hand? Does He record them, each memory pressed between the pages of time? Will they one day be restored to him? Do our memories belong to us alone, or are they so special to God that He takes pains to keep track of each and every one? Before Granddaddy died, he asked me from his hospital bed if anyone needed a good watch and began showing me how his pocket watch and wristwatch worked. His worn hands mimicked the motions of winding and setting a watch that wasn't there. I couldn't take my eyes off his old, rough hands. They'd never attempted anything less than what was decent, honest, and kind. He didn't understand that he had already given me everything someone can give another—unconditional love.

My wife and I had our first child, Morgan, in Mississippi, about one year after Grandaddy died. She was a beautiful blond baby with big blue eyes and I carried her picture on the dash of my car, covering up the fuel gauge. It's odd how you lose one you love, and God puts someone else in your life to help soak up the pain. I sometimes ran out of gas because I couldn't see the needle; I wanted to look at her that much. But now on this Tuesday morning in Jackson, in a starched shirt scratching at my neck and maroon striped tie hearing about the attacks on September 11, 2001 . . . I realized that I was about to head back to CIA, but by a very circuitous route.

I FIRST GOT INVOLVED with Blackwater back around 1998. Law school was ridiculously expensive, especially with a wife and new baby girl, so I had to do something to make extra money. As we sat waiting for Professor Duane's criminal law class to begin, I was complaining about making ends meet. A fellow classmate and former SEAL told me about part-time work as a role player at a place just opening up. I knew nothing about

Blackwater—it wasn't in the news yet and had been open for just a few months.

Blackwater . . . the name—from swamp water colored black by tannin; the logo—from black bears roaming the area; the idea—from a SEAL named Al Clark from Dallas, Texas; the money—from Erik Prince's inherited fortune. Those were the ingredients for Blackwater in the beginning. Erik Prince, heir to a fortune made by his dad in Michigan, paid roughly $900,000 for 3,100 acres from an old potato farmer in Moyock, North Carolina, spurred on by an idea from Al Clark—a guy who doesn't always get enough credit when it comes to telling the story of how Blackwater was formed. That original plan didn't involve security services or any of the things for which Blackwater is now known; it all started with the simpler notion of opening a world-class private training area for the Navy Special Warfare community that was within driving distance of Little Creek, where 99 percent of the SEALs on the East Coast were based.

Al Clark, a SEAL NCO, met Erik at Little Creek Naval Amphibious Base and took the young officer under his wing and planted the seed for Blackwater. Erik apparently figured it was a good business opportunity, and he hoped to outdistance the competition by placing a better facility, with better ranges and better instruction, closer to the navy than the competition did. He started Blackwater and hired Al as director of training.

By the time the Blackwater Lodge and Training Center officially opened on May 15, 1998, it had grown to five thousand acres and Erik had sunk in $6.5 million. Twenty-seven major armed conflicts in twenty-six locations throughout the world occurred the year Blackwater opened, a substantial jump from the year before. Eighteen terror attacks were carried out around the globe, including al-Qa'ida's bombing of two U.S. embassies in Africa, events that collectively killed 255 and wounded more than 4,000. America was slowly coming to understand that we were at war in a way we had never been before; a new reality had sneaked up on us and we faced a hatred we didn't fully understand. Our leaders called it a war against terrorism, but that was politically correct crap designed to keep certain segments of society appeased. This war wasn't a war against terror—how can you have a war against an idea? This was a war against radicalized militant Islam and we had to broaden our battle against it and the group that embodied it—al-Qa'ida. All this meant training more troops, and Blackwater was poised to fill the need.

When I called the number my classmate gave me, I got a guy named Gary Jackson, who said that if I'd come help out, I could take any course for free. I had taken enough courses: I was in law school, not training to be a better shooter. But, in hopes of eventually landing a paying part-time job, I showed up. A young woman took me back to meet Gary, then vice president of operations. He was an energetic, tall, lean guy with tightly cropped jet-black hair. Shaking my hand, he graciously welcomed me; he sported a tight, reptilian grin that spread across his face as he introduced himself, and then he called in Al Clark.

AL WAS AN AMAZING SHOOTER and tactician from DEVGRU (previously SEAL Team 6) and combat veteran of Operation Just Cause in Panama. We called him the "Michael Jordan of Ass Kick." He was the only man I've seen who came close to shooting as well as my old agency boss, Mack.

Al had a biting wit, and you either loved him or hated him and he wasn't about to be ignored. Many called him "Abrasive Al," but he became a good friend. Once, a young army lieutenant came out for a week of handgun training with him. The lieutenant was a small guy—he had Vietnamese parents. Al saw him coming out with all his gear on and started in on him.

"I've never seen somebody like you. Are you old enough to drive? How'd you get here? Do you want a crayon?" said Al.

Later, when everyone was starting to fill out the liability waivers, Al again asked the lieutenant if he wanted a crayon. The week didn't get any better for the kid. But Al was brutal to everybody—it was his way of getting the best out of students, using humor and getting under their skin. Once when we were commuting together to work, he and I stopped at my house in Sandbridge, a beachside community south of Virginia Beach that backs up to Dam Neck Naval Base. We were done for the day but had been talking shop—about shooting, fighting—and so when we got to my house, we decided to practice. We shoved the furniture in my den aside and started grappling in front of the big picture windows overlooking the Atlantic Ocean. We slung each other around, battling for the clinch and the choke. It was a workout.

My wife, pregnant with our second child, came home with our daughter in hand from a grocery run to find two grown men dirty, sweating, rolling around on the hardwood floor trying to choke each other out. Unfazed, she kept moving to the kitchen and said simply, "Hi, guys. Don't break anything." We looked at each other for a second—stopped, helped bring in the groceries, and then finished the fight.

I LEFT GARY'S OFFICE WITH AL and went down the hall to his little corner of the kingdom, where he kept the training programs running. Al was roughly six feet tall and wore the Blackwater (BW) uniform of Royal Robbins khaki pants and a BW short-sleeve T-shirt stained with perspiration. A weathered, faded, sweat-stained BW ball cap sat cocked back atop his head, crowned with a pair of mirrored Oakley blade sunglasses resting on the bill. He handed me a script and a scene-by-scene breakdown of what he needed me to do for this role-playing job I'd signed up to do. My parts were highlighted in red, and what the students were expecting was in green. I was to play the part of a U.S. Department of Defense attaché flying into a hostile country. I'd be picked up by the students in the class from SEAL Team 8 out of Little Creek who'd take me to a few meetings; then I'd be ambushed, they'd have to save me, I'd fake a heart attack, they'd perform medical work on me, and then they'd evacuate me, all while defeating the attackers. It was a two-day exercise.

The SEALs were going through a PSD (protective security detail) course. It was six days long, and I was joining in on the tail end. A scene that Al had worked into the exercise involved the security detail of SEALs escorting me, the attaché, to a bar in nearby Elizabeth City, North Carolina, named Headlights. I understood the name better once I got inside the dark space and saw the stripper poles on top of the raised runway, inhaled enough secondhand cigarette smoke to require an iron lung, and felt my boot slip on beer pooled on the hard tiled floor. The thumping beat of the music in my chest reminded me of a chaotic current of water slamming into me. I stepped aside as a thickly built waitress with peroxide hair, cigarette dangling from her lips, in skimpy shorts straining to contain the load, and carrying a tray of wobbly drinks and hot wings weaved her muffintop between tables of overweight drunk guys with apparently nothing better to do on a Friday afternoon. Earlier, Al had spoken to a dancer and paid her to help our exercise. I was wearing a radio with a one-way earpiece so I could hear him, but I couldn't talk back to him. He'd just give me instructions on what he wanted me to do over the air.

I was sitting right by the raised runway near the main pole where the dancers gyrated to the techno-junk under the flashing strobe lights as the DJ urged everyone to "give it up" for some girl named Shareeka. My SEAL PSO (personal security officer) was next to me in a chair wearing a Hawaiian-style button-up shirt to hide his radio and SIG P-226 handgun. The boy was trying hard to pay attention for signs of any oncoming threats, but he was also trying to keep his eyes from roaming the stage. The rest of the SEALs, also in plainclothes with radios and SIG pistols outfitted to shoot Simunitions (tiny paintballs, essentially), were scattered about, trying not to be distracted by the abundance of uncovered boobs moving around the room. It was hard labor, to be sure, and the guys were stoic—none smiled, none drank anything but water, and it was obvious they weren't the usual patrons. In other words, they weren't blending in at all.

"Okay, Sapphire is going to come over to you and sit on your lap. I want you to start acting like you're getting drunk, acting stupid," Al said into my earpiece. "When she sits down, reach up and grab her tit. She's gonna slap you—got that?" Despite the blaring music, I could hear him laughing and I looked up nonchalantly across the runway and spotted him seated against the rear wall with another instructor, both with the biggest grins on their faces as he lifted a Corona my direction. I nodded slightly. "What I want to see is how your PSO handles it—does he take her to the ground or does he let her slide 'cause she's a naked chick?" I could barely understand him over his laughter and the bedlam of music.

A few minutes later, a tall, bronze-skinned woman with masses of dark hair, eyes like pale emeralds, and more curves than the Nürburgring racetrack appeared next to my table. My SEAL stood and started to intervene, but I held up a lazy hand, gave a droopy-eyed smile, slurred my words, and waved him off. The stripper sat on my lap with nothing between her and the Lord but a smile and three pieces of strategically placed duct tape. She slipped a glittering arm around my shoulders—she apparently was wearing lotion with metal flakes in it and it felt rough. Then she leaned her décolletage my way, placing her head next to my ear. "You know what you're supposed to do, right?" she whispered, smiling and acting like she had just said something terribly wrong. She was a good actress for Elizabeth City.

Laughing, smiling, and acting wasted, I slurred as loudly and obnoxiously as I could, "Oh, I know exactly what I'm doing, woman!" With that, I reached up and placed my hand on her massive breast, just as I'd been instructed to do—all for the good of my country.

The slap that followed could be heard throughout the bar, and I even thought she might have dislodged a filling or two. My PSO was up and on her in a flash, but he didn't quite know what to do with his hands—he held them back from her like she had leprosy or the bird flu. Then he finally grabbed her shoulders, taking care to avoid her now-flailing other upper-body parts as she feigned anger and whirled around on her high heels toward him.

His teammates seemed to materialize from thin air and surrounded us, with everyone trying to figure out how to move this nearly naked, green-eyed Amazonian stripper who was, by now, putting on her best *Jerry Springer Show* audition, complete with racial epithets and words that would make sailors blush . . . which a few were doing.

"Oh my God!" I could hear Al laughing through my earpiece. I figured I must have passed my employment interview.

SHORTLY AFTER THAT I was invited to take the Instructor Development course, which covered how to teach the Blackwater way—which was really Al's way. I was joined by a dozen or so other prospective instructors. Some would make it and others wouldn't. Blackwater was staffed by a lot of SEALs, but simply being a SEAL doesn't mean you can shoot or teach, any more than going to church means you're a Christian. I wasn't a SEAL, but I got a job. I was to be an assistant instructor on the shooting range. Eventually, I was given courses to teach on my own and started making decent money. I worked up to regular hours that I could count on to put food on the table back home when I wasn't hustling to law school classes.

A TYPICAL BLACKWATER COURSE would start in the classroom with a welcome and safety brief, then we'd move to the paper target range. We'd gauge the student's capabilities and work up from there, concentrating on building accuracy and speed by having them shoot three-inch paper dot targets, which are basically the size of the bottom of a Coke can.

Once they had that down, we moved them on to larger eight-inch paper dots—roughly the size of a human head at twenty-five yards. The course progressed to static steel targets and then moving steel—the steel allowed immediate feedback when struck because you could see it and hear the metal being hit by the bullet. We pushed the guys hard: speed, accuracy, and movement; slow is smooth and smooth is fast—those were our maxims. We used competition shot timers that recorded the time it took a shooter to react and fire. We created man-on-man competitions to build speed, and we designed stress courses to place the students under pressure.

A normal student goal was to get a first shot off in 1.5 seconds or less. We wanted our instructors to get their shots off in 1.25 seconds or less. I consistently drew, fired, and hit an eight-inch target at ten yards away in under 1 second. My recorded best time was .74 seconds—that's hearing a buzzer, drawing the gun, and shooting a target the size of a dessert plate thirty feet away in less than three-quarters of a second. I guarantee it was not talent—just long, hard work.

But the mark of a good shooter isn't just how fast he can draw and hit one target on a sunny day standing still, but whether he can do multiple things quickly when everything is going wrong and still make his hits. To measure that, we used many drills, but my favorite was called the "El Presidente," where the shooter stands thirty feet away with his back turned to three steel targets spaced roughly three feet apart. On the buzzer, he turns, draws, and shoots each target twice, reloads, and then shoots them twice again.

The students were expected to get this drill done in under 10 seconds; instructors, under 7 seconds, but we regularly got between 4 and 4.5 seconds. The shotgun version was two shots to the first target, two shots into the second target, one shot into the third target, reload one shell, and fire again into that third target. Once I did it with a Remington 870 pump-action shotgun in 3.73 seconds. A friend and fellow instructor, Chris, beat me by just one-quarter of a second.

All the instructors were excellent and I certainly wasn't the best by far, but I tried hard. You couldn't skate by—the peer competition and ribbing were too severe. If an instructor missed just one shot while performing a demonstration in front of a class of students, his name would become a verb in the chow hall that day. We were teaching the best in the world, and we expected our staff to be the best instructors in the world.

I MET ERIK PRINCE a handful of times back then, and he was a nice, polite guy and generally came across as a likable, patriotic American. He was just about my age, too. But during the spring of 2000, Al had a falling-out with the leadership. I really don't know what happened, but heard that it had something to do with Gary. I couldn't imagine Erik and Al having problems, since Erik was rarely at Blackwater in the early years. He spent most of his time in Tysons Corner, Virginia, at the Prince Group and tending to his first wife, Joan, who'd recently been diagnosed with cancer; so I assumed whatever bad intel he was getting about things going on in North Carolina must have come through Gary.

Gary had started out as the operations manager at Blackwater, and he kept the website afloat. Then people above him started getting fired and surprise—he wound up getting the job in the corner office. Al got so fed up with the internal political games being played that he quit and Erik fired him—all about the same time. I was sorry to see Al leave, but it opened things up because it put Gary in a bind. He'd sold training courses to customers, but he had no director of training or lead instructor. Other than Al and a dark-haired young fella who helped him out, the rest of the staff were part-time and unavailable due to their day jobs. The only two guys who could reliably help out were Chris—the Virginia Beach police officer who beat me in the shotgun drill—and me. It was my last semester of my third year of law school so I basically had a lot of free time on my hands.

My wife delivered our second child, a son we named Cole, as I was graduating. Since our oldest daughter, Morgan, had been born in Mississippi, I asked dad to send me some Mississippi dirt for the birth. He did—in a red Folger's coffee can. During the delivery, I set that can under the delivery table so that my son could always claim to have been born over Mississippi soil—just like his sister. The kids gave their mom a pass, trying to overlook her misfortune of being born in the second-best state in the country—Texas.

With Al's departure, I continued to teach part-time at Blackwater during law school, until the last minute, when my family packed up a U-Haul and headed out of Virginia. We went straight south to get them settled with family, because I had been accepted to a yearlong, postgraduate tax law program at Boston University School of Law, during which I took a foreign tax course at Harvard Law School. BU had one of the best programs in the country and it was the opportunity of a lifetime, but the pain of once again leaving my family behind was rough; still, them being with family made me feel a little better. Then roughly one year later, in 2001, I headed home to a new job in Jackson, Mississippi.

Soon after moving into our new house in Jackson, my wife told me she was pregnant with our third child. For the first time we asked about the sex of the baby and found out that another boy was on the way, but nine weeks into the first trimester we lost him. We named him William, after Alli's father, an outstanding architect and fine Christian man with a wonderful sense of humor and unquenchable fondness for his home state of Texas. Sadly, Alli's dad would pass away after a courageous cancer fight in 2013.

SOON AFTER 9/11, when Erik called with a full-time job offer, I was a sitting duck. The salary sounded good and I was definitely taking the offer seriously—but money really wasn't the only factor. I had to find out what my family thought, because if Momma's not happy, no one is. We prayed about it and tried our best to think it through, but she knew where my heart was and that our nation was going to war. She also knew that I was going to serve somehow.

I called Erik back a few days later and said I'd take the job, contingent on one thing. "Erik, BW is a great asset—the name, the facility, and the instructors are top-notch. But we need to go beyond selling training and making steel targets. I've got an idea to move into high-risk services like protection, security, private intelligence, and, if we can get the work, special missions through Uncle Sam. We've got the expertise and the government will need the help, now more than ever. Trust me, I can make it work and we can do serious good, but I want to run it," I said, holding my breath as I drove home from the law firm one evening in the pouring rain. This was the first of its kind—a new type of company, a new type of service for a new era. The idea would shape a decade of war and ultimately transform the way the United States projects power for many years to come as Blackwater Security personnel safeguarded CIA stations and bases, and protected ambassadors and other dignitaries ███ ████████████████████.

"Okay, it's a deal—you'll wear two hats. You're vice president of Blackwater USA and you will answer to Gary and then to me. But you'll run the security company yourself." I've got to give Erik credit for taking the chance. Steve Capace, the Prince Group's attorney and a good friend of Erik at the time, sent me the employment agreement and we settled all the details. If I recall correctly, they founded Blackwater Security initially as a Delaware LLC and I stepped in as the founding director. Today, some people try to rewrite this history because of petty rivalries and bad blood. It's a shame and silly to think that tearing someone else down builds you up—I just try to ignore them.

Unknown to me, however, Erik hired me directly without first consulting Gary, and apparently offered me a higher salary than Gary was drawing at the time. It wasn't an intentional slight to Gary, and I wasn't a threat to his position at all. Erik and I just worked it out over the phone and that happened to be the number we reached. Blackwater back then, it was said by those on the inside, was like an old woman's sewing circle—full of backstabbing and gossip. The personnel roster there was like the deck of an aircraft carrier—a guy was like an F-18, there one minute and gone the next. Regardless, it occurred to me that behind the scenes Gary possibly started working to get rid of me—but with a smile on his face like we were best friends. To this day the rumors still float around. But oddly, one thing Gary said applies to that—don't listen to the critics when you are doing well because someone will always try to take you down.

MY VISION WAS for Blackwater Security Company (BSC) to become a top-tier operational services group, offering private intelligence collection, protective and security-related work, as well as kidnap and ransom, logistics, and aviation support. Gary didn't appear to have any faith that it would work and told me to devote 20 percent of my time to BSC, the new company, with the rest going toward the core business—training and developing that work. But within months of coming on board full-time, we had a no-bid, ████████, six-month contract with the CIA—my former employer. We were to provide a twenty-man security and operational support team to augment the CIA ██████████ which secured CIA personnel and activities in Afghanistan, where the Taliban was terrorizing citizens and giving aid and comfort to its al-Qa'ida allies who'd attacked us on 9/11.

This was the first war in the twenty-first century for the United States, and the CIA was running it from its station in Kabul—and we were protecting them. If we failed, the agency's operations and staff would be put at risk and thus the war effort itself. The eyes of the CIA's seventh floor, the Bush administration, and eventually the world would be on us. It was a big job—and I was at the helm of the company with the contract and Erik was owner of it all.

Dave Phillips, whom I hired as my deputy, and I started recruiting the best guys we could get our hands on to staff the first team going to Afghanistan. I reached out to some contacts Gary suggested, other people I knew, and the rest was a word-of-mouth campaign. First, we set about defining the men we wanted to hire: they'd have a minimum of eight years of experience in Special Operations, intel, or SWAT; verified through a background check that they had no criminal background, passed a drug test, had no financial issues, no domestic violence convictions; they would be eligible for a secret clearance; and they'd be in good physical condition. Last, we wanted no one who had been separated from the service for more than five years—their skills needed to be current. If their last deployment was in the 1960s, we thanked them but had to pass. In the beginning, we had crazies show up, too. Once a guy came in who claimed to be former Special Operations with the air force. The first clue he was full of crap was that he came in wearing desert camouflage BDUs from the Gulf War, with his pants bloused into shiny, black combat boots, with a desert camo backpack that he never took off, topped off with a desert camo boonie hat. Then, when the shooting started, he couldn't hit the side of a barn if he'd been put inside the barn itself. I called him into my office after the first day on the range and politely told him, "You've got skills, but just not the skills we need."

We pulled guys in from all over the country—ex-Delta, Special Forces, SEALs, Marine Recon. We wanted experts in demolitions, driving, convoys, motorcades, surveillance, sniping, and assault. Dave and I whittled our team down to eighteen people—Erik and I would make twenty. The men were offered $550 per day with no one deployed continuously for more than ninety days. I didn't want guys getting burned-out. We billed the government $1,500 per man, per day, for a total daily bill of nearly $30,000 for eighteen men, which translated into a monthly bill just over $800,000—we definitely weren't losing money.

I drew up an individual gear list for each man and another for the team equipment, ordering it from Jason Beck, who now runs TYR Tactical, and had it shipped in. Thanks to Jason's expertise, we had the best you could get—the latest and lightest body armor and composite trauma plates, helmets, uniforms, Glocks, Bushmaster M4 rifles, gas masks, Blackhawk bags, CamelBak drinking bladders, SureFire lights, Emerson knives—you name it and we had it. We were better kitted out than the majority of military units going over.

Then we brought in the new men of the team, selected a former SEAL Team 6 officer named Bo as the team's boss. Master Chief Denny Chalker was his second-in-command and we started doing train-ups. Briefers from CIA came down from D.C. and gave us a data dump on the enemy, the compound, and what we were up against. We broke into committees—with one handling the urban movement class, another CQB, another handgun, another the M4 and shotgun, another vehicle searches, and so on. Each committee lead was an expert in that area, and the teams would rotate from one class to another, teaching each other and getting on the same page when it came to tactics and procedures. We were now well on our way. We trained for days, sweating it out on the humid North Carolina ranges until we got the word it was time to move. The CIA was ready, and my team was ready. We dubbed ourselves the Wolf Pack and later the Gladiators, after the movie. We were the first team ever, the plank owners of Blackwater Security Company, and we were about to head into the war zone. I was confident, but confidence is what a man experiences before he learns all the facts.

CHAPTER 19

Going to War

June 2002
Afghanistan Border Area

KANE, THE DEPUTY CHIEF OF BASE, who wore a dark brown Indiana Jones–style hat and was backlit by fires burning trash in fifty-gallon steel drums, met us at the massive gates looking like something out of *Apocalypse Now.* “Gentlemen,” he announced with arms outstretched, “welcome to the edge of the empire!” Three days before our helicopter flight in, a task force patrol had been ambushed. There was a body, one of the good guys—hence the call for the two of us. Erik Prince and I were heading to the most dangerous place on the planet to provide security for intelligence officers conducting the most dangerous missions on the planet—hunting radical Islamist terrorists.

Rarely in my life have I been so cold as I was in that CIA helicopter. The swirling wind clawed at everything inside the loud, lumbering bird and seemed to suck the warmth up from my very spine. We had flown with the huge rear doors of the Mi-17 helicopters open like the mouth of some great whale, from a starting altitude of roughly one mile high and to well above fifteen thousand feet to clear the mountains of the Hindu Kush—the foothills of the Himalayas. Snow powdered the turf like icing on a cake and I was starting to wonder if we’d need O_2 bottles up this high. Erik and I both scrunched down between the spare tires and other resupply equipment packed into the bird as the engine and rotor noise lulled us into fitful sleep. We landed in darkness; the only light was

a three-quarter moon. It was Afghanistan's most evil place .
in this barren moonscape that seemed so desolate that the wind was your only companion. It was also one of the hottest places to work—it took fire nearly every day. Vulnerable to attack from the Pakistani side, which was just a mile or so away, as well as from the Afghan side, the base was a sitting duck. If it was attacked by a determined force we'd just have to hold them off until reinforcements could arrive—from a long, long way away—even by helicopter.

On site was and we were here to link with them. The task force lashed up CIA and Delta Force to gather intelligence and hunt down HVTs (high-value targets) like bin Laden, Afghan mujahideen leader Gulbuddin Hekmatyar, and the al-Qa'ida leadership. It was ugly territory. But D.C. wanted bodies—bin Laden's head on a pike—and we were here to help make that happen.

BLACKWATER AS A COMPANY definitely had its ups and downs, but this first major operation for the company I headed up was a roaring success. A company with no past performance, with no staff but me, Dave, and a handful of contractors we hired, was now providing support to the CIA in a top-secret mission in our war against radical militant Islam.

In the weeks before this mission to the border with Pakistan, the world had shot past rapidly as we left the United States and traveled to Afghanistan—a U.S. Air Force C-17 transatlantic flight out of Andrews Air Force Base, a flash through Frankfurt, then on to Tashkent, a CIA flight on an L-100 into Kabul, all as our team of bearded veterans in jeans and hiking boots crossed the globe to get into the fight. Back in the real world, my sweet, blond-haired, firstborn daughter, Morgan, was graduating from kindergarten in her new dress.

In Kabul was a glaring sun; the land, ancient and mysterious, looked like New Mexico; the remains of the airport, littered with twisted metal from Soviet aircraft, was surrounded by jagged, sharp gray peaks that bit like teeth into the blue sky. Only a few months before, Afghanistan's minister of aviation and tourism had been pulled from his plane, pitched to the tarmac, and beaten to death by a mob incensed that they could not travel to Mecca. Smaller peaks ringing the valley where the city sat were zigzagged with coalition-sandbagged gun emplacements. Along with the roar of the CIA cargo plane's engines came the stink of exhaust and swirling dust. A CIA security officer yelled over the clamor of roaring engines and spinning props for us not to step off the tarmac: land mines were still everywhere. Soon trucks pulled up to meet us—a big Mercedes utility truck and a few Toyota HiLuxes—the foreign version of the four-door Tacoma.

We loaded gear, piled into the pickups, and sped out quickly, turning at Liberty circle and passing AMEMB Kabul—the U.S. Embassy, and made it to a walled compound, a bunker heavily armed and protected, which was vital. February had seen the first attack on International Security Assistance Force (ISAF) soldiers since their deployment in 2001. Just before dawn, a car full of gunmen hit a post in Kabul. Then March brought a green-on-blue attack at a base in an eastern province. A man in an Afghan military uniform had turned his weapon on U.S. and Afghan forces. March was just beginning. Nine Americans had died in Afghanistan in April; Germans troops walking through the market on Chicken Street in Kabul had been attacked with someone running up and jamming a syringe of unknown substance into them, and a grenade had been dropped through the open window of a French vehicle stuck in traffic. The situation was grim, but I'd decided one thing: the next time my daughter graduated, I wanted to be sitting in that school.

As soon as we arrived from the airport, we sent one six-man team out to take up static security posts guarding the entry and exits while another team set to work assembling bunk beds. The team's leadership headed upstairs to the second floor in the main building to meet with the station chief, his deputy chief, and Wolf, who was the officer responsible for security and was our team's immediate superior. I got back late; we were all running on fumes, but it was my turn to patrol, so I slipped on my armor, loaded my rifle, and holstered my pistol. Byrd, Babs, Just, Snake, Don, and I set off on a foot patrol around the compound and the grounds.

The next morning, another shift took over as others on our team started building watchtowers and gun positions, setting up floodlights and establishing sniper hides on top of the building. A dump truck rolled past our position and turned into Hamid Karzai's presidential palace. The truck was guarded by German soldiers piled all over it who'd given us the peace sign as they rolled by. I asked a CIA officer standing next to me what was in the truck. "Money," she said. We responded by holding up three fingers—a "W" for war; the middle finger also had a second meaning regarding our notion of peace. The Germans didn't seem to have a proper mind-set—this was war, not a peacekeeping project. Our country had been attacked and we were here to get payback.

A FEW DAYS LATER Erik and I were speeding back to the airport in another vehicle, taking in the looming shadows of the gray mountains licked with snow that lay in scattered patches like footprints across the granite. Smog-choked Kabul flashed past me.

Ours was a three-truck convoy. I rode in the bed of the first, covering the rear. Following was the COS (chief of station) truck, a ████ armored Toyota, followed by another Toyota HiLux like ours. We roared past Ariana Afghan Airlines and, again, the American embassy, before hitting the ruins of the Kabul airport and turning west. We pulled up to the CIA aircraft staging area on the ████████ edge of the facility.

Erik and I were headed ████████████████████████████. The weather sucked at the small, covert CIA forward operating base (FOB) on the outskirts of the Afghan border with Pakistan. At night it was balls-cold and during the day you roasted. Our orders were to help the CIA officers who were tracking terrorists. That could mean anything from casing meeting sites, to defending the base from attacks, to providing security for the CIA officers as they went about their covert work. It was the beginning of Blackwater Security Company's dip into covert operations that went way beyond just standing guard.

Two Hind Mi-17s—Soviet-era cargo helicopters—waited with engines running and rotors slowly turning. We packed the birds tight with equipment and then squeezed ourselves in, leaving the tail door open. CIA helos flew at night because they knew the enemy would try to shoot us to pieces doing a helo landing in daytime. On the downside, however, the Russian birds didn't have nearly the avionics and visual sensors that U.S. Black Hawks did for night ops. Lifting off from Kabul, I scanned through my PVS-14 night vision for ground threats, but once we climbed up a few hundred feet my weapon was useless. I couldn't hit squat that high with a 5.56 mm rifle from a moving platform. So I settled down, propped my feet up on a spare tire, pulled my hood around my face, and yanked the drawstring so tightly that just my nose stuck out, and froze during one of the longest, coldest helicopter rides I've ever taken.

We banged down on the ground and Rick and another CIA door gunner fanned out, taking a knee and covering the left and right flanks while I took the rear, six o'clock position. Three Toyota trucks rolled up, one driven by an NVG-clad bearded Delta operator called Pope, who got out with his M4 and walked up in his black PT shorts, brown T-shirt, and hiking boots. Rotors still spinning, we cross-loaded all the gear from the bird into the trucks as fast as we could, then made our way to the fort in the dark all before any bad guys nearby woke up and started shooting at us. Once we'd cleared the helicopter landing zone (HLZ) by about twenty yards or so, the CIA Air Branch pilots lifted off, back over the peaks. The whole landing and offloading took just minutes.

We sped up the dusty path to the fort we called Apache (some called it Alamo, but in my opinion that sucked as a name for a fort). As we drove into the massive double doors guarding the entrance, a fire was burning in a barrel on the inside, giving off crazy shadows and orange flickers off the towering tall mud walls. A row of green army tents to the center-left housed the Rangers' Quick Reaction Force (QRF); to the far left against the wall sat the trucks backed up all in a line. On the right were Humvees and a building set into the fort's wall, where the CIA chief lived. The rear wall housed the cook; in the center were the few solar showers made of plywood and a few more tents that served as the task force's Operations Center.

"Gentlemen, welcome to the edge of the empire!" That's what the CIA's 2-IC (second in command) said and I will never get that crazy voice out of my head, because that's what it felt like—the edge of the world.

Also in the fort were Delta, British ████████████ guys, a U.S. Special Forces ODA (Operational Detachment—Alpha), and a CIA officer of Afghan background whom we just called Haji. The CIA 2-IC officer briefed us on what had just happened: just a few miles from the fort, he and █████████ rounded a bend and rolled up on a kid with a horse. They slowed down, and then the kid raised an AK and shot and killed a

Special Operations communicator. The AK-47 round punched through his sternum after blowing through the truck's side mirror.

More enemy opened up from hidden positions on a berm to their flanks. The Americans returned fire in a ferocious fight, at times from only several feet away. One of the SF guys told me later that he'd snatched the pin and swiveled his Humvee-mounted MK19 automatic grenade launcher down and shot a Taliban attacker point-blank in the face, blowing the guy's head apart like a watermelon. It was so close that the grenade didn't even have a chance to arm, but slammed a 40 mm projectile roughly the size of a chicken egg into his head. Following that bit of good news, we were shown to our spartan quarters—a small dirt room in the back left corner of the fort, right under the watchtower. Erik and I stowed our gear, set up cots, and racked out until morning.

The next day I was given the same Toyota truck the operator was killed in as my vehicle to drive. The bullet holes were still in the mirror and front windshield and I looked at them every day, whether I wanted to or not. I don't believe in superstition or luck—just good decisions or ones that aren't. Some people carry a rabbit's foot for good luck—well, depend on that if you want to, but it didn't work out so well for the rabbit. So I took the truck and moved along. Our Delta/CIA/Blackwater team spent our time inside the fort cleaning our weapons, pulling guard duty at night up in one of the towers, lifting makeshift weights of buckets filled with sand, doing pull-ups on a wooden frame we built, or getting a tan as we waited for a call from a spy just over the border in Pakistan. Erik and I were the only Blackwater guys on-site and our mission was to protect the CIA officers from dawn till dusk. If they had a covert meeting with a terrorist informant, we were there. We scouted meeting sites days in advance; we set up the surveillance detection routes and coordinated our movements each day with the Army Rangers' QRF. Very simply, our job was to kill any bad guys who threatened our clients.

One day when we had downtime, I got up on the roof to get some sun. Having no suntan lotion, but thinking any oil would work, I hopped down to the kitchen and asked our Afghan cook if he had any. He gave me a small, plastic bottle of foul-smelling stuff that I smeared on, and within minutes I'd attracted every fly within twenty miles. That was an example of a bad decision.

Finally when the spy did call in, the case officer established a meeting time and location and we geared up to go. Often we had to react so quickly that I only had time to throw on my boots and armor, going out wearing running shorts and a T-shirt. Erik and I would climb a ridge and provide overwatch for the intel meeting, or I'd go down into the meeting site to provide close security while Erik pulled sniper duty, since he'd been through SEAL sniper training.

AS WE GOT CLOSE to the Pak border one day, we saw what looked like a Soviet 12.7 x 108 mm DShK heavy machine gun sitting up on the ridge . . . and it had just swiveled down, aiming at our trucks. That gun was used to blow aircraft out of the sky, chop up tanks, and level infantry; it fired bullets the size of railroad spikes and would definitely have obliterated our soft-skinned Toyotas. We slow-rolled to the outpost to signal that we were no threat. The border guards were friendly and even invited us inside the small stone border post to drink tea. We were the first Americans to make contact with them at this border crossing in the mountains—ever. Our chief went in with another CIA officer by the gate while Erik and I stood with a few other guys from the team, namely a PsyOps specialist and a medic. Inside, the chief worked out a deal to enable us to chase al-Qa'ida across the border if we were in hot pursuit—and a promise that they wouldn't turn that big gun loose on us in the process.

Leaving our new Pakistani friends, we drove farther north to case meeting sites and get eyes on a few locations that Delta operators had identified where al-Qa'ida and the Taliban were crossing in the mountain passes. But as we drove, the case officer received the call on his Thuraya satphone: a foreign agent was finally ready to meet, and he was bringing news of al-Qa'ida and Chechens living nearby and operating against U.S. forces. He'd be coming with one driver in a red truck.

Two roads led north—one was the old road, one was new. We chose the former, thinking there would be fewer travelers on it, which was a plus for our clandestine meeting with this arms dealer in al-Qa'ida and Taliban country. As we drove to the spot Erik and I had chosen for the meeting, I spotted three Toyotas filled with armed men hauling tail and going in the same direction as we were, but on the nearby new road a few hundred yards away. After we rounded a small hill, we lost sight of them.

We hid the vehicles behind a large rock formation. It was a twisting, turning wadi, a dry creek bed, with sheer cliffs on either side going up twenty or thirty feet that gave us a perfect blind spot for protection behind and ahead, and it was ideal for our purposes.

Erik was west on the high ground of the plateau with his scoped HK G3. Mark, a late twenty-something full-time CIA ████████ officer, was on the same ridge, covering the road and the north. Mark was slim in build with a placid—almost antisocial—disposition and curly brown hair—a lot of it. If I hadn't known he worked for the CIA, I'd have guessed he was a hipster college kid. He was armed with an M4 and a ████████ grenade launcher. Mark was also the head guy for the CIA's ███ unit here; after this meeting, the unit would be leaving because Erik and I had shown up. Jim was the third man on the high ground. Also a full-time CIA ██ guy, he was a black-haired fullback of a man with Italian ancestry and an easygoing manner who reminded me of my cousin Kevin. I liked Jim a lot—he was easy to get along with and took it upon himself to make doubly sure that Erik and I were up to speed on the MBITR radios, how to call the fort, or even back to CIA headquarters in Virginia from the device, as well as other duties we were to fulfill after he and Mark bugged out.

Jim was up on a small ridge overlooking the road. I was across the road hiding in the open ground, about five yards in, behind a small cluster of rocks, with my M4 and seven thirty-round magazines. Slung over my shoulder was a separate HK 69A1, a 40 mm grenade launcher that I called "the thumper," and my Glock 17 pistol.

I was trying to keep a close eye on the new road as well as looking north to try to see the approach of our agent. Our security plan was basically an ambush. The case officers would be hidden back in the wadi, waiting on the agent, while the rest of us took hidden positions covering every avenue of approach. If al-Qa'ida followed the guy or, worse, was led to us by the guy, then I'd be front and center at ground level in the rocks, hammering at them while Erik, Jim, and Mark poured fire down from the cliffs in a classic L-shaped ambush. I'd haul my little tail to the wadi where our IOs were and we'd all fight off the bad guys and make a hasty escape.

The meeting had a chance of going bad: al-Qa'ida and the Taliban were paying a hundred thousand dollars for any of our team who was captured and had circulated night letters and flyers to surrounding villages to that effect. These people we were meeting—arms dealers—were loyal only to the highest paymaster, so we had to expect they might bring trouble with them.

The plan for the arrival of our agent was simple—we knew he was ready to meet and he said he'd be coming with just one guy driving him. So we told him that we'd call him to tell him where he needed to be. Then he'd come down the road and from their perch Jim, Erik, or Mark would likely see his dust plume approaching and they'd signal me. They'd perform overwatch as I would step out from my hiding spot into the middle of the road and stop his red pickup truck. I'd get him out, search him, then guide him by foot to the meeting area, where our other guys—the IOs Kane and Lee, and Haji, the translator—would take over. Meanwhile, I'd tell his driver to head on down the road a few miles and pretend to be broken down, lifting the hood and working on his truck until his boss found him awhile later.

It didn't exactly work like that.

Erik was watching through his rifle scope when he nervously reported a red Toyota truck, the same color as the one we were expecting, pulling up on the new road. That was odd—what was our guy doing on the new road? After unloading three passengers, it turned around and headed back north, out of sight. I was within a hundred yards of these guys, hiding in scrub brush among a few rocks, and saw long, rifle-like objects in their hands. I had an EOTech red dot sight on my rifle with no magnification, so I couldn't tell if they were armed or not until I carefully, slowly dug out my small binos, but even then the lighting was so bad I couldn't tell. None of the guys on the ridge could see them. The men began walking south down the road—footmobiles, as we called them. I scrunched down farther to keep myself hidden, but kept them in sight. I suddenly was acutely aware that I was the only American exposed in the open at ground level—the rest of my team was up on the ridge or hidden in the crevices of the wadi. If those approaching saw and attacked me, I'd have to cover fifty yards of open ground just to reach the wadi while the boys covered my movement—not good odds. So I decided that if they were armed and came too close, I was going to hit them hard first, with everything.

Questions started flooding my mind—were these three unknown

footmobiles sent around to come up on us from the rear because the agent was a traitor? Why were they here? I hand-signaled to Kane that I had three men, moving south with weapons. I kept watching them through my binos; they talked, and were not trying to be silent. They never scanned the ridges or rocks for threats—they just walked on down the road.

Then my radio crackled in my ear. The call from the agent had just come in—he was coming our way. *Coming our way? How did he even know where we were? We hadn't told him which road to even be on.* Then down the road came another footmobile, solo. I studied him through my gun sights—no weapons in hand, none visible in his waistline, so I let him pass. The tension was high, as sweat dripped down into my eyes.

Then another radio call, "Truck's in sight, thirty seconds out," said Mark. Again, I wondered how did the contact know to drive down this particular road? Had he purposefully dropped off the other three earlier as part of some plan? Was this footmobile who just walked by also part of this plan? I wasn't liking this at all.

"You're clear—no one in sight, take him down," said Mark over my earpiece.

The red truck came into view and I rose from dust and rocks like the grim reaper and stepped into the road, owning the ground and pointing my M4 at the driver's face while holding up my nonfiring hand for him in the universally understood signal to stop.

"*Wadrega! Wadrega!*" I said loudly, Pashtun for stop. Then armed men began getting out of the truck bed. I saw one man in the passenger seat and a driver—this wasn't the plan. He was supposed to have only a driver, nothing more.

The passenger—our agent—got out and said, "It's okay, it's okay—they are my security."

I heard Mark's voice in my earpiece, "Everyone stay cool, stay cool. Kilo-1 stay cool down there," he said, talking to me. I'd been driving the shot-up truck, which was call sign Kilo-1, so that became my radio call sign.

With my weapon sight on the agent's face, I said, "Get them back into the truck!"

Again, he said, "No, it's okay—they are my security."

"I'm you're security today, but if you don't get them back in that truck, you're going to be the first one to die."

He thought about it for a split second, then turned and yammered some Pashtun at these AK-47-toting thugs and they clambered back into the truck.

"Now tell your driver to go down a few miles, stop, and lift the hood—pretend to have a broken engine," I told him.

Again, he turned and spoke some Pashtun, and the red truck drove on past us in a cloud of dust.

My radio crackled to life again, "Kilo-3, keep that truck in view. Kilo-1 bring him in." It was Mark telling Jim to make sure the truck didn't come back on us and for me to march this guy into the meeting.

I was about twenty yards from him now, the red-ringed circular dot on my EOTech centered on the middle of the man's face. He was frozen with his hands up into the air slightly. He obviously didn't expect to see a bearded, sunburned, dirty, dust-covered armed man rising out of the rocks with a gun pointed at his teeth.

I moved quickly to him, slung my rifle over my back, drew my Glock, and, keeping it tucked tightly by my hip—pointed at him—I patted him down with my nonfiring hand for any weapons, but, more important, for explosives. The last thing we wanted was a suicide bomber detonating—especially in a small space like that wadi. He'd kill everyone.

"Kilo-1, you're still clear . . ." I heard over my earpiece.

Then I pointed to the opening in the rock wall where Kane stood visible waiting and said, "*Zah, halta*," pushing him forward. As he moved toward Kane, I holstered the Glock and raised my rifle again, stepped to the side to avoid hitting Kane if I had to shoot, and kept the sights trained on the back of the man's skull. If he made any threatening move for Kane, I'd send 5.56 mm jacketed hollow points into the guy's medulla. I knew Mark, Jim, and Erik were also covering me and everything within eyesight. He reached Kane, they shook hands, and walked back into the wadi.

"He's in, we got him," I heard over the radio.

Once the guy was with Kane and they disappeared, the guys on the ridge covered down on him. I made my way back into position, settled in, and started looking outboard for any threats moving our way. This would be the time to hammer us, if they were going to do it.

For the next ninety minutes, the two IOs, the agent, and our interpreter talked. The agent stopped at one point, faced toward Mecca, and said his prayers. Then later he stopped again, went behind a rock for privacy, and took a crap—but our guys on the ridge had him in their sights the whole time.

"Hey, guy just took a shit. Don't shake his hand—just friendly advice," Mark joked.

When another unknown footmobile passed by within feet of my position, I sank even lower into the rocks and kept my red dot on him. There was the chance he was an al-Qa'ida scout or the point man for a larger assault force . . . or just a guy walking to the village the long way. He never knew I was there.

But about fifteen minutes later, four large jingle cargo trucks—aptly named due to the bells the drivers hung on them that jingled over the rocks—barreled down the new road. Was this a Taliban assault force coming to kill or capture a bunch of CIA officers and their Afghan spy? The trucks had large cargo beds, but I couldn't see in them. When they roared down the road without stopping, I relaxed: the guy walking was just a pedestrian, not a scout, and the trucks were just delivery trucks, not a bed full of terrorist fighters.

Next a convoy from the local governor's protective detail rumbled by—about eight black shiny vehicles filled with armed Afghans. Four other local cars and trucks drove by—all this while a top-secret, clandestine personal meeting was taking place just a few feet away in the rocks.

The meeting went well and no one was hurt or killed. When it was over, we told the agent to stay in the wadi for half an hour after we left, then call his man to come back to get him. We piled into our trucks and headed back to the fort.

On another June morning, Babs, a blond younger SEAL who'd left the navy a few years earlier, and I were in a truck, rolling out of Apache. Erik was back in Virginia, having left Afghanistan after about two weeks of making sure things got off to a good start. Babs screwed the MBITR's roof antenna cable into the handheld unit: radio check. I drove and Babs monitored the radio link back to the fort, and we were off to set another meeting.

I drove down a bank into the rock-strewn wadis—a safer, less visible way of traveling than the dusty, well-traveled roads. Much of moving around these parts was about being careful, not taking the same route every time, nor setting any patterns that the enemy could rely on that would allow them to set IEDs (improvised explosive devices). It wasn't like Kabul—this was the wild land where the bad guys roamed at will. We made our way to a walled-in compound up on a small knoll that was slated to eventually become a medical clinic for the community. At that point it was just an abandoned building on a hillside, easy to secure and within mortar support from Apache's Ranger QRF. The meeting scheduled here was between four case officers and a former Afghan intelligence officer who lived just over the border in Pakistan and was a suspected smuggler.

Reaching the building, we stashed the truck and cleared the few rooms inside. It was a heap of junk—straw and mud walls, wooden beams hanging from the ceiling with holes in them. It looked like it had been used as both a home and stable for livestock—an assumption supported by the stink, too.

True to form for those parts, a group of shepherds was moving their herd of goats through the area and had to cross the road to the clinic to reach greener bushes to eat, but other than that, nothing was going on. The bleating of the goats keep setting me off—one of them sounded exactly like a woman crying out in pain. I mean exactly like that. If I had not spotted the herd, I'd have sworn someone was lying out there hurt, needing help. Babs and I called in that the place was secure and got comfortable—he covered the rear, I covered the front, as we awaited the rest of the team's arrival.

About ten minutes later we spotted a HiLux dusting its way down the road, heading west toward a small mud building. Babs glassed it with his binos and ID'd it as one of our trucks. It stopped at the building and let two people out; then two more got inside. The truck continued toward our position and pulled through the walled entrance to the clinic. Seeing the base chief and Haji in the front seats, I eased down to just inside the entrance and set security at the front, covering south and east. Babs would handle the two foreigners in the backseats of the truck. What the IOs had done was stop and let out Jack and Kane in exchange for the two agent contacts for our meeting. This was called a vehicle pickup (VPU) and served to prevent the foreign agents from being associated with the clinic by anyone seeing them walking into the area. I covered Jack and Kane as they walked in past me, nodding and heading inside.

The area was small and I heard the IOs, Lee, and Haji get to work. "Thank him for traveling this far and tell him that we are grateful." Haji translated this to the men. "Tell him that we appreciate his willingness to work with us." This too was relayed.

The chief spoke: "Ask him what he does for a living."

The man said in Pashtun that he owned a large truck and made deliveries throughout the area and into Pakistan.

"What did he do before he did that?" said the chief.

The answer—he worked for the Afghan army.

"What did he do for them?" the chief said.

After a rambling couple of minutes, Haji translated this answer—it turned out the man had been a crypto code breaker in Kabul during the long Russian occupation here and managed a garrison for the Afghan army until the regime collapsed when the Russians pulled out.

Once the man's bona fides had been perused and noted, Lee started in on him.

"Has he noticed al-Qa'ida or Chechens in Wana?" Haji dutifully translated this question and the answer was a good one—yes. Yes, al-Qa'ida Arabs from areas other than Pakistan and Afghanistan were indeed in Wana along with Chechens, but they didn't live in the city itself.

"Does he know where they sleep at night?" The answer was the same: yes, he did. The Afghan then began to name different areas. "Okay, I want him to do something for us. I want him to get us a map of the Wana city area and mark on it the places where the al-Qa'ida and Chechens regularly drive, meet, and sleep.

"Also, I want to know who is helping them in the area. Does he know this information?" Haji's answer was yes. A man named Salid was assisting them. The man was known to us already; he had helped corroborate intelligence given by another source earlier. It also spoke to the veracity of this new agent, in that he was giving us consistent info.

Then Lee said, "Tell him that I want specific directions to the al-Qa'ida and Chechen locations so that we can drive there if we need to—not that we are going to, but that's the general idea."

The man then said jokingly, "With all your satellites and electronics, can you not do this already?" Lee said, "Tell him we appreciate humor, too, but we are very serious about this. Look at these men." He pointed at me and at Babs, who was sitting just near the door to the meeting room. "These men are very serious about their jobs—we need to get this information. We are not joking around about this."

The case officers were impressive, scanning across fragments of the conversation, bringing each moment into context, sorting, filtering, and choosing what was truth, what was chaff like a sort of twenty-first-century Solomon.

The meeting wrapped with Lee giving the man five hundred U.S. dollars for his expenses. He gave orders for the guy to get the map, the locations, and directions to him in five days. He was to contact a Pakistani colonel who would tell him when and where the next meeting would take place. Shortly, Lee told me that Babs and I would take the two agents to the mosque and let them out to keep people from seeing them leave this area on foot. We started getting ready to head out, but the two men insisted they would rather just walk away.

A FEW WEEKS AFTER the meeting with the guy who gave us info on al-Qa'ida in Wana, I returned to Kabul. Bo and I caught an agency helicopter and flew up to Bagram Air Base for a chance to get American food and just take a mental break for a few hours. We got strange looks from the air force kids who came out to meet the flight—a Soviet-era helicopter landing and disgorging burly, bearded, dirty Americans carrying AKs or suppressed M4 rifles, Glocks, and wearing no discernable uniforms. We walked right down the main road to the fast-food joints, getting stares and whispers the whole way. Back by our helo I met Martin, a case officer from ■■■■.

We talked about how close we were to being attacked again back home by these guys. Very close, he said. One attack involved hitting a water supply with biological agents. A second was to blow the earthen dams along the Columbia River to allow the water to flood a nearby nuclear waste disposal and storage area and wash all that radioactive crap downriver into the Vancouver, Washington, and Portland, Oregon, areas, contaminating them. The FBI set surveillance on the site and arrested a few members of al-Qa'ida who were busy taking soil samples, ostensibly to determine what types of explosive charges were necessary to blow the dams. Shortly after that, the Army Corps of Engineers began restricting people from enjoying earthen dams at state parks around the country.

MEANWHILE, AFGHANISTAN JUST GOT HOTTER. Back in Kabul, a group of terrorists launched a rocket attack and nearly incinerated part the U.S. Embassy. We had a report of a VBIED (car bomb) heading for the CIA station one day and were ordered to stop all vehicles matching its description.

A guy we called Beantown—a former DEVGRU SEAL who hailed from Boston and always had a joke handy—and I did a vehicle stop on one matching the description exactly—white truck, bed covered with a tarp . . . and we searched it right there in the street, just the two of us, while our teammates covered us with sniper rifles from the protection of the station—and well out of the blast radius. The hair on both of our heads grayed a little more that day. Nearby, in Tarin Kowt, U.S. forces called in for air support during a siege that almost obliterated them all. Later, in Jalalabad, there was another similar incident, and in Kandahar, two RPGs were launched at the U.S. air base. Meanwhile, we pushed our guys out into the mountains to buy back Stingers from informants, sent one guy down to Herat along the border with Iran, began running protective details for the chief, and became literally part of the CIA's operations in the war.

It was a crazy time and we pushed ourselves, thinking that this was about the home front, our people and our kids. I talked every day to my family on the group satphone, telling the kids how much I missed them, but trying to keep things lighthearted. Meanwhile, Washington stepped up the pressure. President Bush wanted names and dead terrorists, and to bring safety back into the lives of U.S. citizens.

CHAPTER 20

Eight Miles to Go

April 2004
Afghanistan

BLACKWATER WAS IN MY REARVIEW MIRROR and my own company was growing. Our latest contract was to covertly infiltrate the western badlands of Pakistan to meet with a local cleric, Bilal Rasheed. He had access to sensitive information on bad guys in that area but the situation prevented him from safely traveling across the border. Our cover for action and status would be as a camera crew, working for a major U.S. news network. We were going into the same area where bin Laden, al-Qa'ida, and the Taliban considered themselves safe—the devil's lair.

The border area is formally called the Federally Administered Tribal Areas, or FATA. Home to about seven tribal groups, it borders Afghanistan and the province of Khyber Pakhtunkhwa, formerly known as the Northwest Frontier Province. The Brits created this area in 1901, drawing a line through the homelands of a number of Pashtun tribes, splitting them between Afghanistan and what was India. Neither the tribes nor the Afghans recognized the Brit-drawn border. Then in 1947, as much as I love 'em, the Brits separated the Muslims in Pakistan from the Hindus in India, starting an era of bloodshed between those two that has not yet ended.

When I was there in 2004, the FATA resembled something akin to an Indian reservation back in the United States. It had its own laws and police force and no U.S. personnel were overtly stationed among the roughly three million inhabitants of this rugged terrain of hardscrabble mountains and sheer cliffs. The people, however, were uneducated, with about 3 percent of the women and 15 percent of the men literate.

U.S. personnel responsible for Pakistan were far removed from the frontier area, stationed mainly to the east in Islamabad, Lahore, and Karachi. Just two years prior, I'd been part of the first CIA team to ever go to that border area, back in the early days of the war.

A year earlier in 2003, the author and CNN correspondent Robert Young Pelton asked me to go with him to the Af-Pak border to research an article he was writing. I'd met Pelton back in Colombia when he and two others had been abducted by the right-wing paramilitary. CNN's Eason Jordan hired me to go in and help get him back. By the time we arrived, he'd been released, so we were asked to escort him home—which I did. We traveled together from Bogota all the way to the back deck of his home in Southern California, overlooking the Pacific. There I met his wife and twin daughters, and we all toasted his return home. He loaded me down with half a dozen autographed copies of nearly every book he'd ever written, for which I was very grateful.

BUT BY THIS TIME, in 2004, it was clear the Paks weren't our friends even though they pretended to be in order to get U.S. aid money. In reality, they mostly sided with the Afghan Taliban.

Their rationale was that when the United States left Afghanistan, India would have increasing influence with the Afghans, and that would encircle the Pakis on both their eastern and western borders. To prevent that, the Pakis funded, trained, supplied, and assisted the Afghan Taliban at every opportunity as a proxy force to destabilize the Karzai government. Pakistan's hidden fears of India drove nearly every major strategic decision taken by their national security leadership, even when it came to the United States and Afghanistan. Pakistan has no economy—they basically produce nothing, export nothing, have few natural resources, and rely primarily on aid money from other governments to stay afloat. The war with the Taliban was good business for them—they pretended to help the United States, allowing goods to be railed and trucked through their country from Karachi's port, through the Torkham border crossing, all in exchange for U.S. money to fight the terrorists—but they did little to stop attacks and looting along the way. They were walking a tightrope—get money from the United States, but try to keep India at bay at the same time.

If we came into contact with an official from the Paki side, we'd be arrested or shot. We'd have the same outcome if we stumbled upon any Taliban or al-Qa'ida, not to mention bandits. In short, there were no friendlies at all over there. But on the upside, it made target discrimination simpler.

Jobs like this were not routine by any stretch. But Pakistan presented a challenge to coalition forces—don't cross it from Afghanistan because it'll piss off the Pakis: that was the general rule. Smaller outposts of SF and CIA along the border crossed in and out but only within a few miles, using the fluid location of the border as their excuse for the incursions. Drones flew into Paki airspace all the time and there was little the Pakis could do about it. But the asset we were meeting wasn't just a few miles over the border—he was more than ten miles inside.

My partner was Two-Ton, a very large U.S. Navy special operator who used to hail from Dam Neck, Virginia. We were dubbed the "Crew of Two," and our plan was to fly to Dubai and then on to Kabul to link with my local contact, Fazal, who worked for Afghan intelligence and would help us get a vehicle and be our interpreter down to Khost. Then we would travel overland, south-southeast, to Gardez, up into the mountains through the K-G Pass, before heading down and east into Paktia Province, where we'd move into our safe house and rest. Foreigners simply did not travel by road from Kabul to other cities, mainly because of fear of being caught in crossfire or being abducted by Taliban, al-Qa'ida, or any of the criminal bandit groups working the roads and mountain passes. Someone once described these areas as off-limits to aid workers and even Afghan government civil servants.

Once we'd reached the safe house, we'd head to the Pakistani frontier, cross the border, and link with the asset on the far side. One advantage was that this time-consuming route created a travel "legend" that backed up our cover as a camera crew.

The rest of our in-country team consisted of Doc, our medic, who would stay in Kabul in case we needed med support. Doc was a character. A former British army paratrooper, he was a solid soldier and outstanding combat medic and fancied himself a ladies' man. Admittedly, he was a handsome guy; he had blond hair and a beard and impersonated Sean Connery in flawless fashion. Trouble was, if injured, we'd have to get ourselves to him—hours and hours away from where we'd be operating; in the meantime he'd be living it up while we scraped out an existence in the foothills of the Himalayas.

Two-Ton and I would enter Khost as journalists, make contact with the local police chief, then take pictures and shoot video interviews to document the happenings in this volatile, Taliban-infested town before meeting and debriefing the Pakistani asset. This would support our cover for status and action. I had made contact with an aggressive female reporter named Darby—a woman driven to get stories with teeth—who was trying to get something on UBL's secret caves, along with video of a battle taking place near Khost. We'd met back in Kabul at the Gandamack Lodge, when our company was protecting different people coming and going in the city. At first she had said her network would not approve sending anyone to such a dangerous place, but she knew our experience, and I suggested training us to operate the cameras was a walk in the park. So she agreed, as did her producer, and they convinced the network to green-light the project and arranged for us to all meet in New York to get things moving.

In Manhattan, Two-Ton and I, lugging rucksacks and wearing blue jeans, hiking boots, and T-shirts with polar fleece windbreakers, hit the network offices, looking as out of place as Jane Fonda at the VFW. Cameras came out swiftly, delivered by a diminutive expert we dubbed Half-Gallon Gary, who was tasked with training us on how to use them. He tried to send us off with massive news-type cameras. The business end of Gary's crack pipe must have been hot to the touch from him smoking it so much because he had to be high if he thought we were lugging around cameras the size of a microwave in Taliban and al-Qa'ida territory. We chose the small Sony palm models instead. After leaving the offices, we caught a cab to Columbus Circle, got a steak at Porter House, and sent a text message back to the Operations Center.

COT@NN-NY.ALLOK

The message was simple and to the point—our team, the Crew of Two, had met with the news network in New York and all was okay, tracking as expected. After picking up our supplies and instructions and a solid night's sleep at the Parker Meridian, we boarded the flight for London. At Heathrow Airport's British Airways lounge we headed over to the sleeping area, where the lights were off and one solo traveler was sacked out against the far wall. Meeting our contact there was a no-go; we'd have to move the site. I pulled out my BlackBerry and sent a text message to the Ops Center back at HQ:

> COT@LHR. Ready2meet/need new site

This meant the Crew of Two was at London Heathrow Airport and we were ready to meet but needed a new site because of a traveler in the sleeping area.

A reply came back within a couple of seconds:

> B@WHSmith—5min. Across frm BAlounge. Have cap on backwrds. Kasra. Recog 9.

So I was to head to the W. H. Smith bookstore in five minutes, have a ball cap on backward, and meet with a guy named Kasra. The recognition code would be the number 9.

Standing near the register at the bookstore, I flipped through a magazine with no idea what Kasra looked like; anyone who approached could be the guy—or gal. A young man looked me in the eye and then broke contact, heading for the tourist books. Then a woman did the same, heading for the register. People make eye contact generally for two reasons in the normal world—either they are marking your position to avoid colliding with you or they're trying to signal perhaps amorous interest. The former make quick eye contact and break it; the latter's eyes linger.

Two girls in their late teens or early twenties were flipping through a gossip magazine and fiddling with a purse, babbling to the point where I questioned if I was losing IQ points standing nearby. I shifted to another spot in the store just as an Afghan in his mid-fifties in a dark navy suit walked up and picked up the same edition of a magazine I was thumbing through.

"Nice hat. How are you sir?" he said, extending his hand. His hair was jet black and combed over in an Elvis-style pompadour that, while not my taste, actually was pretty sharp-looking. A neatly trimmed goatee framed his angular face. We shook hands. "Thanks," I replied. "It's been a long five-hour flight for me," I said, giving him the opportunity to complete the code.

"Yeah, too bad for you, my friend. I was just four minutes away," he said. Adding his four to the five I'd mentioned completed the code of nine. A lock—my tickets and info on our guns were minutes away. It was a simple way to link up—no complicated phrases to remember. If you could add, you could do it—unless you were meeting with a smartass who began using negative numbers. Punch people like that.

We headed down the long avenue of airport shops and security screening checkpoints. "Here are your tickets from Mr. Abdul Kharim for your next flight—you have a three-hour layover," he said, handing me an envelope. "Go to the Gandamack once you land. They have two rooms, both under the name Mohammed Karim," he added.

"Once you get checked in, call this number." He handed me a slip of paper. I looked at it and recognized the +93 as the Afghan country code.

He continued: "Ask for Fahran and tell him what you need. He will come to you and deliver."

AFTER A NIGHT IN DUBAI on the Deira Corniche, overlooking the Persian Gulf, where it was 100 degrees in the shade, we landed the next afternoon in Kabul. I looked around for the familiar, simple airport I'd known so well, but it was gone. The place was like a garden taken over during the night by masses of tangled weeds as security, soldiers, and police stood around everywhere. Kabul was nestled more than one mile high in the mountains and seemed decorated with concrete and confusion, all looking as though God painted everything a muddy, pale brown, a tone that seemed to fit the mood of the region. The only break in the palette came from yellow taxis smeared with axle grease and dirt or battered with the random bullet hole or a spidered windshield from catching a stray rock—or perhaps, bullet. A biting cold breeze constantly reminded me that we were no longer in the tourist town of Dubai, and riding on those gusts floated the all too frequent stench of raw sewage mingled with diesel vehicle exhaust, cigarette smoke, and burning wood. Heavy traffic weaved in patterns barely understood by locals and incomprehensible to an outsider. Traffic lights don't exist and zero police stand guard at the traffic circles and congested intersections. One thing people who've been to Kabul will likely advise is that you should plan to blow your nose—a lot. The fecal matter muddled with smoke, trash, and exhaust collects in your nostrils to the point where breathing is a struggle and when you do manage to blow, you expel a blackened mass of something that never should be in human beings in the first place. Aside from the concrete blast walls, HESCO barriers, manned security posts, and high barricades cutting off views of government buildings, hotel entrances, and embassy enclaves, it seemed like any other third-world city with its billboards advertising cell phone companies; darkened, dirty shops assembled from discarded, battered shipping containers; and carts being pulled by mules or broken down, gaunt, four-legged beasts that could have been horses in another life.

To explain Kabul to the uninitiated, it's best to go by way of example. Mention Beirut to Westerners and the name conjures up kidnappings and terrorist attacks, as well as an astonishing number of fragmented religious factions. In nearly every conflict of the twentieth and twenty-first centuries, there's been a Beirut. In Afghanistan in the twenty-first century it was Kabul.

A city such as Kabul attracts all sorts of players moving through the strange, dangerous undercurrents. In any conflict zone, there are various versions of organized crime—some local, some part of transnational criminal groups. In a collapsed wartime economy, somebody always fills the vacuum, provides what's lacking, whether it's AK-47 magazines or RPGs, trucks, food, drugs, or women. These providers will have economic agendas; others may have nationalistic or ethnic agendas. Many will have a mix of them all, but nearly all will go rogue at a second's notice. Life is cheap there.

Other players in cities like these are national intelligence agencies. Every nation with an interest in the region will have a role. Each of them will have spies collecting information against the other. In Kabul, the Pakistani and the Indian intelligence agencies played cat-and-mouse games, while Afghan Taliban cells hid from CIA hunter teams dispatched to destroy them. NATO's International Security Assistance Force (ISAF) attempted to figure out who was flinging rockets at them, and all the while the Afghan intelligence service, the National Directorate of Security (NDS), tried to watch everything.

Along with the factions of organized crime and spies in places like these, there are expatriates, usually criminals, running from dirty pasts at home, who lie about their backgrounds, hoping to lure unsuspecting businessmen into hiring them for their expertise in the ways of the area. They run drugs, employ prostitutes, and live beyond the law, generally running from one job to another. I ran into one of them back when we were providing security services for one of the world's largest American defense contractors. The guy worked as the in-country rep for a freight forwarding and logistics company, possessed an intellect rivaled only by a garden tool, and claimed he was a spy in a former life. He wasn't.

During the 1990s, war tourism emerged—and Kabul was no different. It wasn't just the tourism that adrenaline-charged authors like Pelton wrote about. The tourists I'm referring to are more sinister. For example, in Cambodia, UNTAC (United Nations Transitional Authority in Cambodia) apparently discovered a version of *The Most Dangerous Game* being played on a remote island, complete with assault rifles and kidnapped teenagers from the hills. In Sarajevo, Bosnian Serb forces were, for a fee, providing Russian tourists with Dragunov sniper rifles and letting them shoot at people in the city.

In essence, these places are, in John le Carré's words, Casablancas without heroes. It's difficult to find stability anywhere; everything shifts. Identities and alliances change. Lies are covered with fresh ones. Which person is the manic PTSD victim armed with a surface-to-air missile and freaking out, shooting at airplanes and helicopters? Who is the black marketeer who profits when the air bridge is shut down because of that very antiaircraft fire? Who is the al-Qa'ida-trained terrorist waiting to knock the air assets of a superpower out of the sky? These are the questions that inform life in Kabul today, that compose a sick soup of corruption, murder, and espionage. God help the civilians.

At the airport, I stepped out into the Kabul sunlight and greeted an old friend, Fazal, who worked for NDS, Afghanistan's domestic intelligence service. Immediately he broke into a wide grin and gave me a huge bear hug.

Initially structured by the KGB when the Soviets ran the place, NDS was in the process of being retooled by NATO folks. The agency had more than thirty thousand employees, and fingers, eyes, and ears everywhere—from maids in hotels, to street sweepers, to employees at the airport, to moles buried up in government departments and even NATO and U.S. military commands.

A Panjshiri-born Afghan native, Fazal had worked with me when I was with CIA in Afghanistan. I introduced him to Two-Ton, and he drove us west down the dusty, potholed Jalalabad road. There were no visible lanes; a large concrete barricade divided the traffic. Fazal's drab, tinted Toyota Corolla bumped along, as people appeared to wander mindlessly into the road, ignoring the fact that cars and trucks were hurtling toward them. But if you lived in Kabul back then, it probably seemed like the only way out. We eventually turned left onto the rutted, rock-strewn Passport Lane. On the right corner was the Indian Embassy. Down the bumpy road on the left stood the entrance to the Gandamack Lodge, marked by a lonely blue-and-white-striped guard box. The place was a fortress in comparison to other guesthouses, ringed by a wall and razor wire and guarded by armed Afghans.

The Gandamack has a unique history. A Brit with impeccable hospitality by the name of Peter Jouvenal once owned and operated it. A war cameraman, he was the guy who filmed Usama bin Laden for Peter Bergen's now-famous interview. Bin Laden was said to have rented the property from Kabul businessman Saeed Hashimi for $150 a month and used it as a home for his fourth wife as well as an al-Qa'ida safe house where Yemeni men stored RPGs. One night in 2001 they all left suddenly in the middle of the night and Hashimi is still angry about it, claiming to be owed five hundred dollars in back rent by the bin Ladens. He'll have a hard time collecting that from a guy with a ventilated forehead and porous chest cavity resting in a weighted body bag on the bottom of the Arabian Sea.

Walking through the double doors into the foyer, I saw the old Afghan cook straight back in the kitchen and waved to him. The one-legged Afghan gatekeeper named Rahman Baig still hobbled around on his peg leg—his real one had been taken off by a Soviet land mine. Fatima was manning the registration desk, and a myriad of waiters shuffled in and out of Flashman's Restaurant.

The first order of the day, after food, was to lay our hands on firepower (which was deniable if they turned up in someone else's hands). I dialed the number Kasra had given me and spoke to Fahran, the arms hookup. He had family from the Panjshir Valley, nestled north of Kabul in the vast Hindu Kush. I told him what I needed. He'd make a call and his family would round up the gear and figure out a way to avoid the police checkpoints and get them into Kabul.

THE NEXT MORNING, Fahran called to say that the weapons, which he referred to as tennis rackets, were in town and that we needed to meet to hand them over. Tennis rackets? It was weak—no one played tennis in Kabul anymore. He might as well have called them speedboats. I told him to meet us at the airport parking lot, not wanting him to know where we were living and he told us what he'd be driving. I borrowed Fazal's car. Two-Ton spotted Fahran on our second buzz of the lot and took a photo of his face behind the wheel, as well as of his car and plate number. We pulled up next to him and he motioned for us to follow him across town, where we met five young Afghan men in a two-story house surrounded by a wall. We walked into the back of the property to a tiny, windowless room completely made of concrete, with a ceiling barely high enough to allow a six-foot man to stand erect.

One of the Afghans opened an enormous Nike gym bag large enough to stuff a body into and brought out an RPG launcher, seven rockets, two pistols, and two AK-47 rifles complete with collapsible stocks, canvas slings, magazines, and ammunition. Christmas . . . except for the RPGs, which we hadn't requested.

Two-Ton and I began inspecting the stuff as the Afghans, impatient, began trying to speed it up. One of them grabbed a beat-up-looking, olive-green RPG warhead and a booster and began screwing the two together, asking the whole time, "You know RPG?"

Before we knew it, the kid grabbed the launch tube, slid the now-armed rocket down into the tube, locked it into place, and slid his finger down to the cocking level to demonstrate how to fire the thing.

What you don't want is for a rocket-propelled grenade to be launched in a room the size of a coat closet, packed with people. The new wall décor will evoke a frog in a blender when you're done. Two-Ton and I were both pissed-off—one wrong slip and the kid would have killed us all from the back-blast alone if that rocket had taken off.

We wanted out of the room.

We paid them fifteen hundred in cash, loaded the bag into Fazal's car, and left that brain trust. Back at the Gandamack we set about stripping the weapons down again and, this time, slowly and carefully inspected and cleaned the parts and every round of ammunition. Once reassembled, we took the rifles and pistols to a range on the outskirts of the city run by the Department of State's Anti-Terrorism Assistance Program (DOS ATAP) and test-fired them. Then we set about finding indigenous clothes on the southeast side of Kabul at a tailor's shop down near what we called Sewage River. There I bought that pancake-shaped hat men wear called a "*pakol*"; we both picked up the cloth headscarves called "*shemaghs*" and each got a pair of "*shalwar kameez*." The shalwar was the loose fitting pajama-like trousers, while the kameez was the long shirt that hung untucked over everything else. We had the kameez slit up both sides and had it Velcro stitched by a local tailor. This let us hide our weapons underneath, but if we needed them, we'd rip open our shirts like a Chippendale's dancer and bring heat to bear on the problem. Fazal found us a Toyota Land Cruiser for rent, with a driver who spoke English, for $110 per day.

Prep work completed, we packed bags into the truck and I sent a text to the Ops Center:

COT@LOD. S4G2G. ETD-05.

Translation—the Crew of Two was at the line of departure. S4 was army speak for the supply or logistics department; we used it as shorthand to report that all our equipment was good to go—G2G—and we were departing in the morning at zero five hundred hours. Not oh-five hundred, but zero. *O* ("oh") is a letter in the alphabet, not a number for telling time, and it makes no more sense than if I were to say it was G o'clock.

THE NEXT MORNING WE rose before the sun and met Fazal, who was accompanying us, and were on the road by 0450, headed south out of Kabul. We climbed steadily into the mountains, aiming for Gardez, which sat at 7,600 feet above sea level, about sixty miles south of Kabul and fifty miles west of the Pakistani border. Gardez is the capital of the Paktia

Province, with abysmal roads that quadrupled the normal drive time. The terrain looked like the moon—or a cross between the Badlands of South Dakota and the Mojave Desert near Palm Springs, California. Our destination was a dangerous town of seventy thousand, Pashtun, and overwhelmingly a Taliban stronghold; it was a place where tribes have feuded with one another for generations and where warlords still maintained private armies. But even before al-Qa'ida and the Taliban, Gardez had been a dangerous place due to its proximity to the traditional smuggling routes into Pakistan through the Parrots Beak area, which leads directly into the Shiite-dominated village of Parachinar—maybe one of the most dangerous towns on earth.

We arrived in Gardez in the early morning hours and drove through the main rotary intersection, passing an open sewage canal that divided the street's two lanes on our SDR, alert for anyone following us. We saw nothing; it looked like we were free of surveillance. After a few more turns, Fazal made a right into an alley out of sight from the street, then another quick right into a tiny, darkened garage; getting out of the vehicle, we pulled the garage door closed and turned on the headlights to light up the place. Inside the bone-cold room, we pulled on our Afghan clothing over our Anglo gear, leaving our body armor and weapons hidden underneath.

To our left was the other truck—a Mitsubishi Montero SUV that Fazal had one of his NDS contacts leave there for us. It was a right-hand-drive stick shift, like something from England, and we started to prep it. Two-Ton, the resident mechanical expert, checked the engine and fluid levels and inspected the tires while Fazal and I transferred the gear from the other ride and rigged up the hands-free satphone.

Inside the SUV, we stored ammunition in every conceivable compartment. AK-47 magazines were in the door pockets, glove box, spare tire compartment, and even the slash pockets on the back of the front seats. As it turns out, Fazal had decided to bring along his own RPG rockets, and these were hidden in the cargo area along with the launch tube inside another Nike bag.

Our AKs were hidden in camera tripod bags with their stocks folded closed, making them easier to hide, but more important—easier to maneuver inside the vehicle. The idea was to have ammunition available throughout the truck because you never knew where you'd be if someone started shooting at you. We also made "wolf tails" for the inside door handles of the truck out of 100 mph tape—the really strong, green, military duct tape. The door handles were small and the idea was that, under stress, a shooter didn't want to be jacking around with the tiny Asian door handles trying to get out while Haji's lighting you up with a belt-fed weapon from high atop some ridgeline. So we took strips of tape and wrapped them around the door handles inside the truck to make them longer and easier to grab in a hurry.

I took another foot-long piece of tape and stuck it vertically to the rear post in the back of the truck, labeling it LEFT, then another on the other side, labeled RIGHT. In a fight, whoever got the unlucky backseat—the trunk monkey position—had to ride facing backward to see what was coming up behind us. The labels were there so that the trunk monkey was able to quickly call out directions to the man driving up front and not screw it up. For example, if a threat vehicle were coming up on the left of the truck, it would be on the monkey's right because he was facing backward. But he just needed to look in the direction of the threat, read the words LEFT from the post, and yell out, "Threat! Left side!" It cut out confusion.

LEAVING GARDEZ IN A DIFFERENT VEHICLE and wearing our local disguises, we set out on the second leg—up the long, treacherous mountainous drive through the Khost-Gardez Pass, which is known locally as the Seti-Kandow Pass or simply the Death Pass by locals. It was basically the only route linking Khost to the rest of Afghanistan. We rumbled along slowly, listening to the strain of the engine and the crunch of gravel and ice under our tires, upward into the cold. Our breath was visible in the truck and had started to fog up the windows and then the fog started to ice up. The gray mountains were a tableau of huge vertical faces, craggy peaks, and sharp ravines where rock slides or freak snowstorms can kill you. The terrain disappears in folds and creases, creating innumerable places for anyone to disappear, unwillingly or otherwise. Guardrails didn't exist, and one slight turn of the wheel would send a driver over the side of the gravel road and down into a one-thousand-foot sheer gorge. If the truck broke down or we came under attack, we were on our own.

As if the cold, altitude, mountains, and razor-thin cliffside roads weren't enough, travelers also had to contend with the militant Islamic terrorists as well as gangs of bandits. Pacha Khan Zadran, an older Afghan, ran illegal vehicle checkpoints (IVCPs) up in the mountain passes. Extortion checkpoints would be a more accurate description. A few months earlier, the Pakis arrested Zadran, and now his seventeen-year-old brother, Wazir Khan Zadran, had taken up the business. This threat was the primary reason for bringing along the RPGs—nothing better to break up an IVCP than a rocket.

We slowly, carefully wound our way up the narrow, axle-grinding path into the jagged granite cliffs that soared above us on our left. I checked the Garmin—we'd climbed nearly two thousand feet since we'd left Gardez and were nearly ten thousand feet up in the foothills of the Himalayas. Sheer thousand-foot drops on our right rivaled any view I'd seen to that point. The gravel road was so narrow that at times you couldn't even see the road out the window, just the gorge hundreds and hundreds of feet below. We all prayed that we didn't meet another vehicle, because in many places there was often simply no room for two cars at the same time. Every now and then through the fogged, icy window you glimpsed the mangled wreckage of a transport truck, bus, or car caught in a clump of trees halfway down the gorge, or hanging in pieces off ledges or resting down in the canyons below. The air thinned, and trees had long since given up trying to grow up here. We rounded yet another bend and started the descent into the floor of the Khost bowl when Fazal spoke excitedly, pointing off to our right across the gorge, where the road snaked down the mountain. From our position with the mountain to our left, the drop-off to a crushing death by gravity to our right, the mountain curved back in a U-shape to our right, creating this chasm we were looking across. It appeared to be about another fifteen minutes of road time, but we stopped and I fumbled with near-frozen fingertips jutting from my wool gloves to pull out my binos for a better look. I took my sleeve and wiped the icy fog away from my window to get a better view as Two-Ton reached into the rear and started unzipping and readying the RPG launch tube and rockets from the cargo area, apparently glad that Fazal brought them along.

I barely make out rocks the size of soccer balls stretching across the road in a makeshift roadblock and two armed Afghan footmobiles nearby in dark clothing. We were sure they had spotted us—the sound up here, plus their sheer boredom, gave them nothing to do but notice movement. But we were well out of their rifle range. On top of that, we were on the high ground, maybe five hundred feet higher in altitude and at least a thousand yards across from them, making it even tougher if they'd decided to shoot us. But, if we turned around to go back, they'd call ahead and we'd get stopped somewhere else, plus there was no way to really turn around. We'd have to back out the whole way. There was no other way to go but forward, so we pressed slowly ahead, readying our weapons and establishing a loose plan as we rolled along.

Fazal would do the talking; even though he was from the northern area of Afghanistan and spoke a different dialect—Dari—than these men, it would at least be better than either of us opening our mouths. Two-Ton and I partially unzipped our rifles from the tripod cases, slipped a loaded mag in, and worked the action to chamber a round. We kept them covered at our feet, muzzles down, the buttstocks folded and the pistol grips within easy reach. Under our outboard thighs—the leg farthest from the door—we both slipped our handguns with the grips barely sticking out for quick access. We reviewed our cover story on the way down—we were journalists heading to Khost for a U.S. news network and Fazal was our fixer—that's all.

The gravel made a crunching sound under our tires as we rolled the final few yards, reaching the checkpoint. Rocks like bowling balls were scattered in a line across the narrow one-lane road. One guy—a teenage kid, really—was on the left, AK on a sling, his firing hand on the weapon, finger on the trigger, and his breath visible in the cold air. It looked like the weapon was on safe, but I couldn't be sure. In the backseat, Two-Ton had already slid over to the right side behind Fazal, who was at the wheel to be closer to his potential target. We both knew what would happen if we had to shoot these guys—I'd take the kid on my side and Two-Ton would ventilate the other guy's head. But that was not the primary plan—we just needed to deconflict this situation and quietly pass through here. Our job was elsewhere, not taking down two kids manning a checkpoint.

We eased our windows down as Fazal flashed a smile and sent out a stream of local chatter. I reached out and adjusted the side mirror, giving a glance to our rear, making sure no one was sneaking up from behind. The men peered into the SUV as we did our best to resemble intimidated journalists, holding up our news network ID cards and letting these guys think we were scared to death, but smiling all the while. Again "playing the rabbit," and sometimes it really can cause the aggressor to relax and take your passivity for granted, giving you just that extra edge. If this kid asked us to open the cargo area, though, he'd find the RPGs and then it was going to be very difficult to maintain our story—likely getting really loud on this tiny mountain road in short order.

"Please, get money out for them now," Fazal said softly. I heard the nervousness in his voice and I handed him one hundred U.S. dollars from my shirt pocket. Fazal showed it to the guy at his window—Two-Ton's target. The teen and his buddy, who walked around to Fazal's window, both smiled slightly, revealing teeth with rot and stains throughout and then held out their hands again, and I coughed up another hundred. Then, thankfully, the young crooks began removing rocks from the road in front of us, and a few seconds later we were on our way. These two didn't look like they could organize a one-man march up a straight driveway, but today's decision was probably the smartest thing they'd do in their entire lives.

A FEW MORE HOURS and thousands of feet later, we climbed down out of the mountains, leaving the cold, wind, and snow behind, and rolled down into the warm, lush green valley containing the village of Khost. Located about ninety miles southeast of Kabul and sixty miles from Gardez, you won't find the King, the Clown, or the Colonel here, just the food you bring, and, unless your system is ironclad and your tolerance for gastro risk is sky-high, you'll look like you ate an unhappy meal if you go with the local fare. This place was rough—open sewers ran down the sides of the dirt roads with wooden planks connecting the dark, dimly lit shops on the other side. It sucked like Gardez, but on steroids. It reminded me of what the Old American West must have looked like along the frontier in the 1830s. The air stank—like all of Afghanistan's urban areas—of diesel, burning trash, and meat cooking somewhere nearby. The warbling horn from a large, gaudily decorated transport truck startled a flock of sheep, sending them scattering to the four winds as their shepherd angrily ran after them waving a stick. A bony, mangy pack of dogs, ribs showing, shot between two buildings, their tails tucked, ears back, and heads low.

We drove north, dodging potholes and debris, toward the town's police headquarters. We quickly rehearsed our roles and cover story one more time, restowed our rifles, stopped short of the roadblock created by a thin, felled hardwood tree, and walked up to the police station's front gates. I asked the guard in broken Pashto and a little sign language to speak to the chief of police, telling him that I was an American journalist. They let us into a small courtyard with trucks parked about the grounds. It looked exactly as it had when I came here with Pelton the previous year. A few men and a boy or two were squatting on their haunches atop a disabled granite fountain in the middle of the courtyard. To the right was a long window of bars running along the entire wall—prison cells. I took one look at the poor fellas in those cells and was dern glad I was on this side. Speedy trial? Impartial judge? Public defender? All a huge question mark here.

A few minutes later, the commander stepped out of a darkened doorway and into the harsh sun. After we requested our interview, he ushered us into his office, where we videotaped a few questions, shook hands, and said that we'd like to come back in a few days when he wasn't so busy.

In the mountains it gets darker faster and the sun was setting as we stepped back into the open air. Fazal was waiting by the truck with two keys to a room at a guesthouse just a few blocks away. Apparently no other guests were staying here. Our rooms were actually two-room affairs on the third floor with a short balcony on the far wall that opened up to the street below. A set of double doors divided the two rooms. We took the rearmost room and Fazal took the one nearest the entrance door leading back out into the hallway.

We scrounged around and found blankets that we draped over the iron balcony railing as if they were drying. This concealed any activities on the balcony as well as the inside of our room from anyone on adjacent buildings so we could leave the balcony door open during the day. Attached to the railing between the rugs with D-rings were two ropes in two bags: if attacked in our rooms, we'd empty our magazines into the attackers, toss the rope bags over the rail to the ground below, and then we'd go over the rail on the ropes to the truck. Inside, we set up the satcom antenna, running the wires onto the balcony and keeping it out of sight—another use for the rugs. Two-Ton performed a radio check back to Doc in Kabul, then sent a POSREP (position report) to the Ops Center via satphone while I staged our weapons and ammo and barricaded the door.

THE FOLLOWING MORNING, Fazal and I went up onto the roof to talk. I gave him some taxi money and told him to head back to Kabul; I explained that we'd be doing things he didn't need to be part of. Later, I heard the rumbling of diesel engines and looked out to see four U.S. Army Humvees rolling through the streets below us. The young soldiers in their helmets, Wiley-X goggles, and body armor manning the .50-caliber machine guns on top of the trucks looked around in every direction with no idea that two U.S. operators were hiding just above their heads watching them, with no backup whatsoever.

Soon, Two-Ton and I drove out of the city toward the border area to conduct a VPU (vehicle pickup) and have a rolling meet with a relative of the cleric. The cleric's sister's husband was to meet us to pass along information about the linkup with the cleric later in the week. The meeting was planned to occur during the dhuhr (noon) prayer time, when everyone was busy heading to the mosque. We'd drive by, pick up the source, get his information, drop him off, and get out of the area.

On the southern outskirts of Khost was a lumberyard; just past it, beyond a hand-pump fuel station, the road made a gentle right-hand turn where a low wall began. The turn created a blind spot to traffic coming from either direction. Two-Ton dropped his visor and turned on the headlights—these were to be the two visual signals to our contact. I was in the backseat and would manage the door for the guy. "Slowing, slowing down . . . there's the wall . . . here we go . . ." he warned.

As we neared the blind spot, I cracked the door slightly on my side. Two-Ton slowed as we came up to the low wall, and a young man who had been crouched down stepped quickly toward us. I pushed open the door wide on his side, propping it open fully with my boot. The Afghan grabbed my hand and the door frame, ran a few steps alongside the vehicle, and hopped inside. I slid across to the other side to make room as he closed the door behind him, all while I was shoving him down into the floorboard to keep him out of sight. If we'd been followed, they'd know we started with two in the truck and I wanted it to remain that way.

I hit him with the mad minute: "Thank you for coming. Listen to me now—we are American journalists. If we are stopped by anyone, you're just getting a ride to the border because you've injured your right ankle. We offered you a ride. Do you understand?" He nodded that he did so I continued: "How much time do you have?"

"I have enough time, enough," he answered.

"How is your relative Bilal Rasheed?" I asked.

"He is well and wishes to meet with you, if God wills it, in the next few days," he answered.

"Please send him our regards, and we look forward to meeting with him very soon," I responded. "I need to tell you where we will meet him, when, and how. Can you remember these things for me?" I asked. He nodded yes.

I gave him detailed instructions on how we'd link up so they couldn't screw this up. I explained the all-clear signal that the cleric should put out for us to tell us it was okay to go ahead with the meeting and more. As Two-Ton drove and concentrated on whether we were clean from surveillance, the kid scribbled down a few notes. "I will send a text message to his number," I said. "Give it to me." He scrawled it down and tore off the number for me. "We will meet three hours after I send that message, okay?" He nodded vigorously. "If we miss each other, we will try again the next day at the same time, and same place—do you understand all of this?" He nodded again, his eyes wide with excitement that he did understand.

"You have done a very brave thing today, my friend. Now I have something that I want you to tell Bilal Rasheed for me. When we meet, I want to know who the important Taliban foreigners are in the Miranshah and surrounding areas. I hear that Zawahiri [bin Laden's number two] is close by. Is this true? How did he come in? Where do they sleep at night? I will also ask about who is supplying them with their information on the Pakistani side. Do you understand all of this?" He nodded his head as I reached under my man-jammies into a pouch on my armor plate-carrier vest and fished out two crisp hundred-dollar bills for him.

We drove him farther down the road and then let him out in a dip that provided us another black spot—a spot where the car was out of sight of anyone on the road. Two-Ton made a quick three-point turn and we headed back in the direction of Khost, minus one passenger. But anyone who saw us during the drive would have only noticed two, because he'd been on the floor the whole time anyway. I watched out the back window as the Afghan man slowly walked in the opposite direction, never looking back once. Good man.

ON THE MORNING OF APRIL 4, I sent the message—we'd meet Bilal Rasheed in three hours. We got a reply nearly immediately—green light. The site was quite a few miles inside Pakistan's porous border—outlaw country. The meet was set.

Shortly after Bilal's green-light response, Two-Ton and I shrugged on our low-profile body armor, checked batteries in all the electronic gear for the thousandth time, rechecked the AKs, yanked on the man-jammies over everything, sent a SITREP back to Kabul that we were on the move, and hid our guns. Mine was slung just over my right shoulder, muzzle down by my right leg.

The meet site sat just on the other side of the first village after crossing the border. I plugged the coordinates into our Garmin and we struck out. The all-clear signal that the cleric was to leave for the meet was a Toyota pickup with the hood open, on the road into the village. If we saw the truck hood up, we knew it was okay to meet. We'd drive a little farther past the truck and the cleric would be walking on the right side of the road, heading east, the same direction we'd be driving. We'd scoop him up as we rolled past.

I drove while Two-Ton rode shotgun, kept track of our time, and navigated. We were on target to arrive and timing was critical, especially for Bilal. He couldn't walk all day along that road and if we were late by as little as ten minutes that was too long for him.

Our meandering SDR took us through a small village, and the road turned to the right, weaving between low mud buildings. As we came around the corner, I practically stood on the brakes, sliding to a stop as a herd of sheep clogged the tight dirt road, which was more like a trail. The road was narrow, and mud walls as high as the truck ran on either side of it for fifty to seventy-five yards. Neither of us liked it—it was a choke point. As the last of the sheep got out of the way, I checked the time on my Suunto watch and pressed the accelerator hard. We hammered down a slope into a creek, sending water splashing, and barreled up the opposite bank.

Four miles to go.

A few miles after the sheep jam, we both started noticing a noise, an electronic clicking and chirping sound—like the sound a car makes when keys are left inside an ignition. It continued, and then the radio, which had been playing local music, started to cut in and out. Then the tachometer and speedometer went to zero, the dashboard lights went out, and the truck engine lost power completely, and we rolled to a stop.

Two miles to go.

I popped the hood release and we dismounted. We'd been heading southeast and had just come down off a rise in the road, heading down a gentle slope, when the truck quit. Two-Ton ran around to take a look at the engine. While he did his mechanical thing under the hood, I focused on the world around us.

To our left was a small ditch, and beyond that was a ridge running parallel to the road. On the opposite side was a large open field, and up ahead I caught sight of another local shepherd and a bunch of goats heading our way. I stood on the roadside, leaning against the truck with my rifle out of sight down by my right side and surreptitiously checked my watch, trying my hardest to look nonthreatening—just a local traveler disgusted with a breakdown and mad he hadn't sprung for AAA.

Two-Ton was an experienced gearhead who knew his way around an engine, and in short order he said he'd found the problem but needed an extra hand for something and asked if I'd help hold on to a wire for a second. If I didn't, it would delay the fix: the meeting would be scrubbed and perhaps screw the whole operation. But if I did, I couldn't maintain vigilance on our security. So I tried to do both and reached around with my nonfiring hand under the hot hood, and he put it where he needed the help. I kept my eyes on the road, and my other hand gripped my AK still hanging out of sight down by my side; I looked up the road at the herd again.

As I reached out I heard a sound like a bee buzzing in the background somewhere. The noise quickly grew louder, and I figured out too late that it was coming from behind us. Two muffled pops that sounded like firecrackers or a car backfiring broke through the buzz at almost the same time as two loud strikes sounded against the metal skin of the SUV, like someone hit the truck with a ball-peen hammer. Then the rear glass shattered, and I was violently shoved from the back just as something else slammed into my left shoulder, bringing with it pain like being hit with a piece of steel rebar. I looked down and was startled to see my own blood pouring from a new hole like someone had turned on a faucet.

"Contact rear! Contact rear! I'm hit!" I yelled to Two-Ton, as I dropped to the dirt. He didn't respond.

CHAPTER 21

"Loading!"

April 4, 2004
Afghanistan/Pakistan Border

I CRANED MY NECK AROUND trying to see if Two-Ton had been hit since he'd not responded to me. I'm not the brightest light in the harbor, but as everything started moving in slow motion, I was quite clear on one thing—somebody was trying to kill us.

I'd dropped to the dusty ground in a heap, trying to get underneath the SUV fast while yelling in Two-Ton's direction. Looking back up the rear where we'd come from, I spotted the attackers—two guys on a beat-up motorcycle. The passenger was shooting while the driver was doing his best to keep the beat-up motorbike moving fast, straight, and steady.

The noise from the bike grew louder as they kept hammering away at us. More slugs slammed into the truck, and dirt kicked up all around me. I'd been hit twice and was down—exposed on the side of the road and trying to squirm under the 4x4 to get out of the way and not get hit again.

Two-Ton had also dropped when I'd yelled contact. He had his pistol out—his rifle was back in the SUV. I looked up toward the front tire where he had been just as his muzzle and right eye popped around and he started sending rounds inches over my head toward the attackers. He emptied his gun in seconds, as I ducked, ate dirt, and wrapped my arms over my head.

"Loading!" he yelled.

The attackers flew right by me, trying their best to kill us both, but Two-Ton's volley of fire had taken the attackers' focus off me and placed it squarely on himself, likely saving my life. The biker crew zipped past us.

I lifted my head, wiped the sweat and dirt from my eyes, and managed to dig out my rifle. I felt no pain in my left arm at all as adrenaline and the desire to survive took over. Popping the folding stock down, I snugged it into my shoulder, flipped the selector switch down, placed the front sight post squarely on the center of the motorcycle's dust plume, and squeezed the smooth metal trigger, firing short, controlled, three-round bursts. But the bike was speeding off; it was at least twenty or thirty yards from us now, putting distance between us with every second that rolled. But that was nothing for the AK-47, whose 7.62 mm round is effective easily out past 400 yards.

"I'm up!" yelled Two-Ton, letting me know he was reloaded as he began firing again, too. "Moving!" he yelled again, as he scooted around to the other side of the truck opposite me to keep it between him and the attackers' new position. I vaguely remember catching sight of his shape off to my right. I kept punching rounds into the riders on the motorcycle, and it wobbled lazily for a second—and we kept firing.

"Loading!" I yelled, rolling up to my right slightly as my left hand went into my tunic. My head up, eyes locked on to the bike, my fingers touched another magazine—just as the rear passenger fell lazily off the back of the bike as it, too, careened into the ground in a cloud of dust. I brought up the new mag, used it to strip the empty one out, rocked the fresh one into place, power-stroked the charging handle, and completed the load.

"I'm up!" I yelled. But they were down, not moving. We'd sent more than fifty rounds of rifle and pistol ammo at these dirtbags in a matter of seconds at distances starting at well under thirty yards—and we'd hit pay dirt. We'd won and it was because we'd responded to the attack with as much violence and firepower as possible, reacting as fast as we could. You have to do that. When you're attacked, you have to hammer back so hard, so fast that they're overwhelmed and either die or go away wishing they'd never, ever run across you—make them think they'd walked into a running chain saw.

"Let's go! Let's go!" Two-Ton was up and moving toward me. "I'm good—get the truck working!" Our hearing was blown from the gunfire ricocheting off the truck's body and into our ears. Two-Ton was up in a flash and working under the hood. I stayed prone, covering the direction where the attackers lay, not moving as blood pooled in the dirt next to me. The key thing was to set security, check for injuries, and get out of the area. Blood covered my entire upper arm and most of my forearm as I quickly glanced back over my shoulder toward where they'd come from in case they were a diversion for the main event—nothing yet. Seconds later, I heard Two-Ton slam the truck's hood shut, jump inside, and crank it on the first try.

"We're up, let's move. Can you drive?" he asked in a calm, relaxed tone. "Yeah, I can do it," I said. We both knew what he was asking and why. He had two good arms for shooting if anyone came roaring up behind us for round two. I had to take the wheel. He squeezed his massive frame through to the backseat and asked, "How bad are you?" as he peered out the hole where the rear glass used to be.

"Not sure; I think I was hit twice. Look at my left arm when we get clear. You hit?" I responded.

"No, I'm good—don't think so. I was behind the truck pretty good," he said.

I put the truck into reverse, U-turning us back for Khost.

As we sped along the broken ground, the pain wasn't hitting me just yet. I reached down into my cargo pocket that held my own GSK—gunshot kit—and pulled out the tan pouch about the height and width of a CD case and thick as a Bible and handed it back. Two-Ton reached up and pulled my tunic off, throwing it into the floorboard, then ripped open the kit, tore a gauze patch out, and slapped it onto the hole in the front of my shoulder. "Hold this in place for a second," he said.

An average man has about eight to ten pints of blood, or a little more than a gallon—lose four pints, or about two IV bags' worth, and you're in hypovolemic shock stage 4—dead. I had one hole that we knew of, roughly the size of a man's index finger. My left arm, shirt, and armor were covered with blood and Paki dirt. I kept the truck moving fast, holding the wheel with my left hand and pinning the blood stopper with my right. The truck just stayed in third gear. From the backseat, Two-Ton leaned up and started cramming his hands down between my body armor and torso, checking his own hands every few seconds for blood from other wounds on me that we didn't know about yet. He did this front and back. Nothing showed up; apparently just the shoulder and arm area had been hit.

"You've got another hole in the back of your shoulder, brother—gotta be the entry. I don't see anything else, but your plate in the back took a hard hit," he said. Splashing water over the holes from a drinking bottle, he tried to wash it clear as best he could, although the truck was bouncing badly; he got more on us than the holes. But he could see the holes better—two, back to front, clean through my left deltoid. Two-Ton took out two tampons that we all carried—they were great for plugging holes and stopping blood. He pressed one into the rear wound, wrapping it with a bandage. "Here, pin this for a minute," he told me. Leaning back into my truck seat, I tried to pin the bandage in place.

He pressed another into the front hole, covering it as well, and then wrapped an ACE bandage around the upper part of the arm, around my upper chest and back area, under my armpit, and eventually tied it off around the other shoulder. This would keep the blood stoppers in place and, hopefully, stem the flow.

"Okay, that'll do for now," said Two-Ton, and he picked up his rifle and spun around to guard the rear as we continued to head west. A mile or two down the road, the adrenaline began to wear off, and the pain really hit me. Then my arm just quit working completely.

"Shift for me, dude, my arm's on fire," I grunted through clenched teeth as we started up a slight grade.

"Roger, hang on a sec." He shifted the rifle around and wedged it sideways in the backseat. "Okay," he said. "Ready."

"I'm in third, put me in second . . . now," I said, clutching the truck as Two-Ton snatched the shifter around, slamming it into second gear without taking his eyes off the rear area of the truck. "Done," he said. I released the clutch and we continued to climb the hill.

"I need third, and stand by for fourth," I told him, looking out across the top of the hill we'd just climbed. I clutched again. "You're in third, fourth on you," he barked, as he put us into gear again. Releasing the clutch again, I pressed the gas pedal harder. The RPMs climbed and soon the engine was ready for another gear. "All right, go for fourth." Two-Ton pulled right into fourth gear, sending us speeding across the dusty plateau.

We dropped off the bank, slamming into the creek bed, sending jolts of pain through me as we bucked and climbed up the other side. At that point, the pain became unbearable. I'd driven my limit—any more just wasn't smart because we needed a fully functional driver as we re-entered the city, so we switched out positions. He drove, and I jumped onto the right rear seat, facing backward, laying the muzzle across the top of the seat pointing out the back, holding it with my right hand.

ENTERING A MUSLIM CITY during the height of dhuhr, midday prayer, is challenging even when you haven't been shot up. But the traffic when we arrived back in the dusty, backwater village was ridiculous. I lowered my rifle as we turned left onto the main street. Both of us badly wanted to turn right and head down to Camp Chapman for aid, but we knew we couldn't—the operation was deniable, unconnected to any agency.

Two-Ton worked the SUV like a NASCAR driver, weaving between cars, in and out of lanes, cutting people off, shooting through the gaps. Beat feet—that was our goal; speed was our security yet again. The mission was obviously aborted. We had to get to our room, collect gear, treat the wound, and get clear of Khost. We didn't know how we'd been compromised or by whom, but we had to assume our safe house wasn't safe any longer and that we were still targets: two Americans, one wounded and bleeding, driving a shot-up SUV through the streets in broad daylight—not a hard thing to spot. Call it flying by the seat of our pants—we called it working under pressure.

Then we got jammed up at a circular intersection with traffic coming from all directions. No one was moving. The sunlight filtered through the dust as horns honked. I smelled my own blood as the iron in it mixed with the oil of my skin, giving off a metallic aroma. Both of us had our heads on a swivel trying to watch hundreds of drivers and pedestrians in every direction. Every car window that was down, head that turned our way, or bicyclist became a possible threat. It was mentally exhausting and we were already wired.

Hurting like I'd never hurt before, I got fed up and started shouting at a driver who looked to be the cause of the traffic trouble. He lifted his hand from the wheel, as if reaching for a gun. Drawing my pistol, I aimed at his face with my good arm. Panicking, he got busier than a cat burying crap on a marble floor as he backed up so fast he smashed into the car behind him. But Two-Ton shot through the gap he created, nudging his front bumper aside, and found a cross street through the traffic. We drove north one block, paralleling the road that led to our building, then cut back south, coming up on it from the back side.

Par for the course so far, but then things continued to go north (not south—that's a good way to go) when we found that the back parking area we'd been using was now blocked by a large jingle truck dropping off goods for a local vendor. No one was in it now—likely headed off to the mosque to pray. Two-Ton didn't miss a beat, though, and took our SUV right down by our building, parking directly beneath our blanket-draped balcony. We grabbed our rifles, dismounted, and hustled down the dirt side road that ran along the building's western face.

Our luck just continued to suck. The metal folding gate that controlled access to the stairs was locked, with no one in sight to unlock it. Two-Ton put his back to the wall to protect us as I kicked the gate, but it didn't budge. We couldn't just leave—we had all of our ops gear upstairs, plus I needed more meds for the long ride ahead of us. "I'm gonna breach it," I said in desperation, and started to raise my rifle just as a local townsman came up and raised his eyebrows and pointed to the sky as if to say, "You wanna go up?" Two-Ton motioned for him to stand back as he delivered a massive mule kick to the door, dislocating the lock from the door frame. We shot up the stairs and into our room.

He gathered equipment while I went into the bathroom with the med kit. I knew we'd be on the road for hours before reaching Doc and decent medical care, so I took a syringe and sunk it into a bottle of lidocaine, sucking the contents out. I pushed the needle's contents back out into a bottle of Rocephin powder and shook up the mixture, combining the two ingredients. Then I drew it back up into the syringe and injected it. Rocephin was a strong antibiotic introduced to troops after the 1993 battle in Mogadishu, Somalia, with the notion that if you couldn't reach medical care for a few hours, you shot up Rocephin to keep infection at bay. The lidocaine only served as a local anesthetic to numb the area and minimize the pain of the wound.

I knew I was supposed to inject this mixture into the affected area—the gunshot zone. But the pain was so bad that I had zero desire to push a needle into it. I knew the meds were intramuscular—meaning that if I got into the bloodstream by injecting into muscle tissue it would do its job. So brilliantly I decided to shoot it into my right butt cheek. Bad move. My butt numbed out on that side and I walked like a gimp . . . but the ride back was certainly more comfortable on my backside.

The gear was staged on the balcony. Two-Ton headed down to the trucks, and I started throwing stuff off the third-floor balcony with my one good arm. We loaded up and pulled out, destination Kabul with a quick stop in Gardez to swap out trucks, heading west back through the mountains and back through Pacha Khan's roadblock extortion zone.

As we bounced across rocks, streams, and potholes, the pain in my upper arm was tremendous and growing by the minute, radiating down to my elbow. The swelling and bruising in my back from where the other bullet hit my trauma plate was also causing me trouble. We'd called Doc, who was sitting back in Kabul, and he denied my morphine request. We all carried the drug on us in injectable form, but Two-Ton suggested I ask before taking it. Doc said that if I did, it might lower my blood pressure and, coupled with the blood loss, I could die. I had to suck it up.

But, man, I was in pain, so again brilliantly, I swallowed nearly half a bottle of Motrin over the course of the six-hour ride back over the mountains—which did nothing but make me drowsy, damage my liver, and thin my blood, and make my wounds leak even more. But I have to say, even though I was in and out for most of the ride, Two-Ton made that drive over those mountains and rocks faster than anyone I've ever seen. I passed out frequently, but he said the extortionists weren't there when we'd come through. I think he'd have run them over if they had been there anyway. Maybe they were at the local saloon spending their money from our first pass through the area. I also slept right through the Gardez stop —never remembering one moment of it.

I'D NEVER BEEN SO RELIEVED to see the lights of Kabul. We headed straight for the Gandamack, where Doc had been preparing, boiling, and sterilizing multiple surgical instruments, borrowing a live-shot light from an actual news crew and setting up a surgical room. He even screwed a climbing hook into the ceiling and hung up an IV bag to replenish fluids I'd lost.

I went into the shower. George from the network had flown in the day before and helped me strip and wash all the dried blood off. Then I got up on the bed, rolled onto my right side, and Doc set to work. He punched an

IV into my right arm just at the crook of the elbow to start giving me fluids. His next problem was that he had to clean the wound out to make sure no pieces of my T-shirt, dirt, or the bullet were left inside my body. At first, he said he might have to slit the shoulder from hole to hole, slicing open the muscle in order to clean out the wound channel. I told him that was not going to happen—I think I said I'd shoot him if he did it. Meanwhile, Two-Ton had taken out his video camera and was capturing the whole medical thing to use as a training tape in the future.

I asked Doc for pain meds again—it had been nearly eight hours since I'd been shot and I'd had nothing but Motrin and lidocaine. He said no; he was still concerned about the blood loss and low blood pressure. I'd have to live with the pain for a while longer.

The Suunto Advizor watch that I wore had a heart-rate monitor feature. So Doc strapped the sensor around my torso and told me to keep an eye on my watch—which received signals from the sensor and monitored my heart rate, displaying it on my watch face. I was to call out my heart rate when he asked for it. Then he took a solution of salt water and sucked it up into a huge turkey-basting syringe and jammed that contraption into the bullet hole in the rear of my shoulder, pumping and plunging the water through so that it came squirting out of the bullet hole in the front. Fire—it was like liquid fire being pumped through my arm and I think it might have hurt worse than actually being shot . . . well, maybe not.

He repeated the turkey-basting torture twice more in that hole and then he came around to the front and did it three times into the exit wound. I was visibly shivering now from the cold water and shock. Doc finished, bandaged things up, and for the third time I asked for something to numb the pain. He gave in, took a syringe of morphine, and shot it into the IV. Slowly, warmth enveloped me from my toes to the top of my head and I was feeling no pain.

Just as I was about to pass out from the drug, Two-Ton held up a jar of Vaseline and the video camera and smiled really big, saying, "Hey, boss, you're drugged, have a good night—we sure will!" I weakly yelled, "Noooooo!" and passed out to nightmares about their intentions.

VERY EARLY THE FOLLOWING MORNING, on the fifth of April at around 0130, I was awakened to rumbling and shaking. "Are we being shelled, Doc?"

I thought we were receiving incoming artillery. "No, brother," he assured me, and told me to go back to sleep. He'd been sleeping on a cot at the foot of my bed since the procedure.

The next day, we learned that a magnitude 6.6 earthquake hit in northern Afghanistan and was felt as far away as Abbottabad, Pakistan. Three people died in Kabul.

Fazal and his partner, a huge Afghan from NDS, showed up later that morning. I was still lying in the bed with an IV in my arm. I shook their hands. "You come to our country to help us, you spill your blood on the ground for us, and the earth shakes, my friend!" Fazal joked about the earthquake.

"Brother, I've got big juju and don't you forget it!" I replied, and we all laughed. I stayed in Kabul for a few more days; with my bandaged arm I went and watched a buzkashi match—that's a medieval version of soccer, with players on horseback, and a goat carcass for a ball. Then we caught a flight to Dubai, and then British Airways back to the United States. On the BA flight the flight crew actually gave me a seat in first class all the way from Dubai to London—something I'd never have been able to afford back then. It was a gesture that has endeared me to that airline ever since.

IN AUGUST 2006, the body of Bilal Rasheed was found dumped on a road in Garhiyoum, about twenty-five miles south of Miranshah, the main town in North Waziristan. A note attached to his body made it clear that his murder was punishment. "Anyone found indulging in espionage will meet the same fate," it said. Several tribal elders have been shot or beheaded since, for allegedly spying for U.S. forces across the border in Afghanistan or supporting Pakistan's campaign against al-Qa'ida and other militants in the rugged area.

CHAPTER 22

Bad Contractors

2005
Afghanistan

THE AFGHANS HAD GUNS. They were pointed at my men, but they appeared to be taking their orders from other Americans. The world where I did my business was becoming as murky as the pond where my dad shot the water moccasins. People were going to die—and, if we weren't careful, not from enemy fire.

There was a lot happening and a dark side was starting to show. The rules were loose, and it was getting ridiculous. By 2005, SCG, LLC was coming up, nice and fast, but the whole industry was enlarging as the world seemed to be becoming one complex covert operation, and spies and operators—sometimes at odds with each other, sometimes at odds with the government of their own country—moved through the landscape, unseen. The rise of the contract operator was fast, as need increased and the reputations of Delta and ■■, two units that stalk their prey for years and operate in complete secrecy, along with ST6 or DEVGRU—where the best outfits drew their personnel—were buffed and polished by movies, TV, and the media. Operations such as Delta rescuing CIA officer Kurt Muse from a Panamanian prison; Delta hunting down Saddam Hussein, or the unpublicized "gray" hunt for Iraq's most dangerous terrorist leader, Abu Musab al-Zarqawi; ST6 rescuing Private Jessica Lynch; or the fact that CIA paramilitary operators had captured or killed more than 150 terrorists since 9/11, all served to deservedly increase the reputations and thus the desire to hire this breed of warrior. It fed the private side, which was getting to be a very competitive world, and the knives were coming out.

Unfortunately, in every industry you have good guys and good companies as well as the bad. The private military and intelligence contracting industry is no exception, and many might argue it's worse. There is corruption, infighting, and, to be very candid, a lot of ugly crap that goes on. With nearly every contract we've ever won, there have been attempts to steal it, subvert it, or damage our ability to carry it out. I learned that there was nothing people wouldn't do, some actions legal, some illegal, and when I'm trying to figure out what is going on, I just follow the coin trail. It usually leads in the right direction.

For example, in 2006, we won a small training contract with the U.S. Navy worth a couple of million dollars over two or three years; Blackwater, also angling for it with a bid and playing hard, protested. That seemed to be their company's modus operandi when it lost a bid; its lawyers filed a protest in hopes that the contract would be put back out to bid and Blackwater would get a second shot at it—after the winner's numbers had already been made public. They'd seek a technicality and in lieu of one that applied, they'd suggest one. For instance, when our contract was awarded to us, a small business, they'd claim it should have been open to all-size businesses, and because of Blackwater executives' pull and power, the government would buckle most of the time and just rebid the contract instead of risking a lawsuit.

Blackwater's attorneys were sharp weapons, and everyone knew that if they didn't win, they'd slow down the process. Sometimes it worked and the contract did go back out to bid . . . but not this time—they lost again. But justice was what we didn't get in Afghanistan, where the guns came out.

In 2005, the year before we won the U.S. Navy contract, we were providing facility security and PSD coverage for one of the largest American defense contractors (whom I'm calling ADC) in Afghanistan. Though our work was for ADC, our contract was not; instead, ADC insisted we contract with a U.S.-based freight-forwarding company—I'll call them SKM—that also worked for ADC. Many large defense contractors preferred this type of arrangement to insulate them from liability. As events unfolded, it appeared that SKM saw the money we were making, decided they were qualified to provide this service themselves, and soon it seemed that they were setting about trying to get us ejected from the contract.

When we won the contract we immediately hired and trained more than twenty Afghans from the Panjshir Valley who lived inside ADC's walled compound, which was as large as two or three football fields. We built guard towers, set belt-fed PK machine guns in them, and installed floodlights to blind people from looking at the compound from the road at night. We constructed vehicle barricades and vehicle search areas, reinforced the gates, installed concertina wire, designed evacuation plans, and provided trained, vetted, armed security, led by former U.S. and British Special Forces personnel twenty-four hours a day, seven days a week—exactly like we set up at the CIA station [redacted] in the days when I was director of Blackwater Security.

But Afghanistan had gone from worse to almost bleaker than imaginable after being declared a "failed state" by the UN in the wake of increased Taliban violence, growing illegal drug production, and crumbling state institutions. It was more like the country of Kabul—and every other region in the country was on its own. During the previous year, the number of suicide attacks, direct fire attacks, and IEDs (improvised explosive devices) had grown significantly as al-Qa'ida, Taliban, Haqqani network, and Hezb-i-Islami sanctuaries increased fourfold. This breakdown and dissent into chaos wasn't because we'd been beaten in battle. In fact, despite the sophisticated IEDs, America never lost a battle against the Taliban. The reason was that many in charge didn't appear to understand that it was a tribal issue at the heart of winning the war in Afghanistan. Certainly many did, especially in the Special Forces community, and this was essential. You had to understand the tribal system and its culture, and then engage the people at that level, but that required a major change in how Washington thought when it came to counterinsurgency warfare.

Doc, the Brit who patched me up after I got shot in 2004, had come to work for us full-time and was managing the project in Kabul, along with Matt Larsen, a former U.S. Army Ranger—the guy who reinvented the hand-to-hand combatives system the entire U.S. Army uses today. All of our Afghans reported to Doc and Matt.

SKM's site supervisor was Milton—who would turn out to be a coward and the same guy who allegedly went around telling folks he used to be with the CIA, apparently in an attempt to get them to rely more heavily on his expertise and his company's services. For some reason he never mentioned that in front of my team when we showed up the first day. But now it seemed Milton conspired to hire another group of Afghan thugs, arm them, and then sneak them into the site, using his position to get them through the gates, past our security guards, who also were Afghans. Once inside, these thugs turned their guns on our people—including the American and British citizens. SKM's plan seemed clear: to boot us off the property, convince ADC we couldn't do the job, and then take the contract and get paid for managing the facility and securing it—a multimillion-dollar score, if they could pull it off.

Doc and Matt called our Virginia Ops Center to report the situation. At the time, Dick Roten and I were just off the coast from Little Creek Naval Base evaluating a new high-speed assault boat with U.S. Navy personnel. I felt confident that I knew what was going on. We'd heard rumors that the freight forwarder was trying to oust us to steal the contract. They saw the money we were making. We'd already had clear indications that they were trying in other ways—including paying us two or three months late so we couldn't pay our people and fall into default, which would give the freight forwarder grounds to terminate us. But we knew they had the money because I called ADC Tampa to check on it. They confirmed that the army had paid ADC on time and that ADC paid SKM on time. They appeared to have tried other things as well, like having the Afghan officials declare us unauthorized to work in the country, despite our having every license required, or trying to have our guards ejected for not being licensed to carry weapons and on and on.

So we instructed our men to retake the ADC facility compound using nonlethal force, then disarm and kick the thugs off the property. In my mind, we protected ADC's property. If these guys turned their weapons on us, they became the enemy. So Doc and Matt kept their cool and began talking and joking with the local thugs while Milton, the wannabe CIA mastermind, left, I presume, to go report to his boss back in the States that he'd accomplished his mission and taken the compound from us. After a few hours, Doc and Matt managed to establish rapport with them and invited them all down into the underground concrete room we called the bunker, for tea. There was only one way in and one way out of that little sweet spot.

Once we got them all inside the confined space and handed out tea, the aggressors took seats on the ground, set down their rifles, and began drinking with our guys. While they were doing that, Matt kept them talking and drinking, and Doc stepped out and had our men move quietly toward the bunker—all twenty of them. Matt was still in the room and had somehow, unbelievably, managed to get the thugs to stack their weapons in the center of the floor—every last gun. That's when Doc signaled our Panjshiri guards, who came charging down the stairs in full force, taking the thugs' weapons, and tying them all up.

When Milton returned he found all the invaders disarmed and in custody. My guys reported that he left immediately, cell phone to his ear, tail between his legs, crying all the way back to his truck, leaving a trail of defeat and dust in his wake.

We reported the situation to ADC, who did nothing except tell us they couldn't get involved in a contract dispute between subcontractors because they didn't have *privity*—they weren't a party to it, in other words . . . and that was the entire concept of that relationship they had structured. It gave them clean hands.

THEN THINGS GOT WORSE—DEADLY. A few months later, it appeared that SKM once again tried to actually take the contract by force and upped the ante in its effort. This time the attack was not limited to Afghan thugs, the Afghans were accompanied by Westerners—who arrived in armored SUVs . . . and the whole group came shooting.

It was late at night and our Charlie shift, the third security shift, was on station in the compound. Doc and Matt had since rotated back to their home countries and had been replaced by Johnny, a retired Brit from the Twenty-Second SAS (Special Air Service) who was our project manager. A guy recently separated from the U.S. Marine Corps assisted him. Johnny and his assistant had hit the rack already when the gang showed in armored trucks and began firing on our compound from the street.

One of our guards was hit immediately by automatic weapons fire. Uncertain if it was ACF (anti-coalition forces) trying to take the compound under the cover of darkness, our men did their job and returned fire to defend the U.S. Army's compound, as per our rules of engagement. A ferocious gun battle ensued—all just off the Jalalabad Road, barely within Kabul's city limits and a few miles from the airport.

Johnny, our project manager, got on his cell and called the Afghan police and Afghan army for support, then he managed to reach the wall and get an eye on the attackers, the darkness somewhat penetrated by our few security lights that had not yet been damaged by gunfire. He saw they were being led and directed by Westerners who were behind U.S.-made armored SUVs. By this time, he had already called the Ops Center, and Dick Roten and I called the shots. We immediately ordered our forces to cease fire before someone was killed on either side, and ordered Johnny to begin trying to communicate with the Westerners leading the attack.

Once we stopped firing, however, the attackers rammed the gate, got inside, and began firing again. We had our men stand down, fearing a blue-on-blue problem—good guys firing on good guys. We didn't yet suspect that this attack could be yet another foray by SKM.

As soon as the compound was overrun, the baseball-cap-wearing Westerners fled and the local thugs stayed behind. Milton, ever the coward, walked into the compound just as the Afghan police showed up and arrested him.

We immediately began filing police reports and requesting assistance from ADC. We also sent e-mails and placed unreturned phone calls to SKM in the States, as we tried to resolve this fiasco of their making—but it was as pointless as a white crayon.

We were in an incredibly difficult situation. We were providing exceptional security for ADC and their ultimate customer, the U.S. Army, at a level rivaled only by the CIA station and the U.S. Embassy, yet it seemed clear we had an American company trying almost daily to subvert our every move in order to take the contract from us. We couldn't prevent SKM from entering the premises, even if we were convinced their employee Milton was trying to sneak in armed thugs. If you subvert your security contractor like they were doing, by default you are placing the facility in danger, which translates into placing U.S. interests in danger. As far as I was concerned, it was completely disgusting and one of the most unpatriotic things I've witnessed, short of outright treason.

Finally, getting no support from ADC and open hostility from SKM, I reported the situation to the U.S. Army to keep someone from getting killed. They investigated and ultimately canceled ADC's contract altogether, resulting in a loss for everyone—including the U.S. Army. I have no idea who the Westerners were, what decent, patriotic, laws-abiding Americans would actively harm other Americans in a war zone working for the U.S. Army . . . excluding, apparently, SKM.

AS THE INDUSTRY GREW, the kinds of companies and the services each rendered became more specialized and varied. You can break private military companies, the entities that hire contractors who aren't otherwise hired by government agencies, into four broad groups:

- "Military support firms," which are used as logistical supporters during conflict (e.g., Kellogg Brown & Root)
- "Military consultant firms," which specialize in training and consulting but are not usually involved directly with conflicts (e.g., MPRI, DynCorp)
- "Military provider firms," which provide security and police services and are involved indirectly in actual conflict (e.g., Sandline)
- "Military full-spectrum firms," which provide training, support, and indirect involvement in actual conflict (e.g., Gray Solutions; SCG, LLC; Blackwater; and Triple Canopy)

One might have thought the increasingly professional profile of the industry would have led to less confrontational behavior. But it was still the Wild West out there. In 2010, almost five years after the freight forwarder incidents, we won a multimillion-dollar contract to train U.S. Air Force personnel at Fort Dix, New Jersey. We brought on a subcontractor, a retired SEAL who owned a small company to teach a tiny portion of the program. We didn't need to hire the guy but did it as a favor to foster a new corporate relationship for future projects. He got greedy, too, and decided to try to wrest the contract away from us by conspiring with someone in the air force at Fort Dix to make us look incompetent; he promised that person a job if they were successful. I'm no criminal law expert, but there was something about that deal that not only sounded unethical, but likely crossed a criminal line or two somewhere.

The old guy screwed up, though, and accidentally sent an e-mail that precisely laid out his plans . . . to one of our company's executives; so much for operational security on his part. The old man lost not only his master plan to take the whole thing, but his subcontract with us as well.

A FEW YEARS AFTER THE AFGHANISTAN GARBAGE, I was in my office when my secretary put a call through from a special agent with the FBI.

This FBI special agent was trying to find a contractor named Chaff, who'd worked for us years earlier in Kabul. I knew immediately whom he meant, but we'd already fired him and a friend of his—both marines. They were conspiring to set up their own company, using a name similar to ours, and planned on raiding our customer base, and all on our dime. They were plotting with none other than the freight forwarder again. Again, e-mails were the downfall of the conspirators, and, again, quite by accident they were sent to the wrong person. So we were in the loop: that errant e-mail contained their entire plan in a thread going back weeks.

Once we found out, we thought it fitting that our retired marine full-bird colonel be the one to recall these two to Virginia to give them the good news. Under the guise of briefing them on a new, supersecret project that would mean a raise for them both, we flew them home—appealing to their greed. Suspecting nothing, they were put up by us at a local hotel on the beach, where Dick met them and collected their contract ID cards under the ruse that we needed to get them updated. We returned the cards to the Department of Defense with a letter to the DOD advising them that the men no longer worked for us and were not to be allowed onto any U.S. military facility under the assumption they were still in our employ. That effectively cut the knees out from under them when it came to getting back on any U.S. bases anywhere. Then we also collected their passports—of course with the intention of getting new visas for them—but unfortunately they were somehow lost in the process, preventing them from traveling back to Afghanistan until they got them replaced. The rumor was that the passports had somehow fallen into a storm drain by accident, but we never managed to verify that unfortunate situation. Yet, we all thought that was a terrible, terrible shame. Chaff later mailed a .45-caliber bullet to me at work in a silly gesture I assumed he meant as a threat, but we simply took it out and fired it off during lunch that day.

I advised the special agent of this brief and unpleasant history with the former young marine. After he stopped laughing, the SA said that if we were in contact with the young man, we should advise him that it was in his best interest to contact the special agent immediately or go to the nearest U.S. Embassy if he was overseas. After we disconnected, I had our personnel department send over his archived 201 (company personnel) file to the government. We found out later from Uncle Sam that the FBI did indeed catch up with Chaff, though—in Kabul. They were trying to find him because allegedly he'd been claiming to work for the CIA. Even if he had wrangled a gig with them by hook or crook, you don't go around Kabul announcing that—if you enjoy living. We later found out that after we fired him, he took a job working for none other than the freight forwarder, the same company where their other alleged superspy employee came from.

Welcome to the rodeo.

IV

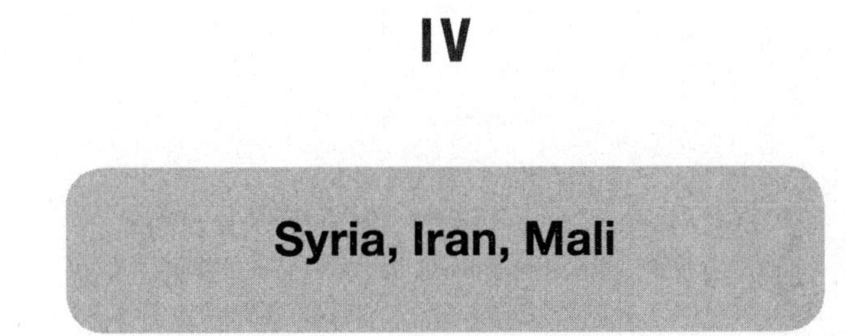

CHAPTER 23

The Iranian Operation

April 2007
Dam Neck Naval Base, Virginia Beach, Virginia

IT WAS FOUR YEARS before Libya ever crossed my mind. Throwing my ruck into the bed of my four-by-four, I climbed in to drive back home. The run this morning had been a particularly tiresome six-mile loop—down Regulus Avenue to the back gate, left over the dunes, up the beach, and winding around the back roads and trails of Dam Neck. Most of my friends thought I was off my rocker to run with a pack in boots at thirty-seven years old. It wasn't an all-out run, just more of a shuffle to keep from blowing out my knees. My usual regimen was weights on base Monday, Wednesday, and Friday, with a ruck run afterward; then on Tuesday and Thursday it was CrossFit. My friends mostly jogged, had personal trainers, or lifted heavy one day and then had their "light days." I ribbed a buddy, asking what a "light day" was—suggesting it sounded like a tampon ad. I just wanted to be able to outrun anyone chasing me and shove a bad guy's head through a wall if required.

As I climbed into the truck exhausted and pouring sweat, I cranked up the AC and turned on the satellite radio, which was tuned to Fox News. The anchor was relaying a short news story about an American—a former FBI agent named Robert Levinson, who had a glowing track record of twenty years of service against organized crime—and now had mysteriously gone missing in Iran. I pulled out my BlackBerry and got online, then pulled up everything available on the story—which wasn't a lot.

The growing theory was that the Iranians had kidnapped him and the U.S. government was trying to find him. Nearly sixty years old and living in Florida, Levinson was a husband, father, and grandfather. At the time of his abduction he'd reportedly been working as an independent contractor investigating cigarette smuggling for London-based Global Witness, an international nongovernmental organization (NGO). Just the previous month, in March 2007, he'd been sent to Iran on a twenty-four-hour assignment where he simply vanished . . . and according to the news, the U.S. government had no leads.

I thought about his family and how I'd feel if that were my dad. I'd want someone to do something. So I decided, sitting there in the truck, sweating and spent, that we would do something—it almost felt like a duty. As I cranked up and headed off base I called Dave Phillips, whom I'd brought over from Blackwater to run our Ops Center, and asked him to compile all available open-source information on the case. The family was in the dark; the U.S. government apparently was at a dead end; the Iranians weren't saying anything. The whole affair seemed to be dying on the vine.

Levinson's last known destination was Kish Island, Iran, at the Maryam Hotel, so Dave researched the air options and figured out that only one carrier—Kish Airlines—had regular flights domestically and internationally. Then we made an educated guess that he'd probably flown out of Dubai.

The next step was a very dangerous move—I wanted to put someone into Iran to pick up the trail.

We kept the operation close to the vest—compartmenting it even from our own people within the company, with only five people involved. We wanted to avoid leaks and were taking no chances. I called one of our operators based out of the United Kingdom. Mila had significant experience working in the Near East, and she spoke Arabic and some Farsi—the language of the Iranians. I asked her if she'd consider a solo job to nose around and collect background information, and being the reliable operator she is, she agreed within minutes.

The op plan called for her to go in with cover as a Brit national seeking employment teaching English as a second language on the island. We settled on this because the office where applicants for such work were interviewed was located near the offices for Kish Airlines, the airline used by Levinson to get onto the island. Before leaving, Mila bought a clean phone, and our tech remotely loaded our GPS tracking software to it. If someone got her phone, the software wasn't visible. She also bought a British phone, and we had her plug it in and leave it turned on back in London. She would send travel pics and text messages and make calls to it as though updating a boyfriend on her travels. It would all look normal to anyone monitoring her outgoing comms, but the travel pics gave her the ability to keep us posted on things. Then she set off for Iran.

BACK IN VIRGINIA, Dave and I stood in the Operations Center, watching the large monitor hanging from the wall: a tiny blue dot moved on a satellite overlay of Kish Island's airport. That blue dot was our girl's cell phone. One monitor displayed her location; other screens were tuned to Fox News and CNN; and a large digital clock displayed the times in Washington, Kish, and London, as well as Greenwich Mean Time (GMT). A watch officer was on duty twenty-four hours a day.

She landed on the tiny island and caught a cab heading for the north-eastern corner, moving through the traffic circle at Amir Kabir Square, bearing left, finally turning off Persian Gulf Boulevard and into the parking lot of the gleaming white, four-story structure. Four massive columns framed the entrance—and what an entrance it was. A red carpet lined the walk through massive wooden doors into a lobby made almost completely of white marble with gold or brass inlays. Stepping inside, she was met by a sprawling center staircase that would have made Scarlett O'Hara drool. She followed the doorman to the right over to the registration desk, just like Robert Levinson had done weeks earlier . . . and she checked in.

Mila made solid progress, meeting two men who actually remembered Levinson—the hotel manager and the manager of the hotel's on-site restaurant, where Levinson ate his last meal as a free man. She struck up conversations about planning to move to the area for work, asking if it was a good place. She was a master of elicitation and they both said it was a great place, but she mentioned her concerns for her safety—after all, according to the news, an American had disappeared there the month before. Both of the managers said they'd seen him and talked to him and there had been no problems—these witnesses' existence, and that information alone, was more than our government had at that point. The two men insisted that Levinson left their hotel via the hotel's car for a ride to the airport and that he'd flown away. Ever the smart operator, Mila asked to take a tour of the island, using the hotel's car. She wanted time with the guy who allegedly last saw Levinson—the driver.

As he drove her around the island, showing her different tourist-type attractions, she brought up the subject of the missing American, asking how safe it was to live there. The driver said it was perfectly safe and that the story was a lie. He claimed to have driven Levinson to the airport and dropped him off, watching him even enter the building. That last part struck her as odd—what driver actually sticks around to watch someone walk inside an airport? That's more like what a relative or friend would do, not someone on the clock doing his or her job. I didn't doubt Levinson had been driven to the airport or perhaps that he'd flown away—I just didn't believe the time or the destination was of his choosing.

Having identified three primary witnesses to Levinson's case, Mila now needed to shore up her cover. She couldn't just fly in, stay at the hotel, talk about an international mystery, and not do what she claimed to be there to do—those would be serious red flags to Iranian internal security. She headed north by taxi toward Sanee Square and turned left into the school where she sat for the job interview. There she met a man who unnerved her. He said he was with the school, but he asked where she was staying; he spoke English very well and began probing her background. Her feeling was that he was from Iran's MOIS, or more formally, the Ministry of Intelligence and National Security of the Islamic Republic of Iran, MISIRI for short. It was just a feeling, but a terrible one that matched the name—misery.

Back at the Ops Center, we were getting Mila's travel pics; but hidden and buried inside them were messages encrypted in the image file itself. You couldn't see it just looking at the picture; it was coded into the file in a technique called "steganography"—from the Greek word *steganos*, meaning concealed writing. This allowed us to decode her messages and read the latest updates. If the Iranians intercepted the e-mails using their eavesdropping capabilities, the only way they would get a clue that we were communicating using this encryption system would be from the size of the picture files, which were larger than normal by a few hundred kilobytes, due to the encryption on the hidden message itself. But detecting that would be a challenge.

But some governments' capabilities in terms of hacking and cyberwarfare border on science fiction. Programs can infect a target computer by posing as a software security update: this operation actually transforms the computer into a massive spying device by secretly turning on the microphone and webcam to record audio and video, take screenshots, and map the local network. It captures e-mail and instant messages, logs Web browsing history, and even copies files. Then the program sends all the recorded data to a command-and-control server before erasing itself—that's pretty high-speed spying.

If you marry up those programs with others similar to the one that Iran claimed was used to attack their uranium-processing facility at Natanz in the summer of 2010, and again in 2011 and 2012, a country could conceivably tear down a nuclear reactor from within by having the computer take control over the centrifuge, spinning it too fast, destroying it. Or perhaps you have the computer controlling the cooling mechanisms shut down, allowing things to overheat.

These capabilities all are part of an overall attack strategy that made better sense to me after I attended a seminar on strategic industrial targeting analysis put on by an army special missions unit in North Carolina. The program covered how to go into a foreign factory on an overt site tour and collect information, such as how to choose targets that would damage the enemy on the macro, strategic scale—like hydroelectric dams, steel production facilities, pipelines or refineries, thermal power plants, and, of course, nuclear power plants. It was about finding the key component that made the whole plant fail if it were broken.

Assume country X has decided to destroy country Y's ability to generate power. A certain power plant is the target in country Y. Inside that power plant are various components that make it work, and you want to hit the key, critical part—the part they can't replace easily or quickly. You have a few ways to do it—drop a bomb, send a cruise missile into it, have a ground team fire a shoulder-launched missile at it, shoot the piece of equipment with something like the Barrett .50, or send in a team to place charges on it or even just break it with a ball-peen hammer. Each of these methods has an upside and a downside, and that was all part of what we learned to factor into a decision.

The decision on which target to hit and which method to use was where the CARVER matrix came into play. All that data is plugged into this simple decision matrix, the letters of which stand for: Criticality—how critical was it to the functioning of the facility? Accessibility—how easy was it to get to? Recuperability—how long would it take to get it back online and working again? Vulnerability—what would it take to break it: a hammer, explosives, or nuclear weapon? What would the Effect on the population be? How would it negatively impact the people nearby, which worked against our overall strategic objectives? Finally, the issue of Recognizability spoke to how easily someone could see and recognize the target in question if they had to sneak in and access it, whether at night, rain, or during a sandstorm. Each potential category on that target was scored with a numerical value based on those six criteria, and the target with the highest score was the one to hit.

The introduction of the hacking capability expanded the CARVER matrix decision on options for hitting the site. Why use a missile, rifle, or team when a few keystrokes from thousands of miles away can accomplish the same thing?

The capabilities only grow from there. Imagine two enemy intelligence officers driving to their headquarters and getting a call from their boss, which the driver answers on a hands-free Bluetooth connection. After hanging up, they brainstorm how to pursue the tip they've just received while another government is actually eavesdropping on their conversation in their vehicle, recording their entire conversation because the Bluetooth system had been hacked, bugging the in-car microphone.

Hackers can hit OnStar and Ford SYNC, unlock doors, kill the engine, turn on the car's microphone, listen to you, and even deactivate the ignition. It's not science fiction—live road tests have proven these wireless attacks can work.

Google Glass, the wearable computer that looks like a cross between something you'd expect to see on Mr. Spock and a PhD candidate at Berkley, provides yet another platform for spying. For years, governments have been able to remotely access computer devices—whether laptops, desktops, smartphones, or tablets—and turn on cameras and microphones and you'd never know it. But that's easily defeated with a Post-it note slapped over the lens and if the mic can detect what's being said.

But with Google Glass, governments theoretically have the ability to remotely turn it on and see everything the wearer sees, does, or hears—and exactly where it's all happening, using the internal GPS without the user knowing it's been activated. Are you in your home having a private conversation with your spouse? Not anymore. Imagine you're in your office working on a sensitive project, or in a board meeting, or perhaps at a doctor's appointment, or discussing legal issues with your attorney that are supposed to be protected by privilege—all of that is potentially accessible. Imagine your fate if companies or bad guys accessed this information about you . . . well, panic, because if they want it, they can get it.

It's not science fiction, either. Governments have even wired the entire ocean with covert underwater microphones a few decades ago to listen for enemy submarines. Some governments have access to every conceivable electronic device that is connected to the Internet, sends or receives signals, or transmits anything over the air or through a cable, to include phones of all kinds, computers, radios, GPS navigational devices, Bluetooth, routers, Wi-Fi—all of what is called the grid. They essentially have the entire earth monitored—ground, air, sea, and even space itself.

But what if you want to get off the grid? Why not buy a new SIM card for your cell phone, in cash, and get people off your trail like in the movies? Nope, every mobile phone has an IMEI number (International Mobile Equipment Identity) hard-coded to that device. The moment you bought it with your credit card and requested that AT&T or another carrier issue you a phone number, you were officially tied to that phone. Replacing the SIM just changes your phone number—you're still identifiable, down to within feet of the very spot you're standing when you put a charged battery in your device . . . even without ever turning it on.

What if you ditched your old phone and bought a prepaid phone from a store with no security cameras, got a new SIM, and did it all with cash—not with credit cards tracking back to you—to throw them off? Sorry, that won't work, either—not if you call or text any of your old contacts with that new phone. Searchers analyze out at least three degrees—meaning the phone records of everyone you called (one degree), the records of everyone they called (two degrees), and finally, phone records of everyone they called (three degrees). This includes the number dialed, who dialed it, how long the call lasted, the cell tower that picked up the signal, the IMEI number of both phones, the latitude and longitude of the callers, and much more—giving tremendous data on both users. With that information your calling pattern would be recognized, your voice matched to earlier calls, your identity nailed down, and then your location determined using the GPS function in the device. Time elapsed? Seconds. But what if you disabled the location services on your iPhone? They can turn it back on and you'll never know it.

But what if you bought a new computer with cash, created new e-mail addresses and a new Skype identity? Sure, but if you e-mailed your old friends and associates, it would again create a pattern pointing back to you; and the same goes for your Skype, IM, FaceTime, and all similar accounts. Guess what else—every computer has a burned-in identity, called a MAC address (Media Access Control), which is assigned by the manufacturer and stored in its hardware. As soon as you connect to the Internet, your MAC identity pops up, your location is betrayed by your IP address, and then your days of anonymity are over—encircled by the tentacles of the eavesdropper like a nest of snakes.

Okay, then how do you get off the grid?

Unless you're ready to give up e-mailing people and ditch calling your family, friends, coworkers, and associates by any method other than a loud yell across the yard, you can't. Don't think using the apparently low-tech postal system is a workable option, either, because every piece of mail, both the sender and receiver's addresses, are photographed and recorded to retroactively track your mail at the request of law enforcement, with no warrant required. That's more than 160 billion pieces of mail just last year, giving the government a pretty good map of your contacts. FedEx and UPS aren't exempt, either. In 2013, they were threatened with criminal charges if they didn't actively police the contents of sealed packages.

The surveillance state has been expanded not only beyond the borders, but within as well, in ways that people probably never expected. Unmanned aerial vehicles fly along the borders with Canada and Mexico scanning for illegal crossings. In most major cities, there are cameras on every intersection, in police cars, on light poles, and in buildings. Through a program called License Plate Recognition technology, or LPR, these cameras see license plates, read them, pull up the ownership information on you, feed that information back to a central database, and match it up with GPS data, all run by your local municipality. It gives the authorities real-time access to where your vehicle is and where it's been and can estimate where it's going, anytime. This technology was used extensively in the hunt for the Boston Marathon bombers. So unless you smear mud on your license plate, you're never going to be able to drive free of surveillance again—and that's just what a local city can do; imagine what a nation is capable of pulling off.

But even if you did ditch it all, moved to a cabin in the Siberian or Alaskan wilderness, relied on solar power, and used carrier pigeons for communicating, if you ever walked into a Starbucks and someone with Google Glass was recording something, then posted it to his or her Facebook page—guess what—your face is there, and you can be placed at that store, on a particular date and time . . . and that's a starting point. Imagine how the steer looks right after the hammer hits him and he's no longer alive but he doesn't know he's dead—that's your right to privacy today.

Yet, following the recent leaks of classified information by the likes of a few traitors, many nations are feigning outrage over this sort of spying. It's not as though they don't do it themselves, nor is it something of which they're unaware. A contact in Sudan sent me a document stolen from their government detailing the monitoring of dissidents—who they called, when, where, how long, and what phone they used. That's Sudan—where they can barely keep the lights on during the day. Developed nations can do things that would boggle the minds of the average citizen.

All countries have friends, allies, rivals, and enemies. There's absolutely no doubt that one of the roles of the U.S. State Department, for example, is to report on what they understand to be the leadership intentions in Germany, despite Germany being a very close friend of America. Is that spying? Where a country lies on the spectrum of friend to foe will determine how the intelligence service gathers information: whether it uses overt or covert methods and how much risk it is willing to take in doing so.

Some countries are just really, really good at this stuff. It's almost like an NFL team playing against a college team, or in some cases, a JV high school team. Imagine marrying up intercepted phone calls, which mention a certain name or topic, with an e-mail on the same topic and then pulling GPS data on the phone and the computer's ISP, colocating them to a known hot spot, and pinging the computer the next time it comes online, mapping the hard drive, turning on the webcam, hearing the voice, running a voice match against a database, and confirming it's a known bad guy. A task force operating in the area is chopped to hit the house that night, and hours later the guy or girl is facing questions. It's a solid system and it's all amazing stuff, and it's only getting better and better . . . or worse, if you're the enemy.

So with those worries it was no doubt that back in Iran Mila was concerned for her personal safety, but despite the anxiety and pressures, she soldiered on. After the interview wrapped up, she walked over to the head offices of Kish Airlines, which sat nearby. The four-story building was topped by the Iranian flag, flanked by two smaller ones all flying above a huge yellow sun affixed to the face of the odd, stair-stepped design of the structure, which looked as if it were leaning back from the parking lot. Under the pretext of coordinating and reconfirming her flight home, she managed to find out that the airline's passenger lists were kept in a large ledger book—not on computers. After getting a look at the list pertinent to Levinson, she surreptitiously photographed it with her phone, checking the date against the time that the Iranians claimed that he left the country. But Levinson wasn't on the list of passengers who flew out that day—a fact that destroyed the Iranian government's claim that Levinson had flown out for Europe. She checked two days on either side of that date—his name showed up on the day he arrived, but he simply wasn't listed on any flight leaving. Robert A. "Bob" Levinson never left the island, at least not by commercial aircraft.

Mila went back to her room and started to unlock her door, but stopped cold in her tracks—a thin hair from her head was lying on the ground near the hinge side. She'd placed it there, just a few inches above the floor, held in place by the closed door. It was her simple telltale she used, along with the "Do Not Disturb" sign hanging from the knob—and its disturbance told her that someone had come in and it hadn't been the maid. She packed quickly and calmly went downstairs and ordered dinner. Her goal was to get photos of the hotel and restaurant managers and then of the driver and send them to us at headquarters.

She'd done all that was possible on this trip—an amazing piece of work, quite frankly. Just consider for a moment that the U.S. government knew nothing except where Bob Levinson had gone, where he'd stayed, and the fact that he hadn't left. They had no witnesses, no trail to follow, basically nothing because they couldn't go to Iran. But in just a few short days we'd infiltrated a hostile nation under cover; gone to the scene of a crime where our government couldn't—or hadn't; found three material witnesses to that crime who were heretofore unknown; and confirmed that the official story being told by the Iranian government about Bob leaving by air was a lie. On top of all that, our operator got photographic evidence to back all these things up, along with GPS coordinates and copious notes.

Anxious for her safety—no, scared out of her mind—Mila sent the rest of her pictures to us and calmly said her good-byes as any traveler would to the hotel staff she'd met, promising to return very soon. Then she got into the hotel's car—the same car Levinson used when he'd been taken—and drove to the airport, just like he'd done. She nervously picked up her ticket, expecting at any minute to have Iranian agents stop her. She moved on through airport security and to the biggest worry—passport control. Was this where Bob had been stopped and escorted off to his private hell? She stood in line, sweating, nervous, scared. She handed the man her passport and waited with a fake smile on her face as he punched keys on his computer. A few seconds later an Iranian official in plain clothes walked up; he looked at the screen, then at her—he wasn't smiling. He whispered something to the passport official and left the booth.

Moments later she was taken. The plainclothes man came up and in perfect English asked her to bring her things and follow him. They walked toward a single door and stepped inside. On the wall was a picture of the supreme leader. A man sat behind a desk and pushed forms across to her while the other official started taking her fingerprints . . . was this the prelude to her disappearance?

After a few minutes of forms and fingerprints, she was released and allowed to head to her gate, her stomach in knots. She never relaxed until the moment the jet's huge tires lifted off the tarmac. Connecting through Dubai, she headed on to Heathrow, where she melted back into her life, ever the gray professional.

WE TOOK THE DATA we collected in Iran and sent the intelligence report directly to the Levinson family in Florida. They sent it to their state's senator, Bill Nelson, a member of the Senate Intelligence Committee at the time, who then apparently contacted the head of the Department of Justice. I was later told by an FBI agent that the head of Justice then asked the FBI director, "Why is this unknown company on the East Coast collecting information that the U.S. government couldn't? Use them."

That's when my phone rang, but it wasn't a number I recognized, nor was I familiar with the caller. It was a Special Agent ████ with the FBI and he wanted to talk.

WHY HAD THE IRANIANS TAKEN LEVINSON? The thread, when pulled, unraveled bad blood between our two nations going back decades, but it had real links to the current war in Iraq.

Since 1979 there have been no direct diplomatic relations between the United States and Iran; the relationship had been tense since the overthrow of the shah during the Iranian Revolution when the fundamentalist mullahs came to power, beginning an era of Shiite Islamic revolt that would spread across the Middle East. The Iranians, intent on establishing a pretext for cracking down on internal dissent, thundered about the arrogance of Americans as they attempted to perpetuate a transformation that would lead to the global domination of Islam and its values. We became the villains, the facilitators of the shah's greed, and the demon behind every problem in the region, according to the clerics running Iran. So when the shah fled to the United States, allegedly for cancer treatment, they took over our embassy, thinking we'd return him to Iran. We didn't and they kept our people for 444 days, releasing them on President Reagan's inauguration day in 1980.

But more recently, the Iranians were trying to build a nuke and that was causing a lot of friction, to say the least. Plus, we knew that the Sepah-e Pasdaran (aka the Islamic Revolutionary Guard Corps, or simply the IRGC), along with a branch of their special operations troops, the Quds Force, were inside Iraq teaching insurgent Shiites how to kill coalition troops. The Iranian intelligence service was working against us there and had set up a special unit called the Ramazan Corps right after Saddam went down; it directed all Iranian operations inside Iraq. In joint operations with the Lebanese terrorist organization Hizbollah, the

Iranians had established, funded, trained, and armed Shiite terrorist groups such as the Hizbollah Brigades, Islamic Jihad in Lebanon, and the League of the Righteous.

Then, in January 2007, U.S. forces in the northern Iraqi city of Erbil captured a houseful of Iranian intelligence operatives, including several high-level Quds Force officers. Among those captured were Mahmud Farhadi, one of the three Iranian regional commanders in the Ramazan Corps; Ali Mussa Daqduq, a senior Lebanese Hizbollah operative; Qais Qazali, the leader of the Qazali network (better known the Asai'b Ahl al-Haq, or the League of the Righteous); and Azhar al-Dulaimi, one of Qazali's senior tactical commanders. Iran said they were diplomats, but they were IRGC working undercover to arm the Shiites to fight coalition troops.

One month later, on February 6, an Iranian intelligence operative named Jalal Sharafi was snatched from his car as he drove through the Karrada District in central Baghdad by members of the Iraqi Thirty-Sixth Commando Battalion, a unit trained by Second Battalion ODA from the U.S. Army's Fifth Special Forces Group. The Iranian had been in Iraq working under diplomatic cover as the second secretary of the Iranian Embassy in Baghdad. Now Iran was stinging from these losses and wanted their men returned, so they responded.

On March 8, almost one month after Sharafi's capture, retired FBI special agent Robert Levinson disappeared inside Iran—just two days before his birthday. Two weeks later, on March 23, eight Iranian boats surrounded and captured fifteen British sailors and Royal Marines from the HMS *Cornwall* in Iraqi waters at roughly 10:30 Iraqi time. They were taken to Tehran, where they were stripped, dressed in prison clothes, held in eight-by-six-foot stone cells, isolated, and interrogated nearly every night. They were given two options—admit to being in Iranian waters and go home, or face up to seven years in an Iranian prison.

Eleven days later, on April 3, Iranian diplomat/intelligence operative Jalal Sharafi was released and walked back into the Iranian Embassy in Baghdad. The following day, the Iranian president, Mahmoud Ahmadinejad, announced the release of the British captives. But there was no word from coalition forces about releasing the five Iranian operatives captured in Erbil, and thus there was no word from the Iranians about Robert Levinson. In fact, the Iranians didn't even admit to having him in the first place—just like when they snatched CIA station chief William Buckley from Beirut that same exact month twenty-three years earlier. It was the same MO they used dating back at least to 1979—blackmail. The Iranians seemed to be saying, "You have something we want, so we'll take something you want until you give us what we demand."

Unless there is another revolution in Iran, I don't believe the mullahs will ever negotiate peace with the West in good faith. They might appear to, but it will be a time-buying ploy to enable them to build their nukes or fulfill other nationalistic goals—not the sign of a true desire for peaceful relations. They are motivated by a warped interpretation of a prophecy that says the West has to be destroyed, as well as all non-Muslims. Before he was elected president, Ahmadinejad was the mayor of Tehran and secretly had a special road built that led to the mosque where the twelfth imam was supposed to go when he snuck out of the well he's said to have been hiding in since A.D. 941. The mullahs and many Iranians actually believe this stuff. Any appeasement or concession they give is only to further that nutball agenda.

So Levinson's FBI background made him, in Iranian eyes, a spy—and the Iranians had a reputation for brutality when it came to American spies: they tortured and killed them.

SPECIAL AGENT ██████ WAS TALL AND LEAN with dark hair, and he was all business. He had a drive to see Levinson returned and was one of the most professional FBI special agents with whom I've ever had the pleasure to work. He was always on time, prepared, and—despite the FBI being a somewhat risk-averse organization—was willing to consider ideas that weren't just out of the box, but ideas when there was not a box in sight. In later years, he never gave up on the case, even when it was transferred to the "cold case" department and long after he'd been transferred to another field office.

But at the meeting we set up in 2007, he and three other FBI special agents from the Washington field office met with me at the Marriott hotel near Fourteenth Street . . . to make sure I wasn't involved in Levinson's kidnapping somehow. Once they realized I wasn't, we all relaxed, and they called again—this time we'd meet in Richmond, Virginia—at the now-defunct Red, Hot and Blue barbecue joint on West Broad

Street. Once again, four of them showed up in khakis, hiking boots, and windbreakers concealing their Glocks. Special agent ████ was a straight shooter and said they wanted to talk to the three Iranian guys we'd identified. *Okay, fine, so talk to them,* I thought. But they obviously couldn't serve a subpoena on anyone in Iran, so they needed another way. Did I have any thoughts, they asked?

As a matter of fact, I did.

I pulled out a pen and paper napkin, pushed the french fries and ribs to the side, and sketched out a loose plan. The only thing I asked was that the government cover our expenses—no profit in this, just our expenses. We'd get the guys and deliver them to the FBI for interrogation—and hopefully help bring this American hero home. They liked it in concept, took a few days to run it up their chain of command for approval, and then we got the go-ahead. It was time to snatch up the bad guys—three material witnesses to an international crime that had no leads, no evidence at all, just a missing grandfather.

A "rendition" in law is a transfer or handing over of persons from one jurisdiction to another, after legal proceedings and according to law. In other words, after a court says you can have "Mr. X," then the host government transfers him to the requesting government. What we were planning was an operation that was a kidnapping, an abduction. In other words, it was a snatch . . . or what the media likes to call an "extraordinary rendition," but we didn't use that phrase.

Deceiving an enemy goes back to biblical days. Rebekah, the wife of Isaac, helped her youngest son, Jacob, steal the birthright intended for Esau, his brother, by deception. Not only did deception happen in families, but also in two of the world's oldest professions, prostitution and espionage. These two occupations share the use of deception: the whore slaps on gobs of makeup to cover years of hard living, while the spy throws down lies to hide his true intent. My team aimed to snatch three people out of Iran, and to do that we were going to have to lie our butts off to every nation we touched but our own.

THE PLAN I DREW UP was to have Mila reach back to the three targets—the manager of the restaurant, the manager of the hotel, and the driver who allegedly took Levinson to the airport. Had they been part of a conspiracy to kidnap Bob? Were they actually Iranian agents? Had the hotel manager given information on Bob after he'd arrived at the hotel? Was the driver truly just a driver, or was he part of the Iranian Revolutionary Guard Corps? Was the restaurant manager part of this trio of intrigue, too? The reality was that the U.S. government knew that one of their own—a decorated, senior retired FBI special agent—had been abducted, the Iranians were behind it and lying about it, and that after many weeks, the United States had no leads in the case that amounted to anything. This was their best—no, it was their *only* option.

Mila's excuse for e-mailing the three men in Kish was that she wanted to repay them for the way they had helped her during her visit. She would tell them that she worked for the owner of a major Middle Eastern hotel chain as a private tutor to his children. This, she would say, allowed her to put in a good word for these three men and she had set up a unique job interview for them—in Dubai.

In preparation for this ruse, we visited the actual website of the foreign hotel chain we were using as the lure and cloned all their fonts, images, and the look of the site itself. Then we bought a domain name on the Internet exactly like the actual hotel chain's, but with the words jobs.com added to it. Now it looked like a website set up to hire for the hotel—a job portal. Then we built an entire website complete with dozens of fake jobs. Buried in that list were three that precisely fit the skills of our three targets to whom Mila sent links to the website. She instructed them to pull up the site, read the descriptions, and—if they thought they were a fit for the jobs—write back to her.

The website served to validate the ruse because I knew from personal experience that, unfortunately, people believe nearly everything they read on the Internet. Once the targets all received the e-mail and visited our website, they e-mailed her back and told her they were interested. How could they resist? We'd set the pay for the positions well above what they were likely making in Iran, and she'd promised them that the hotel would move them and their entire families to Dubai. That was unheard-of in a city where men from all over the third world came to work.

Once we got their interest hooked, we set up the job interviews. They would be flown, at the hotel's expense—which was actually at our expense—to Dubai. They'd be picked up by a hotel limo and taken to a hotel we'd chosen to use, unbeknownst to the hotel itself, where rooms would be waiting. They'd get a complimentary night's stay and the following day would sit for the job interviews. They were promised that the jobs were already theirs, based on Mila's glowing recommendations, and the interviews were mere formalities. Once the interviews were over, they would fly back to Iran, where they would begin making preparations to move to the United Arab Emirates.

I sent our advance team to Dubai and they began setting up the rooms, locking on the cars, and even getting blue blazers with gold cuff links for our team members who would act as drivers.

On the day of the operation, everyone was tense on both sides of the Atlantic. The FBI, CIA, State Department, and my own team who were OCONUS and actually executing this whole thing were all geared up, ready to go. A lot of moving parts were involved and we held our collective breath until we got word from Mila that all three men had boarded their flight from Iran. So far the plan was working.

The targets landed, and the hotel manager sent a second message to Mila—they were on the ground. He sounded excited, even giddy at the prospect of this new job, this new life that he was about to start. I called Special Agent [redacted] and relayed to him the latest update on our targets. He was waiting on us to give them the word that the lobsters were in the pot.

One by one, the men from Iran picked up their carry-on baggage, deplaned, and headed down the ramp, where one stopped to collect his checked bag. The other two walked on ahead without him and got in the line to have their passports stamped. Mila, with cell phone to her ear, was updating me on everything going on from her location, where she stood just on the other side of the glass and waved to the men excitedly. The plan seemed to be working like a finely tuned watch. The first two were stamped and ushered through. Mila hugged them both and told them how excited she was for them. She then pointed them to two of my men, standing just a few yards away holding signs with the men's last names written on them—just like genuine chauffeurs. The first two then walked out of the airport and into the waiting limos.

That's when the plan ran into its first snag. The last man, the one still in the airport waiting in the line for passport control, was taken out of the line by the Dubai authorities. They said something to him, examined his passport, and pointed back the way he'd come. Mila, confused, called him to find out what was going on—she saw him through the glass partition. The young man, who wore a white, open-collared shirt and had thick black hair and a tiny mustache, put the cell phone to his ear. "They are not letting me come in," he told her.

She walked over to one of the Dubai officials and began speaking with him in Arabic, while texting me,

Driver not being allowed thru. Working it now.

I called Special Agent ███████ and updated him that two packages were en route, and that we were working the third, but were having problems at the border. He wrote back,

Copy.

Mila continued to reason with the officials at the border, but it was no use. They simply weren't letting him through. She sent me another message.

RamRod, sorry—he's being sent back. No idea why. What do you want me to do?

If you can't do more at the border, roll back to the hotel and continue w/original plan.

Roger, she wrote and headed out.

I told Special Agent ███████ that target number three was a no-go and we had no idea why. The guy who'd driven Levinson the day he disappeared wasn't being allowed to enter Dubai by the UAE passport authorities. We had two-thirds of our quarry on our turf, but this last one—the last person to supposedly see Levinson alive—wasn't being allowed into the country.

Meanwhile, my men drove the other two to the hotel, all the while under surveillance by both FBI and CIA teams. We'd already pre-checked the two arriving men in and had their hotel keys, so once at the hotel, they were escorted them up to their individual rooms.

D *(left)*, standing with me outside a safe house near Misrata, Libya. He is one of my best friends in the business and a guy I've worked with and trusted for many years now. He was my partner on the Libyan mission in 2011–2012.

Some of our staff, standing on TV Tower Hill overlooking the city of Kabul, Afghanistan, in 2005. *(From right to left:)* Matt Larsen, Randy, and Doc, who patched me up when I got shot a few years earlier.

Note: Omissions have been made in photographs and captions at the request of the Central Intelligence Agency.

D (*right, in sunglasses*) sits atop a captured tank from Qadhafi's defeated army in Misrata, Libya, in 2011. The burned-out, gutted buildings in the background testify to the ferocity of the fighting that took place.

A typical street in the Hay-al-Andalus area of Tripoli, Libya, not far from the house where the sniper was killed.

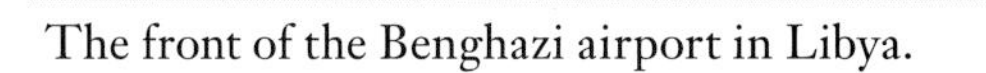

The front of the Benghazi airport in Libya.

D (*right*) and me, standing next to weapons and ammunition piled, unguarded, along a street in Misrata. As we watched, at least two vehicles pulled up and people loaded ammunition into their trunks and drove away. It's no wonder there's a problem with weapons proliferation in the country today.

A friend stands next to a rebel militia antiaircraft machine gun bolted into the bed of a hand-painted pickup truck parked in front of a hotel in Benghazi. These *Mad Max*–like contraptions have been seen throughout the country as late as 2014.

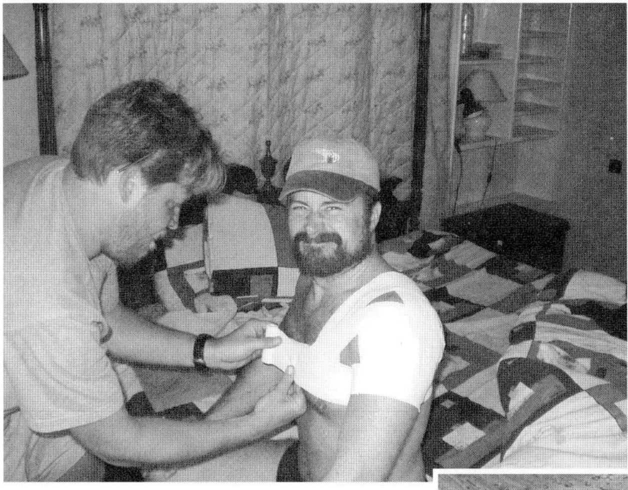

Doc (*left*), changing my bandages back at our safe house in Kabul a few days after I had been shot just over the border in Pakistan in April 2004. Doc was an outstanding medic and former British paratrooper.

Doc (*left*) and me, on the road to Jalalabad in the eastern mountains of Afghanistan in 2006. Rusting Soviet armored vehicles litter the background of this strategic location, warning travelers that this was a dangerous road back then—and remains so today.

Kabul International Airport in 2003 was a strange collection of contractors, spies, military personnel, and journalists. In this photo, taken that year, I'd just arrived from Dubai and was heading into passport control.

Here I'm standing ████████ ████████████████ in Kabul, Afghanistan, in May 2002. The large banner in the background is for the Northern Alliance Commander Ahmad Shah Massoud, who was assassinated right before the 9/11 attacks.

My colleague Two-Ton (*right*) and me, on our way out of Afghanistan in 2004.

We wore local clothing when making road trips through the countryside of Afghanistan. In this photo from 2004, we are heading through the treacherous eastern mountains to ████████ ████████████████ the border with Pakistan.

Visiting with the locals, eating, sharing tea, and making friends was the only way to survive in the mountains of Afghanistan. Here I'm sitting with an elder tribesman ██████ in 2003.

This photo was taken near the gate at the Afghanistan/Pakistan border, where I was part of the first group of Americans to meet troops guarding the Northwest Frontier in 2002. This outpost was attacked a few months later and nearly every Pakistani man in this photo was killed.

From high atop TV Tower Hill, Doc points out key landmarks to a new crew coming into Kabul to work security for us in 2005. We took each new team up here with maps of the city to orient everyone. A good friend, Randy (*far left*), looks on.

Doc (*left*) briefs the day's route to James from General Dynamics (*center*) and a U.S. Army lieutenant colonel as we prepare to take them from Kabul up to Bagram Air Base on a snowy winter day in 2004.

I stopped in at Camp Chapman in Khost, Afghanistan, and visited with some U.S. Army troops guarding the base. Just three years later, it was here that U.S. intelligence suffered its worst loss in twenty years.

Riding atop a police truck after having traveled to inspect a city entrance checkpoint, I snapped this picture of the chaotic, third-world streets of Khost, Afghanistan, in 2003.

Remote outposts in the mountains along the Afghanistan/Pakistan border like this are manned night and day in an attempt to detect and intercept Taliban and al-Qa'ida terrorists sneaking into the country to stage attacks. Firefights are a regular occurrence and hardly ever make the news.

Retired SEAL Command Master Chief Denny Chalker *(third from right, standing)*, plank owner of SEAL Team 6, and I *(fourth from right)* stand with Northern Alliance fighters in Kabul in 2002.

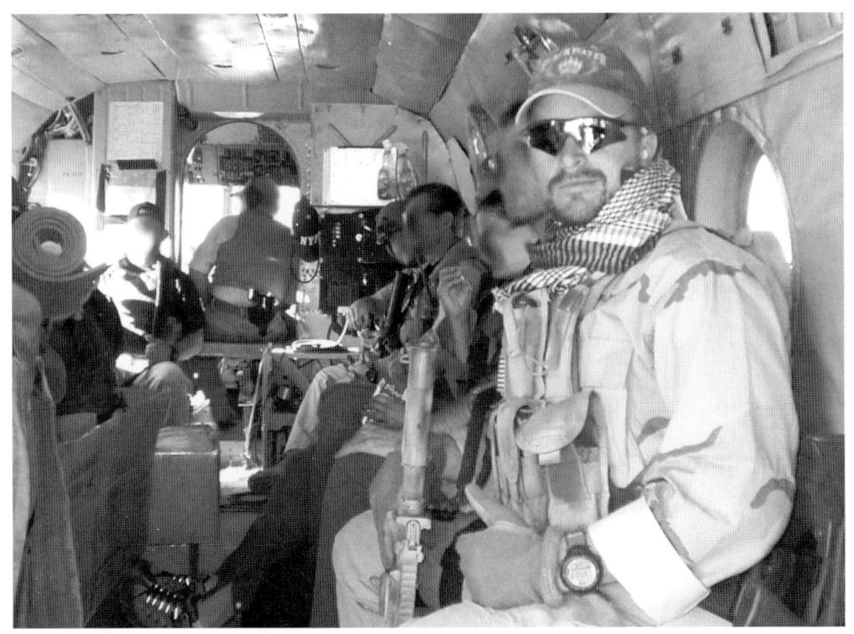

On board a government Mi-17 helicopter flying back from Bagram Air Base loaded with U.S. intelligence personnel in 2002 as part of the Blackwater Security team. The pilots told us, "In the air, we're in charge. But if we get shot down and are alive, we're listening to you guys." I'm on the far right.

I'm standing at an Afghan border checkpoint in eastern Afghanistan looking into Pakistan in 2004. We'd just completed a four-hour ride through the mountains to reach this location for a meeting.

Our trucks, waiting to unload supplies from a U.S. Chinook helicopter just outside our base in eastern Afghanistan in 2002. The pilots preferred the safety of the dark, so it was a rare occurrence for them to fly during daylight.

The first Blackwater Security team, posing after training at our training facility for the deployment to Afghanistan in April 2002. The team deployed on top-secret missions to secure CIA assets in the country. I'm kneeling in the front row, second from the left. Denny Chalker is also kneeling in the front row, third from the right. Erik Prince is in the back row, third from the right.

Some of our team from Blackwater in 2002 atop a mountain northeast of Kabul, overlooking the notorious brick factory from a captured Taliban gun position. I'm third from the right.

Erik Prince, repairing gear in our hooch (improvised shelter). My cot is to the left, in the room that we shared with two intelligence officers in late May 2002.

Like everyone else, Erik Prince pitched in to help build guard towers and improve security in Kabul as part of the overall security project in 2002.

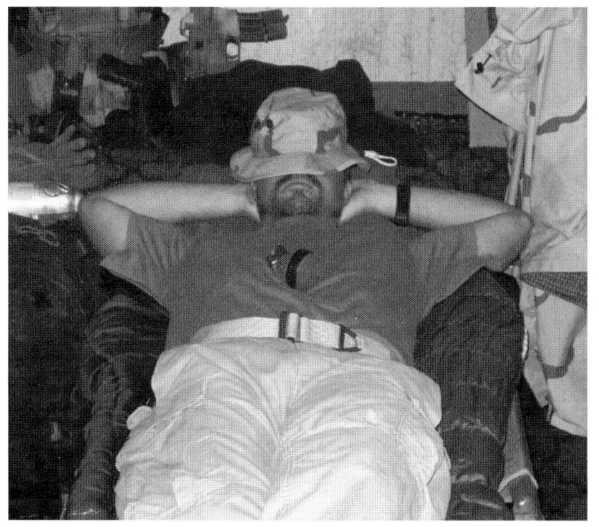

As I took a quick nap following a hot morning of work, Erik Prince slipped a grenade onto my stomach and used my camera to take the picture. Practical jokes were part of what kept us sane in a hostile environment during that summer in 2002 near the Pakistani border.

At my own company in 2007, I'm teaching a carbine course to students. We grew steadily during those early years, with word spreading about our PSD (protective services detail), tactics, and weapons training programs. We soon had students inquiring about training from around the world.

In this photo from 2010, I'm initiating a range drill by firing a Glock 34 for some of our students going through PSD training. At the sound of the gunshot, they assumed they were under attack and began an aggressive sequence of movements to evacuate their VIP.

In this photo from 2007, D *(left)* is with two other students as they hustle a VIP *(center, in white hat)* out of the danger zone in an evacuation drill. Shortly after this evaluation course, D was offered a full-time job.

Just two years later in 2009, D (*facing the camera)* is teaching a tactical handgun course to a mixed class of men and women at our range facility in Mississippi.

D (*second from right)* is observing as students engage moving steel targets from behind a simulated disabled vehicle. The team has bailed out and half are preparing to move to a safer location, while the other half provides covering fire for them.

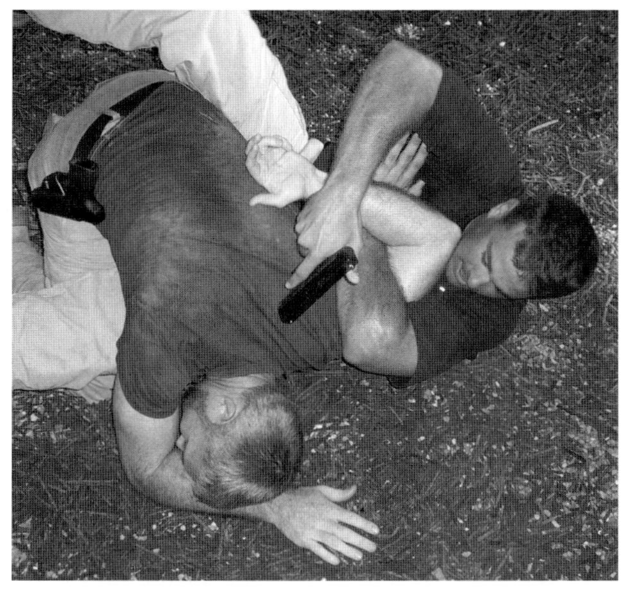

As my friend Matt Larsen says, "You only fight long enough to allow your buddy to show up and shoot the bad guy in the face." In this photo, Kendrick (*with gun*) and JJ are training in combatives, and Kendrick has managed to gain the upper hand—literally. In real life, this fight would be over with just a few pounds of trigger pressure.

Cold and tired, D (*right*) and I stop for a quick, early-morning picture in northern Iraq as we head south, away from the border with Syria and Turkey, following the Syrian mission in 2012.

Robert Young Pelton *(left)* and me, upon arrival at LAX. Eason Jordan from CNN hired me to go to Bogota, Colombia, and bring Pelton home after he'd been kidnapped by United Self-Defense forces. He was released and we escorted him all the way to his front doorstep in 2003.

Twenty-four years of foreign places, missed moments, and tearful good-byes truly brings home the reality that ". . . being forever available to the rest of the world is overrated." Today, I try to spend as much time as I can with the ones I love in quiet, peaceful places, ignoring the critics and enjoying the second half of this game of life that God has given me.

As soon as the doors were closed behind them, the FBI team ████████—who also had keys to the targets' rooms—burst inside. They questioned them for hours about Levinson's whereabouts, and my team and I never heard or saw those men again. Not knowing whether they were taken to Guantanamo or some other facility, and knowing the driver had been turned back, my concern was damage control. We had to preserve our relationship—Mila's relationship—with the driver. I saw two things we needed to prepare: an explanation for why he wasn't allowed into Dubai, and a story in case the other two guys ever got released and returned to their old jobs and ran their mouths off to the driver.

We found out a few days later the reason for the third man being turned back at the border: the FBI had been required to tell the State Department that an operation—*our operation*—was taking place on UAE soil. State Department officials then decided that they had to tell the UAE, who had then been given the list of our targets. The UAE decided that the driver, an actual Iranian passport holder, wasn't going to be allowed entry; they didn't want any political fallout from the Iranian government—which sat just forty miles north across the Strait of Hormuz from them.

The other two guys were allowed to enter because though they lived and worked in Iran, they were actually ████████████████ citizens holding ████████████████ passports with Iranian work visas. My frustration was at its peak, but there was nothing we were able to do. The UAE put target number three, the driver, back on the next plane to Kish and he was out of our grasp.

Our damage control plan was simple—Mila called the driver and told him that the reason he'd been denied entry was that the other two guys lied to the Dubai authorities about him to keep him out of the country. Mila told the driver that the other two guys did it because they wanted a family member of theirs to get his job—in other words, we sowed a little greedy discord to increase the driver's desire to work with us and, hopefully, to drive a permanent wedge between him and the other two guys. I wanted him to hate them to the point that he'd never give them the time of day, much less an opportunity to hear what they had to say. It worked—he did. It turns out that he'd quit his job at the Iranian hotel the week before he flew out, giving it to his brother. Once he failed to get the new job, he was unemployed and had to move back in with his family at their village in a remote part of Iran, having lost face and his job . . . and he blamed them.

WE CONTINUED TO WORK THE LEVINSON CASE for the FBI for the next year, and then, in November 2008, a family friend of the Levinsons who also was a former federal prosecutor, David McGee, contacted me. He'd been the one who pushed our report to Senator Nelson, I would later learn. He was now asking us to escort him and an associate to Cyprus—he said he had a lead on Levinson. I spoke to the FBI and told them what McGee requested. The FBI didn't think his lead was credible, so I promised to keep them informed of anything that we learned during the trip. So D, another employee named Rocky, and I headed to Cyprus.

Once on the ground, McGee told me of how he'd gone through Bob's personal safe and his e-mail accounts and discovered that he'd actually been working for the CIA as a contractor. That made more sense to me than this silly cigarette-smuggling story, but I couldn't understand why the CIA wasn't doing the legwork to gather the intel to get back one of their own. So I asked McGee.

"Bob wasn't supposed to go to Iran. He was working for an office in the CIA that had no authority to send him overseas. He was working for a woman in the analysis division, not the operations side. When he disappeared, the woman in charge of that office did absolutely nothing—she acted as if he never existed, never worked for her, never had any connection with CIA—probably because she knew she'd screwed up by sending him in the first place. There's a massive internal investigation going on; she's been reprimanded and likely will be fired," he said.

So apparently the CIA couldn't help with the case because it was being investigated and there was, essentially, a conflict of interest. I reported back to the FBI by phone what I'd just been told, and we continued with our mission to protect McGee and his associate in Cyprus. They met with a Syrian businessman and big-time gambler—Fouad al-Zayat—whom we dubbed the Fat Man, at his offices in Nicosia. He'd reached out to McGee offering to help find Levinson, saying he had a connection in Lebanon who could get us a meeting with Hizbollah, who'd set him free.

The meeting with the Hizbollah rep would take place in Nicosia at the Fat Man's office. I would be with McGee posing as an associate attorney with his law firm, D would be a paralegal, and Rocky a law firm investigator. I put D and Rocky in a vehicle running countersurveillance on the office, keeping watch for Hizbollah thugs who might try to do harm to McGee or follow us when the meeting broke up.

McGee and I went in to the meeting on the upper floor of the Fat Man's office in a small, bland conference room that was like a missile frigate stripped for action. Inside around a small circular table sat a man claiming to be Hizbollah from Beirut and another man who said he was a retired colonel from the Jordanian Special Forces. Acting in my role as an associate attorney, I said nothing while McGee and the two Arabs spoke—until they said they could deliver Levinson to McGee if he'd go to Beirut with them. That was where I drew the line and broke my silence for the first time.

"That's not going to happen. Mr. McGee will not be going to Beirut. If anyone is going, it'll be me, but not before we have something more than your word that Bob's even alive, or that you have the ability to deliver him."

Both men looked almost startled that I spoke, not to mention what I'd said. McGee looked at me and then back at them and simply said, "He's right." The two Arabs whispered for a moment, then asked to take a break to make calls back to Lebanon. As we were leaving the room, the Jordanian pulled me aside and said, "I didn't think you were a lawyer" and he smiled. I called D and Rocky, telling them to be on their toes, that the bad guys now knew McGee wasn't just here with office staff.

The Arabs disappeared, claiming they needed to go back to Beirut to coordinate Bob's release and speak to their leaders. But before they left that night, they came to McGee's hotel to meet once more—and we set up surveillance. I'd told McGee to hold the meeting in the lobby of the Hilton. D, Rocky, and I were on the upper floors, which overlooked the lobby, taking photos and video. McGee had an ink pen I'd given him that was recording everything they talked about. When the meeting was over, I collected all the audio and video files while D and Rocky drove McGee and his partner to the airport for their flight out. While they did that, I went to another hotel and, for the next several hours that night, sent the files to the FBI. I'd recorded every conversation we'd had.

D and Rocky came back from the hotel and went to the room they shared. They heard a knock on their hotel door. They opened it and eight thickly built Arabs, armed, pushed into their room, frisked both men, took their cell phones, and disabled the hotel phone.

They claimed to be Cypriot National Police investigating the murder of someone in northern Cyprus, but Rocky noticed none of their weapons matched. D later said that he noticed none of them called in by radio or cell phone to a central dispatch to report anything, either. D spotted his personal folding knife on top of the nightstand and noticed the men didn't move to secure it—all these things actual police officers should have done. What they did, however, was to begin questioning my guys about who they were and why they were in Cyprus, and then they started going through their computers, BlackBerrys, and cameras. But they found nothing—both men had removed the micro-SD storage chips and given them to me earlier that night, then they'd wiped their phone logs. D would later tell me that he'd slipped over to the nightstand and secretly tucked his knife into his pocket. He calculated that there'd be a lot of blood from eight bodies and they'd simply decided they'd have to burn the hotel down to cover it up. That's how my men look at things—no one is taking us anywhere, and we'll win, even with odds like that, at all costs.

The Arabs finally decided to leave after interrogating the guys for nearly six hours. The next morning I got two pieces of bad news—my candidate had lost the presidential election, and D telling me what had happened to them the night before. We knew we'd been compromised and were in a dangerous situation. The men who'd held them that night were likely Hizbollah—and that was not good, at all. D and Rocky had scheduled flights that next morning, so we did major surveillance detection routes to throw off anyone following us, got them to the airport, and they took off. I, on the other hand, had a flight leaving the next day. So alone, with Hizbollah in town, I called my office and had them make a reservation for me at yet another hotel—this one close to the airport—and checked in. I didn't poke my head out until the next morning and caught a flight out with no problems.

THE FAT MAN LIKELY HAD GOOD INTENTIONS with regard to Levinson, but my impression was that McGee thought he was just trying to get in good with the U.S. government by helping find him in hopes that it would help him in some high-stakes litigation he had pending in New York. At the time, we assumed Hizbollah and the Jordanians were likely just trying to lure McGee to Beirut, where he'd be abducted and held for yet another payday in the crazy world that is Lebanon and the Middle East, or they thought we were CIA sent to help recover Levinson. In that case, a trip to Beirut would have had far more dire consequences for us.

The situation also turned sour on a financial front. My company spent quite a lot of money on travel and hotels, and when we submitted the bill for the work, to include the time of three of our top people, the family refused to pay, saying it was too much. We tried talking, then threatened to sue but never really meant it—I couldn't do that to a family going through such emotional turmoil. We tried to set up a website to raise money for them and hopefully get reimbursed for our work, but they objected to that, too. Ultimately, we ended up eating the cost of helping them to the tune of tens of thousands of dollars.

The Levinson situation would turn out to be one of the biggest scandals in recent CIA history. At least three people would be fired and seven more reprimanded, and new rules were crafted to govern how the agency worked with contractors. The CIA even wound up sending someone to personally apologize to the Levinson family along with a $2.5 million settlement in lieu of a lawsuit that would expose the situation in open court. But all that would happen many months later.

I WASN'T CRAZY ABOUT THE END OF THIS PROJECT. I'm somewhat of a perfectionist; I like things to end as planned. I want to hit my target. The fact that the driver escaped questioning bugged me; it kept me up nights, particularly given the fact that the outcome was jeopardized by what I considered mere bureaucracy, my least favorite entity. We mounted other covert operations in the three years that followed, even proposing an Argo-like op before we even knew about the movie or the older mission. At one point, we even had intelligence from a source who had recently left Evin Prison in Iran who reportedly saw Levinson in person. We briefed the Washington FBI field office on almost a monthly basis, but Robert "Bob" Levinson remains missing and the Iranians have never acknowledged they have him—but they do.

At this point the Iranians will only release him if they have a way of saving face. If the United States changed its approach and requested the Iranians' help—perhaps not alleging they kidnapped him—it might allow the Iranians to "find" him or to "rescue" Bob and return him to his family.

The man is elderly and ill and is the longest-held hostage in U.S. history. He is of no intelligence value to Iran after this long. He's missed weddings, graduations, and births. His situation is truly nothing more than a last-ditch, backdoor bargaining chip for the Iranians to use if they truly get behind the eight ball—a sad, pathetic strategy by a government claiming to be honorable and acting in good faith. Bob's story and our involvement will perhaps one day be told completely, and there is a lot more to it than what I can write here, but I'm not at liberty to go into more detail on our involvement in trying to win his release on behalf of the family or the U.S. government.

CHAPTER 24

Rendition

December 6, 2004
Railway Station, South Asia

IT WAS A SNATCH JOB, and we'd gotten very good at it. This story remains classified, so I have to blur the details.

A massive South Asian city with ancient roots, it was a capital, the seat of one of the oldest civilizations on earth. The pollution-filled sky slammed the heat down on its citizens. Tracey wiped her forehead with her sleeve as she pushed her way through the crowd. A veteran female intelligence officer, she was running surveillance on someone for us—a PONI, person of national interest. She struggled to keep her target—Lal—in view. Our team was tasked with picking him up and delivering him for questioning, and our girl was on his trail. We knew where he lived and, through a contact, Tracey had found out that he was about to make a trip on the 0800 train to a smaller city to the southwest where tourists flock to see temples and mosques.

Tracey had already advised the Ops Center of her plans; now she was fighting what looked like a losing battle to keep the man in sight. She'd barely managed to get a ticket for his train. She must have felt as though she would be crushed by this crazy third-world parade of men, women, and children. Hundreds of people were carrying boxes and suitcases on their heads, rolling barrels onto carts, and lugging everything you can imagine. Dirty, smelly beggars extended bony hands from underneath ragged shawls. There was an odor of diesel fumes, cigarettes, and unbathed bodies. It was like a mass exodus with thousands of people fleeing with all their worldly possessions. But it was just a normal day.

Tracey had last spotted Lal walking out onto the big train platform and up the open-air staircase to the catwalk. There were multiple tracks with trains on every one of them. To reach a train on the other side of the track you had to walk up a ramp, across the catwalk, and down the ramp on to the other side. Tracey shoved and slid through the crowd, receiving glares, stares, and curses.

She reached the top and made it to the railing, looking over the edge down at the platform below for signs of her target. The crowd was overwhelming; everyone seemed to have on the same color clothing—dark with a light touch of dirt. For a moment she thought she saw a man who resembled Lal standing partly behind a bulletin board reading the train schedule. She strained for a better look, but just as she was getting into a better position, she was bumped out of the way by a man carrying a large trunk. Then two small girls and their mother wedged between her and the railing, and no sooner had that happened than was she swept back into the stream of the crowd, losing sight of the man again.

At last she made the turn on the other side and began the descent down the ramp to the train platform. She broke free of the crowd, hurrying over to where she last spotted Lal, but he was nowhere to be seen. This was not how she'd trained to do this back at Fort Monckton, near Portsmouth, England. At the British intelligence training facility she'd been with a team of her fellow students and they had radios to coordinate movement, but here she was all alone trying to follow a guy in a hastily planned surveillance operation with no backup.

Just as she located her train, she spotted him—between two posts littered with handbills on the other side of a large pallet that was being rolled by two national army troops. Lal, slight frame, black hair, five feet, four inches tall, mid-forties, was wearing brown slacks and a collared shirt unbuttoned to mid-chest, exposing a stained V-neck T-shirt. He was standing near the train car, smoking and talking to two young, white, female tourists.

Tracey quickly rechecked her ticket; her first-class train car was the one Lal was standing next to. It seemed he would certainly board. She slid her left sleeve down a bit to expose the tiny passport-size photo of him affixed to her wrist. She compared the photo to the man in front of her—definitely the same guy. She lowered her gaze, reached into her shoulder bag, took out the local newspaper, and began to read. Then she reached down to her touristy fanny pack, which was strapped to her waist, and pushed a concealed button on the video recorder hidden inside. A wire ran from the fanny pack underneath her shirt, attaching to the sunglasses she was wearing.

The sunglasses, fashioned after the popular massive frames worn by the celebrities and wannabe celebs, served no medical purpose whatsoever. The wire from the recorder was attached to the end of the right arm of the glasses, all covered by her long dark hair. The frame arm had the wire from the recorder inside, which was connected to a fiber-optic camera lens and recorded video images of anything she turned her head toward. Just looking at her, no one realized that this woman in her thirties was anything more than a graduate student on a weekday outing. The camera lens, no larger than a pinhead, was completely hidden from sight.

Tracey made her way to Lal, who was talking to the tourists. She was pretending to read as she walked. She stopped, folded her paper, and took out her tickets—pretending to be trying to find her car. She overheard Lal as he spoke to the girls, asking to be of assistance to them. "Oh, you are English, perhaps Australian? This train system can be very confusing, indeed. Do you need help?"

"Yes, we're British; thank you, and, no, we're quite fine. But thank you for asking."

The girls were trying to ignore him and had turned their backs to Lal. Tracey walked over to the other side of the platform to keep a better, more discreet eye on things. She craned her neck to read his lips, the camera recording every detail of his face.

". . . so, you are going to [redacted] to see the [redacted] or maybe the temples?"

"Yes, we are." The girls were obviously getting annoyed and pretended to find their car on the train; he simply followed them as they walked. The guy would not quit.

"No. Thank you all the same." Then the shorter of the girls grabbed her companion's sleeve and pulled her away. Lal pulled out his ticket. His train was the same as the English girls', and Tracey's car was just one down from Lal's; they were connected, which made things much easier.

She waited until the conductor called for last boarding before she jumped on, just in case Lal changed his mind. Once aboard, after the train had pulled out, she made her way to the passage between the two cars, where many passengers gathered to smoke. There was also a small room in the passageway where the toilet was located. It was just a hole in the floor with molded outlines of feet next to the hole. Looking through the hole, the tracks running below the train were visible.

She stood in the drafty passage with two local men who were smoking; a small, old woman was squatting over the hole and her sort of ugly wasn't just a light switch away, either. Tracey leaned against the wall as the air blew in through cracks in the door. She positioned herself to keep a good watch on Lal as he continued to flirt with the poor girls. For the next three hours, she leaned against the train wall and watched him . . . all the way to the railway station.

When the train stopped, the passengers started exiting. Tracey's muscles were cramped from standing, but despite her physical discomfort, she was the first out the door and quickly took up a position on the steps to see above the heads in the crowd. She caught sight of Lal as he ran across the platform, through the train station, and out into the dirty yard. He rounded the corner of a plaster and cement building and waved to a cabdriver.

Tracey was quick on his heels, hailing a cab of her own and jamming bills into the driver's hand. She ordered him to follow Lal's cab and he did, but a few minutes into the ride, Tracey began to worry for her safety. The driver was a madman. He honked his horn at everyone, bumped an old man pulling a rickshaw out of the way, nudged a herd of sheep with his bumper as they crossed the road, and generally drove like a nut. Concerned about keeping a low profile, Tracey asked him to be more careful and lay off the horn.

In about ten minutes, they reached the middle of the city. Lal's cab pulled over to the side of the road in front of a hotel that looked like a shack or a whorehouse. She watched as he jumped out and yelled something back at the driver, who waved at him and turned off his engine. Tracey motioned for her driver to also pull over and park behind a large wagon full of vegetables. She gave him more money and told him to stay put, that she'd be right back. Lal had slipped down a staircase into the lobby of the run-down building. The stairs actually led down to a restaurant that was connected to the hotel. Tracey gave Lal enough time to get inside and then, slipping out of her taxi, hustled through the dusty streets past the sidewalk vendors' carts and entered the building, too.

Scanning the dark interior of the restaurant, she saw no sign of him. She sent a quick text back to headquarters asking whether to press on or let him go and pick him up tomorrow. No, we might not have another chance. Find him.

The place was almost completely empty, except for the two young locals sitting in the corner staring at her and the old woman behind the cash register. To her left, she heard steps out in the hall, going up the stairs. She made her way into the hallway and looked up between the stairs to see Lal disappear into a room on the third floor.

Softly, she walked up the staircase, located the door to the room, looked around for anyone who might be watching her, then put her ear against it. Inside she heard Lal's voice. He was talking to what sounded like an older man. Her language skills were now once again paying off.

She heard the older man tell him about a quantity of opium and then she heard Lal say, "Yes, yes. Okay. How much is it?" in the local dialect.

Lal was a drug dealer—add that to the mosaic of what we knew about the guy. Jobs like this didn't come with much information other than who the target was, where he lived, and where he was to be delivered. We were tools used to perform a specific task and, as such, weren't usually privy to anything about why he was wanted or what he'd done wrong. It was called "compartmentalization"—keeping information restricted to those who needed to know.

Quickly unplugging the wire running from her glasses-camera to the fanny pack, Tracey connected another wire attached to a thin, flat, black, one-inch-square piece of plastic. A fiber-optic fish-eye camera lens was fixed in the plastic. She slid the plastic square under the door and pressed record on her fanny pack again. The fish-eye lens would record a panoramic view of the inside of the room from underneath the door, without revealing her presence. She then put her ear back to the door, took out her notebook, and began taking notes on the conversation while the camera did its thing. When she had recorded enough, she walked back out, called the Ops Center, and delivered a SITREP, then got back into her cab and waited. There was now a fix on his next hard set of plans, and that was where the team would come into the picture.

A FEW DAYS LATER, four men sat in a dark gray Toyota Land Cruiser, sweating right through every layer of street clothes they had on, jammed together, shoulder to shoulder, parked near an apartment building. Behind them was another Land Cruiser with more fellas. The air was hot and the windbreakers worn to hide equipment didn't help. Under the jackets, they wore radios with covert mics and earpieces, Glock 17s, pepper spray, collapsible batons, and numerous pairs of plastic flex cuffs. The last two guys in the second truck wore the same but each also carried a UMP—a suppressed submachine gun firing .45 ACP—in addition to their regular load. These last two men were backup and security for the rest of the team.

The snatch team was following up on Tracey's legwork. She wouldn't be part of this today, too much of a chance that Lal, the target, might recognize her face at the last minute and get spooked, which would mess up the entire operation. No, surveillance teams didn't participate in the actual operational work when at all avoidable.

Lal had citizenship in the country they were visiting, but he was about to find out how interested the nation was in him. Earlier, they had visited the American Embassy, entered the main building's front doors, and gone down to the basement and walked into a vaulted door beyond. U.S. military personnel called the place home. They'd laid out once more the plan to get the guy and got the final green light.

Lal enjoyed dual citizenship in this country and one other as a result of his marriage and, for this reason, had apparently attracted attention from local midlevel drug runners who promptly offered him work. His family wasn't well-off, by any stretch of the imagination. So he became a courier in the drug trade. When a dealer needed to send a sensitive message, he called Lal; when he needed to move a shipment out of the country, he called Lal, who was paid to take the risk of strapping the drugs onto, or inserting them into, his body and breezing through customs checkpoints. In repayment for his work, they gave his family a new apartment. But Lal wasn't wanted because he carried drugs in his colon. Sources indicated that he also ferried messengers to the real bad guys—terrorists.

This morning the eight-man team was in two trucks near a five-story concrete apartment building that was protected by a concrete wall on three sides and a fence on the street side. The team in the first

Toyota slowed to about 10 mph as they approached the fence. The dome lights in the truck had been disabled and to be extra-cautious they'd covered it with 100 mph tape and taped the switch off too, all to prevent a "light ND"—a negligent discharge of light. They also disabled the rear brake lights. With the door cracked open, they slowed down, and one of the guys, call sign Blacksmith, dismounted into the darkness and scaled the wall. Once he was clear, the Toyota picked up speed and drove on down the road, never once coming to a stop. The second truck drove past the building and turned on the other side of the block.

The report from Tracey said Lal would be leaving early to catch the 0500 bus for a city close by. Supposedly, he was to make a pickup there. Now, with Blacksmith on the inside, the two teams of operators sat waiting for the word to move in and grab Lal.

They'd practiced and rehearsed the upcoming assault dozens of times back in the States and again after arrival. Everyone had a job; everyone knew their jobs. There was no need to talk. Each guy had a door he would take; one even would check the ground right before they pulled away for anything that might have fallen out of a vehicle or off a person, to make sure they didn't leave behind evidence. Both drivers stayed with their SUVs, while another guy would jump into Lal's car to drive away once they had him in custody. It was all as choreographed as a presidential inauguration ceremony.

Normally, SWAT members assault a vehicle from the rear, where the driver can't see them. They might toss a flash-bang over the top of the car toward the front so it explodes above the driver's windshield, causing him to look up toward the front while the team hits from the rear. Bunched up tightly, everyone would approach right up the centerline, then fan evenly out to the left and right flanks in a loose V-shape. If shooting, the outmost guys of the V would handle the driver and front passenger, the two inside the V standing by the rear fenders would be responsible for the backseaters. If there were hostages or someone to pull out of the vehicle, two more would come up between the shooters, yank open the door, and rip the person out onto the ground while the shooters covered the dead and dying. Today, there'd hopefully be no shooting . . . the target was alone and there was no way he was not coming with them.

The inside man landed feetfirst on the other side of the fence and crouched down behind two parked cars. He immediately reached to his ear and his left hip to make sure his radio and earpiece had not fallen out.

"Anvil, Blacksmith. Bingo. Am oscar mike," he whispered over the team's net, reporting he was inside and on the move.

"Roger, Blacksmith. Anvil standing by," came the reply from the lead truck.

Hunched on all fours, he got still and looked around for anyone who might have noticed or heard his entry to the grounds. He would be the inside man, tipping them off when the target was coming out. When Blacksmith decided everything was normal, he trotted across the concrete lot, his feet crunching bits of gravel beneath the soles of his shoes. He headed toward the only entrance to the apartment building, which sat atop huge concrete columns, creating an open breezeway where the staircase and elevator were located. No lobby, no front door to worry about, just over the wall, straight to the elevator.

Blacksmith, crouched low, ran toward the building. He noticed a Mercedes 300D matching Lal's off to his left as he moved. He had drawn to within ten yards of the entrance just when he caught sight of a glowing light that appeared in front of him—the elevator indicator light.

He stopped and heard the mechanical drone of the hydraulic elevator as it descended. He was about to be caught in the open, and he moved quickly, looking for a place to hide. He rushed into the hallway, bypassed the elevator doors, and bounded up the first flight of stairs to the landing, out of sight from anyone exiting the elevator.

There was a low ping, then the scraping, mechanical sound of the antiquated doors sliding open. Blacksmith saw the glow from the elevator car's lights. He heard what sounded like two people talking—an elderly male's voice and a reply from someone else he also couldn't see.

He listened as one of them exited the elevator and walked off. The other man stayed on the elevator car and went back up.

Blacksmith cautiously stuck his head down, peering around the corner at the elevator area. He only saw the bottom of a man's pants cuff as he passed out of view. Keeping his eye glued to that opening, Blacksmith crept down the steps and looked. He dropped to the ground and looked around the next corner. The man had the dark hair and skin of our target . . . he had the right height and build . . . and he was getting into Lal's 300D—it had to be him.

"Anvil, Blacksmith. I have the eye on Fragile . . . he's going mobile . . . he'll make a left onto the street now . . . I've lost the eye . . . and am oscar mike for pickup," said Blacksmith, his eyes locked on to Lal's aka Fragile's taillights as he moved to the street to be scooped up by team Hammer's truck.

The team in the first Toyota—call sign Anvil—inched up a side street until Max the driver had a clear view of the street running in front of Lal's apartment building. Anvil spotted the guy's car as it pulled out and headed in their direction.

"This is Anvil. I have the eye. Fragile is oscar mike, our direction. Hammer, copy? Over," the Anvil team leader asked Hollywood, who was seated in the front right in the Hammer truck.

"Roger, moving now, over," came the response from Hollywood. Hollywood actually was from California, had jet-black hair, and had the looks of an actor to the point that folks just started calling him Hollywood. But in the gym the man was probably able to squat a Ford pickup truck, and when other people asked for a bar pad for their shoulders when doing squats, he gave them a look that could stop a train and said, "Grow some traps." On top of that, he shot the El Pres drill clean and faster than anyone I'd ever seen.

Fragile drove on, unaware of the danger down the street this early, muggy morning. He approached the traffic circle. Normally, at this time of the day, or anytime for that matter, locals didn't heed the speed limits. Knowing this, Anvil's driver gunned the engine and shot across the curve of the rotary, blocking Fragile's path. The startled guy stood on the brakes cursing, his eyes wide as sand dollars as he blasted his horn indignantly. His car skidded sideways into the curb to avoid hitting and being hit.

Hollywood's team roared up behind Fragile's car, screeching to an angled halt, boxing his car in and preventing him from backing out. Almost before the sound of screaming tires left the air, they were out and swarming his car. The man who'd been sitting behind the Anvil team leader reached Fragile's door first as planned, yanking it like a breacher would on a building, stepping aside just as the team leader came barreling in and fist-punched the target twice in the side of the neck hard, stunning him. At the same time, the passenger door of his car was flung open as Hollywood piled in from that side, punched Fragile's seat belt release, and shoved him as they dragged him out onto the ground. It was like a torrent of water was washing him out of his car and into the street—there was no use resisting; he was coming out. Then four arms simultaneously seized his wrists, arms, and head in what must have seemed like a vise. In seconds, they'd ripped him out and he started screaming, so the team leader braced his neck on one side and slammed another quick fist into the opposite side, sending him into a spasmodic jerk of silence. His face turned almost green and his eyes rolled back into his head as what looked like a wave of nausea swept over him.

Silence is golden but 100 mph tape is green, and that's exactly what he got slapped over his mouth as they threw him into the back of the Anvil truck. Two guys taped his mouth, flex-cuffed his hands and ankles, then connected them to each other behind his back—the PONI was now hog-tied. The last thing he saw before a hood was yanked over his eyes was a blue-eyed man holding a black thing with metal prongs sticking out. Then the team leader decided not to use the Taser and just punched him again instead. It was just too much gadgetry to fool with in a confined space for his liking. He might have ended up zapping myself by accident.

Hollywood jumped behind the wheel of the target's Mercedes as the rest piled back into the Toyotas and all three vehicles raced away through the streets. Mission accomplished . . . in less than sixty seconds. Whatever messages he was passing, that loop was broken.

CHAPTER 25

Syria

February 2012
Homs, Syria

SOMEONE ONCE SAID that the road you didn't travel is always smoother, and after our mission in Libya, my company was next tasked with learning more about Iran's involvement in the escalating situation in Syria—a road certain to be full of unexpected potholes along the way.

In February 2012, we entered Syria to establish whether Bashar al-Assad's merciless campaign to remain in power was being aided and abetted by the nation that may perhaps be the greatest threat to American interests in that region: Iran. If we were apprehended in Syria, it was simple: we died. It was going to be incredibly difficult, dangerous, and like looking for a needle in a hay field.

In 2012, if you're an American white guy with a CIA background who used to be vice president of Blackwater USA and was the founding director of Blackwater Security, you can't just jump a plane to Damascus unless you're into being hung from a ceiling on meat hooks. The Syrian internal security apparatus—the General Security Directorate, or GSD—is brutal and efficient. For this mission, D and I planned to fly out of D.C., through London, and on to Turkey and into northern Iraq. There we would connect with the world's best smugglers—the Kurds, who live along the border with Turkey, Syria, and Iran. If they smuggled sugar, cigarettes, and coffee in and out, they could do the same for us and get us into the land of Assad. We would land at night in frozen Erbil, the capital of the Kurdistan Regional Government (KRG) in northern Iraq, on a flight in from Istanbul.

Bordered by Iran on the east, Syria on the west, Turkey to the north, and Baghdad's Iraqi central government to the south, the KRG—an independently governed, federal region within the nation of Iraq—is run by the Barzani family. Massoud Barzani serves as its president while his son runs the region's security apparatus. The Kurds gained their freedom from Iraq in 1992 when a new Iraqi constitution was drawn and elections held. In 2005, after another election, the KRG's status was again modified, and it grew beyond its original definition into something more independent—and ambitious. Today, the KRG conducts separate diplomatic relationships (independent of Iraq) with more than twenty countries. Currently in the midst of building up its own military, intelligence, and security forces, the KRG appears determined to counter any aggressive moves by the Iraqi government to the south, in Baghdad, where the Kurds' rich petroleum reserves are coveted.

But this wasn't the first time I'd infiltrated hostile territory.

CLINT AND I WERE commandos, special operators—in our minds. We were both fourteen years old, best friends, and, as many boys did in the 1980s, we'd go to each other's houses, put on all the OD-green and camo junk we'd bought at the army surplus store, grab our toy M16 rifles or BB guns, and hit the woods. With camo face paint, floppy boonie hats, tiger-striped pants, jungle boots two sizes too big, and Vietnam-era web belts with canteens clamped to them, we were ready for anything.

Clint's house was our forward operating base and we'd creep through barbed wire fences that in our minds became electrified hostile Soviet border crossings. Now in enemy territory, we observed two men in an aluminum fishing boat floating in the middle of a neighborhood pond. The enemy.

We took up firing positions on the small hillside, crunching leaves as we nestled into place. The assault began as we fired BBs at the enemy fishermen. A weak, pathetic little BB would land near them disturbing the water. The fishermen turned to look at the ever-increasing ripples in their perfectly still fishing spot. Another volley from our sniper hide resulted in one landing in their boat with a tiny, metallic clinking noise.

We had walked our rounds in. We were on target . . . but were soon wishing we weren't.

Their outboard engine was yanked to life, and the enemy craft swiveled in our direction, heading full speed in a flurry of whitewater rooster tails and curses.

"They see us!" Clint yelled.

"Let's go!" I yelled back.

We both leaped to our feet, this no longer being fun, and started sprinting down the hill back toward the border, toward the safety of the base—Clint's mom's kitchen. Guns in one hand, hats in the other, we ran, slipped, tumbled, and fell down the hill toward the ditch below. If we could get there, we could lose them in the twists and turns of the gulley. We were on our own—every man for himself.

"Meet you at the house!" I heard him yell. Just then I heard men screaming curses at us to stop. They'd spotted us, made landfall, and were giving chase. Clint and I both came to the conclusion that it was better to hide and let them search than outrun them. Maybe we could have, maybe not. But we'd watched *First Blood* and that's exactly what Rambo did—run, hide, and then just disappear—so it had to be right.

I found an old log lying on its side and crawled up into it. I heard the two men running around cursing. Then I heard Clint's voice—my teammate had been captured. I shrank farther into the log. The voices faded—what were they doing to him? Taking him back to the enemy boat for interrogation? Torture?

I knew I was outnumbered and couldn't help, so I waited a few minutes more and decided to get reinforcements—his mom. I slipped out of the log and, hearing nothing, began running through the woods. My empty, Vietnam-era rucksack swung wildly back and forth as sweat poured and muscles screamed for relief. My canteen rattled and everything seemed to snag every vine, twig, and bush along the gauntlet back to safety.

After what seemed like a marathon distance, I reached his house, out of breath, dirt and mud clinging to my pants and face. I was scratched up and worn smooth out. I didn't want to, but I had to tell the ambassador—his mother—what we'd done. My partner was in desperate peril and needed all the help I could get for him. In I went . . . only to find Clint sitting at the kitchen table, eyes downcast and shoulders slumped in a most defeated posture. Mrs. Susan stood with her hands on her hips in the pose moms take when their kids were screwed. His BB gun stood silently in the corner behind her. He'd not been caught but had taken a shortcut home.

His mom interrogated him and was now mad at us both—our visit was over. The ambassador summarily declared me persona non grata, and we all piled into the maroon family sedan—official embassy transportation—and she drove me home.

Clint would go on to graduate from Ole Miss and become a law enforcement officer, where he would be assigned to a federal task force hunting fugitives a few years later, just like we were pretending that day.

First lesson? Don't get caught.

AFTER A FEW MEETINGS IN LONDON, D and I landed in Erbil in northern Iraqi Kurdistan and moved through passport control and met Hardy, our Kurdish contact, who had earned the nickname in wartime after opposing forces were exposed to his resilience and toughness. A former translator for a Special Forces ODA, he had worked with the State Department as a local security guy and had grown up a smuggler in the northern Kurdish and Turkish border areas.

Sleeting rain fell from the inky black sky and quickly formed ice patches waiting to send a biped slamming to the ground. Security seemed to own the tiny airport—you couldn't even park your cars near it. Carefully navigating the black ice with our sixty-plus-pound rucks, we made it to Hardy's Toyota Prado SUV and drove into town. The Kurds had reserved hotel rooms for us a few miles from the airport at a modern, squat, blue-glass-sheathed building called the Lamussu.

The next morning, we set off for Duhok in northernmost Iraq to meet with a Kurdish man who had earned the trust of forces in Iraq during the war and had connections to other Kurds inside Syria. He was a former Iraqi general acquainted with General David Petraeus, who was the current CIA director. I hoped to use the man to recruit Kurds for a guerrilla force we would train and send back into Syria. Now he just had to help us get over the border.

Encircled by mountains, the town of Duhok—on the Tigris River—has more than a quarter million residents and is the capital of a province by the same name. It reminded me of a Colorado ski town nestled amid scenic mountains. We rolled in late in the afternoon the same day to clear blue skies. Hardy was on his mobile phone from the minute we hit the outskirts of town, setting up the meeting with the general. Syrian intelligence knew the Kurds were a threat, and the general was heavily monitored. His life, at this point, was about moving from house to house, place to place. We hoped he could safely light in one spot long enough for us to meet him.

We finally got a firm fix on the general from his son, who was acting as the go-between, communicating with Hardy by phone. The general was moving at the very last minute as a precaution, creating headaches for us as we stopped, turned around, and drove in circles until he finally stayed in one place. Then we headed into a residential neighborhood, where we entered a modest home set on a gentle incline.

We were shown in by a short, thickly built, serious-looking man I guessed to be in his late forties or early fifties who greeted us warmly. The back of his thick neck bulged at the base of his skull like a scarf of muscle. With a firm handshake I'd just made the acquaintance of the general's point man inside Syria, a former senior noncommissioned officer (SNCO) named Bassam, also a Kurd, and who worked for the general back when he was in the Iraqi army.

Inside we took seats in a small living room smelling from years of cigarette use and crammed with too much furniture. The décor would have made the Pink Panther proud—the lower half of the walls was covered by a pale pink marble, then white plaster ran up to meet more pale pink crown molding. Smack in the center of the ceiling hung a brass-plated chandelier with one side dipping lower than the other; spotlights punched into the ceiling—all turned off—looked down at the burgundy-checkered carpet. On the right wall a matching pale pink entertainment center sat crammed with books, DVDs, a small dusty television, and assorted components, topped off by a gaudy, store-bought black-and-gold decorative fish. Snapshots of three small children were taped to the upper edge of the glass. In the corner was an end table partially blocking a door. A folded prayer rug lay on the table waiting for the next round of supplications. Above the door hung the faded yet ever-present picture of Barzani, leader of this part of Iraq. A few seconds passed, and then through the door the general entered the room carrying a large black, leather-bound notebook. Sporting a few days' worth of stubble and dressed in dark gray wrinkled pants with a striped sweater pushed up to his elbows and a gold digital watch on his wrist, he shook hands with us. His face was quiet, angular, with piercing dark eyes like those of a statue, all framed by three noticeable birthmarks—two moles on either side of his long nose and one right between his eyebrows. He took a seat across a glass-topped coffee table from me in a large, comfortable-looking chair with oversize burgundy studded leather armrests. Bassam sat to his right in the chair's twin, with Hardy sitting next to him by the corner of the front window of the house, which was covered by a drawn sheer curtain. D stood to my left in the opening to the room next to the front door of the house—always on the alert and ready to control our exit point. I noticed no other sounds came from the house—no children, no voices, no smells of cooking from a kitchen—just the five of us in a tiny, crowded room and the smell of stale cigarette smoke.

We made our introductions. I showed him the letter—a new one specifically for the Syria project—from Congresswoman Myrick and he showed me a picture of him standing with General David Petraeus from years ago, before Petraeus became director of the Central Intelligence Agency. Then we got down to business.

"General, I understand you have sources inside Syria?" I asked.

"Yes, we have many people there, and Bassam goes there for me." This sounded like he was coordinating something, despite being out of the military.

"We are hearing reports that Iranians are helping Assad. Is this true? Have you heard this or do you know anything about it?"

"They are definitely there. Bassam has seen them—in groups of six to twelve men. They move through, crossing the border from Iraq and making their way to fight for al-Assad. But they do not cross from this part, but south of here," he answered, as he pulled a cigarette out and lit up, blowing a long stream of smoke toward the TV. He offered one to me; I took it, as did Bassam and D. I don't smoke—I've heard it's bad for me.

His point wasn't missed—the Kurds weren't tolerating Iranian activities on their soil—at least that's what they wanted people to believe. The reality was that they were there and the Kurds really couldn't do much about it. This was in stark contrast to the Baghdad-controlled Iraq, south of here, where Iran had cozied up with the Arabs. The Iranians had been inside Iraq since the fall of Saddam in 2003, but after the White House pulled the last U.S. forces out of Iraq at the end of 2011 the Iranians moved in like Occupy Wall Street protesters. Arizona senator and war hero John McCain would later say, "When President Obama withdrew all U.S. forces from Iraq in 2011 . . . many of us predicted that the vacuum would be filled by America's enemies and would emerge as a threat to U.S. national security interests." In 2012, Obama made numerous speeches about how he'd ended the war in Iraq—a war that Obama had called "a dumb war"* when he was a U.S. senator. Dumb? Hussein was one of the most vicious, cruel dictators of modern times. Certainly, invading Iraq can be argued as to whether it was necessary at the time. But what was done was done, and Obama inherited that issue. If anything was dumb, perhaps it was not maintaining a stabilizing force to prevent the growth of al-Qa'ida in the region and to blunt the influence of Iran. Just two years later in 2014, ISIS/ISIL would be sucking up large parts of Iraqi territory while the Iraqi central government was practically powerless to stop them. If U.S. forces still maintained a presence there, that wouldn't have happened.

"Where are they?" I asked.

"Many places, but the closest is in al-Hasakah, Syria," he said. But we couldn't just take his word for it; we needed to see it for ourselves.

"General, can you get us into Syria—show us the Iranians?" I asked.

The general answered without hesitation, saying Bassam would take us. I noticed that Bassam, like a good soldier, didn't object. The general said to be ready early the next morning, and we set about devising plans on the coffee table in the cramped living room.

When I asked the general to show me where Iranians were positioned, he brought out maps—Iraqi military maps—and proceeded to show me precisely where they were holing up. We wrapped things up after about two hours. After shaking hands with the general, I told him we'd be in touch. The man clearly had access, knew his business, and, being a Kurd, was in sync with our goals.

The Kurds saw the Syrian revolution as an opportunity to establish a Kurdish zone in the northeastern area of Syria, near their fellow tribes-

---

* http://warontherocks.com/2014/01/losing-iraq/.

men in northern Iraq. The 25 million Kurds are the largest ethnicity in the world without a state of their own. They were promised, but never granted, a state after World War I. Now the Kurds reside in parts of Turkey, northern Iraq, Syria, Iran, Armenia, and Azerbaijan. Saddam had hammered them while Hafez al-Assad used them as a tool against the Turks. Now the Kurds, searching for a place to finally call their home, saw their chance.

I saw the Kurdish situation as a strategic lever and hoped that, ultimately, we could convince the Kurds to open a second front against Bashar al-Assad, forcing him to stretch his military—and, more important, his logistical train—from Damascus on the west coast, all the way out to the northeast to fight a new, second enemy. I envisioned Kurdish leaders, along with Arab representatives of the Free Syrian Army, visiting senators and representatives in Washington together. The ramifications of an alliance against Assad by these longtime enemies would be a demoralizing new problem facing the dictator—a strong psychological blow. In hindsight, it also might have been a deterrent to ISIS/ISIL if Kurdish forces had been forward deployed into Syria's western regions.

After leaving the general, the three of us headed to Zakho, a town at the tri-border area of Iraq, Syria, and Turkey. Zakho, part of the Duhok Province, is separated from Turkey by the Little Khabur River, which flows west into the Tigris. This location has made it a long-standing center for smugglers. Until its closing in 1996, the base there offered safe haven to Kurds fearing reprisals from Saddam. Six years later, the town offered us a safe house and smugglers who knew how to cross the border unnoticed. Sugar, tea, tobacco, guns, or operators: the residents of Zakho could get anything into Turkey or Syria with relative ease. They had centuries' worth of experience.

THE NEXT MORNING—AT AROUND 0200—Hardy, D, and I headed west out of town on Road 2, ultimately reaching the moonlit Tigris River—the border with Syria. We cut the lights, easing into a small clearing off the dirt road. D told Hardy to position the truck so that no headlights from passing vehicles would illuminate our reflectors. To be extra-cautious, we covered the tail and brake lights with 100 mph tape. Then we shouldered our smaller packs—D carried the CamelBak Urban Assault pack while I continued to carry my trusty Kifaru Tailgunner—and made our way to the water's edge, leaving our larger rucks behind at the safe house.

The Tigris was shallow here. I'd photographed it and videoed it the day before as we'd moved toward Zakho, stopping at an ancient Christian church that sat on the riverbank. You could cross the border at any number of places—in the desert on sand dunes, near formal border crossings, or in crazy, out-of-the-way places like this. We wanted to cross at a place as far from civilization as possible, in the company of someone who did it all the time: mines littered the area. Sandbars were visible; the water flowed at a gentle pace—nothing required ropes or a boat. On the other side, in Syria, was a small village called Khanik, with an electrical substation and a small river patrol.

We walked to the river's edge and Hardy, covering his phone to keep the light from the screen out of sight, made a call. We waited until we saw a red light on the other side of the river blink three times and then Hardy told us to go. D and I stepped off Iraqi soil into the biting cold water flowing at knee level toward Syria. My Salewa boots filled with the frigid dark water immediately, soaking my wool socks.

We pushed across to a sandbar in the middle of the river, officially standing on Syrian territory at that point. To our right, about twenty yards away, was a Syrian communication outpost ringed with a white fence, standing in a copse of fir trees. Directly ahead was a huge berm of gravel or dirt—I couldn't tell which. That was our destination, where we'd seen the flashing light signal. We stopped, took a cold, wet knee, and listened, hearing nothing but the rushing water. Moments later, we were scrambling up the bank to Bassam and a waiting Toyota Corolla on the other side. Thankfully, he had disabled the dome light—a detail I noticed, and appreciated for the professionalism it demonstrated. But just for insurance, I took out my roll of 100 mph tape, ripped off a piece, and slapped it across the light. Bassam handed us both headscarves as we headed west. After breaking out the Garmin to keep track of our route, D and I hunkered down for a long ride and tried to sleep. No one said a word.

We drove in the darkness through village after village, over the flattest terrain I've ever seen. Assad must not have considered the Kurds a threat, as there were no checkpoints and no roadblocks. For that I was thankful. Many hours later I could see a glow in the western sky from a town up ahead—al-Hasakah.

Bassam dowsed the headlights; we crossed a set of railroad tracks and pulled off the road down into a wadi—another dry riverbed, places that I seemed to live in these days—where we slowly crawled over the smooth stones for another twenty minutes before I felt the worn old Toyota angling upward again. We eased down a dry, smooth dusty road, our lights still off. To our left, I could make out the silhouette of a building or three. At a fuel station—a Syrian version of 7-Eleven that was more like a 6-Ten—Bassam pulled into one of the garage bays, got out, and pulled down the roller doors, shutting us inside. D and I unfolded from the car and stepped out into the frigid dawn air, our bodies stiff.

Bassam wasted no time, quickly pulling a nylon tarp noisily off an old delivery-style dump truck. We helped, stowing the covering in the bed. Bassam, in his badly broken English laced with Arabic, told us to get into the back of the truck and dragged an old, musty-smelling canvas tarp to cover us up. A few seconds later, the diesel truck cranked up and we were off again—my Garmin showed a southwesterly heading now.

The ride was freezing cold even under the tarp as the wind blew straight over the top cab and never stopped hammering us, whipping and snapping the canvas, nearly tearing it off. The wind managed to slip in on the sides, slapping us with a gust of misery every few seconds as we both scrunched down farther into our collars like turtles in our shells to cover our necks. With wet boots, socks, and lower legs, we sat like statues leaning against each other and the cold, vibrating metal of the cab. Just once did I summon the cojones to pull back the tarp and poke my head above the cab to see where we were going—I was rewarded with a blast of frigid air full in the face that essentially froze my lips shut and dried up my eyeballs. Ahead, light poles lined the right side of the road, casting a sickly orange glow over a four-lane highway divided by a median strip of dirt where scruffy shrubs struggled to survive the desert clime. I sat back down and watched the seconds on my Suunto creep along. Time and timing go together but are not always the same, as that second ticker seemed to just sit there. D was asleep and I envied him for it, but it was a good idea. So I scrunched back down, pulled the tarp back into place, and tried to get rest. But I just couldn't get my mind off my dern wet socks, and boots that were nearly frozen stiff.

WE AWOKE AT THE SOUND OF THE BRAKES squealing or perhaps it was the vehicle slowing. Was it a checkpoint? I looked out the slits in the bed on my side. The tailgate was tall—no one was able to see into the truck without climbing up on it. It looked as though there were a crater or volcano off to our right. Bassam pulled the truck farther into a mud garage structure, parking right next to an old tractor.

I heard Bassam's squeaky door hinge scream in protest as he got out and slammed it shut. The gravel crunched along D's side and then the Kurd climbed up onto the tailgate, whispering and motioning to us to get out. Throwing off the tarp, we tossed our bags over our shoulders and buckled our waist belts as we climbed out of the truck. The sun was rising slowly.

Bassam said that this was a Kurdish farmer's place; the truck would be hidden and safe here. We'd be on foot the rest of the way. He eased out of the mud garage, looked around, and then waved back at us to follow. All around us I saw farm machinery, orchards, and fields of crops. We set off through the darkness down a dusty trail running alongside a pond to our right, a trash heap on the left. No one was moving about yet, but we heard the sounds of the place waking up. We ran quietly from one covered position to another in short bursts, trying our best to dodge rocks or other debris that would make any more noise. Out of twenty years of habit I repeated the old mantra, "I'm up, he sees me, I'm down," as we ran low, crouched across the desert ground.

We ran southwest toward the volcano-like mountain through the scraggly, rock-strewn countryside. We entered another orchard at the base as we started our climb. Six rows deep of olive trees concealed our movements for now, but if we didn't move faster we would be easily spotted as the sun began to rise—three guys crawling up the smooth, flat surface of a volcano or whatever this thing was. We had to move faster and Bassam knew this, too. I saw the look of concern on his face. We had to get up the mountain before the sun came up and people spotted us.

Higher and higher we climbed, my thighs burned as we worked our way up to the top of the crater's rim, then we crested it and began a fall, roll, and run down to get off the ridgeline and out of sight. We all stopped, gasping for air. Bassam drew a rough circle in the dirt representing our crater, an X for where the truck was parked, and then another larger circle out in front of the one we stood in, saying that was the other crater, which stood next to a military base.

We were at the north end and needed to push across to the opposite side—the southern edge, roughly a three-hundred-yard movement. But we didn't need to drop all the way down into the bottom and come back up the other side. That was just more work for us. As long as we stayed just below the lip, down inside this bowl, it was possible to move unobserved. So we started our run around the left edge of the crater's bowl, finally reaching the southern edge. We stopped again and caught our breath as we grabbed bottles of water from our packs and drank.

Bassam got flat on his belly and motioned for us to do the same as he slowly moved up toward the lip and a large grouping of rocks to our left side. We had no weapons other than our pocketknives and my Medford TS-1 fixed blade. Though it was an awesome weapon that I'd used to chop through wooden doors before, it wouldn't do us much good if a Syrian chopper spotted us. Bassam pointed to the southwest.

The sun was just up now, illuminating the large, flat valley below us. Fields were at the foot of our hill, but about a third of a mile off to our front right sat a Syrian military base, encircled by a large dirt berm, obviously pushed up by dozers, which acted as a wall around the compound. Syrian armor was clearly visible. I counted at least fifty tanks on the northern end alone, parked side by side, turrets facing out. Gun emplacements were dug in between the base and our position—they looked to be antiaircraft guns, the ZSU-23s, perhaps, and were oriented east, toward Iraq.

I took out my 8x25 Steiner binos and started glassing the area while D got out his notebook and pencil as I called out information. The sun was to our backs (and in the eyes of anyone looking our direction) so we weren't concerned about giving our position away from reflection. But just out of caution, the bino lenses were covered with two pieces of ladies' tan pantyhose, secured with rubber bands. Our dark headscarves we draped from our heads down to our hands covering my binos, all to break up our silhouettes.

We counted tanks, gun emplacements, and communication towers as we sketched the place out. It was designed much like a tree and all surrounded by a massive, long wall. Inside that wall, one main paved road—the tree's trunk—came from the foot of the other volcano and ran right up the middle of the compound. Smaller paved roads—the limbs—branched off to the left and right, ending at clusters of one- and two-story buildings that reminded me of clusters of leaves. I counted eight such branches.

Bassam glanced down at the sketch and waved his finger, shaking his head back and forth. "That's not the entire base," he said. Then, with a sweeping gesture, he pointed out past the buildings, indicating that it covered many square kilometers. We were just on the eastern edge where the Iranians have been spotted. He pointed to the large volcano, as I'd started to call it, and the communications tower on the top.

"That's where they are," he said. I shifted my binos and saw a tall, silvery communications tower soaring into the sky and a smaller red and white one standing to the left of it. Six support buildings were clustered around them, likely housing generators and switches. One or two looked large enough for men to stay inside, but there was no way to be sure without going there—and we weren't doing that today. What looked like a single-lane, paved road led up to the top and snaked down the hillside back into the main armored compound below us. I started redrawing my western boundaries. We spent the next hour or so sketching, noting, and observing.

I was drawing and D was glassing the northern area of the base when Bassam tapped his shoulder and told us to look toward the volcano. Two large vehicles were moving up from the base, climbing the hill. They made twisting, snaking turns, disappearing for a moment as they passed around a bend. Then they came into view and parked by one of the buildings. We were a long way off from the comm towers, but it was a clear day, the sun was shining right on them over our backs, and we were able to make out some things.

We saw the drivers wore the Syrian army's olive-colored winter uniforms. They climbed out and milled around for a moment. Then more men started coming out of the buildings—lots of men, armed men. I counted at least one dozen. From our distant position it looked as though many wore beards. None wore the monochromatic clothing of the drivers—they were dressed in a mix of colors—tans, grays, and blacks. They looked civilian, rather than military.

Bassam pointed and said, "Iranians."

Climbing into the back of the trucks, the men took off again, heading down the hillside, turning left at the foot. Then, heading back down the main road, they made a right turn back into the army base. We tried to follow their route but lost them a few times as they drove behind a building or two. Finally, we saw them stop and get out, with all the men walking into one large, tan flat building. Perhaps a chow hall?

They were closer now, though, and we were able to get a better look at them—at least better than before. They did have beards—nearly all of them had thick, black ones. They looked fit, like soccer or rugby team fit. They carried their weapons with a professional air—not pointing their guns at one another when they talked. They filed into the building and we didn't see them for two hours, at least. I asked if a closer, better look was possible, but Bassam was having none of it. He said it was dangerous just being this close. We would stay here until the sun set, then make our way back down the volcano, get into the truck, and head back.

The day went by slowly. We saw the men come out of the chow hall, as I had started calling it, and move to the truck. Obviously, it was not a chow hall since no one eats all morning long. They were then driven to another building on the western side of the tree, where they once again filed out. They didn't come out again for the rest of our time there.

We rotated security up on the crater. One of us would watch our rear in case a farmer, shepherd, or kid made his way up to the top. We had noticed a trail when we were coming up the first time, so someone had been up here enough to wear out a groove. Every so often, we'd rotate the security job out. By the afternoon, we'd decided to bag the surveillance of the base. We'd seen what we needed to see—plainclothes, bearded men that Bassam claimed to be Iranian shooters at a remote Syrian army outpost close to the Iraqi border—no doubt from where they'd crossed.

Mercifully, the sun started setting, the sky glowing a pinkish red in the clouds near the horizon. Lights started coming on throughout the valley and in the base below. The red blinking lights on the comm towers came on to warn aircraft away. We let the sun fade from the sky before we slowly got up and started moving back toward the north end of the crater. Staying in position, we watched the area for any signs of trouble. Everything was still, so we slipped down the hillside, through the orchard, down the trail past the garbage piles, and back into the garage through the side door. D and I weren't looking forward to the frigid ride again, but we climbed over into the bed anyway and pulled the tarp down while Bassam opened the big door, got in, cranked up, and backed out. I took a hit on the Garmin after a few minutes of driving—just to be sure we were heading back to the border. Trust is earned, and while Bassam had proven himself a good ally so far, you never knew.

A few hours later, we relinked with his car at the 6-Ten fuel station and headed down into the rocky gully and then back on the paved road. About forty minutes out from the tiny village where we'd crossed the Tigris, Bassam made a call, we hoped to Hardy, who would be in Zakho—giving him enough of a heads-up to link with us on the other side.

We reached the village and Bassam cut the headlights as we made our way to the water's edge and crouched on the muddy bank. His phone vibrated and in response he hit his red-lens flashlight three times, just as before. On the opposite shoreline, we saw a red light respond with two quick winks. Bassam said, "Go and I see you soon, my friends."

D and I slipped back into the black frigid current and slowly trudged to the first sandbar. I kept my eyes on the horizon, where I had picked out a shadowy landmark just above where I'd seen Hardy's lights. We kept moving toward that spot and made it to the river's edge. There was Hardy, alone and smiling, ready to take us back to Zakho, a warm house, and dry clothes.

We'd come to northern Iraq, linked with Kurdish resistance, taken a report from them on Iranians operating inside Syria, and then we'd infiltrated deep into northeastern Syria, seeing what appeared to be Iranians operating out of a Syrian army base. The Iranians were likely using it as a layover point, coming into Syria through Mosul, Iraq, an Arab city unlike the rest in the north, which were mainly Kurdish, Assyrian Christian, or Yazidi. I figured the Iranians would lay up there, rest, and then start making their way toward the west in Syria, to Aleppo, Homs, or Damascus.

THE IRANIAN CONNECTION in the Syrian conflict was significant. A relationship between Shiite-led Iran and predominantly Sunni Syria might appear unlikely; however, Assad is an Alawite, who are closely aligned with the Shia and an enemy to the Sunnis. Both also despise the United States. For three decades, Syria and Iran have remained allied, despite attempts to rip them apart. Together, they have not only helped fund the Iranian terror group Hizbollah, but also have pooled political leverage and military resources to enhance their positions, build a network of surrogate militias, and frustrate the plans of their enemies, whether they be Israel, Iraq under Saddam, or the United States. Today, perhaps the main reason the Iranians are opposed to ISIS/ISIL invading Northern Iraq is because the group is Sunni and they're standing between Shia Iran and Al-Assad's Syria.

Together Syria and Iran ensured that Saddam Hussein's Iraq, which bordered both countries, did not become the predominant regional power. They forced the United States out of Lebanon in 1984, using Hizbollah to blow up our embassy and U.S. Marine barracks in 1983, and they thwarted Israel's effort to bring Lebanon into its orbit during an eighteen-year occupation that finally ended in Israel's unilateral withdrawal in 2000. The odd bedfellows together sired or supported—in addition to Hizbollah—Hamas, Palestinian Islamic Jihad, and an array of radical Palestinian groups. All reject peace and together have inflicted repeated setbacks on six American presidents. Since its inception the Iranian/Syrian alliance has lacked one thing—an unbroken geographical link between the two countries. Now Iraq was becoming that link.

Once Iran and Syria saw the United States invade Iraq, remove Saddam, and begin to set up a new government, they saw their chance to create an unbroken roadway from Iran through Iraq, into Syria and then Lebanon directly. This uninterrupted land bridge would open a path all the way to the Mediterranean Sea for the Iranians, allowing the uninterrupted flow of cash, killers, and Kalashnikovs straight from Supreme Leader Khamenei's front door, through Assad's Syria, direct to Hassan Nasrallah's Hizbollah terrorists, and on to Benjamin Netanyahu and Israel's back porch.

This was one reason why the conflict in Iraq drew so many participants, including Syrians and Iranians, all attempting to destabilize the country, kill U.S. troops, and gain influence with Maliki—the feckless leader of the Shiite-dominated government in Baghdad. Iran was working under the concept that the United States would leave

Iraq if they inflicted enough violence on American troops . . . so Iran and Syria poured resources into the region . . . and it worked. President Bush started the war and was keen to see it end, but Obama accelerated a premature withdrawal of our troops from Iraq, which allowed the Iranians to move in. It is now Iran who effectively controls the Shiite-dominated government in Baghdad—a reality that even folks who eat soup with a fork should understand to be horrifying. In fact, no matter how many democratic revolutions or freedom revolutions are seen and undertaken in the Middle East—whether in Iraq, Syria, Libya, Egypt, or any other place—there will never be anything close to peace until Iran is freed from the rule of the mullahs and the people of Persia have their country, their proud heritage, and their history returned to them.

Northern Kurdish Iraq remains the one, tiny stumbling block for the twin bad guys. The Kurds, progressive Muslims, have little in common with Iranians, Syrians, or Iraqis. The Kurdistan Regional Government (KRG) is doing its best to beef up its military to counter any aggressive moves by the Iraqi central government to the south. As the Syrian conflict grew, Baghdad attempted to move forces into the north to gain more control in the Kurdish region, particularly of their petroleum resources. The Kurds would have none of it—at least someone had cojones in the region and still stood up to the tyrants.

FOLLOWING OUR RETURN to the safe house in Zakho and a good night's sleep out of the cold, D and I made our way back to Erbil, where we received a call informing us that KRG president Barzani's representative had agreed to a meeting. In Hardy's Prado, we drove from our hotel back toward the airport, to another hotel just off the main road, where I touched base with the manager and D scouted meet locations. We were about to sit down with the Kurdish equivalent of the U.S. national security adviser or perhaps the president's chief of staff.

D waited on the steps of this next hotel while I was inside the lobby. Within fifteen minutes, he poked his head back inside: "Boss, we got company—our guy's here." In the door walked a distinguished gentleman wearing gray slacks, a powder-blue collared shirt sans tie, and a dark blazer. Sharp, almost angular features of his face were framed by jet-black hair sprinkled with hints of gray here and there along the temples. He came alone—no security, no escort—and I got the impression he was either going to, or returning from, some family event. The manager, who beamed, couldn't do enough to help the guy out, and allowed us to meet in his office.

I got down to business and told our visitor that the Syrian Kurds needed a place to train and launch operations, a safe haven for medical treatment and resupply. I wanted a firm agreement that the KRG would supply that just inside their border with Syria. He asked what the KRG would get in return. This was feeling like déjà vu à la Cairo. I asked what they wanted and he—from memory—gave me a list of weapons ranging from sniper rifles to antiaircraft missiles, just as the Libyan general back in Cairo had done a year earlier. I told him I would see what was possible, pressing him for a commitment if help with the weapons was even a possibility. He said he wasn't in a position to make the decision but would find out. Same tent, different Arab? In one sense, yes, but in another no, because these were Kurds, not Arabs, and they had a whole different set of problems caused *by* the Arabs.

I understood the KRG's problem. They were sandwiched between Syria and the Turks, both of whom hated Kurds. The Turks labeled them terrorists, and Syria hammered them at every opportunity. So if the KRG helped the Kurds in Syria, they would be accused of harboring terrorists by either nation. But if we legally located the weapons for them, which they wanted to strengthen their security, then I thought they'd be more agreeable. Illegal weapons weren't even up for discussion—we didn't get involved in that sordid trade.

Meanwhile, former CIA officer and author Bob Baer and I had been working on developing sources within the al-Assad regime while our advisor Dr. Walid Phares spoke with dissidents, defectors, and former officials in the regime. So far, we'd had successes. We knew that Syrian officials of consequence had sent small groups of family members to Dubai to purchase property and set up living arrangements for key families closely connected to the regime. We were hearing good news, such as that Majd Bahjat Suleiman, the oldest son of Syria's former head of internal security, was leading the first wave of Alawites and their grown children to Dubai. We knew they had arrived on private aircraft with considerable cash and set about purchasing homes for themselves and others fleeing Damascus. That was good—it showed a lack of confidence within the family at various levels.

We also knew that members of Assad's inner circle were trying find a way out of the quagmire. Syrian deputy minister of defense Assef Shawkat and Mohammad Nassif, a veteran operator for Assad's father, had reached out to a few former CIA officers whom they had known for many years. Assef Shawkat contended that they had been unable to get anyone in the U.S. government with authority to describe what Washington wanted to see happen in Syria. That was incredible to us. Shawkat had even asked us verbatim, "Do you want him [Assad] dead? Just tell me and it will happen." On order from me or Bob, this Syrian would have put a bullet into Assad and ended the revolution. He also told us that Obama's call for the regime to publicly break with Iran simply wasn't going to happen. "It's not a viable course of action at this time," he said. "If we say that publicly, we have to start killing Iranians and those loyal to Iran." We were connecting the dots in a region where the hard part, as Bob reminded me constantly, was just figuring out what was a dot to begin with. What Shawkat had just said tracked with what I'd seen already and was yet another indicator of a sizable contingent of Iranians inside Syria—in February 2012.

The substance, despite his offering to kill Assad, was that Shawkat and his men were thugs who had been part of the savage inner circle in Syria. But they were increasingly concerned about having a means of escape or surviving the violence that was growing each day. Pictures of the last moments of Saddam and Qadhafi were fresh in their minds and they were starting to get the picture that the 401(k) program for dictators was becoming increasingly difficult to redeem.

Washington stayed silent and Shawkat would be assassinated later that summer. If the government had acted on what we were passing to them in February, we literally had the power to tell Shawkat to kill President Assad, and conceivably, with the head of the snake cut off, Syria's civil war could have possibly been over in days. But that didn't happen—it wasn't something we would do without U.S. government authorization, and that wasn't forthcoming.

Maher al-Assad and members of the Makhlouf family (relatives, by marriage, of the dictator's family and part of the nation's security apparatus and business activities) were also reaching out, through contacts in Beirut, seeking help in moving financial assets out of Lebanon. Bob, Walid, and I continued to pass on these nuggets of intelligence to those in the U.S. system, but I've had more meaningful conversations with door stops.

In Syria, there was an air of increasing concern within the regime about how to continue fighting the uprising. Defections within the Syrian army were continuing steadily and Alawites were killing Sunnis. We knew that if this continued, more Sunnis would depart the army. The ranks of the rebel Free Syrian Army were growing steadily, and normal Syrians were growing increasingly angry, willing to take risks for the sake of peace. A recent attack in Homs on the Syrian intelligence building—which was being used by the regime as a sniper platform—demonstrated to us the resolve of the revolutionaries and the cracks starting to show in the regime.

Everyone with an IQ above room temperature saw the magnitude of the situation—Syria posed the most serious strategic threat to Iran's ability to project its power through the region. Cutting the overland logistics and financial bridge between Iran and Lebanon put the Iranians' position at risk. The loss of Syria would deal a significant blow to Iran's ability to orchestrate and support frontline operations against Israel via Hamas and Lebanese Hizbollah.

There were other positive implications: the downfall of Assad's Syria might embolden the two main Iraqi political parties to withdraw from Maliki's Iranian-led coalition, potentially collapsing that regime and enabling the rise of a new governing coalition that might not align itself with Iran. This was a way of salvaging something positive for the long term from the hard-won fight in Iraq, which seemed to be slipping away due to the White House's orders for the premature pullout.

These factors, all within the sphere of American influence, provided strategic opportunities for pushing American security interests forward in the Middle East. If significant internal security issues inside Iran were exacerbated, this could force them to pull their resources and focus away from their nuclear program. It was possible to influence the security situation inside Iran without the need for a large, sustained conventional military aerial campaign. But all this was predicated on the U.S. administration waking up to the problem and the possibilities. However, motivating a president facing reelection is complicated . . . and in this case, impossible.

Two years later would see nothing change, as Obama refused to seriously engage ISIS/ISIL until election season had passed.

D AND I RETURNED TO WASHINGTON in March 2012 to brief the Congressional Anti-Terrorism Caucus staff with Dr. Phares. Jana had the PowerPoint presentation primed, I spoke first. My main point was that the United States needed to vet, supply, and arm the Syrian rebels that we could trust. I drew a parallel between events in Libya and those in Syria, pointing out the opportunity to reduce Iran's influence. I told them about the Iranian presence we had seen in Syria and reminded the group assembled in the Cannon House Office Building that our nation was engaged in a simmering covert war designed to keep nuclear weapons out of Iranian hands. Taking the time to figure out the good guys and arming them in the Syrian resistance provided a platform to dull the Iranian knife without more U.S. troops getting cut.

I talked about Hizbollah, puppets of Syria and owned by Iran. I made the case that arming the resistance and changing the regime in Syria would remove Assad, one of Hizbollah's major patrons, cut off their supply lifeline from Iran, and effectively put them out of business in that area.

I wrapped up the briefing with this point: once Assad was gone and if we came to the rescue of the Syrian people, we had the opportunity to create a lingering, positive memory in the collective mind of the Syrians—and the rest of the Arab world—fostering the development of yet another U.S. ally in a volatile region where such allies are sorely needed.

There are two obvious possible outcomes in Syria: Assad remains in power or he's defeated. If the West continues to do nothing, we risk giving Assad the victory and perpetuating Iranian influence. If he'd been killed early on, whether removed by our assets inside the regime or by a U.S. Reaper strike, his underlings could likely have secured a peace with the rebels and worked things out before the radical jihadis and militant Islamists solidified the foothold they've now built. Now the West watches as Assad uses the jihadis to battle against the rebels. They are unwittingly doing his work for him, degrading the rebels who are now fighting two wars—one against Assad and another against the jihadis. However, most believe that, ultimately, Syria will see regime change—

after a lot more death and carnage. If the United States continues our current course of inaction, the Muslim Brotherhood and al-Qa'ida will assume overwhelming influence and transform Syria into a safe haven for terrorists. Jihadis will subvert any new government and create an Islamist state. U.S. influence will be nominal. Weapons will fall into the hands of unknowns. Look at Egypt, look at Libya—it doesn't take a rocket scientist to figure these things out. In fact, this boat may have already sailed—we may already have missed our opportunity in Syria.

I told the caucus that we had to act, mentioning opportunities created by providing humanitarian aid, the need to show public support for those fighting the regime, that we needed to take the risk of identifying friendly, trusted rebels, and then start supplying arms to the opposition, and providing covert operational support to the resistance forces. If we put CIA and Special Forces teams on the ground to help better organize and train the fighters, we could control who got what, as well as make a positive impact on ending the war far faster. I recommended giving air support, as well as intelligence support. My travels had convinced me that the challenges there were hardly insurmountable and that we had a golden opportunity to sever Iran's geographic connection to the Mediterranean Sea, thereby significantly reducing its ability to threaten Israel and U.S. interests. If Iran were a vampire, we ought to be the garlic, daylight, and a wooden stake all at the same time and run them out of the region and back to Persia.

STANDING ON THE SIDELINES is no way to run a foreign policy. At that time, the civilian casualties in Syria were at least twice those of Libya, where we had acted with our allies to help the people out. The events in Syria were a tragedy—but also were an opportunity that we overlooked at our own peril. Sitting around, refusing to engage, and hoping things worked themselves out only created a vacuum in the region—and one that al-Qa'ida and their affiliates would fill. My frustration had reached a new level as I left Washington once more, this time headed to northwest Africa, the new front in the U.S. battle with al-Qa'ida and radical, militant Islam.

CHAPTER 26

Targeted Killing

2013
Mali, Africa

THE POOR NORTH AFRICAN NATION OF MALI sweltered with waves of heat from the Sahara that pressed against the contractor's skin. He sat in a small green Renault, parked near Centre Ville in Bamako while his Malian partner waited across town, watching the jihadi target's apartment and his yellow taxi. When the cell vibrated, he noticed the +223-655 country code and prefix of his partner's Malitel cell phone. The African reported the target had just pulled away in his cab. He'd follow and let the contractor know when it was time for his part in this drama.

The contractor wore a brown wig pulled back in a ponytail, John Lennon–style brown-tinted sunglasses, and flip-flops. In his right front pocket was an Emerson P-SARK folding knife. His black T-shirt was untucked, and a white hand towel from the hotel was draped around his already sweating neck. A beat-up Makarov pistol with electrical tape wrapped around the grip to hold it together was tucked in a holster at the small of his back.

The contractor wiped his eyes to get the stinging sweat out. His T-shirt stuck to his back and rivulets of perspiration ran down, soaking his butt. By the time he'd arrived in North Africa, it was winter in the United States, but hotter than two rats fighting in a wool sock in Mali, where gold once built an empire enriched by salt and served by slaves owned by their own African brothers.

Bamako, on the Niger River, is Mali's capital city, and the name means "Crocodile River" in Bambara, though French is the official language of the country. On this day in 2013, the sights and sounds of the place assaulted the senses of the contractor. Car horns cut through the air, fighting for attention with engine noise and loudspeakers blasting crazy music. Debris littered the steps, sidewalks, and roadways. Mopeds of all makes and models zipped and sputtered through the streets, passing battered, antiquated Mercedes sedans, which seemed to be the national car of Mali. Western Union appeared to own every corner with its ubiquitous black-and-yellow signs beckoning customers needing cash. Rugs and laundry hung from balcony railings everywhere he looked. Men and women milled about in brightly colored patterns, passing the unemployed, drunk, or lazy who seemed to fill every step, nook, and alley. Bamako was a swirl of activity, but it was relatively calm at night except for a few cats screaming and roadblocks designed to extort francs from drivers. Beyond the capital, the situation was much more dark and unstable toward the east and northeast, and it was best not to travel after the sun fled the horizon. The Islamist jihadis in the capital hadn't tried anything major . . . not yet.

IN 2013, THE U.S. GOVERNMENT was swaggering about the Middle East and North Africa like a blind dog in a meat market. The war against radicalized, militant Islam had completely consumed so many that the ability of America's intelligence organs to understand other developments in the Muslim world was limited. In almost every country it felt like they had been running behind the action.

Now the runoff from revolutions in North Africa was leaking into Timbuktu in Mali, Niamey in Niger, and other places like Burkina Faso. Many members of the U.S. Congress had to consult their maps to locate the nations now being drawn into the sphere of influence of Iran and the jihadists. Mali had come into play after President Amadou Toumani Touré—who had instituted a new constitution and free, multiparty elections—led a revolution against the dictator, Moussa Traoré, in the 1990s. But President Touré had been ousted in 2012, in a coup led by a military empowered by the poverty-stricken nation's overall instability and triggered after more than eighty Malian soldiers were massacred along the frontier with Niger. The president went into hiding until finally reemerging to announce his resignation and his self-imposed exile in neighboring Senegal. Touré, who had ruled since 2002, had not been able to maintain power in the face of the burgeoning Islamist presence and the rebellion of the Tuaregs, Berber nomads who move through Mali and other countries of the Saharan interior, including Niger, Algeria, and Libya.

Estimates put the jihadists' strength at around five to six thousand in the country. Around 1,250 were from Mali itself; others came from Chad, Nigeria, and elsewhere. That's a lot of heavily armed, hate-filled bad guys concentrated into one country. The French understood this, inserting about twenty-five hundred troops, plus four hundred more European Union (EU) troops who'd flown in to help retrain the Malian military.

Mali has a strange shape to it—kind of like a lopsided butterfly. The entire country is roughly twice the size of Texas, with the largest part lying to the north-northeast, looking on the map like a massive right triangle. To the southwest is the rest of the country, where the capital, Bamako, lies; just northeast of that is a tiny area just around two hundred miles across that resembles the waist of a fat man and connects it all with the strategically important town of Mopti, sitting smack in the middle where the belt buckle would be.

The confused state of the nation following the coup was just what the jihadis wanted. The existing leaders in Mali were in no position to establish central political or military control. So the jihadists were able to launch strategic offensives and had quickly assumed control of key cities with minimal opposition, destroying ancient historical artifacts in the process. Control of cities, particularly Gao and Timbuktu, gave the Tuaregs and their jihadi compatriots control of northern Mali almost entirely. Now in 2013 they were moving west-southwest toward the fat man's waistline and Mopti. If they captured it and broke through on the western side, it would be a short, fast road trip into Bamako for yet another coup d'état. They'd own the place—and an al-Qa'ida-run, radical, Islamist, jihadi state in Africa would become a reality . . . can you say "Afghanistan"?

If they took Mali, they would throw their support behind Boko Haram—the militant jihadi group that was trying to shoot down a civilian plane at an international airport near Niamey or N'Djamena. Our private intelligence sources were reporting that they had enough arms and ammo for ten years and were armed with sophisticated Libyan MANPADS like the SAM-7 and the deadly EGLA-18, which was capable of taking out slow-flying passenger jets in a heartbeat.

They were killing those who spoke out against them. But Mali was just the beginning. Once they took it, they planned to expand to Senegal and Burkina Faso, with the main prize being Morocco and Mauritania, along the western coast. The nation the contractor entered was in a state of emergency, and curfews had been imposed. But while this hot war was breaking on the desert plains to the east of the capital, another battle was playing out in the shadows . . . a war of assassins and spies.

ON DECEMBER 2, 2012, Malian colonel Elhadji Ag Gamou left a house in the Niger capital city of Niamey, with his bodyguard leading the way. As he reached his car a man on a motorcycle unleashed a hail of bullets. He missed the colonel but not the bodyguard.

The Malian colonel's militia had extensive knowledge of local conditions and combat experience against Tuareg fighters, and he posed a serious threat to the jihadi terrorists in Mali. They tracked the colonel to Niger, then ordered the assassin to take Gamou off the chessboard permanently. They hadn't succeeded against Gamou yet. But chess requires two sides, and now the contractor and his team were tracking the terrorists.

Their job was to hunt down jihadi sleeper cell agents in Bamako, like the guys going after Gamou. Orders were to capture some, get rid of others, but the overall idea was to take out the enemy's eyes—their spies, their communications, and their access to information. Sleeper cell agents had been used to take Timbuktu, Kidal, and Gao in 2012. These terrorist spies lived undercover, collecting intelligence on Malian and French troop strength and rigging up sabotage and assassination operations. Should the jihadis go for the capital, these fighters would become the front line.

One target was a jihadi in his late twenties, a thin black guy with closely cropped hair who drove a late eighties yellow Mercedes taxi. They'd been following him for three days to learn his schedule. On the fourth day it was decided to move on the target. The French were hammering the enemy to the east, and the concern was that the enemy would get desperate and activate their agents. The contractor's team observed him leaving his little apartment block and walking toward his car, which he would drive to the Centre Ville, by the Place des Trois Caimans.

The contractor's cell phone buzzed again: the jihadi taxi driver was turning into his area. The contractor hung up, took a deep breath, pocketed his keys, and left the truck, walking toward the taxi zone where the target had parked for three days in a row. Taxis in Bamako come in two shapes—with or without a sign on the roof. If you see a sign, the vehicle is shared and can take multiple passengers. No sign means the vehicle is private and reserved for one fare only. He knew from earlier surveillance that their boy had no sign on his taxi . . . and that was a good sign—for them anyway.

As he pulled up to the curb in line with a gazillion other cabs, the contractor headed straight for him. Lighting a cigarette as he sat in his car, the driver spotted him approaching as the white man waved his hand like a naïve tourist. The cabdriver's face lit up with his pearly white teeth against his ebony skin. He dropped the match out the window, nodded, and motioned toward the backseat. Most drivers did that—they tried to get you in and then start driving without prenegotiating the fare. Normally the contractor wouldn't go along with it, but he wanted this guy relaxed, thinking he had a simple, potentially lucrative patsy on his hands.

The contractor closed the left-side door and sat directly behind the driver, patted him on the left shoulder, and said, "*Merci, emmenez-moi au supermarché*," telling him to head to the supermarket. Again the contractor patted him on the left shoulder. The inside of his cab was neat, despite the green shag carpet covering his dashboard, likely hiding cracked leather from the blistering sun. An air freshener packet dangled along with blue and red beads from his rearview mirror, and the decor was rounded out with a few stickers adorning the right edge of the windshield.

As they drove, the contractor slid to the center of the rear seat and made eye contact with the driver in the mirror, as he smiled and pointed to a building off to the left, asking him what it was called. As the driver looked off toward the building, the contractor's right hand reached back and retrieved the gun, sliding it under his right thigh. The jihadi agent mumbled something in French about the building the contractor asked about and returned his gaze to the road ahead as they continued.

They drove across a set of railroad tracks. Vendors littered the sides of the road, selling everything from handbags and bananas to teapots and goat meat. All around them traffic swirled. At a light, they slowed to a stop as mopeds and minibikes weaved their way between the vehicles. A slender young black man with glasses pulled up next to his window on a moped. Behind him his wife was dressed in a bright yellow outfit with matching headpiece and held on to him with one hand while cradling her baby in the other. When the light turned, they all edged up to the front and headed off.

A few minutes later, the contractor saw the right turn coming up that he and his Malian government partner had identified the day before. He patted the driver on the left shoulder again and said to turn there instead, pointing while pulling the towel off his shoulder and folding it into a tight square. They turned down an empty, narrow side street. Halfway down the dirt road, the contractor smiled and asked the cabdriver to stop, saying this was where he was going and told him to pull over. "*Combien?*" he asked, for how much, and the driver told him the fare was 2,500 francs—West African francs, just about five dollars American. The contractor pulled out two blue 2,000 CFA notes and handed them over. It was too much—but he'd planned it that way. The driver pulled out a money pouch, put it in his lap, and looked down to get his change.

As soon as the contractor heard him unzip the pouch and look down to count the money, he quickly took the towel square and placed it over the nose of the pistol, leaned forward, bringing both up to the base of the man's skull, and fired two fast shots, point-blank. The towel muffled the noise and served to catch the blowback of gunpowder, skin, and blood, but the shots were still loud and his ears were ringing with the familiar high-pitched whine. The target's shoulder simply slumped, his money pouch fell from his lap, and coins clattered on the floor mat. The body started falling toward the car horn as the contractor grabbed his left shoulder, pulling him to the right so that he fell onto the passenger seat. The familiar, bitter smell of gunpowder filled the car.

The two rounds had passed through the driver's brain stem, scrambled his medulla, and exited through his teeth, but the contractor wasn't able to see where they'd landed inside the car. He'd angled the shot downward to avoid spidering the windshield. Blood, tissue, and pieces of teeth clung to the steering wheel and the instrument gauges. There was a trickle of dark blood coming out of the two holes in the back of the driver's head. Pulling his phone out, the contractor took two pictures of the dead terrorist's face, then grabbed his money, leaving a few coins on the seat to make it look like a robbery.

As he looked around quickly, he saw no one at either end of the street and slid over to the right side to exit the car near the building. There he walked on down the alley, reached the end, turned right, and hopped into his Malian partner's black government Peugeot, which was waiting just out of sight. He slipped in the front seat and they pulled away. One sleeper now slept permanently. This is how it works sometimes in this war against radicalized militant Islamists that people mistakenly characterize as a war against terrorism.

CHAPTER 27

MANPAD + Bad Guy + Jet = Bad Day

2012
North Africa

BOB BAER AND I usually talked once a week during this time, catching up on family news or just to see how things were going or complain about stuff to each other—but today's call was not social. *Al Akhbar* newspaper published reports that I was involved in assassinating Qadhafi. Their source came from e-mails illegally obtained by WikiLeaks in a hack on the corporate intelligence firm Stratfor's e-mail systems, with which we'd been in contact. But more pressing was information suggesting that an American passenger jet was being targeted by al-Qa'ida out of West Africa, and as dramatic as it sounds, we literally had days to do something with that information.

We had a contact in the government of a West African nation with access to a top figure in al-Qa'ida in the Islamic Maghreb (AQIM), the al-Qa'ida group based in Mali and elsewhere in the North African region. AQIM extremists had declared their intentions to attack American, French, Spanish, and Algerian targets, and we knew they drew recruits from the South Moroccan Sahrawi and Algerian Kabyle tribes. Our contact was very well placed: he was the official go-between for his government, who had attempted to negotiate with AQIM and the terrorist organization.

Bob was calling to tell me to check my e-mail, that the notes from the debrief were in my inbox. The debriefing read in part:

Plan to attack Niamey and other southern towns in Niger in order to attract the army and security forces into a defensive position, thus emptying the north and facilitating the northern route between Mali and Libya. Plan to open a front in Chad and work on the Tobou [an ethnic group in Chad] dimension and also to support Boko Haram. They will attempt to shoot a civilian plane, near an international airport, such as Niamey or Ndjamena soon. They are receiving recruits from Egypt, Libya, Yemen, Somalia and Senegal. They have Libyan MANPADs; we have photos of SAM-7 and they affirm they have the EGLA-18.

Our source had pictures of the missiles—the EGLA-18, in particular, was deadly and currently fielded by the Russian army. It was an infrared homing surface-to-air missile that flew at Mach 2.3 and took out planes up to eleven thousand feet in the air. It wouldn't bring down fighters, but slow-moving passenger jets and lumbering cargo aircraft were sitting ducks. AQIM had bought or stolen these from Libyan stockpiles and the rest were being moved ironically by the *Al-Entisar* out of Libya and up to Syria. We had warned the United States about this possibility of North African attacks earlier in our Libya briefings, and now a passenger jet was in the crosshairs.

THE NEWSPAPER ARTICLE out of Lebanon about my being part of the assassination of Qadhafi—a lie—was not good news, either. Just a few weeks earlier, my teenage daughter had been standing behind our house in Virginia Beach on a rainy morning when she saw two men in camouflage hiding in the woods across the creek, watching the back area of our house—and it wasn't hunting season. I was there at the time and grabbed my Glock, jumped in the truck, and headed to find them. On the way, I called my good friend Jimmy, who was on the city police force, and he vectored two cars to me. We searched in the rain for an hour, but the surveillance team was gone. It wasn't the first time my family told me they'd seen people in dark or camouflage clothing across the creek, watching the house.

I went back to my home office and checked the security cameras mounted on every corner of our house—nothing. Two years earlier, when I'd been told that al-Qa'ida had put a bounty on my head, along with those of CEOs from companies supporting the U.S. war against radical militant Islamists, I had replaced all our locks, installed a mag-lock on the front door with only a combination lock for entry, and put up a wall and gate to prevent drive-ups along the street. Our K9 group sent over two serious dogs; we fenced off the rear of the property with chain link and barbed wire and even brought in an armored B7 Suburban for my family to use. We lived in a compound—a nice one, but a compound. The Suburban would stop anything but an RPG. I had weapons in every room, hidden in specially constructed places by a friend who did custom cabinetwork. I was armed every time I left the house, even when I went to church, and every member of my family had a GPS beacon with them at all times that I could pull up on my iPhone. After the surveillance scare, I had two men cover my house in a low-profile security role that my family never knew about—I didn't want my kids to fear playing in their own backyard.

By this time, I owned a number of different companies and was busier than a one-winged bird. Two of the companies I owned were SCG, LLC, which was based in Virginia and handled our government contracting work; and SCG International, LLC, which was a Mississippi-based company designed to handle debt and other high-risk ventures, to include some foreign work. Early on I co-owned SCG, LLC with a medically retired Marine NCO and we briefly were a service-disabled-veteran-owned business, but I recovered all my shares from him and we dropped that identifier. During this time I made two decisions that I regret to this day. The first was hiring the son of a former dean of my old law school in late 2008. He'd been a respected attorney in Virginia Beach, but had since been accused of misconduct, lost his license, and couldn't hold a job. He had a new wife and a lot of kids from a previous marriage. I knew his father, a well-respected lawyer and a man I truly admired, and assuming a man innocent until proven guilty, I hired his son to help him out. The son didn't tell me he had court-ordered conditions on what he was supposed to do. When I learned this important fact, I let him go. Later he was tried and found guilty and sent to prison.

The second decision I regret started back in 2007, when SCG International, LLC, the Mississippi company, received a loan from a

Pennsylvania man. To say things didn't go well from there is an understatement. To say this turned out worse for me than any life-threatening undercover operation I have ever been on is a lot less of one. In short, the guy sued, my company ended up on the losing end of a massive judgment, I ended up pilloried in the press as having defrauded the guy, and both SCG, LLC and SCG International, LLC were destroyed. And the air force canceled our contract due to the civil court's ruling for the guy. But that was something they had to do—it was their SOP. But it was not because we'd acted improperly with respect to our contract with the government. In fact, the student reviews were glowing. I do not believe justice was done. But I didn't have to go to law school to know that this book is not the place to try to set the record straight.

I have even managed to let my anger go, because as a wise man once said, "Holding on to anger is like grasping a hot coal with the intent of throwing it at someone else; you are the one who gets burned."

More important, I've moved forward helping to establish a new, fresh offshore venture called Gray Solutions, which is providing training, intel, and security services across Africa and the Middle East.

BUT BY 2012, THE ONGOING LITIGATION, on top of all these other worries around the world, was pressure I did not need. So I consulted with Colonel Cantwell, my staff, and Myrick's office on the terror threats in North Africa involving the airline attacks, as it had materialized into something against a named U.S. airliner, United Airlines, which had just recently merged with Continental, creating the world's largest air carrier. At the same time this was happening, because of the ludicrous Lebanese newspaper article about my assassinating Qadhafi, the radicals' bounty on my head, and sightings of strange people at our house, I decided that my family needed a more anonymous and off-the-grid location. But everything had to happen rapidly, because I still had work to do.

Bob's information indicated that other surface-to-air missiles sold to Libya back in 1982, notably SA-7Bs, were being refurbished for use. They, too, had been stolen from the armories of Qadhafi. We learned that AQIM had linked up with Boko Haram, a Nigerian-based militant Islamist group known for attacking Christians and bombing churches across the region. Their very name showed their Stone Age thinking—"books forbidden," from the Hausa word *boko*, which meant figuratively "Western education," and the Arabic word *haram*, "sinful" or "forbidden." They were yet another example that this war wasn't a war against terror, but a war against radical, militant Islam. They had been responsible for more than 620 deaths in the first six months of 2012 and over 10,000 more in the previous few years. They kidnapped Christian women, beat them until they converted to Islam, and then used them as bait to lure in followers of Christ from local villages, who then had their throats cut in an effort to rid the region of Christians. All this—the missiles, the threats to the passenger jet, the growth of the jihadis and al-Qa'ida in the region—needed to be reported.

I told Bob I was going to call Colonel Cantwell so he'd speak to the DCI (Director, Central Intelligence Agency). Bob said he had tried his government contacts without much success. "But I'll bet United will be real interested when they lose a plane because no one paid attention in D.C.," he said.

We both worked our contacts as hard as possible, agreeing to speak the next day. But our plans were OBE (overtaken by events): our contact came back with more news, not only confirming that United was being targeted; now we also had a specific flight number and date range and specific method of attack—a surface-to-air missile. It was scheduled to leave West Africa in two days and would land at JFK Airport in New York City. It was time to sound the alarm. We contacted the Transportation Security Administration; Colonel Cantwell touched base with the seventh floor at Langley while Bob and I reached out to others in the federal government.

But because of the ticking clock, we decided to cut the red tape even more and called Congressman Michael McCaul from the Tenth District of Texas. He'd spent six years as a member of the House Committee on Homeland Security and he was currently serving as the chairman of the Subcommittee on Oversight, Investigations and Management—he had oversight authority over all Department of Homeland Security operations. We figured he definitely would light a fire under someone.

We relayed it to the representative and whatever he did from there, we never knew, but rumor was that he'd called the airline directly about the threat and the threat never materialized after that.

THIS WAS THE FUTURE, America's and mine: Africa, which the terrorists were trying to turn into the new battleground. After getting my family to a safe, guarded place, I reached out to Mila and sent her to northwest Africa. Her job was to scout suitable locations for an office—a facility from which the new company, Gray Solutions, would operate, as well as to lock on transportation, food, and housing. That meant locking on logistical supply routes. She hit the ground running, examining options in more than four countries in just a few weeks, finally narrowing the list to two locations.

The war against the terrorists in North Africa was intensifying with the Maghreb becoming, along with Yemen, the setting for the new war against al-Qa'ida. Geographically, the Maghreb, whose name translates as "land of the setting sun," was nearly everything in Africa west of Egypt and north of Mauritania. The word came from the Arabic word *Maghrib*, which described the western areas that fell in the seventh century during the Islamic invasions. These were the Moors—the Islamists out of North Africa who invaded Spain and Europe.

These same forces were once again on the move in the twenty-first century, seeking—as the Bible might put it—whom they might devour in a modern-day attempted Islamic invasion. They preyed on weak, almost-failed states such as Mali. In short, they wanted to re-create the Islamist state—the old caliphate empire, run by hard-line fundamentalists, that spanned all the way from the Middle East to North Africa—just like it had been hundreds of years earlier.

The radical, hard-line, fundamentalist, militant Islamists were impossible to deal with—if it's not a video* they don't like, then it's a cartoon.† If it's not a cartoon, it's a teddy bear.‡ If it's not a teddy bear, it's a billboard§—it never mattered, they always found something over which to be angry, something over which to commit violence. Human beings have the right given by God to speak freely in opposition to tyranny,

* http://www.huffingtonpost.com/2012/09/17/innocence-of-muslims-protests_n_1889679.html.

† http://news.bbc.co.uk/2/hi/4684652.stm.

‡ http://www.dailymail.co.uk/news/article-497490/Thousands-Islamic-fanatics-wielding-knives-demand-jailed-teddy-bear-teacher-executed.html.

§ http://screen.yahoo.com/billboard-u-troop-embracing-muslim-175854022-cbs.html.

oppression, governments out of control, and on any other topic they choose, as long as it doesn't harm another person. As my granny would say, "Your rights end where my nose begins."

Fundamentalist Islamists are the bullies of the world. They want their way and attempt to get it through threat or infliction of violence. They justify their savagery by saying it's their religion and that the world should simply buckle under and look the other way, giving them what they want.

No.

The Libyan people fought against a dictator who denied them freedom. The Syrian people are similarly engaged, as are the Afghans, the people of Mali, and people of other countries around the world. To allow savages who claw for power, many under the guise of religion, to take over any country is a morally bankrupt idea.

Mila went through a law firm to rent the property, allowing us again the cloak of anonymity, and that equaled security as we undertook the mission of working against AQIM extremists in Africa. Our office was in a great place—near the Mediterranean with a great view of the sea, isolated with three ways to get in or out, on a mountaintop, thus elevated enough to enable us to see visitors approaching from a long way off. My cover would be that of Canadian tourist—my first time in that country actually, but what a great place it was. To make it as strong as possible, I caught a one-way flight into Ottawa, debarked, and got a hotel nearby. I had a travel agency buy a ticket to Europe in my name the next day using cash.

Sure, I came through passport control into Canada as an American, of course, since that was what my passport said. But once on the ground in Europe, I became Canadian and had the Air Canada tickets showing my point of origin as Canada, got a Canadian passport cover, and made my way south by rail, crossed the Mediterranean—but this time by a real ferry and not the *Al-Entisar*. Once on the ground in Algeria, I began setting up links to the sources in the target country, Mali, as well as back to Libya, since Libya was where the MANPADS reportedly came from.

I also needed ways to communicate with sources that we developed, so once again I set about establishing webmail drops, as well as choosing neutral cities where our contacts traveled for anything urgent or compelling. We set up a schedule for touching base with each other on a weekly basis, as well as a method for signaling if something was needed urgently.

I started making connections and met people with influence in Mali and Mauritania. In the course of my travels, I moved frequently into and out of Europe, Libya, Egypt, Mali, Morocco, and Mauritania. It was the second half of the same game and I was still on the field.

ON ONE OF MY TRAVELS, I drove through the enchanting kingdom of Morocco. I was bumping along through the peaceful, bucolic back roads, passing olive orchards, mud huts, and farmers harvesting their year's supply of wheat. I heard a few people singing harvest songs that rose through the sleepy sunlit air as sheep roamed in search of shreds of grass. An old man in a djellabah with his pointy hood folded back rode sidesaddle on his donkey laden with massive twin saddlebags of green grass, as he beat the animal's flanks with a switch. Nothing, it seemed, could mar this serenity, but I wasn't here to admire that sort of thing.

Morocco is predominantly a French- and Arabic-speaking country, but many also speak Berber. The kingdom rests along the northwestern coast of North Africa and I'd driven its entire length quite a few times. On the northern coast, you can see the famed Rock of Gibraltar across the water of the azure Mediterranean that I knew so well from earlier days. The country was a mix of emaciated mutts, mules, and mutated versions of French automobiles. Take a drive in cosmopolitan Casablanca next to a Jag or Merc and then a few miles down the road have to stop for a herd of goats crossing the road. Once I saw more than three dozen camels lazily sauntering along the middle of a major roadway, chewing on something they'd ripped from the ground, watching with sad eyes as tanker trucks, cars, and mopeds worked their way between them.

Called Berbers today, a form of the Greek word for "barbarians," because the locals refused to adapt to Grecian and Roman ways, the people in Morocco had converted to Islam centuries earlier when the Arabs invaded and foisted their beliefs on them. It had been an easy choice for most—convert to Islam or be killed. Today, many Berbers hate the name itself and instead choose the term *Amazigh* or *Imazighen*, which translates as "freemen," to describe themselves—with *Berber* considered an insult.

Regardless of nomenclature, the people were helpful, gracious, and kind. The country folk lived in modest one- or two-room homes made of plaster and cinder block with a metal teapot, plates, and few other utensils resting on shelves bolted high on plaster walls. I've sat cross-legged on their concrete floors around small tables while the wives heated up milk and handed out individual Nescafé instant coffee packets, cashews, and store-bought cookies. A dear friend, Abdullah and his wife, Zaina, shared their home with me for a time, right after the birth of their daughter Fatima. This was a land of good, hardworking, peaceful people—friendly people.

But despite this hospitality, there was a subtext: this country was the Achilles heel that threatened Europe's security. It had become a channel for North African terrorists who wanted to get into Europe.

During the course of my work, I visited a little-known Spanish territory sitting on the continent of Africa just across from Gibraltar called Ceuta, or, if you are in Morocco, Sebta. It's one of three Spanish protectorates on North African soil surrounded by Morocco ever since the sixteenth century—and has been a sore spot between the two nations ever since. But once you walked about twenty yards and stepped across an unseen line on the ground into Ceuta you were technically in Spain . . . in Europe, the EU.

That meant that after catching a quick ferry ride across the Mediterranean you were literally on the European continent and free to go anywhere in the EU without passport checks. The challenge was getting from Moroccan land across that unseen line into Ceuta. But it was not hard to do.

I crossed through the Ceuta border post often, going back and forth from my home base in Spain. Since it's my job to notice details, I noticed that the border was less than secure—on both sides. Sure, both countries have the requisite "3-Bs" for securing a position—boys, bullets, and barriers. Winding its way between Ceuta, Spain, and Morocco, there was a double fence topped with razor wire, reminding me of the U.S.–Mexican border. There were guard dogs, spotlights, riot vans with their windshields covered in steel mesh. There were men on both sides armed with submachine guns; there were metal detectors, there were multiple steel gates, and it all made the border appear well protected. But in reality it wasn't. The metal detectors on either side were turned off nearly every time I went through. A well-dressed bad guy with nice suitcases could bring weapons or anything else across without much trouble at all—just by giving off the *good citizen* appearance. But there was something even simpler, something worse.

Assume for a moment that Libya has surface-to-air missiles, MANPADS, floating around in the hands of radical militant Islamist bad guys (which they do). Then assume that a group of those bad guys wants to strike Western targets, killing as many as possible (which they do). How do they do it? Sail across the Mediterranean Sea? No, they'll be boarded by a NATO warship, arrested, and thrown in jail. Take a ferry out of Benghazi? No, they'll be stopped at the port in Europe.

First, they head southwest, crossing into Algeria, where they sell or transfer the weapon to al-Murabitoun—the main al-Qa'ida jihadi group in Algeria—who then continue the trek southwest, crossing into Mauritania at the porous border near Chegga. Once inside, they make their way to Nouadhibou, an Atlantic port city just a few thousand yards south of Western Sahara—which is essentially Morocco. They hire a simple wooden fishing boat, push out into the Atlantic, head north a few miles, and beach it on the Moroccan Atlantic coastline of Western Sahara. Fishermen are everywhere along that area, so it's nothing out of the ordinary. The terrorist, having coordinated a vehicle with sympathizers in Morocco, heads north up through the modern highway to Agadir, turns right for Marrakech, hangs a left toward Casablanca, and then Rabat, all the way to . . . you guessed it, to the northernmost point of Ceuta, Spain . . . yet still on the African continent.

But you can't just walk through with a five-foot-long surface-to-air missile—that'll draw attention whether the metal detectors are on or not. But again, that crossing point has water on the eastern side. They go to a Moroccan tourist shop, buy an inflatable pool raft, wait until dark, and float the weapon twenty yards north from one side to the other, passing the border station to the Spanish side. Kick their way back to shore, knife-sink the raft, hail one of the dozens of cabs that make a U-turn at Martinez Catana Avenue looking for customers, and the bad guys are technically in Spain—the EU. Once inside, they catch one of the daily ferries leaving the marina at Puerto de Ceuta for mainland Spain, and there'll be no further checks on the other side of the ferry ride—they, their weapon, and their evil intent are in Europe. It's like catching a bus to go from Madrid to Barcelona, or from Canton, Ohio, to Chicago—no checks.

Once on the mainland, they are able to go anywhere with anything, crossing borders unchallenged all across Europe, to airports in Spain, Italy, France, crossing through the Chunnel into England and armed with a shoulder-launched missile capable of blowing a slow, fat passenger jet completely out of the sky. How many Ceutas are there? How many holes, how many threats around the world? Lots—and they are simple to exploit.

From my experience, the simple plans work. Box cutters took down three jet airplanes on 9/11; simple trucks with explosives destroyed our embassy and marine barracks in Lebanon in the 1980s, and the Murrah Federal Building in Oklahoma City was taken out by a rental truck parked out front in 1995. Simple works.

Bad guys could shut down mighty LAX—Los Angeles International Airport—or any airport in the United States with a spray bottle filled with ammonia nitrate. A bad guy need only crush up the small white balls out of the one-use instant cold packs that you can buy at almost any CVS or Walgreens pharmacy, or buy a sack of fertilizer and then mix either with water. Then walk through the airport and spray it on the floor, call in a bomb threat, and the K9s will indicate bombs everywhere. The authorities would tear the place to the ground trying to find bombs that don't exist—simple works. Get that mixture into the wax used to polish the floors and that airport will be razed.

Bad guys with half a brain can walk through airport security, head to any Hudson News snack store, and buy all the supplies needed to make a deadly blowgun, a functioning frag grenade out of a coffee thermos, an incendiary carry-on suitcase, and even a functioning shotgun just using Axe body spray, lithium batteries, a hair dryer, a handful of quarters, and a few other items. Simple works.

The sniper attacks in the Washington, D.C., area in October 2002 were carried out by two guys whose collective IQ was probably no larger than their shoe sizes, yet they took a rifle, hid in the trunk of their Chevy Caprice, and shot people from a hole bored out next to the license plate. These two moral midgets managed to effectively shut down the nation's capital. It was the sort of operation that, if deployed across the country in teams, would lock the nation in fits for weeks, shut down commerce in major cities, tie up law enforcement, and cause significant economic damage . . . for the cost of a few rounds of ammunition.

I hope the good guys realize these weaknesses, because the bad guys do and are always looking for more. As the late, great British prime minister Margaret Thatcher said long ago, the bad guys only have to be right once, but the good guys have to be right all the time.

MALI HEATED UP as soon as I got settled. Then came the attack on the U.S. Consulate and CIA annex in Benghazi, Libya, on the eleventh anniversary of 9/11. It didn't have to happen: once again, information that we had attempted to pass along nearly one year earlier was ignored, and suddenly people were dead as the powerful ran to take cover from the fallout. We had reported the militias' connections to al-Qa'ida, the fighting between the militias, and the weapons being stolen, sold, and proliferated around the region. We had described the pile of weapons on that street in Misrata, the guns and other hardware available to any child, zealot, or madman. We told them about the boat—the *Al-Entisar*—that crisscrossed the Mediterranean Sea delivering fighters and weapons hidden among medical and food supplies. We had offered our government access to the sources and contacts that we had developed inside the militias but it was like screaming underwater—pointless.

Soon the United States was yanking personnel from Benghazi—and appearing to be running from the fight, which is exactly what the radical militants wanted. They wanted to hit us, drag American bodies through the streets, and watch us run out, leaving them to build, work, and develop their capabilities. I hope we don't fall into that trap. I hope I live to see the day that our government can truly say that it has moved beyond the politics that endanger the lives of Americans and others all across the world and has truly decided to step up and defeat these radical Islamist enemies of mankind.

I'm in a risky industry, wanted by terrorists with a bounty on my head happily supplied by both al-Qa'ida and Hizbollah. I've taken steps to protect my family and myself, but the danger remains real. I created a company more than a decade ago that set the tone for the future of U.S. power projection. We introduced contractors and private, black-side operators into the strategic calculus of the United States in a way never used previously. We've hunted terrorists, captured bad guys, recovered deadly weapons, negotiated important deals and truces, guarded our nation's most critical intelligence facilities and personnel, and executed successful operations in places not many Americans would dare set foot. War will always exist until the Lord returns, and as a result, so will honorable, skilled, mature men and women willing to fight them. Private contractors are among those men and women.

Today, the words of one of my favorite songs rings ever true to me as I spend yet another holiday away from home, from my family, because I've traveled here and everywhere following my job, but . . .

> *. . . anywhere I'll ever go and everywhere I've been, nothing takes my breath away . . . like my front porch looking in.*

RECENTLY, MORE INTRUDERS have been taking more photos of the back of our old home—but no one is there. As I write this from Cairo, the situation becomes more complicated. When I rise and when I lie down, I pray for the safety of my family and the world. I think of my grandfather, clutching his Bible, trying to be a good man in a world where so many couldn't claim that designation. I think of my father in Mississippi in the days of my childhood, there on his tractor, ballcap on his head, eyes squinting as he aimed his Smith & Wesson revolver at the dark, dangerous snakes that swirled through the waters where we had once safely played. Again and again, he took aim, shooting those water moccasins, and he did his best to protect his family. All I am doing is shooting snakes. All I ask for is a little help.

EPILOGUE

TEDDY ROOSEVELT ONCE OBSERVED that life's greatest gift is the opportunity to work hard at work worth doing. I will always treasure my opportunity to do that.

I've learned quite a bit about how things work behind the scenes. I realize now that governments don't just do things out of kindness—aid money flows to get something in return, such as that new military base or port access, military cooperation, access to natural resources, or a favorable vote in the UN on a pet project. Every operation, battle, or war has a secret undercurrent moving, flowing, and searching out its objectives. When a typhoon hits Myanmar or an earthquake levels Pakistan, the United States sends help.

When the West slaps sanctions on Iranian oil and banking endeavors, you learn the backstory, that the Iranians, who now control Baghdad, have bought up many small Iraqi banks and trucked Iranian money across the border for laundering. I've come to understand how they mix their oil with Iraqi oil and sell it at massive discounts to Gulf oil middlemen. I learned how Pakistan, driven by its fear of India gaining influence in Kabul, actually hates the United States and never wants to see a stable Afghanistan. So they help the Afghan Taliban with money, training, intelligence, sanctuary, and supplies as the Taliban kill more coalition troops. In my job, there's always something hidden in the background; the story is always more complicated than it appears.

Small but crucial events, conversations, and ideas, placed at the right time, can change the course of history. I have been blessed to be at the right spot, at the right time over the course of the last twenty-plus years. From Blackwater's direction, to Libya and Bob Levinson, those ideas knocking around in my north Mississippi noggin some say have helped shape a decade of war, and in some small way have influenced the way our nation projects strategic influence. I've made mistakes and failed at times along the way. I'm in good company though—Machiavelli was one of Florence's leading diplomats who had his career ended abruptly when the Medici family falsely accused him and jailed him . . . and during that time he wrote *The Prince*. I'm certainly no Machiavelli. I'm just a simple, Christ-following American from Mississippi who saw things needing to be done and I have tried my best to do them—most often in an unconventional way. Yes, I've been blessed with success, but I have also experienced quite a few failures and dealt with some pretty underhanded people. But you can't be afraid to fail. It's okay to fail, because if you're not—you're not growing. As Ortega y Gasset said, "It is from failure that human and personal progress are made." Failure and errors of judgment don't make you wise, but if the person is willing to use such setbacks to grow, they can lead to wisdom. It's what you do after you fail that determines the man or woman you really are.

PRIVATE MILITARY COMPANIES

The world isn't getting safer; it's more lethal than ever. Threats from terrorist groups, rogue nations, lone-wolf killers, and organized crime are affecting states and companies doing business abroad, nonprofits and individuals alike. But states increasingly can't meet the threats alone and, like any other need in the market, if a service provider steps up, someone will buy. Every Olympic Games has hired private security for years because the host country can't do it unless they bring out the military, like the United Kingdom had to do in 2012 because the security company dropped the ball. But the military is designed to kill people and break things—not police drunks at a swim meet.

The trend to use private military and security companies will continue to grow and shape international security. In defiance of the traditional ideas of state-centric security, these private security actors pose real challenges to effective regulation of the services they provide, particularly when it comes to accountability for violations of human rights and remedies to victims. But these organizations can also challenge the security community in a positive manner, through innovations and the possibility of cost-effectiveness that may be welcome in difficult economic times. The recent trends toward privatization of security and the impact of international business on the enjoyment of human rights have also served as the impetus to forge surprising alliances among states, industry, and civil society groups. These multi-stakeholder efforts may be able to find real solutions to these challenges, building innovative and flexible frameworks that can respond to global, economic, and human security needs in the twenty-first-century world.

THE PRESS

Of the souls who reside on this earth who are not in the employ of a government agency or military, none are more intrepid, resourceful, and bold—even fearless at times—than those who deliver the news from around the world. These folks go with little support or security and no weapons into the heart of darkness. I've dodged their crews to preserve my cover and mission at times, and at others I've sought them out because they often have contacts and insights that can't be gained any other way. People open up to reporters and tell them things that they wouldn't tell their preacher. Reporters—the good ones—understand that you only get good information from people; eavesdropping systems and satellite imagery don't tell you what someone is thinking, intending, or intimating. That only comes from having people on the ground meeting other people. They are an indispensable part of our world and, with but a few exceptions, contribute to the safety and security we all enjoy—governments and intelligence agencies should learn much from how they operate. Sure, there are bottom-feeders out there who seek only to make a name for themselves by tearing down someone else, or intentionally twisting what is said to promote an agenda—and I've experienced those sorts, too. But by and large, journalism is an honorable profession. I applaud them and respect the risks they take.

THE CENTRAL INTELLIGENCE AGENCY

When things go wrong, the CIA gets shot at by everyone from politicians covering their rear ends, to the press, and by everyone in between. But we rarely hear when things are done correctly, which is far more often than not, and that is how the agency would prefer it. The CIA is at the top when it comes to ranking the best intelligence agencies in the world today, in spite of often-feckless political leadership. That's just a cold, hard reality and is not based on any biases I hold. They simply are the best—with their global reach, excellent people at collecting information, and near geniuses at conducting analysis. The CIA, with the skills of its personnel and a mountain of cash to back things up, has paramilitary capabilities that can win wars and defeat armies, and is ever increasing its achievements in the digital age. There is simply none better and I'm proud to have been an officer in its ranks.

Certainly, there are a number of other good services in the world today and many with global reach, such as the British, Russian, and Chinese. Then there are crack outfits like the Israelis and the Jordanians, but they have both been historically focused on their regions, and for good reason. No doubt Britain, Jordan, and Israel all land in the top five or six, despite their shortcomings in other areas. Which country's intelligence service is the worst? That's a more difficult question to answer—do you include their counterintelligence capabilities or their covert action programs, or lack thereof? Many services don't get involved in those things at all. It's a race to the bottom.

The CIA has a long, proud history of providing vital information to our leaders, and while not perfect, they get way less credit than they deserve. The CIA led and won the war in Afghanistan, found and killed bin Laden, and pioneered the arming of drones, [redacted] [redacted].

I was overseas in 2011 when Usama bin Laden's worthless life ended. But when I got back to Virginia Beach, I took my son for a ride over to Dam Neck to show him ST6's new headquarters building. We linked up with a friend from the Team and took in the memorial garden that has a massive piece of the Twin Towers standing in the ground, like a massive trident pitchfork. The names of the JSOC operators killed in action since 9/11 from all the services were etched into a stone wall surrounded by the individual team plaques—Red, Gold, Blue, CAG, SOAR, and more. We walked back by the firing ranges where ST6 had developed the precision skills used to end bin Laden's theft of this earth's oxygen. Then we drove the sandy road farther back to the obstacle course and Cole climbed a few walls and cargo nets, just like the big boys.

Killing bin Laden showed the American public a glimpse of what the new fight is like. The science, the skill, the training, and the people are unlike anything our nation has ever produced before. The CIA operation that killed UBL was as ordinary for the shooters in terms of its complexity as putting on their boots. They'd executed thousands of missions since 2001, and when the CIA and the SEALs finished killing him, the corpse was flown by V-22 Osprey to the nuclear-powered aircraft carrier USS *Carl Vinson*, lowered to the aircraft hangar deck by elevator, and shoved overboard for a twenty-five-foot fall into the waves, where the scumbag sank to the bottom of the sea. In other words, he was dumped from the ship, the same way the navy handles its garbage.*

Modern-day Spartan warriors—our men are no longer just men, they are weapon systems, with millions of dollars of training, research, and historical precedent invested into each one. They are treated like professional athletes, with professional trainers who develop exercises specific to the mission, locker rooms like NFL players to store gear, support staff to keep everything in good working order. Then, when game day arrives, which it does multiple times, day or night, they go at it full-bore.

The CIA's Counterterrorism Center, which had three hundred employees on the day of the 9/11attacks, now has more employees than al-Qa'ida's core worldwide.

But no organization is perfect, and weak political leadership coupled with CIA's kinetic operations pulled the agency from its traditional espionage mission, undermining its ability to interpret global developments such as the Arab Spring.

However, the CIA is a reflection of America, and just as our country rises to the challenges and adapts, overcomes, and plows ahead, so does the agency. It's learning from the mistakes, improving, growing, and getting better by the day. With competent, bold leadership on the sev-

* http://www.navy.mil/submit/display.asp?story_id=2712.

enth floor, and hopefully on Pennsylvania Avenue one day, the CIA can get back to doing what it's done so well for so long—protecting the nation from enemies abroad by providing the president with solid intelligence and carrying out covert operations to blunt the enemy's attacks before they ever see our nation's shores. The CIA has been protecting America with outstanding success since this war began and I hope the American people remember that.

THE DEPARTMENT OF DEFENSE

No more lethal organization has ever existed on planet earth than the U.S. Department of Defense. We ought to consider renaming it the Department of Offense or the War Corps because our men and women in uniform have been developing the most lethal killing machine the world has ever seen and putting it to use against more bad guys and breaking more of their hardware than any other nation, ever. Is that something to be proud of? Absolutely! Our service personnel are all volunteers and are simply staggering in their commitment, courage, and overall conduct. But as Robert Kaplan put it, defense experts understand the importance of "presence"—having enough ships and jets in a region to reinforce American diplomacy, reassure allies, and deter possible adversaries, such as the Chinese. But the people, the public, will ask, Why can't we reduce the number of those ships and jets if there's no obvious and direct threat to the United States? The American public has never been enthusiastic about defense unless the threat against the homeland is concrete and immediate, as 9/11 and the years since have demonstrated. So the armed services and the politicians must learn how to explain why armies are required for emergencies—which do happen; why navies and air forces are required for guarding the sea-lanes; and why they're essential for preserving the global system, upon which America depends.

But they need to be forthright and up front when they give their explanations—not trying to pass off a war against radicalized militant Islam as a war against terrorism. I have posed this question to myself as well as friends of mine with whom I share similar backgrounds. If our objective really is the destruction of radical, militant Islamists, then we simply cannot rely on superior intelligence and military capabilities alone. What we often forget is that in war, our military might is confronting an ideology that is, more often than not, pursued by unemployed youth in third-world countries. An argument can be posed that an ideology, regardless of how extreme, is only successfully fought with an equally effective opposing idea. President Reagan and Prime Minister Thatcher proved this theory during the Cold War. Yes, it was necessary to have all the right military hardware, but eventually communism crumbled because its political, social, and economic framework was unable to sustain itself beyond a set limit. People living in Eastern Europe soon realized the values and necessities of having a more open society that offers superior education and subsequently greater economic incentives.

Not many of us on this side of the fence like to acknowledge that our war machinery has cost a great deal more than what it costs our adversary to put a man in a ragtag army. Our political elite understand all too well how to manipulate the masses for their own gains. But they would do well to remember that while terror plots will continue to be discovered and disrupted, don't expect to achieve anything spectacularly different in terms of results in another ten years. Don't expect that we'll kill them all, because as soon as one high-value target is taken out, he's replaced by the next man standing in line, ready to hatch the next plot and create the next emergency.

But when those emergencies do occur and America sends Delta Force operators to hunt down another Saddam Hussein, or the Eighty-Second Airborne to bring the pain to another Taliban, or the Sixth Fleet to smoke another part of Qadhafi's air force out of the sky, or the U.S. Marines to plow through more terrorists like in Kandahar, or when we need more of the 280 U.S. Air Force personnel running sixty-five round-the-clock MQ-1 Predator and MQ-9 Reaper drone operations every day, no military compares to that of the United States of America—none. Simply put, we kill people and break things better than anyone else, even on Christmas . . . just like our first president showed us how to do back in 1776, when he crossed the Delaware. When the next emergency, terrorist strike, or genocidal war breaks out, the American people will demand and cry out for those men and women, machines, and weapons to protect them, to keep them safe—but you can't cut it to nothing now and expect it to be there tomorrow. There is no more noble calling than to be a soldier in our nation's military, because they are some of the finest men and women in America.

CONTRACTORS

Fires require firefighters. The civilian who responds to a need by signing a contract to work for a company filling that need is not a bad guy or girl just because he or she is armed as part of their job, any more than a police officer is bad for being armed and getting paid to stop crime as part of his hiring contract, or a soldier signing an enlistment contract to get paid to fight wars. The weapons we carry are tools, just like the hammer is for the house builder—another contractor, just working in another field. Contractors have been around in one form or another since time began—just like spies, preachers, politicians, and prostitutes. The American Continental Army depended on civilians for transportation, engineering, meals, and medicine—not the military. In fact, a crew of French contractors led by the Marquis de Lafayette set sail for America to fight in the American Revolution against British colonial rule in 1777.

Today, contractors are a needed, indispensable element of the modern battlefield. Getting them out is like removing the color from Kool-Aid. These warriors, many retired from military service, are seeking ways to continue serving their country. They are away from their families, often lacking the support they need, and when they get shot they bleed like anyone else on the battlefield. When contractors are killed, they are just as dead as a soldier, sailor, airman, or marine who dies.

Like anything else, though, it can get out of control. When companies are able to go into a country in chaos and appear—to the leaders of that nation at that moment—to be the only viable option for holding on to their power, they can be allowed to run loose, and that's where the problems sit. Patriots or mercenaries, professionals or "cowboys"—most Americans have an opinion of these warriors without uniforms. Most of those opinions are based on media articles, Hollywood's portrayal, or a politicians' comments. Other opinions may be based on a single tactical failure that grabbed worldwide attention for a few days. But judging these people based on a few sensational headlines, without truly understanding them or the circumstances that brought them into this war, is akin to judging our entire Department of Defense on the events at Abu Ghraib.

Other industries capable of doing harm are regulated—such as lawyers and doctors—and its members are held accountable for their actions, wherever those actions take place. They can be punished for bad behavior by their home state's bar, board, or prosecutors by losing their license, being fined, or doing prison time. U.S. military contracting companies are also subject to the law of their home country, and in some cases, the laws of the country in which they're working. But perhaps to level the training field state-based boards are created and standards for training are set, licenses for operating are agreed upon and codified by the state's legislature, and remedies for negligence are prescribed. Is it a place for the federal government? Certainly, if the contract is with a federal entity, then yes; but otherwise I'd say no. There are too many areas of life where that behemoth already intrudes and the states have shown acute wisdom in handling their own affairs over the last two-hundred-plus years.

It's not popular with pockets of the public to have people in this gray area. Perhaps it's because money is being made when a war is going on, or it's politically based resentment because it blossomed under a particular political party's rule—I'm not sure. But I do understand that without that gray work, you can't have the black-and-white that makes life so easily understood and enjoyed by the folks back home in their recliners sipping a cool glass of Lipton on a summer afternoon under the magnolia tree. Our nation has always had—and always will have—men and women who have one foot in the civilized world, but who keep the other foot in the savage world, kicking the enemy out, keeping them at bay. It's dangerous work—hard work. But it's hard work worth doing. One day I hope my children look back at me—like I do with my own father—and say their dad worked hard at work worth doing.

If you can keep your head when all about you
Are losing theirs and blaming it on you,
If you can trust yourself when all men doubt you,
But make allowance for their doubting, too;

If you can wait and not be tired by waiting,
Or being lied about, don't deal in lies,
Or being hated, don't give way to hating,
And yet don't look too good, nor talk too wise

If you can dream—and not make dreams your master;
If you can think—and not make thoughts your aim;

If you can meet with Triumph and Disaster
And treat those two impostors just the same;

If you can bear to hear the truth you've spoken
Twisted by knaves to make a trap for fools,
Or watch the things you gave your life to, broken,
And stoop and build 'em up with worn-out tools

If you can make one heap of all your winnings
And risk it on one turn of pitch-and-toss,
And lose, and start again at your beginnings
And never breathe a word about your loss;

If you can force your heart and nerve and sinew
To serve your turn long after they are gone,
And so hold on when there is nothing in you
Except the will, which says to them: "Hold on!"

If you can talk with crowds and keep your virtue,
Or walk with Kings—nor lose the common touch,
If neither foes nor loving friends can hurt you,
If all men count with you, but none too much;

If you can fill the unforgiving minute
With sixty seconds' worth of distance run,
Yours is the Earth and everything that's in it,
And—which is more—you'll be a Man, my son!

—RUDYARD KIPLING
"If: A Father's Advice to His Son"

ACKNOWLEDGMENTS

FRED BURTON INTRODUCED ME to my literary agent extraordinaire, Jim Hornfischer, and for that I thank you. I wish to thank David Highfill, and the professionals at William Morrow, who took a leap of faith when he bought the publishing rights, and his editorial guidance was priceless. Thanks to George Hodgman, for his initial editorial work and patience with me, as well as to Dale Rohrbaugh, Laurie McGee, and Candice for their keen eye for detail and making sure dates and places tracked accordingly.

Any errors in this book are mine. However, I know there will be those critics who inevitably will attack me personally and try to discredit this work. In fact it already happened, months before the book was even published. But these are stories, my stories, going back more than two decades, and stories are what I've endeavored to tell, not furnish an historical account or a geopolitical treatise. I was fortunate to be part of a program in the U.S. intelligence apparatus that was canceled following the Gulf War. My class was the final one, and while many will say the government would never hire a college student for covert work, you only need to look at the Defense Department to realize that men and women as young as eighteen sign up every day, going into Special Operations and intelligence work.

I would like to thank my former colleagues at SCG, CIA, and FBI who devoted their lives to protecting America. Many of the things they achieved will never be made known to the public and they are the true heroes. Equally, I wish to thank Ninj, because I couldn't have written this book without your support, encouragement, and advice—because "Hey, hey, hey—that was the plan, Stan." In addition, special thanks to Bob Baer and two other CIA colleagues who wish to remain anonymous, for their advice and encouragement, Colonel Richard Cantwell (USA Ret) and Miles Adler (USN SpecWar/SEAL), as well as D, Epp, Admiral David Anderson (USN Ret), Doug, Alan, Clint, Jimmy C., Jack A., Chris H., George, Mike, Leonard, Tripp, Ed L., Brent, Todd, and Ellen.

Finally, thank you to my family. You shaped me, impressed upon me, guided and loved me—nothing is more important. Finally, I wish to specifically thank my parents, Jamie and Bonnie, for the example they set of Christ-centered, hardworking parents who sacrificed many things for us. Bebo couldn't have asked for more.

GLOSSARY

AD—"Accidental discharge"; also referred to as an "ND," or "negligent discharge." It refers to the discharge of a firearm involving culpable carelessness, but the term can also apply to allowing noise or light to escape through negligence. Example, "he had a light ND when his flashlight turned on," or "he had a noise ND when he slammed the car door."

AG-1—A pack by Kifaru designed specifically to be worn atop body armor.

AK-47—*Avtomat Kalashnikova*, refers to the year 1947, when it was introduced into service in the Soviet Union. The AK-47 is a selective fire, gas-operated, 7.62x39 mm assault rifle. It is one of the hardiest weapons ever created.

Al-Entisar—Boat placed into service for Libyan rebels to transport equipment, aid, and other required items into Libya during war to oust Muammar Qadhafi in 2011.

Al-Qa'ida—A global militant Islamist organization founded in 1988 by a guy who was correctly and righteously shot in the face by U.S. commandos in the spring of 2011.

Ambien—Brand name for zolpidem, an outstanding drug for knocking you out ASAP. (See ASAP.)

ASAP—As Soon As Possible, or how fast you'll go to sleep with Ambien.

A-6—An American, twin-engine, midwing attack jet built by Grumman Aerospace and discontinued in 1997.

Atmospherics—Information on attitudes, tribal influences, and figures of influence.

BM-21 Grad—*Boyevaya mashina*, Russian for combat vehicle, is a truck-mounted 122 mm multiple rocket launcher. The nickname *grad* is Russian for hail.

BDU—Battle dress utilities or uniform.

BOB—Bug Out Bag, an escape and evasion bag filled with gear needed in order to leave and survive.

C4A—Cover for action. The lie an operator tells explaining what he's doing. Perhaps he's conducting surveillance on a target building, but he's pretending to be a street sweeper. The action of sweeping is the cover for the surveillance.

C4S—Cover for status. The lie an operator tells about his employment when he's on a mission. Perhaps he's pretending to be a casket salesman, [redacted] or an arms dealer. It gives him a reason to be in a certain place.

CH-47—An American twin-engine, tandem rotor heavy-lift helicopter manufactured by Boeing, also called a Chinook, S#!t Hook, or Flying School Bus.

CIA—Central Intelligence Agency.

C-130—A four-engine turboprop military transport aircraft designed and built originally by Lockheed, now Lockheed Martin. Also known as the most terrible plane to ride in as a passenger.

CONOPS—Concept of the Operation; Defense Department terminology for a verbal or graphic statement that clearly and concisely expresses what the joint force commander intends to accomplish and how it will be done using available resources.

CQB—Close quarters battle; combat in a confined space.

Crye—The best uniform and equipment maker on the planet.

CS—Countersurveillance; a team watching your back for signs you're being followed by surveillance.

CTC—Counter Terrorist Center, located at HQS, CIA.

Delta—First Special Forces Operational Detachment-Delta (First SFOD-D and also formerly known as CAG—Combat Applications Group) is one of the United States' secretive tier-one counterterrorism and special mission units (SMUs). The unit's new name has been changed to ACE (Army Compartmented Element).

DEVGRU—The U.S. Naval Special Warfare Development Group (NSWDG), or more commonly known by its former name, SEAL Team 6 (ST6), is one of the United States' four secretive counterterrorism and special mission units (SMUs). This unit's official designation has also been changed.

DIA—Defense Intelligence Agency.

Dragunov SVD—Literally "Dragunov's sniper rifle" is a semiautomatic sniper rifle chambered in 7.62×54 mm and developed in the former Soviet Union.

D-ring—An item of hardware, usually a metal ring shaped like the letter D. It may be used at the end of a rope or strap. Also can refer to one of the corridor rings at the Pentagon.

DShK—A Soviet heavy machine gun firing the 12.7×108 mm cartridge.

EOD—Explosive Ordnance Disposal, the guys who disarm bombs.

F-22 Raptor—A U.S. single seat, twin-engine, fifth-generation fighter using stealth technology manufactured by Lockheed Martin/Boeing.

GPS—Global positioning system, also known as SatNav.

Hellfire—The AGM-114 Hellfire is an air-to-surface (ASM) missile developed primarily for antiarmor use but has multi-mission, multi-target capability and can be launched from a variety of air, sea, and ground platforms.

HK G3—7.62x51 mm NATO assault rifle manufactured by German company Heckler & Koch.

HUMINT—Syllabic abbreviation for HUMan INTelligence, referring to the gathering of intelligence by means of interpersonal contact, gathered from and provided by human sources.

HQS—Headquarters.

ID—Identification.

IO—Intelligence officer.

IR—Infrared.

KGB—Intelligence and security agency of the former Soviet Union from 1954 until 1991. Short for *Komitet Gosudarstvennoy Bezopasnosti*, or Committee for State Security.

Kifaru—The best pack and gear-hauling manufacturer on the planet.

LIFG—Libyan Islamic Fighting Group, a terrorist organization.

L-100—A civilian version of the C-130 (see above).

MANPADS—Man-Portable Air-Defense Systems; shoulder-launched surface-to-air missiles (SAMs). They are typically guided weapons and are a threat to low-flying aircraft, especially helicopters. Examples include the U.S. Stinger and the Russian SA-18.

MDACC—A concept of evasive movement when under fire; stands for motion, distance, angles, cover, and concealment.

Medford—Knife and tool maker out of Phoenix, Arizona, that makes the best edged weapons anywhere.

M4—A gas-operated, air-cooled, magazine-fed, selective fire, shoulder-fired weapon with a telescoping stock. It is essentially a shortened variant of the M16A2 rifle. It has a 14.5-inch (370 mm) barrel, allowing a shooter to operate more efficiently in confined spaces.

MICE—A short explanation for why some chose to spy; stands for money, ideology, compromise, ego; add revenge, and it's MICE-R.

MiG-23—A third-generation Russian variable geometry fighter aircraft. MiG is short for the *Mikoyan-Gurevich* design bureau in the former Soviet Union.

MOLLE—Modular Lightweight Load-carrying Equipment, pronounced "molly." The system's modularity comes from rows of stitched nylon webbing allowing the attachment of compatible pouches and accessories. It is the de facto standard for modular tactical gear today.

NATO—North Atlantic Treaty Organization.

NOD—Night observation device, aka night vision.

NSV—A 12.7 mm heavy machine gun of Soviet origin, named after the designers, Nikitin, Sokolov, and Volkov. It was designed to replace the DShK machine gun and was adopted by the Soviet army in 1971.

NTC—National Transitional Council, sometimes known as the Transitional National Council, was the de facto government of Libya for a period during and after the 2011 Libyan civil war.

NYPD—New York Police Department.

OCONUS—Outside the CONtinental United States.

OD—Olive drab.

Oi—Short for Odell International.

ONI—Officer of National Intelligence.

Ops Center—Operations Center.

Op Order—Operations Order, also referred to as OPORD, is an executable plan that directs a unit to conduct a military operation.

OODA—Observe, orient, decide, and act; refers to a decision-making cycle the human brain undergoes before performing a task.

OSC—Operator Selection Course.

PIT—A pursuit tactic by which a pursuing vehicle can force a fleeing vehicle to abruptly turn sideways, causing the driver to lose control and stop. It has a number of different meanings, depending on the agency using it or the school teaching it. The most common meanings are: precision immobilization technique, pursuit immobilization technique, and pursuit intervention technique. Whatever you call it, Roscoe P. Coltrane could've used it on Bo and Luke and it would've shut down their antics in Hazzard County.

PK—A 7.62 mm general-purpose, belt-fed machine gun designed in the former Soviet Union and currently in production in Russia. PK is short for *Pulemyot Kalashnikova* or Kalishnikov's machine gun.

Predator—An unmanned aerial vehicle (UAV) built by General Atomics and used ████ by the United States Air Force (USAF) ████████████. Initially conceived in the early 1990s for reconnaissance and forward observation roles, the MQ-1 Predator carries cameras and other sensors but has been modified and upgraded to carry and fire two AGM-114 Hellfire missiles or other munitions. The aircraft has seen combat over Afghanistan, Pakistan, Bosnia, Serbia, Iraq, Yemen, Libya, and Somalia.

PSD—Protective services detail, personal security detachment, or personal security detail is a protective team assigned to protect the personal security of an individual or group.

PT—Physical training, aka exercises.

Reaper—an unmanned aerial vehicle (UAV) capable of remote-controlled or autonomous flight operations, developed by General Atomics Aeronautical Systems (GA-ASI) primarily for the U.S. Air Force, but also in use by the U.S. Navy, Customs and Border Protection, and NASA. The MQ-9 carries a variety of weapons including the GBU-12 Paveway II laser-guided bomb, the AGM-114 Hellfire II air-to-ground missiles, the AIM-9 Sidewinder, and recently, the GBU-38 JDAM (Joint Direct Attack Munition). Tests are under way to allow for the addition of the AIM-92 Stinger air-to-air missile. In essence, a bad guy's worst nightmare.

Red-Teaming—Practice of viewing a problem from an adversary's perspective.

RFI—Request for information.

RPG—*Ruchnoy Protivotankovy Granatomyot*, meaning handheld antitank grenade launcher; a Russian shoulder-fired, antitank weapon system that fires rockets equipped with an explosive warhead. These warheads are affixed to a rocket motor and stabilized in flight with fins.

SAC—Special Activities Committee, the current name for the CIA unit responsible for covert/clandestine operations known as "special activities" and formerly known as SAD and prior to that, MSP (Military Special Projects).

SAD—Special Activities Division, the former name for the CIA unit responsible for covert operations known as "special activities" and now designated as SAC (Special Activities Committee).

SDR—Surveillance detection route; a preplanned, timed route of travel and stops, executed to detect and, if necessary, manipulate surveillance to accomplish an operational objective.

SEAL—U.S. Navy commandos unit tasked with maritime Special Operations.

SF—U.S. Army Special Forces tasked with unconventional warfare, special reconnaissance, foreign internal defense, counterterrorism, and direct action.

SITREP—SITuation REPort.

SMU—Special mission unit; in the U.S. military an SMU is a Tier 1 U.S. SOCOM asset under the control of Joint Special Operations Command. SMUs are specially selected and designated units, which are tasked with "special missions," sometimes referring to unconventional warfare, counterterrorist activities, direct action, and/or black operations.

SOCOM—United States Special Operations Command.

SOP—Standard operating procedure.

Stig—A personality on a BBC show *Top Gear*.

Suunto—The best watchmaker on the planet for special operators, adventurers, and folks who just want a watch to work and last for a long time. Based in Finland.

SWAT—Special Weapons and Tactics; teams who respond to situations requiring additional skill and training.

Thuraya—From the Arabic name for Pleiades, the astronomical Seven Sister star cluster in the Taurus constellation; a UAE-based satellite telephone service provider.

Tier 1—Tier status is based on a combination of national necessity and funding. Tier 1 includes Delta and DEVGRU and others. Tier 2 are Rangers, AFSOC forces, and the regular SEAL teams.

Toughbook—Ruggedized laptop made by Panasonic.

UAV—Unmanned aerial vehicle, such as the Predator and Global Hawk drones.

USB—Universal serial bus; in this book it refers to a memory stick that plugs into a port on a laptop.

USG—United States government.

VIP—Very important person. An example would not be the author of this book; he would be a VUIP.

Zodiac—Manufacturer of boats, but in common terms generally refers to a rigid-hull inflatable boat used for maritime insertion and extraction operations.